WAKE UP, AMERICA

WAKE UP, AMERICA

My Four Years in Hell

Paul A. Mostowski

VANTAGE PRESS
New York

Published by Vantage Press, Inc.
516 West 34th Street, New York, New York 10001

Manufactured in the United States of America
ISBN: 0- 533-12641-X

Library of Congress Catalog Card No.: 97- 91327

0 9 8 7 6 5 4 3 2 1

Contents

Part Three: Christmas Day Enroute to Bataan

Part Four: General MacArthur Arrives in Australia

Part Five: The Fall of Bataan

Acknowledgments

All credit must go to my wonderful wife, Lorraine, who deserves all the credit that I can bestow for her constant compelling voice that got me started on this book again after almost fifty years since I wrote the first lines. I was forced to stop at the very start because of what it was doing to my health by reliving the memories of the horrors we as prisoners of the Japanese were put through. Even to this day, I get tears in my eyes writing about the days spent under the rule of the Japanese as a prisoner of war. Credit must also be given to all those wonderful people who kept asking me about my book, thus prodding me on to get it into print.

About the Author

On 21 August 1906 at 3:32 A.M., I entered this world as the son of George Mostowski, a Russian emigrant who arrived at Ellis Island in New York in January 1898, in the dead of winter after a very rough crossing of the Atlantic Ocean. Upon being released from Ellis Island in New York, he went to Oyster Bay with Mr. Catalioti, an emigrant from Italy, whom he met on the ship while crossing to America. That same year, he married my mother, Lillian May Elliott, who was fifteen years of age. My mother was a native, hometown girl of Oyster Bay. She was the descendant of English, Irish, and Welsh parentage. She was just a child herself when I was born, barely twenty-three years old. I was her sixth child. With my father being a staunch Roman Catholic, she knew there would be more.

In those days, there was no such thing as birth control. She decided six was enough. So she ran away with a friend, Gene Platt, a traveling salesman.

In those days, a laborer got eighteen dollars a week. With that kind of salary, it was utterly impossible for my father to hire someone to take care of his family while he worked. So we were made wards of Nassau County, Long Island, New York. My father never got over losing his family. He died, heartbroken, within a year.

At the tender age of six months, I and my sister Sarah, eighteen months old, and my brother George, three years old, were placed in the Home for Destitute Children, in Brooklyn, New York. My older brother and sister were placed in another home. I never learned where they went.

When I was about three years old, I was transferred to The State Agriculture and Industrial School, a home in upper New York State, in Industry, about six miles west of Rochester. It consisted of 1,500 acres of land that had been donated to the state of New York by a very rich lady for the sole purpose of giving shelter to destitute boys, giving them a chance to learn farming or a trade that would prepare them for the outside world.

When I reached thirteen years of age, I was placed on different farms, where I worked for room and board to learn farming. At the age of seventeen, I was given one hundred dollars and told everything that they could tell me about myself: my true name, birthday, where I was born, and so on, after which I was on my own.

Not knowing where my brothers and sisters were or, for that matter, if they were still alive, I started to think about my future. I headed for Oyster Bay, New York, the place of my birth and also the place of birth of the twenty-sixth president of the United States, Theodore Roosevelt.

A Bit about This Great President,
Theodore Roosevelt

Theodore ("Teddy") Roosevelt was elected the twenty-sixth president of the United States. He remained in office from 1901 until 1909. Teddy was born on a farm of about one hundred acres, Sagamore Hill, in Oyster Bay on the twenty-seventh day of October 1858 and lived there until his passing in 1919. His home on Sagamore Hill, where he romped and played while growing up into manhood, is surrounded by giant sagamore trees, and is open to the public daily. Teddy himself named the place "Sagamore Hill" when he was a little boy, in honor of those great, giant sagamore trees that graced the land all around his home and farm that he loved so dearly.

Teddy married a hometown girl. Her family had settled in the Carolinas more than a century before. From this union, there were born six sons and one daughter. When Teddy was in town, he and his family attended the Christ Episcopal Church in Oyster Bay Village every Sunday. I was baptized and confirmed in the same church. It had twelve large, beautiful stained-glass windows with figures of Jesus and his disciples. They were donated and dedicated to Teddy, his wife, and to each of his sons and grandchildren by the parishioners.

Teddy's remains lay in state in Christ Episcopal Church for several days so all who loved him could pay their last respects to that great man. He was laid to rest outside his home on his beloved Sagamore Hill in Oyster Bay under those giant sagamore trees, where he had spent his boyhood days. His wife and six sons are also buried there. One of the saddest things that happened to Teddy was the loss of five of his six sons while fighting for their country in the First World War.

The day that Teddy was laid to rest, the United States mourned the loss of a great patriot and one of the greatest presidents this country has ever known or ever will know. He refused to accept any favors or currency to aid him in his elections. He owed allegiance to no one, and he let his conscience be his guide. He refused to be a puppet. He was his own boss, with no election debts to repay.

By his own convictions, he kept this country strong. He built up an army and navy that was the envy of the world. Although Teddy Roosevelt was the head of the Rough Riders in the U.S. Cavalry, his love was for the U.S. Navy, and he proved it by building it up into the greatest fleet of ships and iron men the world had ever known.

Teddy Roosevelt's dream was that when he became president of the United States, he would immediately start working to make this country strong and gain the respect of the rest of the world by beefing up the army and navy, which he surely did. He built it according to his belief that "in order to have peace, one must be strong." When the navy was ready to be shown off to the whole world, Teddy had all the American naval ships painted white. They became known as the "Great White Fleet."

In 1905, while acting in his capacity as the commander in chief of the armed forces of the United States and in keeping with his motto, "Speak softly and carry a big stick," Teddy sent the Great White Fleet on a cruise around the world. He wanted the whole world to see this show of force and to let them all know that the United States had grown up and was now a country to be reckoned with. He wanted to show the world that although we were a country of *peace,* we were still ready to protect ourselves in any conflict that might arise.

It paid off. He gained the respect, as well as the fear, of the rest of the world by parading the Great White Fleet around the world. Teddy was a peace-loving man, but he believed that to have peace, one must be strong. Then no one would dare tread on your toes.

When the Great White Fleet got to Japan, they ran out of money to pay for rations, and coal to run the ships. Teddy went before Congress and told them he had run out of money and requested the Congress to give him the funds required to fuel and provision the ships to enable him to bring them home.

Congress, which was up in arms when the president ordered the Fleet to tour the world in the first place, was now more than ever up in arms. They flatly refused his request. They told Teddy they wanted their Fleet home and demanded that he, as the commander in chief and the president of the United States, get them back in any way that he could.

With Congress up in arms and refusing to grant him the funds to bring the Great White Fleet home, Teddy calmly said, "Okay, leave them there to rot. I sent them there; you find the funds to bring them home." They found the funds in a hurry. To this day, some seventy-five years after his demise, our beloved Teddy is still known as he always will be, "The Father of the United States Navy." His birthday, the twenty-seventh of October is known as "Navy Day." No president of the United States has ever done half as much as Teddy did for the navy. May God bless him and allow his soul to rest in peace forever.

Dedication

To those brave heroes, the "Battling Bastards of Bataan." Let us who are living pay tribute to those boys who fought their country's battles in the trenches, on the beaches, on the ships, and on Corregidor in the Philippines in their last-ditch effort prior to surrendering. They served their country faithfully in time of strife and in the heat of battle and made the supreme sacrifice by giving their last ounce of devotion while fighting to preserve the freedoms that we all now enjoy. They are now serving on the staff of the Supreme Commander of the universe. May they rest in a well-deserved peace, wherever they may be.

I think General MacArthur said it best when speaking of the courage and *needless* great sacrifice the boys of the Philippines made on Bataan, Corregidor, and the beaches. "Corregidor needs no comment from me. It has sounded its own story at the mouth of guns. It has scrolled its own epitaph on enemy tablets. But through the bloody haze of its last reverberating shot, I shall always seem to see a vision of grim, gaunt, ghastly men, still unafraid."

Preface

This story is written by one who has returned from four years of enduring the horrible torture of hell at its worst as a prisoner of war under the hands of the Japanese military. It is written with the hope and prayer that no man or group of men from this country shall ever be left in such a disgraceful condition again as we were in the Orient and the Philippine Islands. I used the word "hell" for lack of any word or group of words that could express the horrible ordeal we went through because the U.S. Congress refused to give us adequate weaponry to defend ourselves. The Congress of the United States, long before the shooting started, had plenty of time to remedy the terrible tragedy of the Philippines in 1941.

The question to ask ourselves is who was to blame? That answer is: Every American citizen was to blame for reelecting those officials who vote year after year to scuttle our defense system while they raise their own pay and put money into their pet projects at home to enable them to garner votes for their next election. Once elected and seated in Congress, they immediately start looking out for their own interest, not of this country's as a whole.

Practically all intelligent people carry life insurance to protect their loved ones. Our armed forces are our "life insurance." If that insurance is kept strong enough, no American blood need ever be spilled on a battlefield again. *Peace doesn't come without a price.* America must remain big and strong, allowing no nation to invade our shores. Remember, the weak fall by the wayside; only the strong survive. It is the contention of the author that as the battle cry before Pearl Harbor was *"Remember the Alamo,"* the time has come to change it to: *"Remember Pearl Harbor and the Fighting Bastards of Bataan."*

When Congress is debating about the military, they should be reminded of the deplorable conditions they left us in the Philippines. There should be a resolution that the United States Congress shall never be allowed to again dub another group of the military *"The Expendables"* or the *"Suicide Fleet,"* as they dubbed those who were serving their country faithfully in China and the Philippines. When debating the status of the

xix

military, let Congress be reminded of what Teddy Roosevelt once said, "Speak softly and carry a big stick."

Let it be resolved that no president or Congress of the United States shall ever allow this country to become so weak that it must accept apologies when humiliated, as it did when Japan was building up, grabbing off pieces of China, and engaging in the barbarous treatment in the raping of Nanking, China, in 1937 or in the sinking of our ships and the treacherous strafing of our boats when loaded with wounded as they did on 12 December 1937 of the U.S.S. *Panay.*

It is a sick delusion to think that just because the Communist Soviet Republic has collapsed and the dark clouds have passed over, we can just relax and drop our arms, and it will be just beautiful sunshine from now on. The questions to ask ourselves are: Has Russia really collapsed? Who controls the arsenal of bombs still pointed at America? What about Japan? How can such a group of high United States elected officials become so stupid to close all our bases and scrap everything?

Take a look at the two countries we defeated in the last great war, namely Germany and Japan, *or did we?* They are very rich and getting stronger every day, while we find ourselves *trillions* of dollars further in debt. We are building a hole we can't climb out of. Yet almost every day, we read in the papers that the president and Congress are promising to give some country millions of dollars. However, not a cent to the boys who allowed them to keep their freedom and their jobs. It's about time to *wake up, America.*

Let our lawmakers never forget the words spoken to them by that great American, General ("Storming") Norman Schwarzkopf, who said, in speaking of his troops who fought under him in Saudi Arabia, to the combined Houses of Congress: "By their example, we should all remember that the freedoms we enjoy today in this great country of ours do not come without a price. They are paid for and protected by the lives, limbs, and the blood of American servicemen and women." Then he went on to say, "We ask God to grant a special love to all our fallen comrades. We also ask that God grant special strength to our comrades who are still in the hospitals with wounds and injuries they received in the war." Then he continued with, "America, take care of your veterans and the military in time of *PEACE,* and they in turn will take care of you in time of *WAR.* Above all, always remember the promises you make to your servicemen while they are in the heat of battle. These promises should not be forgotten after the war clouds have disappeared. I pray that our great nation doesn't continually forget them, as they have in the past."

"Forget them, as they have in the past" are the key words. Let's quit giving away the wealth of our country until we have taken care of those who fought this country's battles on the land and on the sea. They are now living in the streets, some without clothes on their backs to keep them warm, no decent home to go to, and wondering where their next meal is coming from. They have been forgotten already by the government they fought for.

General MacArthur was promised so much, but he was forgotten also. What a humiliating situation he was put in by putting his faith in those promises from Washington. He had publicly sworn to the Filipino people that the United States would indeed defend every inch of the Philippines and would not allow anything to stand in their way. The United States would not let them down. They would not be allowed to suffer defeat. In hopes that America would change its mind and send some help, which they promised they would do, MacArthur would himself go over to the front lines in Bataan and mingle with the troops in the field. He kept making false promises to keep up their morale. He kept telling them that tomorrow or in the next couple of days, help and supplies would arrive to relieve them. He had promised so much to the Filipino population and especially the boys serving and dying on the front lines of Bataan. He just couldn't bring himself to believe that President Roosevelt would write the Philippines off so easily.

Many of us today still feel down deep inside that America could have saved the Philippines if they had only listened to the pleas of those two great soldiers General Jonathan ("Skinny") Wainwright and General Douglas MacArthur. The loss of those troops in the Philippines represented sixty-five hundred more than were lost in World War One. Why? Yes, why did our commander in chief, the president of the United States allow it to happen?

If a U.S. Senator or Congressman could have seen the filthy sayings written in American blood about them on the walls of the latrines in the prison camps and in the death cells, their faces would have turned crimson from pure shame. Then maybe, yes, just maybe, today they would think twice before they vote to reduce our armed forces and close all our bases. Are we going to allow this country to grow weak again as we did back in the 1930s and have Congress name another group of fighting men, "Suicide Fleet" or "Expendables" in some other part of the world?

I implore our lawmakers in Congress to heed the warnings of President Teddy Roosevelt and General Norman Schwarzkopf. Yes, it is true that the money spent on our armed forces in times of peace is tremendously high, but should this nation be forced into war because of its weakness? The price would be ten times greater, not only financially, but also in needless loss of the lives of so many of our youth on the battlefield. There never would have been a Pearl Harbor if we hadn't gone to sleep and let our arms down while others were secretly building up their coffers for war.

Watch those same countries. The Japanese are not sleeping. So I say loud and clear, *Wake up, America.* The time has truly come for you to wake up. When the Fighting Bastards of Bataan were released and arrived home, there were no ticker-tape parades or any fanfare for those who had fought there so bravely. To add to the insult, more than fifty years later, the United States government is doing nothing to comfort them as the sun sets on their lives.

So I say, Shame on you, America.

I served my country in the malaria-infested jungles of Nicaragua in the early 1930s, then on Bataan and Corregidor in the Philippines in 1942, and later was a Japanese prisoner of war, and now, at ninety-one years young, I can't even make an appointment in an *emergency* at any military hospital. Thank God, I am not reliant on the government for help. But there are many others who are not as fortunate as I am.

General MacArthur said, "I shall return," as he was about to board the PT-41 boat in his daring escape from the Philippines, while standing on the shores of Corregidor Island. Three years later, he did return, thereby keeping his word. Later, standing in the halls of Congress of these United States, as he finished addressing the combined Houses, he said, "Old soldiers never die, they just fade away," which he also did. May his soul rest in peace. God bless him. He truly was a great hero, a soldier I shall never forget. If, we carry the "big stick" that our beloved Teddy Roosevelt had in mind when he sent his Great White Fleet around the globe, there would be no need for war, no need to shed the precious blood of our youth on a battlefield again. If the U.S. Congress had given us the necessary fire power on the Asiatic station rather than just cast us aside as "expendables," this story would never have to be written.

However, our country is going down the same path again, so I must speak out. Hence this story, "Wake up, America." The following poem, written by a war correspondent, pretty well describes the feelings of most of us who were fighting a losing battle on Bataan, with our backs to the wall.

No mama, no papa, no Uncle Sam;
No aunts, no uncles, no nephews, no nieces;
No pills, no planes, no artillery pieces;
and nobody, yes nobody gives a damn.

To the many whom I had the pleasure of serving with in the armed forces, I say "God bless all those Fil-Americans wherever they may be and let them live in well-deserved peace. And God bless America, may her colors fly high and never be forced to touch the ground again."

Fond Memories of My Tin Can Days

J.D. Harp (Originally appearing in *Our Navy* magazine, circa 1945)

There's an old four stacker tin can
Sitting out in Frisco Bay,
Her decks are all rust eaten,
And her paint job's washed away.
She isn't much to look at,
After twenty years at sea,
But she's a rugged little tin can,
And she was home sweet home to me.

I've stood upon her pitching decks.
I've watched the salt water spray,
Across her rolling fo'csle,
From Shanghai to Bombay.
I've cussed her skipper and her chow,
Clear around the Philippines,
But she's the best old tin can,
I guess I've ever seen

From the Asiatic Station to Java we did go,
Sumatra and Celebes and back to Borneo,
From Guam to Bali Bali, where the
Southern trade winds blow.
I can't think of any places,
That old tin can didn't go.

Now she's sittin' out there swingin'
Round her anchor chain,
When I think of what they're gonna do,
It fills my heart with pain
For they say they're gonna scrap her
And do it right away,
But to me she's still the best Tin Can,
Out there in Frisco Bay.

WAKE UP, AMERICA

Part One

Japan Vows to Avenge the Humiliation Caused by Commodore Perry's Actions

1. Japan Invades Manchuria

On 5 July 1853, Commodore Perry sailed into the Japanese harbor with his guns manned and pointed at their batteries along the shoreline. Japan, although declaring it to be an act of war, found herself not in a position to wage war openly with the West at that time. However, they vowed that someday the West must pay for the humiliation this act had caused them. The Japanese knew it would take many years to actually get in shape to avenge themselves on the West, but they vowed that the United States must pay for their humiliation from the actions of Commodore Perry. Perry's rank at that time was commodore, but the shogun chose to called him "Admiral." This embarrassed the commodore, but he accepted it, figuring it would help to make things easier in his quest to open the ports of Japan to the West. However, to his friends here in America, he was known as Matt.

Then again, at the turn of the century, the Japanese were once more humiliated when Admiral Dewey, commander of the American forces in the Philippines, befriended the Russians in Manila when the Russian naval armada arrived in there. Dewey fueled and provisioned their ships with food, knowing they were on their way to engage the Japanese fleet. This humiliated the Japanese and started their swords to rattle again. They started immediately to prepare for war against the West, meaning the United States. The proof is that they stored guns and ammo in caves on the ocean side of the Mariveles mountains, wrapped in newspapers dated 1906.

When, as a prisoner of war in Japan, I was walking around the shipyard in Osaka, I asked the Japanese colonel, my camp commander, whether the Japanese had started to prepare for war against us when they stored all those guns and ammunition that we located in the Mariveles mountains. He said, "Yes, that is true." He told me that in 1853, Japan immediately set out to avenge the humiliation they had suffered at the hands of those two Americans, Commodore Perry and Admiral Dewey. I was told in no uncertain terms, Japan never forgets, even if takes one hundred years. He also told me that I should always remember those words. I hope and pray that America does not forget it either and stays *awake*.

3

So with Admiral Dewey's actions in providing fuel and provisions to the Russian Fleet as they lay at anchor in Manila Bay, the emperor immediately started to prepare his country for war. The shogun said, in 1853, that "even if it took one hundred years, the West must pay." And it did take almost one hundred years; it just lacked twelve years. So you see, Japan never forgets. They will never forget General Douglas MacArthur either. So again I say, keep a careful eye on Japan, and wake up, America.

The emperor and his warlords just could not, and would not forgive the United States for those two deeds that had so badly humiliated their country. Admiral Dewey's aiding the Russian fleet, really put the frosting on the cake, especially since Japan was in a declared state of war with Russia. The emperor and his warlords, felt that Japan could not match, or would be able to, fight a long war to avenge themselves on the West without first conquering the Eastern world. They knew they must defeat China first, then the rest of the East could be conquered easily. With this accomplished, the road would be open and their dreams of their long-awaited war for vengeance on the imperialistic and barbaric West, as we were called at that time by the Japanese, would be just a matter of time.

The emperor, in the late 1920s, feeling that Japan was strong enough to start on their plans of bringing China and the East under their control, sent Colonel Ishihara to photograph and map out Manchuria for a later invasion. Incidentally, Colonel Ishihara, who mapped and photographed Manchuria, was the same Colonel Ishihara who masterminded the attack on Pearl Harbor on 7 December 1941, some seventeen years later, and who was now advanced to the flag rank of general.

We have only to look back to recall that in 1896, Japan started trouble by causing little incidents with China and also with the United States and England by invading the Yangtze River and harassing our men and patrol boats that were stationed on the Whangpoo and Yangtze rivers in Chinese territory for the protection of American and British interests. American and British gunboats were there with the consent of the Chinese government.

Several times, notes were sent to Japan by both the United States and England, asking her to insure the safety of American and British personnel and their properties in that area. When an incident would occur involving Japan, we always got the same reply: "So sorry, please," and it was accepted by this country and England. Japan had no intention of accepting the pleas of either the United States or England.

4

Japan knew that both these countries had weakened their military forces to the point that they were helpless to repel her actions in her determination of conquering the East. With this knowledge, they kept on causing these little incidents. When questioned, the old reply was always the same: "So sorry, excuse please."

In 1896, Japan began taking territory away from China. They took just a little piece at a time. First it was Taiwan and Korea, then a piece of Manchuria in 1931, a little more of Manchuria in 1932, then Jehol in 1933, then inner Mongolia in 1935. This went on and on over a period of forty years. This territory was needed to aid them in conquering the East to put them in a better position to be ready when the time came for revenge on the barbaric West.

The above was all in their planning stage, so that when it was strong enough and the East had been won over or defeated, Japan would be in a position to go to war with the West. Which was their main objective all along. Every time they would grab a little more of China, they felt that they were nearing their goal. Each time getting off scot-free with just an apology. The United States and England, feeling that they were to weak too do anything, just stood by and watched the slaughter of the Far East.

In 1935, Emperor Hirohito directed his general staff to map out plans to prepare for war with China as soon as possible. The general staff went to work, and the plans were completed as early as the spring of 1937. In the early summer of 1937, Emperor Hirohito, seeing that the United States and England were accepting his apologies time and time again, and knowing they were both much too weak to put up a front, ordered his troops to invade and capture the rest of Manchuria, in accordance with the plans that had been mapped out as far back as 1925 by Colonel Ishihara of the Japanese imperial headquarters.

According to the wishes of the emperor, Manchuria was invaded, along with some more of China. Once again the United States and England stood by and did nothing but protest, which was expected by the Japanese. So once again, the Japanese said, "So sorry, please," and once again England and the United States accepted their apologies. Knowing that the so-called League of Nations at that time was proven a flop, Japan knew no threat would be forthcoming from that quarter, and none was, from no nation. The United States and England were too weak to raise a finger.

5

2. Japan Seeks a Way to Start a War with China

With Manchuria conquered, the emperor now found himself in a terrible situation. What to do about China? This was the big apple, and he knew that Japan must control all of the Eastern world before they could even give a thought about going to war with the West, the emperor's ultimate goal. That was the big question, which gave him many sleepless nights. Emperor Hirohito didn't have any animosity toward China. In fact, he was very friendly with Chiang Kai-shek, the ruler of all China at that time. However, friends or not, the emperor insisted that war must come and China must be conquered as planned to enhance the holdings of Japan.

Defeating China had become a necessity in the national program that he inherited from his grandfather and his great grandfather after Perry's entering Japan's harbors at gun point. Hirohito's great-grandfather had sworn an oath, with all those around him, that the red-headed barbarians must be driven into the sea and destroyed. He also vowed that someday the West must pay for their actions.

In the early 1920s, the emperor and his great leaders had decided that the program set by his great grandfather could not be fulfilled without adding the Indies to his empire. To accomplish this, they needed ports all along the South China coast to keep the barbarians away.

So the emperor ordered his generals to find a way to create a war with his good friend Chiang Kai-shek, the ruler of all China. He said that "China must be taken by force if necessary," because without China, the emperor wouldn't be in a position for an all- out war with the West, to avenge themselves on the United States for the belligerent actions of Commander Perry in 1853 and Admiral Dewey's befriending the Russians in Manila Bay, Philippines. He must fulfill the vows of his great grandfather and grandfather.

However, with the emperor being on such friendly relations with his neighbor, China, and his friend, Chiang Kai-shek, he was in a quandary of how to get a war started with such a good neighbor, one he would like to be allied with, but which was an impossibility. He felt that he couldn't have a partner in such a great undertaking. It was better for Japan to conquer all of the East, and to go it alone if he was ever to have his dream come true.

But how to get a war started with his good friend Chiang Kai- shek? That was the big question. The emperor held a conference and ordered his high command to find a way to get the war started with China by 7 July

1937. He wanted it started by using the "three seven" system. Japan believes in the principle of the seventh son of the seventh son of the seventh son. The Japanese try to do all of their great undertakings by using this principle. So the date and time was set for the seventh month (July) on the seventh day (Sunday) at seven in the evening, and in the year 1937. This gave the emperor an extra seven to boot, making it four sevens.

But then the question arose of how to get it started so that the rest of the world would put the blame on China, not on Japan. After a few months of study, the war lords came up with a plan that was sanctioned by the emperor. They would cause an incident that would force China to fire the first shot, thus engaging herself in a war with Japan. That way, Japan would not be to blame, and the world would see China as the one who started the war. Japan would, by this method, create sympathy for its own people. They also figured that if need be, if things really got tough and went awry, they could possibly convince the United States to help them. Then they could turn on the West after they had fully conquered the East. Cunning, those Japanese—*wake up, America.*

The plan was for a Japanese private to leave his unit at exactly seven, Sunday evening on July seventh and go into the woods to urinate. It was also planned that at that exact time, some of the men who were stationed in a Japanese garrison nearby in Tientsin, just outside Peking, would fire their weapons in the air to scare the Chinese, who, thinking that the Japanese were firing at them, would in turn open fire on the Japanese, thus starting the war the emperor so badly wanted with China. This went off as scheduled, except, however, the Chinese didn't open fire as planned.

The high command in Japan failed to notify the private's platoon commander in the field that when one of his men went into the woods to urinate, the Japanese garrison nearby would fire a round of shots in the air. In fact, the platoon commander was kept in the dark; he was not told a thing about the plan of getting the Chinese to open fire first so they would get the blame for starting the war. So not having been made aware of what was happening or what had been planned by the high command, the platoon commander, when hearing the bursts of gunfire and thinking his man who went into the woods was being fired upon, he in turn ordered his men to open fire on the Chinese. Thus the war had begun, with Japan firing the first shot. The missing soldier had rejoined his group long before. But it was a perfect reason to start the war. However, it backfired on the Japanese, and the whole world condemned Japan, putting the blame where it rightfully belonged.

When this incident happened, I was serving on board a destroyer, the U.S.S. *Barker*; we were tied up to the dock in Shanghai, China. You should have seen the Chinese workmen who were on board the *Barker* abandon ship that day. The Japanese, to this day, call the war with China an "accidental war." But in reality, although it backfired, it was just what the emperor wanted in order to hasten the day for that war with the West. Oh, yes, the Japanese are cunning, and I caution the world that they are not to be underestimated. Japan is like an elephant, it never forgets, which is why America should never forget the sneak attack on Pearl Harbor. It is one of the main reasons for this book. Also, we must remember that Japan will not forget the forced humiliation on the United States battleship, the U.S.S. *Missouri,* in Tokyo Bay, at the hands of another great American, General Douglas MacArthur, by the signing of the peace treaty that ended that phase of World War Two with Japan. Keep your eye on Japan. She never forgets; it may take one hundred years, but they will try one day to avenge their humiliation by the West in 1945.

3. Japan Invades Nanking—Starts War with China

On Sunday, 7 July 1937, the evening that the Japanese did eventually invade China proper, neither the United States nor Britain were prepared to help China; both countries had depleted their armed forces to a disgraceful condition. And so, because of Japanese activities in various parts of China, due to the weakness of these two super powers not wanting to have an incident occur, those ports of call had to be restricted to the Americans and the British. Yes, I'm sorry to say, our Congress had weakened our armed forces so badly, we just stood by and allowed the Japanese to have a free hand in China in their massacre of civilians. Are we heading down the same path again? You bet we are. It's time to *wake up, America!*

Chiang Kai-shek was forced to flee from his headquarters at Nanking, China on or about 10 December 1937. The Japanese troops under Prince Asaka, the nephew of the emperor who relieved the ailing General Matsui of his command, moved in. The men were given a free hand and, in fact, were encouraged to carry out their barbaric and hideous crimes on defenseless Chinese men, women, and children. It was sickening for each and every one of us Americans and British who were out there serving on the China Station to just stand by and actually watch the raping of Nanking in 1937 while neither the United States nor Great Britain raised a hand to help our Chinese friends.

It was very hard for our officers and men to comprehend that the military position of our country was in such a deplorable state that we had to accept their apologies over and over. What a shame for this country to allow Japan to go into Nanking and, literally, rape men, women, and children. Yes, that was rape all right. We just stood by watching the Japanese under the control of the emperor's nephew, Prince Asaka, as he not only allowed, but encouraged his troops in 1937 to proceed to massacre some 100,000 to 200,000 Chinese, troops who also raped some 5,000 to 6,000 young men, women, and children before killing them. This went on until the last girl and boy had been raped. It was not uncommon to see a string of Chinese bodies that had been beheaded lying in the streets and just left there in the gutters, and it was not uncommon to see Japanese officers as well as enlisted men waiting for their turn to rape some Chinese woman or child still in one of the houses. The Japanese made it mandatory that all the Chinese men be registered and each day fifty to one hundred of them were selected for a beheading party to take place that night.

Although the ailing General Matsui, who was the overall commander, voiced his disapproval to both *The New York Times* and to the emperor, it didn't do any good, the crimes kept going on and on just the same. And as usual, we Americans had to drop our arms and just stand by and watch this horror taking place day after day and do nothing about it. Why? I asked myself that question over and over again. How in the hell did we allow our armed forces to grow so weak as to allow those atrocities to happen? I pray *this shall never be allowed to happen again*. That is why I say again and again, *wake up, America*. To think that Japan had the audacity to condemn the war trial sentencings in 1948, after all their atrocities committed in Nanking and in China proper, let alone in other parts of the Asiatic world, such as the Philippines, etcetera, to say nothing about their atrocities to prisoners of war, killing us in cold blood, running bayonets through the prisoners on the death march from Bataan, among others.

4. Joined the Navy—Assigned to "Old Rocky"

I became an orphan at the tender age of six months and was placed in the Home For Destitute Children, along with my two brothers and two sisters, at 217 Sterling Place in Brooklyn, New York. When I was five years old, we were separated, and I was transferred to the State Agricultural and Industrial School at Industry, New York. It was about six miles northwest of Rochester. When I grew older, I was taught farming, by being placed on farms in the nearby communities. When I reached the age of sixteen, I started to grow restless and wanted to go out and see the world, also to see if I could locate my brothers and sisters, or anyone of my family still living.

When I was released from the orphans' home at Industry, where I had been raised, I returned to Oyster Bay. Upon finding myself all alone in the world, not being able to contact any of my family with the exception of my grandmother, or even know if any of them were still alive, I decided to make the U.S. Navy my career. So on the third of December, 1928, my pal, Alley Catalotte, drove me from Oyster Bay to Brooklyn, New York, to the Naval recruiting station in Borough Hall, by the Brooklyn Bridge, where I joined up as a coal passer.

The navy had several coal burning ships still on active duty back in those days. I was sent to do my boot camp training at the Naval Training Station, Newport, Rhode Island. Along with our drilling and other instructions, we were taught to sing navy songs and little ditties to help keep us from getting homesick. We were all young men, seventeen or eighteen years of age, and most had never been away from home before and found it very hard; a lot of the fellows were homesick. It didn't bother me because I never had a real home with a mother and father. Among the several songs we were taught and sang was this one:

We're just a bunch of rookies going to Newport, Newport
We're just a bunch of rookies going to sea.
We're just a bunch of rookies going to Newport, Newport
To show the gals how happy we can be—can be—can be.

We were paid twenty-one dollars a month, but they took back all we earned the first two months. The first month, our twenty-one dollars was spent as follows: five dollars for four haircuts (our heads were kept shaved all the time we were rookies); five dollars went for a galvanized bucket and a bar of salt-water soap and a scrub brush to scrub our clothes with, using salt water, a Gillette safety razor, shaving cream, and a bar of face soap. Six dollars went to putting heavy-duty soles on our new shoes for drilling purposes. The other five dollars was to get three white stripes sewn on our dress blue uniforms, which we received upon graduation from boot camp. The second month, the whole works, the full twenty-one bucks went for a

10

peacoat, for which, we had been informed, Uncle Sam would return to us later, with interest. Did we ever get it? What do you think? When does Uncle ever give anything back, especially to the military? They just take; they don't give back.

Upon graduation, after ten weeks of hard drilling, we were given the rest of our pay, which amounted to eleven dollars, and a leave of absence for ten days to allow us to visit our homes before going to sea. But there was a catch; before they would let us go, we had to produce a round-trip ticket to get back to Newport, Rhode Island. Well, my round-trip ticket cost five dollars and ninety-five cents on the overnight Fall River Steamship Line to New York. This left me with the grand sum of five dollars and five cents to last me ten full days to pay for room and board, and maybe take a gal out. I wasn't lucky like my other shipmates; I didn't have a home to go to. I went anyway to Oyster Bay to see the friends I had made there. But being broke and not having a red cent for food, let alone for lodging, and not wanting to sponge on my friends, I cut my leave short and returned to the naval training station after three days.

A few days after I returned to the training station at Newport, I was handed my first assignment, ordering me to the tropics down Panama way for a tour of duty aboard the U.S.S. *Rochester,* in the Special Service squadron, known as the "banana fleet" and which is what they called us in those days. I was a happy kid, having my first set of orders and ordered to sea duty as a tar in Uncle Sam's navy. The U.S.S. *Rochester* was a coal-burning ship; she boasted of a glorious history.

When the contract was awarded to the New York shipbuilding company to build the *Rochester,* no one believed that a ship built of iron would float. All the politicians were up in arms and threatened to sue and recall Benjamin Harrison, the president of the United States at that time, for awarding a contract to build a heavy cruiser made of iron—no way would it float. The president refused to concede; he stood his ground and ordered that the ship be built. After the next election and Grover Cleveland took office as the president of the United States, all the politicians started after him to stop that nonsense of building a ship of iron, but he too held his guns and refuse to intervene, so the ship was built on schedule.

When the ship was completed, the Congress of the United States, being still very mad and skeptical about this ship made of iron, all went down to Brooklyn on the day of her launching to watch it *SINK,* they thought. However, as this majestic ship slid off her moorings on being christened, there was absolute silence. To everyone's amazement, she floated into the water as gracefully as the young lady that she was. She was christened, the U.S.S. *New York*. All the politicians were astonished to see it stay above the water. In a very few moments, loud cries went up, "*It floats, it floats.*"

That day in 1893 was a glorious day for Past President Benjamin Harrison and his successor, Grover Cleveland, who also refused to listen to the senators and congressmen to give orders to stop building the ship. Both presidents rejoiced at seeing all the newspaper editors of the world utilizing their whole front page with words in huge type, "*It Floats—It Floats.*" They also rejoiced in seeing the politicians eat crow, for their disbelief.

She was the first armored ship to be built in the world. She was equipped with torpedo tubes down in the bowels of the ship, and two eight-inch gun turrets graced her decks both fore and aft. She also had eight gun emplacements with portholes located on each side of the second deck. In all, she was the finest cruiser the world had ever seen.

My first assignment on Old Rocky was in the black gang as a coal passer. In those days coal passers were called "snipes," so I was known as a "snipe." The U.S.S. *Rochester* was the last survivor of the coal-burning ship days in the U.S. Navy. Her home port was in the Canal Zone at Balboa, Panama. It was a great honor to serve on board the U.S.S. *Rochester,* due to its great history. It was the first ship to carry the name U.S.S. *New York,* in honor of New York State since she was built in the Brooklyn Navy Yard, in New York.

In those days, they didn't name ships as they do today. Ships were mostly given the name of the city or state of the shipyard where they had been built. When they started to build battleships, they changed all that. They decided to name battleships after states, and cruisers after large cities. Airplane carriers after famous battles, and submarines were given names of fish. So the U.S.S. *New York,* being a cruiser at the time they started to build battleships, was renamed the U.S.S. *Saratoga.* Then when they started to build light cruisers, she was again renamed: the U.S.S. *Rochester,* because Saratoga was a famous battle, and the names of famous battles were going to be reserved for airplane carriers, which were to be built in the future. For Old Rocky, as she was affectionately called, this was another first; she was the only ship to have her name changed, and not just once, but three times.

Old Rocky was always a flagship. There was always some admiral's or squadron commander's flag flying on her mast, signifying there was an admiral of the fleet or a squadron commander on board, this went on throughout her naval career. What an honor to serve on board her. I stayed with her down in Central and South Americas for over three years. The *Rochester* carried a large contingent of marines. In those years, we were engaged in fighting the Sandino forces in the jungles of Corinto and Bluefields, Nicaragua, for which I received the Nicaragua campaign medal with five stars.

The U.S.S. *Rochester* was still on active duty and serving her country on the China Station as late as 1942, at the start of the war with Japan. She was purposely sunk prior to our surrender of the Philippines to block the harbor of the Olongapo shipyard, off Luzon Province in the Philippines. And so, from 1893 until 1942, for over fifty years, the U.S.S. *Rochester,* the first ship in the world built of iron and clad with heavy armor, a ship that the world thought would never float, served her country with honor. Even at the end of her career, although she couldn't serve her country with her guns blazing, she served by blocking the channel with her hulk. What a record and what a great ship and what a grand old lady she was.

Even today as I write, the U.S.S. *Rochester* is still in the news. Divers are bringing up treasures that went down with her when she was scuttled off Olongapo for her last assignment. They say even though she has lain there in Davy Jones's locker some fifty years, she is still not yielding to the waters below but is still in good shape, with the exception of a few barnacles growing on her sides. Down in Panama we all used to sing the following song to the tune of the "Marine Hymn." More than a half a century later, I still have that same feeling I had then for Old Rocky.

> Oh, the flagship of our squadron,
> Is known as Old Rocky
> She's the finest cruiser in her class
> That sails the seven seas.
> From the barrooms of old Panama
> To Corinto, Nicaragua, or at sea.
> We'll uphold old Rocky's honor, wherever she may be.
> And if we ever leave these tropic lands
> And go back to God's country,
> We'll leave our mark on old Broadway,
> *For one damn good liberty.*

5. Enroute to the Asiatic Station for Duty

In the early spring of 1936, I was attached to a destroyer doing duty at the naval academy at Annapolis, Maryland. One day I received a set of orders to the naval training station, San Diego, California, for a course of instructions in Gregg shorthand, which I had requested in order to better prepare myself to be able to act as a court reporter at an officer's general court martial anytime my services would be required. At that time, military law required a naval officer or a senior chief petty officer to serve as a reporter when an officer was being tried by a general court martial.

One beautiful spring morning upon returning from a weekend of liberty in Los Angeles, while I was awaiting orders to go back to my destroyer at the naval academy after having completed the shorthand course, I heard someone yell out loud as I walked in the door.

"Hey Ski, I hear you're China bound." I didn't pay any attention, thinking *Oh, yeah.*

Then another one.

"Gonna bring back a Rooskee princess for your wife, hey? Those Rooskees will get you, baby, if you don't watch out."

I was subjected to this kind of ribbing coming at me from all sides for several minutes. "Okay," I finally said, "where the hell is all this dope about China coming from? Where did you guys get this scuttlebutt from, anyway? Maybe I should go have a drink from that scuttlebutt myself. You guys are nuts. I'm heading back to my four-stack destroyer at the naval academy."

"Sure, you bet you are. It'll be a destroyer all right, but not where you think. It will be a little four-stack torpedo boat, as the gals in New Orleans called them. It'll be right out on the Asiatic station in the Philippines."

So I decided to go over to the executive officer's quarters to check up on all this ribbing and to get the straight dope and find out for myself. What they were telling me proved to be true. They had my orders to the Asiatic station all right.

On 1 June 1936, a couple of weeks later, I left San Diego and was on my way to the Philippines via the U.S.S. *Chaumont,* a U.S. Navy troopship with orders to report to the commander in chief of the Asiatic station for assignment to duty. The U.S.S. *Chaumont* was captured from Germany during the First World War and was pressed into service by the navy where she remained as a troopship in World War One and was still on duty in

World War Two. The U.S.S. *Chaumont* carried about 1,500 passengers on this trip and about a ship's complement of another 600 to man the ship.

The passage from Long Beach, California, to Manila, Philippine Islands, normally took twenty-six days. We played all kinds of card games, such as poker, blackjack, pinochle, read books, told cock-and-bull stories, and slept; it helped pass the time, which at times became pretty damn monotonous, to say the least. They were a long twenty-six days. Seven days after we left Long Beach, we sighted the Hawaiian Islands, and after clearing the breakwater, we were moored to a dock at Pearl Harbor.

We remained at Pearl for three days, which allowed time to fuel and provision the ship. Also it allowed time for the crew and passengers to go on liberty and stretch their sea legs a bit on the beach. The tenth day found us out on the high seas heading toward our destination, which was Manila in the Philippines. On this leg of our trip to Manila, we stopped at Wake, Midway, and Guam Islands. The U.S.S. *Isabella* was stationed in Guam. She carried passengers going on vacation or, as they say in the service, some good old R&R, rest and relaxation. She also carried the mail from Guam to Manila and the China station at Shanghai, and vice versa.

The U.S.S. *Isabella* was formerly a yacht converted into a small passenger boat. It served that purpose to a tee. She made a round trip each week. Guam had only a small dock, and the U.S.S. *Isabella* was tied up there. So upon our arrival in Guam, we anchored out in the harbor. From there, all the mail and stores that we had brought from the States and Hawaii and the marine personnel replacements for the company of marines that were stationed on the island had to be ferried over to the beach.

Guam was a small island, mostly all natives who worked for the United States, so we stayed only long enough to take care of the required chores. The troops were granted liberty for a few hours. From what I had heard about Guam, I remained on board, feeling there was nothing there for me. That evening, we cleared the breakwater and headed out to sea to continue our trip to Manila.

6. Crossing the International Date Line

One day while at sea, I couldn't believe it when I heard the chief boatswain's mate pipe over the loudspeaker, "Now hear this, now hear this, church services will be held on the first Sunday of this week. The second Sunday will be treated as just another work day." Then I suddenly realized

15

we must be at the international date line (the 180th meridian), where one gains a day going to the Orient and loses a day on their return. Sure enough I had made the right guess; we were approaching the 180th meridian, the international date line.

When a vessel approaches the international date line, they have entered the realm of His Royal Majesty the Golden Dragon, and he will not suffer a lowly neophyte to go beyond the 180th meridian without his permission. If there is anyone on board the vessel who has not crossed the date line in the past and is not a "subject of the Royal Golden Dragon," then that vessel cannot proceed until it has his permission, which will not be granted until everyone who is not a subject of His Majesty has been initiated into his court by his court jesters.

So upon reaching the international date line, all vessels are stopped dead in the water by the orders of His Royal Majesty. He then goes on board over the bow of the ship and demands to see a roster of the personnel on board to make sure that no neophyte, if there be any, will pass through his realm without becoming one of his subjects by being duly initiated into his court. As I had never crossed the 180th meridian before, when the names were presented to His Royal Majesty, my name was on that list, so I was called upon to be initiated by the orders of His Royal Majesty.

I immediately informed him that I was a shellback, and that I was a subject of His Majesty King Neptune, who resides at the equator and controls the seaway at the equator, that he was the real king of all the seven seas, therefore he was inferior to His Majesty King Neptune. I soon found out that was the wrong thing to say. A shellback is one who has been duly initiated in the Court of His Majesty King Neptune as he crosses the equator, which I had done on my way to Rio de Janeiro, Brazil, when President Hoover made the U.S.S. *Rochester* his home for two weeks while visiting South American ports. President Hoover chose the *Rochester* to enable him to stay in touch with Washington. The *Rochester* was the only ship at that time that had enough power to relay to, and receive, messages from, NAA, the naval radio station in Washington, D.C. The President also was initiated as a shellback, along with the rest of the crew in 1928.

King Neptune, like the Golden Dragon, stops all shipping and demands that all neophytes who enter his realm of authority be duly initiated into his court. So I had been initiated by orders of His Majesty King Neptune, and I kept a certificate with me at all times while at sea to verify that I was indeed a bonafide shellback. It was also recorded in the service records of all naval personnel who have crossed the equator; the only way

16

they have to determine who is to be initiated is by checking the service record of all on board.

I was on my way to present my certificate to the His Majesty the Royal Dragon, but before I got there, he became furious and demanded to know who this upstart was. Who dared to say that he was inferior to some low-down who calls himself a king and ruler of any part of the seas? He kept ranting and raving and demanded that upstart to be brought to him so that he may cast his fury upon him. All of a sudden, I was grabbed by some of his subjects and taken before him. When I got there, he demanded to hear what I had to say in my defense. I first showed him my certificate proving I was a shellback; this made him all the more furious. He took my certificate and threw it back at me.

"I don't want to see such trash," he said. "What else do you have to say? Speak up, you upstart."

I then repeated that King Neptune was the ruler of all the seven seas in the whole world, and that he had no jurisdiction over me.

Upon hearing this, he went into a rage and jumped off his throne and ordered his subjects to get me out of his sight immediately and to give me the full works for my insolence. To this, I vehemently objected, but to no avail. He ordered that I be hauled off to the royal doctor, because, in his opinion, I must have been insane and needed to be placed under a doctor's care. He said that "no one in his right mind would have the audacity to oppose the orders of His Royal Majesty the Golden Dragon or to say that he was inferior to someone else."

I was immediately rushed off to the royal doctor, who took good care of me all right. He gave me some large pills made with some gook and red pepper, which I was forced to wash down with a very bitter drink. I was then rushed off to the dentist, who had an electrified toothpick, which he used to probe my teeth and with the electric juice, would give me a good jolt each time as he turned the juice on.

Next, the Royal Dragon ordered that I be put into a barrel filled with water and pushed under until my hat floated. When that was done, I was taken before Buddha, who demanded I get down on my knees and kiss his belly button.

Then I was tossed through a chute into a dark room, where some of his subjects had brooms and kept swatting at me while I groped in the dark trying to find an opening to get out. I finally got out and immediately landed in a pool of gook, consisting of mustard, eggs, catsup, etcetera, you name it, and in this mixture were also paints of all colors. What a mess that was.

17

You couldn't stay on your feet, it was so slippery, you couldn't get your balance to try to get out of there. To make matters worse, they had six or seven of His Majesty's subjects, dressed in red devil suits, and with long electrical probes, jabbing us all the time, which kept us off our balance. When I would finally get to the point where I could stand up, I'd get another shock from one of the red devils, and down I'd go again. When I did succeed in getting out, I was covered from head to foot with that mixture; it was in my ears, hair, eyes, nose, and mouth. Well, needless to say, after that episode, I was ready for the showers.

There was much more to the initiation that I won't divulge at this time, because some day you might cross the equator or the international date line; therefore, I must leave some of the best things as a surprise for you. There were about 400 of us initiated that day and it lasted all day. It took almost three hours for me to get through the initiation. Then it took another couple of hours to get showered and clean the gook off. Our clothes were beyond saving, so we just tossed them away. What a day, but it was a lot of fun for everybody and, of course, broke up the monotony of our crossing to the Orient. When it was over, I was given my King Neptune certificate back to prove I was a shellback.

After crossing the international date line and things were back to normal, the seas were very calm, as if we were floating on a sea of glass, not even a ripple in the water. The only thing that attracted us was a ship passing now and then going in the opposite direction or porpoises diving in a straight line, about twenty-five or thirty on each side of the bow. They stayed with us for miles and would return each day. It made one feel that they were leading the ship.

Other than that, we just fell into the old routine of playing poker, reading, sleeping, eating, etcetera. Every night after dinner, as soon as it got dark, we would all go up topside to see a movie, which was shown every night. It was like being at an outdoor theater at home, with the moon shining brightly overhead. Well, not exactly like home; at this outdoor theater, we were missing a thing or two, such as an automobile with a pretty nice young chick by our side; however, we were content to just sit or lie there on deck with a blanket. Those movies were a big help; they took some of the monotony out of the long trip at sea; especially when one is not assigned to any job, the time just drags on. And the last few days did drag on and on. They were very monotonous, with nothing to do, just the same old routine. I just kept yearning to get to our destination, mostly to get off that crowded

18

ship so I could stretch out a bit and get rid of those sea legs. But I was also getting a bit anxious to be assigned to duty, just to have something to do.

7. History of the Philippines

As I traveled on the U.S.S. *Chaumont,* those last few days, it struck me one morning that here I was, heading to a place for a tour of duty of which I knew nothing. I had never read a book or tried to equip myself with any knowledge of this strange land, the Orient, or the Philippines. I also wanted to acquaint myself with some knowledge of Manila, of which I had heard so much about but couldn't fancy what to expect. I remember the Congress of the United States wanting to know "where the hell Manila was." So I thought, *Paul, here is a chance to find out for yourself where the hell Manila really is.*

Before this, I had never given the Philippines or any part of the Orient, for that matter, a second thought, but here I was, heading to the land that in 1898, some thirty-eight years ago, had startled the halls of Congress of the United States upon the receipt of Admiral Dewey's famous radio message during the Spanish-American war that was delivered to his commander in chief, the president of the United States, which read, "I have just captured Manila, and it is ours." Upon receipt of this message, the members of the Senate and Congress of the United States exclaimed, "Where the hell is Manila?"

As I was doing nothing but leaning on the rail of the ship, just wasting my time in watching the porpoises swimming or just looking out at the sea as the ship wallowed in the waves, I set myself to thinking just what the hell this place Manila is all about. I didn't know a darn thing about this place where I was being transferred to. Therefore, now being curious and also feeling that as long as I was going to live and serve Uncle Sam in doing my duty in that part of the world, I thought this would be a golden opportunity for me, while sailing on board the U.S.S. *Chaumont,* to enlighten myself as much as possible about its history.

Each day thereafter, I would go down to the ship's library and spend as much time as I possibly could studying everything I could find about the Philippines and the Orient in general. Thus, I gained a lot of useful knowledge that I could use while in the islands. I found out that the Philippine Islands, in the sixteenth century, were named after King Philip the Second of Spain, who reigned at that time. I also read that Spain had jurisdiction over

19

the islands for approximately 250 years up until the time the Philippines were captured in the Battle of Manila by Admiral Dewey in 1898, when the Philippines became a possession of the United States. It was made a Commonwealth of the United States, with a high commissioner from America having sole authority.

In my search, I also learned that the Philippine archipelago consists of approximately 7,000 islands and are bounded by the Pacific Ocean, the South China, Celebes and the Philippine seas, and on the northern tip lies the Luzon Straits. It is approximately 115,000 square miles and approximately 1,200 miles wide. The Philippines comprises some 22,000 miles of coastline. The islands are mostly small. Many have an area of approximately only one square mile, and there are a few of about one thousand square miles. Many of the islands have no name at all. Mindanao and Luzon are large islands and account for about 75,000 square miles of the 115,000 square miles of the Philippines.

The Philippines are considered a rain forest and are mostly tropical. They have an average rainfall of eighty inches, which occurs mostly in the summer, and have an average temperature of about eighty degrees Fahrenheit, with a high humidity. The mode of travel on the waterways or rivers is mostly by *bankas,* boats, built from a hollowed-out log, with an arm on each side, such as an outrigger, to keep the banka from tipping over. They are mostly rowed, but some of them have sails.

The islands have many large areas of dense jungles, which are found mostly on Luzon and Mindanao islands, as are huge mountains. The mountains contain many areas of vast forest land along with the dense jungles, which are full of snakes and wild animals, such as wild boars, etcetera.

The population of the Philippines are mainly the Tagalogs (pronounced Ta-gal-lic) on Luzon. The Ilocanos live in the Cagayan River valley, and the Visaya on the central islands.

There are many smaller groups of people, such as the Moros, who are of the Muslim minority. There are the Malays, which are ancestral to the rest of the Filipino groups. There are also the Igorots who live in the mountains, mostly on Mindanao, and are head hunters and always carry a large bolo knife or swordlike weapon. They wave these bolos over their heads and can cut one's head off with one swipe of the bolo.

A couple of friendly native tribes still exist in the Philippines, living in the jungles. They get their subsistence from the fruits of the land. One tribe is the Negritos, pygmies, about three feet tall, who live in Oceania and the southeastern part of Asia and are Aborigines. I had the privilege along with a buddy of mine to visit the Aborigines on Luzon Island for two weeks, which I will elaborate on later.

When Admiral Dewey captured the Philippines back in 1898, the United States, believing in the freedoms of people and, therefore, not about to control other peoples or their land, assured the Filipino people that they would be given their freedom and be granted full independence as soon as they were in a position to govern themselves. That day came on July 4, 1946, when the Philippines became a sovereign country, by being granted its independence, as had been promised by the United States. It was a glorious day for the Filipino population, and they had something to really celebrate, because on that day they had become a free nation for the first time in over 300 years, after having being held under the rule of Spain for over 250 years, then with the winning of the battle of Manila under Admiral Dewey, under the jurisdiction of the United States for another 48 years. However, under the United States, they were as free people, because we did not exploit them or drain them of their wealth; in fact, it cost the United States quite handsomely to keep the high commissioner and troops there to protect the islands. That day, the Fourth of July, 1946 will go down in Filipino history as their independence day, a free nation at last, and as the "Republic of the Philippines."

8. Corregidor Island Spotted—Joined the Asiatic Fleet

I had been sleeping outside the cook shack on deck; for the past week or so it was too hot to sleep in my bunk down below decks on board the U.S.S. *Chaumont*. In the wee hours in the morning of the twenty-sixth day after leaving the States, I woke up and, looking out across the ocean, the Philippine Islands started to loom into view. I immediately got dressed and went over to the rail to get a good look-see of the shores of the country that was to be my home for the next few years. As we steamed up the coast, we passed *Fort Drum*. *Fort Drum* was a concrete battleship built on the tiny island of El Fraile, which guarded the entrance to Manila Bay.

In a few more moments, Corregidor island was spotted. What a sight was this island fortress, which comprised twelve-inch guns, with the Fifty-ninth and Sixtieth Coast Artillery companies manning them to protect Manila Bay. As we sailed past Corregidor while we stood on deck, looking across the waters and admiring the island, I never had the wildest dream that in five years I would be forced to surrender to the Japanese forces, and become a prisoner of war on that magnificent island fortress.

As we got inside the harbor, we passed the Cavite Navy Yard. It was there that I got my first glimpse of Manila, the home of the Asiatic Fleet, of which I was soon to become a part. The Asiatic Fleet, as it had been known for many years before the beginning of World War Two, got its true start by Caleb Cushing, a descendant of John Cushing who came to the United States in 1638 from Norfolk, England. Caleb Cushing graduated from Harvard University and later was elected to Congress from Massachusetts in 1835. He was appointed by President Tyler in 1844 to be the first envoy to China. It was there that he negotiated and signed treaties that opened the door to that vast country for our warships.

The first treaty was signed on 3 July 1844, which allowed our warships to lay at anchor in Chinese waters, along with the Portuguese, who arrived at Macao in 1557, and the English, who arrived in 1635. Although American ships had visited Chinese ports for many years before, we had never signed a treaty with the Chinese. Upon my arrival in Manila in the spring of 1936, I reported to the commander in chief of the Asiatic Fleet for assignment to duty. I was given orders to report to the Commander Destroyer Squadron Asiatic Fleet (ComDesRon AF) for duty. I was further ordered by ComDesRon AF to report for duty to the commanding officer of the U.S.S. *Barker* 213, of the thirteenth division of the Asiatic Fleet.

This division consisted of four destroyers, namely, the U.S.S. *Barker, Whipple, Alden* and *Bulmer,* all very old and obsolete destroyers. The Asiatic Fleet consisted of the following ships: The U.S.S. *Augusta,* a heavy cruiser of the 10,000- ton class, which served as the flagship, carrying the commander in chief of the Asiatic Fleet Admiral Harry E. Yarnell, on board. There were four divisions of destroyers, the thirteenth, fourteenth, fifteenth, and sixteenth, and four destroyers in each division, plus the U.S.S. *John Paul Jones,* which made thirteen destroyers in all.

ComDesRon, of the Asiatic Fleet, made the U.S.S. *John Paul Jones* his home and the flagship of the destroyer squadron. The destroyers were all of the 200 class; they were pre-World War One vintage, hence, very, very old—ancient, rusty, and practically worn out. The U.S.S. *Black Hawk,* which served as the destroyer tender, also was from the First World War vintage. She too was on her last legs. She leaked so badly that her bilges had to be continually pumped out, day and night.

We had six submarines of the S-Type, of World War One vintage. All were so old that they were leaking and were continually breaking down and were constantly under repair. The U.S.S. *Canopus* served as the submarine tender, she too was very old and obsolete. For our navy air force, we had a squadron of PBYs, with the U.S.S. *Langley* as their tender, built in 1912.

All of the above ships were based at the Cavite Navy Yard, across from Manila in the Philippines. They all should have been sold to the Gillette razor blade company and cut up into razor blades years before. In China, on the Yangtze River, we had four light gun boats and four river boats. They too were built long before World War One. They were charged with the patrolling of the Yangtze and Whangpoo rivers, carrying mail, stores, and other materials, and for the protection of the U.S. Embassy and all American properties along the rivers.

Just a few months before the outbreak of the war, Congress thought they had better beef us up out in the Asiatic station to upgrade our spirits, so they dispatched a squadron of very modern V-type submarines, with the U.S.S. *Otus* as their tender. The U.S.S. *Otus* was a fairly new, modern ship compared to what we already had in that part of the world to fight a war with if need be. They also dispatched eight PT boats and ten more PBYs. This gesture made us feel a little more secure in trying to fight a war should the one that was brewing become a shooting war.

So you see, every naval vessel serving on the Asiatic station was pressed into service prior to World War One, and all should have been retired with the exception of the U.S.S. *Augusta,* the U.S.S. *Otus,* and the squadron of V-type submarines, which were the only ships that were not obsolete and which were assigned to the Asiatic Fleet. However, the destroyers' sailors, being well trained, more than proved themselves against the Japanese when called upon, as will be told later.

The Asiatic Fleet was assigned the task of protecting the American consulate generals, their staffs, all U.S. owned property, American citizens and their property on the islands of Wake, Guam, and the Philippines, also all of China and all the countries of the Malay archipelago. Quite a vast job for a bunch of worn-out ships. Oh, well, Congress called us the "expendables." Those were the ships that Congress gave us to protect and safeguard the lives and property of our citizens in that part of the world. The Asiatic Fleet was known throughout the navy as the "expendables," or the "suicide fleet," names given to us by none other than the U.S. Congress. We were so far from the United States, it would be hard to get help to us in time of war, and they refused to beef us up in times of peace.

Later on, we were called the "the fighting bastards of Bataan." This latter name was given to us by the Japanese General Homma, who found out the hard way, by allowing us free passage into the Bataan-Mariveles peninsula, which later cost him over 20,000 of his crack troops, and their three well-seasoned commanders, who came up from Singapore. The Asiatic Fleet was given a mission to perform should our great country ever be under attack and forced into a war with any nation in that part of the world. But Congress didn't see fit to give those on the Asiatic Station the proper tools to carry out that mission—they just gave us a bunch of obsolete ships. To top it off, just before the war started, they assigned my old happy home the U.S.S. *Rochester,* built in 1890, to be a part of the Asiatic Fleet. What a laugh.

When the war came to the Philippines, the navy had pilots and gas galore, but just a handful of planes. Why? We are hearing today the same old story that we heard back in 1940 when the war clouds started to loom over the Asiatic Station. The words of "fortify the Asiatic Fleet" would come up in the halls of the Congress, and the responsive cry would always be, "We are a peace-loving nation. We might offend our good neighbor, Japan," or "we might offend Russia."

In Korea, when China was bombing our troops in South Korea from Chinese soil across the Yellow River, General MacArthur was told he was not to cross the 39th parallel because we might offend China and drag her into the war. General MacArthur wanted to bomb their base across the Yellow River and stop the slaughter of our troops in South Korea. If China wasn't already in the war with her big bombers, then what the hell did they call it. When will we ever wake up?

Congress was blind to Japan's fortifying up to her teeth, buying shipload after shipload of scrap iron, etcetera, from America and around the world, all the time getting ready for that war for which they had been preparing as far back as 1853 against the United States, or the "imperialistic West," as the Japanese called us. I hate to think that our congressmen and senators whom we elected were really that stupid that they could not see what was coming and prepare those they had put on the Asiatic station by arming them properly to enable them to do the job that was expected of them. Instead, they just classified us as "expendables."

In the spring of each year since 1898, when Admiral Dewey, during the Spanish-American War, steamed into Manila Bay and captured the Philippines, it was the custom for the Asiatic Fleet to spend the summers in China and winters in the Philippines. So in April of each year, we would weigh anchor and head for our summer maneuvering grounds in China. It was also the custom, prior to the fleet going to their respective Chinese summer maneuvering grounds, for the entire fleet to first go to Shanghai for a ten-day period of recreation and relaxation, which was something all hands looked forward to.

Upon arrival in Shanghai each spring, several Chinese workers would come on board, the same ones each year. All the ships had their Chinese workmen. For lack of a name, we called them all Charlie. After our ten-day stay in Shanghai, the Chinese workmen would follow us to our summer maneuvering grounds at Chefoo, China, We had names for all of them, such as "No Squeak" for the shoe repairman, "Sew Sew" was the tailor, and then there was "Scrubby Scrub" for the laundryman, and so forth. We had a lot of fun with the Chinese workmen.

In the fall of the year, for fun, we would ask them every day, "How cold today, Charlie?" They would count the number of coats they had on. If they had on six coats, they would reply "sic coat cold." The coats they had on were very thin, a little thicker than a bedsheet. Sometimes they had on as many as twenty such coats. Which gave us a big laugh. They were a great bunch of fellows.

Every day, we would give them a lot of food, among other things, to take home. When we arrived in port, upon anchoring or if we moored to the dock, two or three sampans would come alongside and drop their anchor or tie up to the ship. They would wash the outside of the ship or scrape and paint it where necessary. Some of the sampans would comprise the whole family, including the grandparents. It was their home; they were born on it, and they died on it. Each ship would drop all the leftover scraps from the tables into the slop chute, which was located on the fantail of the ship. Sometimes the cook would offer them a whole roasted turkey or chicken, or a few loaves of bread. They would insist that everything, no matter what, be put in the slop chute, and they would catch everything in their drip net, They washed everything in the dirty Whangpoo River before they would eat it. So we used to sing:

Meet me by the slop chute on the old Whangpoo,
Bring along your drip net, there'll be chow for two.
We'll have some sweet potatoes and some good old Irish stew.
If you'll meet me by the slop chute, on the old Whangpoo.

25

It seemed that they were always happy, smiling, and joking with one another. We liked them and were glad to see them when we arrived in China at our summer maneuvering grounds. They were always there. Almost everyone in the ship's crew had a rickshaw coolie who was very loyal. When we went into town, they would ask "Where you go, master?" After we told them and were seated in the rickshaw, we'd say, "Chop-chop," and they would start running and never stop until our destination, regardless of how far. I don't know how they did it.

If one went into a house to stay for the night, they would take all your money and ask, "What time shipside, master?" No matter what time you told him, regardless of day or night, Charlie was there to make sure you got back to your ship on time. He would break a door down if need be, and they sometimes did, just to get you back on time. When you came out in the morning, he would give you back your money, and not a cent would be missing, regardless of whether the sailor was drunk or sober the night before. They were very honest. When the ship was in port, Charlie was right there all the time. He slept in his rickshaw, at the dock alongside your ship. They were very dependable. We paid them eight *mex* a day (about fifty cents gold), which they called American money.

When we left China for our winter home port in the Philippines, we gave them all the Chinese money we had left, to keep them for the winter. Sometimes it amounted to about thirty-five dollars gold. After our usual stay at Shanghai, we would break up and sail for our regular summer ports, the destroyers would go to Chefoo, the submarines to Chin-huang-Tao, the flagship the U.S.S. *Augusta,* with the commander in chief of the Asiatic Fleet on board, summered between Shanghai and Tsingtao. Some of His Majesty's ships of the British Royal Navy that were serving on the Asiatic station summered at Weihaiwei, and some went to His Majesty's Royal Naval Yard at Hong Kong.

9. Trip to Vladivostok, Russia

In June of 1937, Franklin Delano Roosevelt, the thirty- second president of the United States, and his cabinet, were trying to strike a deal with Russia that would eventually lead to our recognition of that country. Just about the time that America was getting ready to vote to recognize Russia, the Russian government sent an invitation to allow a division of American destroyers to visit Vladivostok on a good will mission, as a gesture of their good faith.

The invitation was gladly accepted by Admiral Harry E. Yarnell, who was the CINCAF at that time. As no other United States naval vessels had been allowed in a Russian port since 1923, the Admiral deemed it an honor that the Russians would even think of allowing a group of the United States naval fighting ships to enter a Russian port. Admiral Yarnell, in accepting this invitation, also figured that since no other American men-of-war had been allowed to enter a Russian port in over fourteen years, this would give the United States a golden opportunity to get a first-hand look-see in a country that up until now had been closed to the whole world.

The Thirteenth Division, which comprised the U.S.S. *Barker, Bulmer, Alden, Whipple,* and the destroyer flagship, the *John Paul Jones,* were given the nod to accompany the commander in chief of the Asiatic Fleet on his voyage to Russia. I was serving on board the U.S.S. *Barker* (213) at that time, and along with my shipmates, was delighted to know that we were going to make this trip.

The division of destroyers, with ComDesRon AF on board the *John Paul Jones,* left Chefoo, China, and headed for Vladivostok about 5:00 P.M. on Friday, the twenty-third day of July. ComDesRon AF was under orders to rendezvous with the U.S.S. *Augusta* at a prearranged location while enroute.

About midnight the next day, Saturday, the twenty-fourth of July 1937, the U.S.S. *Augusta,* with Admiral Harry E. Yarnell, CINCAF, on board, and commanded by Captain R. P. McConnell of the U.S. Navy, left Tsingtao, China. The U.S.S. *Augusta* joined up with the division of destroyers on Sunday afternoon, the twenty-fifth of July at the prearranged location. This was the beginning of the typhoon season, and the seas were starting to kick up their heels; however, all went off without a mishap. At about 1600 hours that afternoon, we ran into the edge of a typhoon off the coast of Japan. The winds were so strong that all shipping in the area were tied up either at Shimonoseki or Fusan, Japan. However, we continued on.

At about 2000 hours that night, on the twenty-fifth of July, the winds were blowing in full force and the seas were getting very rough. I thought for a moment that we too would be stopped in our tracks and be forced into a port for shelter. But we were very fortunate in escaping the fury of the storm's center, the eye of the storm, and we were able to continue toward our destination.

Wednesday, 28 July 1937, in the early morning hours, as the armada of American ships, consisting of the U.S.S. *Augusta* and the five destroyers, approached the shores of Vladivostok, we were met by a Russian destroyer, the U.S.S.R. *Stalin,* about twelve miles out at sea. After acknowledging each other, the Russian destroyer escorted us into the port of Vladivostok. This marked the first time in over fourteen years since the U.S.S. *Sento* served there as a station ship for the American crew operating off a nearby Russian island wireless station that a U.S. naval vessel had been allowed to enter a Russian port.

As the armada of American warships steamed into the harbor, the Russians announced our arrival by firing a national salute of twenty-one guns in honor of the president of the United States, whom we were representing, and also honoring Admiral Yarnell, our commander in chief of the Asiatic station. Upon entering the harbor of Vladivostok, it made one think of the striking resemblance to the harbor at Constantinople, the entrance through East Bosporus into the Golden Horn.

The harbor was about four miles long, a mile wide, and extended from the Bay of Peter the Great to Amur Bay. There were excellent facilities available for docking, handling cargo, and marine work. Icebreakers keep the harbor open during the winter months. The Russians exported mostly soya beans, lumber, and fish from this port; hence, it must be kept open all year round for shipping. The city was built on the slopes of a ridge of hills. Its population numbered over 100,000. This sight was selected for an outlet for Eastern Russia after the Treaty of Aigun in 1858. It has been the far Eastern terminus of the Trans-Siberian Railroad since 1917; however, rail communications were established with the Trans-Baikal district via Manchuria in 1857.

As soon as the *Augusta* had been secured to the dock at about 10:00 A.M., Admiral Yarnell, commander in chief of the Asiatic Fleet, and the commander of the destroyer squadron, disembarked to make various official calls on the commander of the U.S.S.R. Pacific Fleet, the garrison commander, the Far Eastern representative of foreign affairs, and the president of the city council, who was also the mayor of the city of Vladivostok. All of these calls were returned that afternoon by the various Russian representatives of the U.S.S.R. just mentioned.

When all the formalities were over, the crews were granted liberty, which was about four in the afternoon. We were given free tickets to a Russian circus, which offered some outstanding acts, such as acrobats, trick riding, tight-rope walking, trained dogs, and stunts that in United States circuits would make vaudeville headlines. We were furnished refreshments, which included ice cream, cigarettes, soda water, candies, and many varieties of cakes before, during, and after each of the performances.

We were treated very kindly by the Russians. But even back in those days, they were cunning. During the two weeks of our stay there, with the banquets, shows, dances, and, as an added attraction, a circus, for which the Russians are famous, we were entertained royally from early morning to midnight each day, which gave us hardly any time for ourselves to shop or walk around on our own to really see what Russia was like. Of course this was the Russian plan for us, to keep us busy. It was their intention to keep us occupied, and that they did, by mapping out our time to serve their own interests, not to allow time for us to go our own way and see parts of Russia they didn't want us to see. Such as how the population really lived, how they fared, etcetera.

But I and a couple of my buddies skipped some of their hospitality in order that we may get a little glimpse of just what gives in Russia. The Russians, young and old, were led to believe that Americans were very poor. They did this by not giving us the proper exchange for our money. The money exchange was part of their idea of utilizing our time. With a poor rate of exchange, we wouldn't have enough money to spend, thus making us look very poor. So an exchange booth was set up on the dock to exchange our money into rubles.

As we came down the gangplank from the ship, a lady was there to exchange our money before we could go into town. I had five dollars in U.S. currency and, not knowing the score immediately upon landing, exchanged it right there on the dock. We were not informed that if we went to the bank, we would get the same exchange as the Russian people. The exchange at the bank was at that time about eighty or ninety rubles to one U.S. dollar. At that rate of exchange, my little five dollars would have gotten me four hundred and fifty rubles, whereas they only gave me twenty-six rubles and twenty-five kopeks. What a difference. We were given what they called the international exchange which was five rubles and twenty-five kopeks for one U.S. dollar.

The next day, the twenty-eighth of July, 1937 we were granted permission to take cameras ashore; did we use them? I'll say we did. I myself used up many rolls of film. However, we were only allowed to go and see what was planned. In the afternoon of July 29, we were entertained by the Russians with an exhibition soccer game in their athletic stadium, followed by an exhibition softball game put on by the crews of the U.S.S. *Augusta* and the U.S.S. *John Paul Jones.* On July 30, the Russians gave another circus performance, along with refreshments, for those who didn't have liberty the day before, so all hands got to see the circus. There was also a presentation of the Self-Activity Concert of the Red sailors and officers' families, including singing and acrobatic and native dances. I must say it was outstanding.

Having already seen the circus with the first group, I, along with a couple of buddies, went to a hotel restaurant, and upon being seated, we ordered a glass of vodka and a steak dinner. While we were waiting for our dinner and enjoying our vodka (or were we?—it sure was a strong drink), an American merchant marine sailor from a Standard Oil tanker came over and spoke to us.

"Hi, sailors, what rate of exchange did the Russians give you guys?"

We told him five rubles and twenty-five kopeks for one American dollar.

"Holy smoke," he said. "You guys must have a lot of money to be able to drink vodka at the rate of exchange you guys got."

"Why do you say that?" we asked.

"Do you know that that small glass of vodka you guys are consuming is costing you about thirty-five rubles—about seven bucks American money according to the exchange you got." In the same breath, he asked, "What did you order for your dinner?"

"T-bone steak, what else?" we said.

"Steak! Are you guys mad?" he yelled out loud. "T-bone steak will cost you about eighty rubles, or fifteen bucks, so with a vodka and the steak, it will run over twenty-two bucks American money without even a tip for the gal. Where do you guys in the navy get that kind of dough to be living that high on the hog?"

We were all so dumbfounded, none of us could give him an answer. The meal we ordered was costing each of us a little over twenty-two bucks in American money, while that same meal would have only cost a Russian two dollars and nineteen cents with their regular rate of exchange of eighty rubles for one U.S. dollar. Brother what a difference. We rushed over and thanked the guy. You never saw three guys scramble as fast as we did to get the heck out of there. We left, leaving the steaks behind; we had already drunk the vodka before the sailor informed us about the rate of exchange.

We got lost in a hurry in the crowd on the street outside the restaurant, because we had left without paying, and were in fear of being caught. We didn't even have enough to pay for the vodka, which we had already deposited down the hatch. That was too rich for our blood at the rate of pay,

Uncle Sammy paid us. Right after leaving the restaurant, we ran into a Chinese man with a little black bag; he was exchanging American money for rubles at the rate of sixty-five for one. We told him, "too late, Joe, the gal on the dock got our money."

In looking over these prices below, one can easily see that with the rate of exchange they gave us, our money wouldn't go very far in Russia. They certainly did make us look like paupers to their people. The stores were mostly empty and with hardly anything to sell. What they did have was of poor quality and very costly, as shown in the table below.

Item	Regular price	Russian pays	American pays
Pair of shoes	180 rubles	$2.11 US	$34.28
Men's suit	450 rubles	5.63 US	85.39
Shirt	35 rubles	0.44 US	6.64
Hat	70 rubles	0.88 US	13.28
Necktie	20 rubles	0.25 US	3.80
Meal	60 rubles	0.75 US	11.39
Mask	29 rubles	0.36 US	5.50
Can of sardines	40 rubles	0.50 US	7.59

The USSR fixed the rate of wages and exchange for their people from day to day, as they saw fit. They tried to stop us from really seeing Russia and its failure under Communism by not giving us the same rate of exchange for our money as their own people received. If we had only known and gone to a bank in town, maybe the Russian gals and others on the street would not be so sorry for us *poor* Americans.

From observing the people as I walked the streets, it seemed that the average Russian had but the barest necessities of life. We saw as many as six separate families living in the same house. Rooms had bunks jammed against each other, about four high, so one could hardly crawl into them. I really didn't see how they managed, especially with each family having four or five children. Which meant, counting the husband and wife, it would make six to seven in one family, and some couples had many more children than just four or five; some had seven or eight. However, with just four children to a family, and six families living together, that's thirty-six people living in the same house. And the houses in Russia were just about the same or smaller than the average house here in America. That was the kind of thing they didn't want us to see.

But my buddy and I sneaked away and got a good look, which gave us the opportunity to really see how the other side lived under Communism. Building repairs were long overdue. I didn't see a single home that was fit to live in. They were in such horrible shape, yet five, and sometimes six, families lived together, or rather were crammed together. The stench was horrible as you walked past some of the houses, almost unbearable at times. What a life.

The main street of Vladivostok was cobblestoned; the side streets were dirt and muddy; the sanitation was bad everywhere you went. All the buildings looked unsanitary and filthy; and no matter where you went, the stench was there. My buddies and I kept our handkerchiefs over our noses most of the time. Looking into the faces of the crowds of people as I walked down the streets, they presented a picture of hard-working men and women with a look of desperate determination. However, it seemed they were burdened too heavy to smile even a little bit. You saw very few smiles.

Each day as I walked the streets with my buddy, I kept saying to myself, "there is definitely something missing." I kept wondering and searching my mind as I continued looking at those people, trying to find out what was missing, what it was I was looking for. Finally, it hit me like a ton of bricks. There it was, staring me right in the face. It was that "the jovial, bantering characteristic for which our people in America are known." That was what was missing. These people were depressed and wanted to speak out to us Americans but were in constant fear for their very existence. There were military men walking four abreast down each street about a block or so apart. Each carried side arms, and a rifle on their shoulder. Their uniforms were dirty and disarrayed.

On 31 July 1937, in the morning, we were entertained by the Red army in the Red naval fleet garden. That afternoon they held an international swimming meet for our pleasure and entertainment. In the evening, they all invited the ships' crews to attend a Russian musical comedy. Both the musical comedy and the swimming meet were very nicely done and enjoyed by all. The Russian commander of the U.S.S.R. Pacific fleet held a banquet in the house of the Red army and naval fleet building for the American officers on Friday, and for the U.S. Navy petty officers on Saturday. They were scrumptious banquets, for which Russian hospitality had been famous. As we were enjoying this banquet, one couldn't help but wonder and feel pity for the ordinary Russian persons in the street who were going hungry while we were being served all those platters of gourmet food. Such lavish entertainment by the U.S.S.R. even bewildered the Russian people who served the food and otherwise worked there. It was a rare experience for them. It was evidence of the Soviet's desire to prove their hospitality and friendship. However, even back then, it gave one the feeling they were trying to show their people that Communism was the only way to go, that the capitalistic people were very poor.

Some nights we would be taken to a dance pavilion in a park. They had two bands set up at each end of the pavilion; one would play for ten minutes and stop, then the other would start up and play for ten minutes. As each band stopped, before you could get your breath, bingo, another girl would latch onto you and keep you dancing. After about an hour or so, I finally said "enough" and quit. The high command made it look as if dancing in the streets and in the parks was very popular in Russia with the younger set. But we found out later that such was not the case, because there was nothing to dance about in their way of living, that it was just a show for us poor Americans.

There were plenty of girls made available as dancing partners for the American visitors. I was told by several girls who could speak a little English that for a couple of weeks before our arrival, those girls had been taught and rehearsed over and over on how to dance. The young ladies were beautifully dressed. One young lady who spoke broken English told me that the dresses were loaned to them for just this one occasion, that they were just for show. She also told me that the dresses had to be returned as soon as the American ships left her country.

She and several other people whom I was able to talk to were very bitter against their own people but were not in a position to do anything about it. If they complained they would be banished to the salt mines. The girls were also given money and instructed to buy drinks for us, having been told that the Americans were very poor people and couldn't afford to buy a drink. Even the motion picture houses refused our money and courteously invited us to come in and enjoy their programs free. They even gave us free sodas and popcorn. When we tried to pay for something, they would say, "You keep your money, you need it badly." The average Russian felt the same pity for us poor Americans; they believed that we were in a far worse position than they, a belief imbedded in their minds by their superiors. They had been brainwashed about how poor we Americans were long before we had arrived in the port of Vladivostok.

I noticed that all the churches and synagogues were closed and boarded up. So I inquired of the girl I was dancing with about religion in

33

Russia. She told me that the Russian people were not allowed to hold religious services of any kind, but that religion flourished in their minds, and they held clandestine meetings wherever they could, which was not too often. In Russia, it seemed that sons, brothers, sisters, and even mothers and fathers were spying on one another, so one was afraid to say a word in his own home, for fear of being turned in by his own family and sent to the salt mines to perform hard labor. When they were sent to the salt mines, they never returned, neither were they ever seen again. The salt mines were feared by everyone, because they all knew that they used only slave labor, and one worked until he dropped. There was no hospitalization for those sent there, just slave labor.

This trip was a rare experience and a golden opportunity to visit a city of the U.S.S.R., to be able to observe their struggle in trying to make Vladivostok the commercial, naval, and military center of the Far East.

On 31 July 1937 at about 11:30 A.M., Admiral Yarnell gave an official reception on board the U.S.S. *Augusta* to our Russian hosts. Immediately after the formalities, open house was held on board the *Augusta* for about four hundred Russian visitors.

Although we had accepted the invitation to visit Russia for the full period of two weeks, which was from 27 July to 10 August 1937, the sanitation was so bad and the streets so filthy, Admiral Yarnell cut our visit nine days short; five days was all we could stand smelling that stench. Admiral Yarnell gave the excuse that with trouble brewing between China and Japan, we had been ordered back to Shanghai.

As we returned to our ships for the last time, we noticed that the Russians had changed the large sign over the money booth that had been set up on the dock to exchange our money when we arrived. Upon our first arrival on the docks at Vladivostok, the sign read, "This bank is for your convenience—exchange all monies here." It now read, "The ruble is solely for internal exchange. It is therefore unlawful to take Russian rubles out of the country. If you have rubles left over, they will not be redeemed. They must be deposited in the box provided."

Well, as they shortchanged us upon our arrival with their rate of exchange, we decided to spend every ruble, and not give them back. So I stayed on the dock that night and helped collect all the rubles we could from those who did not want to take them home as souvenirs. When all the ship's company had reported back on board that night, and we had collected all the rubles we could, we sent a gob ashore to spend the money any way he could instead of our returning it. We bought little cans of sardines,

34

which at our rate of exchange was seven dollars and fifty-nine cents a can; the same can of Norwegian sardines in the U.S. was only ten cents. However, we decided we were going to get something for our rubles, and *we did.*

On 1 August 1937 the admiral issued orders for all ships to make preparations to put to sea and to proceed back to their summer home ports in China. So that afternoon, the destroyers headed for Chefoo, their summer maneuvering grounds, and the *Augusta* headed to Tsingtao. As we were steaming out of Vladivostok harbor, Admiral Yarnell, on board the U.S.S. *Augusta,* sent this encoded message to all the ships that had accompanied him on the visit to Russia: "God save us from Communism is all that I can say." I shared the admiral's sentiments. I once again bowed my head in prayer and thanked my Heavenly Father that I was born in the United States of America, as I had done many times during my four-year tour in Central and South Americas when seeing how the people were forced to live. I thanked Him for my not having to live like that, and for my being an American and being privileged to live in this great country of ours, under the Stars and Stripes. I have often said that those people who advocate the overthrow of Democracy and replaced with Communism, or another ism, should be forced to go and live under those conditions. They would soon be begging to come back to America, to the "land of the free and the home of the brave." To honor our country's flag, which so many have given their lives for, and not burn or trample it under their feet. To all this I say, "Thank God I am living in a free country and not under Communism or a dictatorship."

Later, Admiral Yarnell, in describing our visit to Vladivostok, wrote:

> There are two main streets paved with cobblestone, the remainder are dirt roads. The buildings are unkempt. Sanitation is at is lowest ebb. The goods in the stores are few, and what were there was, was of poor quality and high in price. God save us from Communism.

Admiral Yarnell also wrote about Russia that "in order to make a success of this form of government; first, you must kill off the intelligentsia. Second: destroy all churches and deny anyone from practicing any type of religion. Third: discourage family life by crowding the populace into poor housing, with several families residing in the same house. Fourth: have one-half of the people watch the other half and report what they see to the commissar." Incidentally, Rear Admiral Robley "Fighting Bob" Evans, in writing of his experience in 1902 after also taking some ships of the Asiatic Fleet under his command to Vladivostok, said:

> The city is a lake of mud. Many large buildings were going full blast, with the attraction being wine, women and song. With champagne and vodka flowing over the doorsill of the saloons, which were everywhere. Prostitution was on a rampage. The stench was so horrible, one could hardly stand it.

So with the prostitution and filth in the streets being so bad, he too, cut his visit short and headed for home.

With our visit, some thirty-five years later one would think that all which Admiral Evans had witnessed would have changed and the Russians had become more civilized. Well, nothing had changed in those thirty-five years between Admiral Bob Evans's visit and ours; the streets were still dirty, and the unbearable stench was out of this world.

A friend of mine made a recent trip to Russia and told me that everything was the same today as it was when I was there more then fifty years ago. The good thing that our visit accomplished, if nothing else, was that it was good for the ship's complement; it afforded the personnel the chance to see for themselves, first-hand, real Communism at work in Russia. They were now in a true position to tell their friends and the world the difference between our two systems.

10. Stranded up the Min River in China

Two days after leaving the Russian port of Vladivostok, while en route to Chefoo, China, our summer home, we received a message from the division commander ordering the U.S.S. *Barker* 213, the ship I was serving on at the time, to proceed to Tsingtao, China, for repairs. Upon arrival there, the ship was put in drydock and remained there for one week. Upon completion of the ship's repairs, we again put out to sea and were heading back to our summer maneuvering grounds. While enroute, we received orders to proceed to Foochow, a city up the Min River in South China.

Things were getting pretty hot in that area, with the Japanese moving in fast. Our duties were to relay messages for the staff of the American Embassy who were stationed there and, in general, do any duty required by the American consulate. We were to stand by to evacuate the American consulate general and all American nationals should it become necessary. We were being placed at the disposal of the American consulate general in Foochow, in the Fukien province.

After being up the Min River a couple of months, we started to run short of food. We finally got to the point that something had to done. We reported our plight to ComDesRon AF and requested supplies immediately.

While we waited, we were playing baseball one day in a cow pasture. A cow loomed into view. Instantly, that cow was butchered. It had hardly hit the ground before the men were cutting steaks off her rump and throwing them onto an open flame. Being a farm boy, I did everything in my power to stop them from eating that meat. I told them that all red meat should be hung at least fourteen days before being eaten. Fourteen days is the least amount of time it takes to get the animal heat out and make the meat safe to be eaten. Hey! You try to tell that to a bunch of half-starved sailors. I did, but got nowhere, it was totally ignored. I was told to get lost; they were hungry, and steaks it was going to be for dinner that night. Well, the boys had the steaks on the grill and devoured within two hours from the time we saw the cow grazing in the field.

Well, needless to say, we had a bunch of sick sailors and marines on board that night. The ship's doctor was mad as holy carey and gave them hell, which they justly deserved. Being an ex-farmer I knew better, so no way was I going to partake of those nice juicy steaks, so of course, yours truly didn't get sick.

A couple of days later, we received a message that the U.S.S. *Parrot* would relieve us. We were told that upon being relieved, we were to proceed to the British Crown Colony, Hong Kong, to provision and fuel the ship and, upon completion, to report back to ComDesRon for orders. The captain of the U.S.S. *Barker* had the boilers lit off and got the ship underway as fast as he possibly could and headed down the Min River. Upon arriving at the mouth of the river, there we found ships that the Chinese had brought in and sunk to keep the Japanese out. But it backfired—the blockage had us locked in.

This was bad. We were almost completely out of food and had no way to replenish our stock. We were forced to return back up the river and wait for the Chinese to clear a passage to allow us access to the open seas. The Chinese brought in huge cranes to raise the sunken barges and ships. It was a godsend that the British destroyer, the H.M.S. *Darling,* also was there performing the same duties for their country. It was a good deal for us that the British came prepared to stay awhile; they had plenty of food for themselves. Therefore, we used our ingenuity and invited them to come and see our movies at night, and they in turn invited us over to partake of their food. We had only six movies on board, so night after night we showed them our movies (all six). We showed them over and over. Then we would take a reel of one and a reel of another to make our own movies. It was entertaining, and a lot of laughs were had by all, because no one knew what was coming next. One minute a girl was being shot, and the next minute she was being loved to death; it was entertaining.

In the daytime, we taught the Limeys how to play baseball, after a couple of games, we played them for beer. Of course, you know who won. We won, who else? After all we taught them the game.

The Chinese worked very hard to open the mouth of the river for us. Well, they finally got an opening wide enough to let us out and the U.S.S. *Parrot,* our relief ship, in. By the time we were in the open sea, we were completely out of food. We had been locked in for over three months, The chief commissary steward reported that he had only enough rations to feed the crew for one more day.

The next morning, our relief ship, the U.S.S. *Parrot,* was sighted. When she got near enough, we received the following signal:

"We are out of provisions. Give us all you can spare, also your movies that you have on board."

"Boy, oh, boy," we said, "what chow?" We sent back a message.

"We have six movies, and our food supplies consist of two cases of baking powder."

When the U.S.S. *Parrot* cleared the entrance to the Min River, we transferred to them the movies and whatever else we could find that they needed. After our captain gave all information to the relief captain about the conditions, we headed out to sea. And as soon as we cleared the entrance to the Min River, the captain's first order was full steam ahead, as he hadn't fared much better than the crew regarding food. We must have broken a few records in racing toward Hong Kong; we needed some good nourishment.

Upon our arrival at Hong Kong, we were met by the U.S.S. *Neches,* a naval oil tanker, who fueled us. Upon being refueled, we proceeded into port. The U.S.S. *Chaumont* was there, and she gave us the necessary food and provisions to last us for three months. As soon as the ship was fueled and all the stores were on board, the paymaster from the U.S.S. *Ashville,* which was anchored in the harbor, came on board and gave us our three-months back pay. Liberty was granted immediately, and yours truly hit the beach pronto to find a restaurant, among other things. Food and more food was about all I had on my mind at that particular time.

That night, our captain sent the following message to both the commander in chief of the Asiatic Fleet and to ComDesRon AF which read, "Arrived in Hong Kong. Crew paid. Liberty granted, and the crew has received a big feed of chicken with all the trimmings, including ice cream and cake." I thought, *what is this Navy coming to? Are we turning into a bunch of cream puffs? "Ice cream and cake."* However, such was not the case, when a few years later, as proven in 1942, in the Java seas, when those tin-cans (destroyers) were put to the test and went into action against the enemy. More about the tin-cans later.

After five days in Hong Kong, while we were enjoying a little rest and relaxation, or R&R, we received orders to return up the Min River to relieve the *Parrot.* She was now in the same condition as we had been, no food, no pay, or relaxation. They also had been on a mission such as we had been on for over three months with no place to draw stores, etcetera, before being relieved by them. Now it was their turn for a little R&R.

In compliance with the orders of ComDesRon AF, we weighed anchor and headed back for the Min River to relieve the U.S.S. *Parrot.* We arrived at about 1400 hours. They were happy to see us steam into the bay of Amoy. As soon as the U.S.S. *Parrot* had been refueled and provisioned with enough stores to last a few months, she came back up the Min River to Amoy and relieved our ship, the U.S.S. *Barker,* which had been ordered back to Philippines for a tour of duty and R&R upon arrival of our relief.

11. Two Weeks with the Pygmies (Aborigines)

While on one of the tours in the Philippine waters, I and a buddy had the privilege of spending two weeks with an aboriginal tribe on Luzon, an island near Manila in the Philippines; it was very refreshing. I learned a lot about them. Their teeth are all jet black, from chewing betel nuts, which is the seed of the betel palm. They chew betel nuts together with lime and the dried leaves of the piper betel, a climbing pepper plant. It is chewed as a mild masticatory stimulant. This is a common practice of southeastern Asians, which includes Pygmies, Chinese, and Filipinos. The Pygmies are a primitive race, aborigines. They are very small. When fully grown, they're about three and a half feet high. I found them to be an arduously working and happy group of people. They were always smiling, laughing, and gibbering in their native tongue. Neither my buddy nor I were able to understand them, but the head of the tribe, their chief, spoke with a mixture of his own speech, a little broken English, and Filipino Tagalog, pronounced (TA-GOL-LIC). So we kept pretty close to the chief because of that and because we were his personal guests.

Their clothing consisted only of a loin cloth, which is worn like a diaper. Some wore makeshift sandals on their feet, but most of the men went barefoot. The women dressed the same as the men, just a loin cloth, no upper clothing, barefoot, some wore sandals made of bark. Every day, they built several fires to cook their food and used the warm ashes at night to sleep on. They didn't have any matches to light their fires with; this was done by rubbing sticks together or hitting stones to get a spark, almost the same as our Boy Scouts are taught to do when out on a survival trip here in America.

We had a couple of books of matches, which we gave to the chief. He sure was grateful. They were like a toy to him.

"I keep till water come down and stick wet," he said. I laughed.

The forest provided all the food they needed, which consisted of wild boar, snakes, berries, herbs, and fruits; all grew wild in the forest. Their main diet consisted of herbs and fruits that the men gathered in the forest when they went hunting, which was every day, rain or shine. They had traps set to catch the wild boar. The wild boars liked to wallow in water holes. So the Pygmies would dig large holes in the ground and fill them with water. They would then cover the hole with coconut palm and let it hang over the top of the hole. Then, when a wild boar would get in the hole to wallow, a cord would snap and down would come the covering. The Pygmies would then shoot the wild boar with bow and arrow while he was still in the hole, before they took the top off. My buddy and I got to see them get a wild boar this way. Very interesting.

One had to be very cautious when out in the woods away from camp, because there were a lot of large snakes, pythons, that hung down from the trees. The Pygmies were so small, they could be swallowed by the larger snakes. I was told by the chief that this actually happened occasionally.

In their village, they put together large coverings of coconut palm leaves, which they string from one tree to another to shelter them from the hot sun in the summer months and the rains in the winter months. This serves their purpose to a tee.

40

There were many small huts made mostly from banana and coconut leaves, but I hardly saw anyone using the huts to sleep in while I was visiting them. Of course, we were there during the summertime, and the nights were as hot as the days. Also, it seemed they mostly preferred to live and sleep out in the open under the stars. Maybe, when it rained they used their thatched huts. I don't know, because it didn't rain during the two weeks my buddy and I spent with them.

I inquired as to how they kept warm in the winter months and during the rainy weather? The chief told me that in the winter months, when the weather got cold, they made a bed on the warm coals that they had cooked their meals on. They would level out the coals, lie down on them, and also use some to cover their bodies with. Although their skin is a deep brown, the ashes gave their bodies a peculiar look, sort of like a milky chocolate color.

The women stayed in their village and did the required chores, mostly consisting of cooking, and sweeping the grounds within the boundaries of their housing area. The women were excellent cooks; at least, that is what my buddy and I thought. Whatever they cooked was very tasteful and delicious. They were lucky gals: no clothes to wash, no housework to be done. They tended to the little ones, and there were many of them running around the camp. Their babies looked like little baby dolls as they ran around playing.

They were a happy group of people, very content with their primitive world. No radios or electricity, hardly any contact with the outside world, not a worry about worldly affairs, the only water was from the nearby river. They didn't have any piped water or showers. They never had those things and so, never missed them. They had outhouses, or "chick sales," as we called them.

When I was kid in New York State, living on a farm, we too were without the things mentioned above and were happy. Back in the early 1900s, we didn't know about the things we have today. We caught rain water in a big vat in the basement and pumped it up to the sink in the kitchen for washing dishes and cooking. We carried a bucket of water into the house from the well for drinking. We used kerosene lamps to light our way around the house and barns. We had a chick sales out in the yard for our toilet. So the Pygmy way of living was not far different from mine back at the turn of the century when I was boy. An exception is that we had a cook stove, and washtubs for a bath on Saturday nights, whether we needed it or not. We also wore clothes. We had party-line telephones, such as they were in those days.

The Pygmies didn't have any contact with the outside world, whatsoever, no newspaper, no radios, no television. They took care of all their own medical needs, and I might add, they appeared to be a very healthy group of people. The two weeks with them went flying by, and before we knew it, it was time for us to return to the U.S.S. *Barker*. We had enjoyed so much being with them, we hated to have to bid them farewell. It was hard to say good-bye to those little guys and gals. As I was saying good-bye to the chief, tears actually came to my eyes. They were great little people. We had a wonderful visit with them; we were treated like kings; and we came away much enlightened about the Pygmies and their habits.

12. Battling Worst Typhoon in History with *Hoover* Rescue

One morning, after about a year of rotation duty between the Philippines and China stations, the thirteenth destroyer division, consisting of the U.S.S. *Barker, Bulmer, Whipple,* and *Alden,* was tied up to the dock at the Olongapo Navy Yard in the Philippine Islands, waiting for a new assignment in the China seas. About four o'clock that morning 10 December 1937, the commander of the destroyer squadron of the Asiatic Fleet (ComDesRon AF) on board the squadron flagship, the U.S.S. *John Paul Jones,* sent his flag secretary to Olongapo Navy Yard with confidential orders for the commanding officers of the U.S.S. *Barker* and the U.S.S. *Alden* for those two ships to prepare to get underway immediately.

I had stayed over on the beach that particular night, enjoying a little liberty. I was awakened by someone in the street below my window, yelling.

"Hey, Ski, wake up." I poked my head out the window to see what was going on, and this guy said, "Hey, Ski, come on, all hands of the *Alden* and *Barker* are being ordered back to their ships. We have been ordered to get underway as soon as possible."

"What the hell is all the rush about. What's the score?" I yelled back.

"I don't know. It's a big secret," the messenger replied, "but I think something must have happened in China with the war going on there, or it could be somewhere else. Hurry, hurry, come on, Ski, let's go, come on, let's go."

Feeling that something big must have happened, I jumped up, got dressed, and went outside. There I saw another messenger who was riding a bicycle, ordering all hands from the *Barker* and the *Alden* back to their ships as fast as possible. As this was to be a secret mission, they couldn't order the men back to their ships via radio, as they usually did, but had to resort to using messengers.

Everyone on board was asking one another what's up. What happened? Where are we headed? And all sorts of questions were forthcoming. We got a lot of answers that were just plain guesses, because no one really knew. Someone said, "Maybe something big happened in China, and we are being sent back there, or maybe Japan or Germany declared war on America." It seemed that everyone was saying "or." No one had been told a thing, not even our skippers. Our skipper was to be told after we had cleared the breakwater. After being up until dawn, dancing and having a good time, I had never seen a ship's complement get back to the ship and to their stations as fast as they did, especially when we were all were half asleep and it was so early in the morning.

However, we were back on board ship and underway in less than an hour after the flag secretary had come on board. In no time flat, the old *Barker* had her steam up and was ready to do Uncle Sammy's bidding. As soon as our skipper got the word that the destroyer *Alden* had steam up and was ready to go, he issued orders to get underway and head out into the open seas. We still weren't made aware of what had happened or where we were heading.

As we left the docks, we were ordered to disregard the harbor three-mile-limit and make all possible speed. We did. Before we had cleared Olongapo harbor, we had all boilers lit off and were making top speed, I think over thirty-one knots. However, it was all a four-stacker could make. The stacks were red-hot; I thought they would melt right then. As we cleared the breakwaters of Manila Bay, we were met by the U.S.S. *Alden*.

Would you believe it—the flag secretary had come on board at 4:15 A.M. to give us orders to get underway, and we had gotten the crew back on board and the boilers lit off and the steam up and cleared the breakwater at exactly 5:11 A.M. in less than one hour—what a record.

The captain of the *Alden* was ashore that morning and, I guess, didn't get the word; anyhow, he wasn't on board when the *Alden*'s fire room reported all boilers lit off and steam up, ready to get underway. Our skipper who was the senior officer present had been ordered to take command of this mission, so he ordered the executive officer on the U.S.S. *Alden* to not

43

wait any longer for his skipper. He was ordered to take command and to get the ship underway. He was further ordered to take his orders from the commanding officer of the U.S.S. *Barker*.

The captain of the U.S.S. *Alden* had stayed at the officer's club in Manila that night and finally got the word that his ship was leaving without him for an undisclosed destination. However, he was not going to be left high and dry while his ship was headed for some unknown destination without him at the conn. He grabbed a taxi and rushed over to the Nichols Army Air Force Base, which was just outside of Manila, and got an army seaplane to fly him out so he could board his ship at sea.

The U.S.S. *Alden* received a radio message that the captain was being flown to his ship by an army air force seaplane. The executive officer, upon being made aware that the plane carrying his skipper was about to land in the water, maneuvered the ship, swinging hard around, in order to make a smooth sea for the plane to land on. The plane came in low, and the skipper of the *Alden,* not waiting for the plane to land, just dove into the water and swam to his ship to take command. A big cheer went up as he climbed up the cargo net that had been lowered over the side to allow their captain to board his ship.

It is only natural that captains want to be with their ship when emergencies arise. He wants to be at the conn and the ship and crew entrusted to his care; he feels the responsibility.

The captain was a good swimmer. Everyone used to enjoy watching the *Alden* skipper each morning as he swam around his ship when she was lying at anchor in a port. Well, it finally paid off. The captain's swimming ability allowed him to catch his ship in an emergency while out on the high seas.

After we were several miles out to sea and clear out of sight of the beach, the skipper of the U.S.S. *Barker* received a coded message from the commander of DesRon AF, explaining our mission. So now the straight dope was finally out and all the anxiety and excitement was cleared up. We were on a mission of mercy. The S.S. *President Hoover,* an American passenger ship of the Dollar Line, had gone on the rocks on Japanese-held Formosa, and we were on a rescue mission.

We were told that the crew was out of control and were looting the ship and raping the women and that we must get to her as soon as possible. So the order was given, "Flank speed ahead." The steamship, S.S. *President Hoover,* was heading for the United States. She was a magnificent luxury liner, the best the United States had at that time; she was carrying passengers and a valuable cargo. The word was out that she was carrying gold bullion from the banks of China to the United States for safekeeping for the Chinese people so it wouldn't fall into the hands of the Japanese, now that they were at war with China.

At about 2200 hours on the ninth of December 1937, the winds started to pick up, and at about 0300 hours on the tenth of December, we ran into one of the worst typhoons in history as soon as we got clear of the territorial waters of the Philippines and out into the open sea, heading to rescue the S.S. *President Hoover.* It was a storm that was later recorded as the worst storm in history in the China Seas.

The *President Hoover,* in battling for her life, plowing through the terrible typhoon, the likes of which one had never been seen before, was thrown off her course several degrees by the green seas and angry, howling winds of that terrible storm that landed her on the rocks of the Japanese-controlled island of Formosa. She was breaking up badly, so the two destroyers, the U.S.S. *Barker* and U.S.S. *Alden,* were dispatched to get to her rescue as soon as we possibly could.

Upon leaving the territorial waters of the Philippines and once out in the open China seas, we knew that we were in a storm and that the time was at hand when we must fight to not only save our good ship *Barker* by keeping her afloat, we must also fight for our own lives. It was like all hell had broken loose. What a storm. I had been in many bad typhoons as a destroyer sailor serving on the China station, but nothing like that one, nor have I seen the likes of it since and never want to again. It was hell's worst fury, and we were just entering the edge of it.

As we were starting to plow our ship's bow into the mighty waves, I started to wonder if it is this bad now, what the hell will it be like as these two ships plow deeper into this storm? The captain ordered all hatches battened down, all watertight compartments closed, lifelines to be strung, and all necessary preparations made for heavy seas. By this time, although our engines were laboring hard and we making all possible speed, we were only moving about three knots ahead, which is about all this old ship could do in such a ferocious storm. I knew right then that little old me was in for one helluva ride. I could hear some of the fellows up on the poop deck yelling, "ride 'em cowboy," but that soon died down. It was no longer fun; it was getting quite scary.

The messages kept coming in from the desk jockeys in Washington for us to keep full steam ahead. That is one time in my life that I wished they were here instead of me. Our skipper was ordered to keep the State

45

Department informed as to our longitude and latitude at all times. They kept telling us to go faster. Yes, "faster" was all they would say. I, for one did a heck of a lot of praying. It was so bad, our lifeboats were taking on water. When a storm is so bad that the ship rolls over so far as to dip water in the lifeboats, it's got to be bad.

The seas, on the second day, got even rougher, and only yesterday, I thought how can it get any worse than it is now? About all that one could do now was to keep his head on straight, stay as calm as possible, and put his trust in the Almighty; we were in His hands now more then ever. The officer of the day, in order to conn the ship, was forced to go up to the flying bridge, (a small platform attached to the foremast about ten or fifteen feet above the regular bridge deck). Mattresses were brought up and placed in position all around the flying bridge deck. For fear of the helmsman and the officer at the conn being washed overboard, they had to be lashed to a stanchion. The officer at the conn couldn't see a darn thing and had to rely on his charts to conn the ship, and sometimes his charts would get a soaking from the seas coming over the bow. The helmsman couldn't see anything either; he could steer only as directed by the conning officer, but just keeping the ship on course as instructed was itself no easy chore, as the mighty waves just tossed us around as a toy boat. The seas just kept washing over the bridge deck, and sometimes, the heavy green seas got so high, they even hit the flying bridge deck. The *Barker,* it seemed, was under the water more than on top. It was a terrible storm. It was so bad, the navigator had to almost guess his course, due to not being able to shoot the sun by day or the stars at night.

But through it all, we did not lose our sense of humor. We were under the water more than on top; one sailor said to me, "Ski, I didn't ask for submarine duty, but I guess I'm in a submarine now." As frightened as I was, I still got a big laugh out of that. The ship was laboring hard. As we plowed through, the seas were continually washing over the ship's bow, and sometimes giant waves would smash into the flying bridge. The officer at the conn couldn't get relieved for fear that if he untied himself, he would be washed overboard. He said, "Hell, I guess I'm here for the duration, just throw me a sandwich now and then." We got a big laugh out of that one. We would latch onto anything to get a laugh, anything to help us forget how scared we were.

The seas were hitting the flying bridge very hard by now. The lifeboats were taking on water badly. Most of us wondered each time the ship rolled so far on its side, whether it would recover, with all that water the

46

boats were taking on? I considered myself a darn good tin-can sailor. I had weathered many bad typhoons in a tin-can during my career, and some of them had been fierce, especially out there in the China seas, but never had I been caught in anything like that one. Those other storms didn't faze me a bit. However, on that trip I thought I had met the storm of storms, and I, for one didn't give myself much chance of ever seeing shore again.

The sea was real angry and showing it, too. I could now see why the S.S. *President Hoover* went on the rocks. As I said, I considered myself a well-seasoned destroyer sailor, but this typhoon was the worst. I had never in my life found myself so frightened as I was at that time. I cannot even really describe that storm and how frightened I was. As I went about my work, and I must say, I just did only what work had to be done and no more in this storm, during that time, yours truly never stopped praying. There must have been a lot of conversations besides mine going on between the other sailors and the good Lord above, and not only from the U.S.S. *Barker,* but also from those on board the U.S.S. *Alden,* which, according to reports, was breaking up badly.

The bridge windows on our faithful old *Barker* were knocked out by the heavy seas. Stanchions were bent in the lower compartments, but the good ship *Barker* kept her nose headed into the angry seas, just kept groaning and groaning as she carried on. Our captain, all praise to him, never left the bridge during the worst of the storm, which lasted five days. He had a cot brought up and placed in the navigator's shack on the main bridge and was able to doze off now and then during comparatively calm spells, which were few and far between, and so intense that those calm spells were likened to a lesser typhoon. So there was really no such thing as a calm spell.

The captain told me later, jokingly, that during the fury of the storm, he sometimes thought he was in a conning tower of a submarine, because in the navigator's shack where he stayed captive those five days with the seas washing all around, he was under water more than he was out. I then told the captain what a young sailor had told me about him not wanting submarine duty, but that he thought he had it anyway. The skipper got a big laugh out of that one also, same as I did.

On the second day out, the U.S.S. *Alden* fell way behind and finally out of sight; she too was having her troubles. She lost both her anchors (we lost one), her bridge was a wreck, and her stanchions were badly bent below decks, so bad that she requested to turn back but was ordered to carry on by the officials of the State Department in Washington, D.C. They were probably sitting in the noonday sun, smoking fine cigars, and having a shot or two of good scotch or brandy while ordering our two ships to go faster.

One day in December 1937 while we were at sea fighting this terrible typhoon, we received word from Washington that the Chinese were being routed very badly, and the Japanese were closing in on Chiang Kai-shek so fast that he was forced to vacate his headquarters at Nanking and flee to Taiwan, where he was setting up his new headquarters.

On 15 December 1937, after being tossed about and fighting to stay afloat in that terrible typhoon, we finally reached the island of Formosa, where the steamship *President Hoover* of the Dollar Line was beached on the rocks, and here we were, two very badly battered destroyers, carrying her tired and weary ship's complements from battling the worst typhoon history has ever recorded, none even coming close to this one.

Both destroyers made a beeline for the *President Hoover,* which was on the leeward side of the island, and where we would be sheltered from the still raging seas with its mountainous waves. But we were not to stay there for long; oh, no, two Japanese destroyers and two heavy cruisers loomed immediately into sight. As soon as they got close enough, they ordered us via semaphore to go back out to sea, beyond the twelve-mile limit. Being so badly outnumbered, there was nothing for us to do but head back out into the open sea and into the storm.

Well, twelve miles is a heck of a ways out, especially in a typhoon like this. The storm had not subsided at all. It was still as angry and raging a sea as it had been for the past five days. The sea was breaking over the bow and washing down the passageways, taking everything in its path overboard. We got into a trough that was so bad that it broke the remaining dishes and things that were saved those last few days while we had been battling the fury of the storm trying to get to Formosa. It was so bad, we didn't dare stop our engines, because we had to keep our nose headed into the storm. The chief boatswain's mate had to keep the lifelines strung about the decks, for fear of our men being washed overboard. The captain issued orders that no one was to be on deck unless it were absolutely necessary to perform his duties, and then, to keep hold of the lifelines at all times.

We repeatedly requested the Japanese to allow us to proceed and anchor on the leeward side of the island, where we would be sheltered from this terrible typhoon. We told them about the condition of our ships, that the stanchions below decks had buckled, our anchors lost, etcetera. They flatly refused, saying that this is no longer Chinese territory, that this island had been captured and now belonged to Japan. They told us we were in Japanese waters and to stay out beyond the twelve-mile limit.

They made us stay out in the open seas while the big Japanese cruisers kept harassing us by continually steaming around and around us. We explained that we were on a mission to rescue the passengers who were shipwrecked and to give them food, clothing, medical care, and ample protection, but the reply from our so-called civilized friends was still the same, "remain where you are." And to insure our staying out in the angry open sea, more Japanese men-of-war kept arriving on the scene, all the while staying on the sheltered side of the island while keeping our ships out in the open sea. To insure that we stayed out there, they had two big Japanese battleships steaming around us, having relieved the two Japanese heavy cruisers, which were now on the sheltered side of the island and out of the storm's fury. The big Japanese battleships were being tossed around, but nothing like our small tin-cans.

After about six hours of this terrible ordeal, our commander succeeded in getting a radio message to the United States, via the U.S. Embassy in Tokyo, explaining our plight and protesting the Japanese actions. Our skipper explained that this unusual treatment by a so-called friendly nation, by keeping us out in this terrible storm, was causing great havoc to our ships. The State Department finally succeeded after about five or six hours in getting permission from the Japanese high command in Tokyo to allow us to seek shelter on the leeward side of the island. This was transmitted via Tokyo radio transmitters to both the United States commander and the Japanese commander of the Japanese fleet off Formosa Island.

Upon receipt of this order, the Japanese sent us a signal, via semaphore, allowing us permission to leave the rough seas and to proceed to the sheltered side of the island. A big cheer went up when we got the word below decks. As soon as we were anchored on the leeward side of Formosa, everybody started to yell, "let's eat," since we hadn't had a decent cooked meal in almost a week. And the cooks started to clean up the kitchen so they could prepare us some decent food for a change.

While the *Barker* was getting ready to drop her one anchor that she had left, the Japanese sent over two motor launches, which arrived before we were anchored. They were carrying three Japanese naval officers with side arms. They told us we were free to go to the aid of the S.S. *President Hoover*. They also told us what we could take with us, how many men we could land, and that no one under any circumstances, would be allowed to carry side arms on this mission. But they themselves had on side arms.

The *Barker* dropped her one anchor, and the *Alden,* who had lost both her anchors in the raging storm getting to Formosa, tied up to the S.S. *President Hoover* with one large hawser, and another tied to the rocks on the beach. That was all she needed to hold her, the ocean being almost calm on the leeward side. As soon as the U.S.S. *Barker* was anchored, the captain ordered a boat lowered to take him over to the *Hoover* to see what shape she was in and what was needed to be done. He took along with him the chief boatswain's mate, the executive officer, me, and a contingent of ten sailors.

Upon boarding the crippled *President Hoover,* we found that none of the information we had received back in Manila about the looting and the raping of the women was true. We found the captain to be in full control of what was left of his ship. The passengers were all safe out on the rocks, with all their belongings, plus bedding that had been removed from the ship, with the aid of the ship's crew. Most of the crew were out on the rocks, tending to the passengers' needs and making them as comfortable as they possibly could, and the rest of the crew carrying food and hot drinks to them. This was all being done in an orderly fashion.

Lt. Comdr. Leland Lovett, my commanding officer, told me to take the ship's logbook and to gather up all ship's papers and any orders of the day that I found in my search that were not recorded in the ship's log in the past forty-eight hours that may have been promulgated to all the watch officers on the bridge prior to the fateful tragedy that had befallen the S.S. *President Hoover,* forcing her on the rocks on Formosa Island. It was very important that the above information along with the ship's log be preserved; it must be presented to the board of inquiry, which would take place as soon as possible to ascertain why the ship was so far off course, causing it to hit the rocks on Formosa. We also took other valuables, which included the ship's manifest, etcetera.

On December 16, 1937, a sister ship of the S.S. *President Hoover,* the luxury liner S.S. *President McKinley,* stood in to rescue the passengers and what they could of the cargo. With the aid of the crews of the *Barker* and *Alden,* the *President McKinley* took all the passengers and most of the remaining valuable cargo off the crippled S.S. *President Hoover* and proceeded with them to Manila. The *Hoover*'s captain and crew remained with the ship until the rest of its cargo could be salvaged and loaded onto a cargo ship when it arrived in a day or so.

With the departure of the S.S. *President McKinley* for Manila, the commanding officer of the U.S.S. *Barker* sent a radio message to Com-DesRon AF (Commander Destroyer Squadron of the Asiatic Fleet), describing what had taken place and that the *Hoover* was waiting for a cargo ship to arrive and remove the rest of its cargo, and requested further orders. ComDesRon AF radioed back to our commanding officer that one ship was to remain with the *Hoover* until everything had been secured, and the other was to proceed to Olongapo Navy Yard in the Philippines for repairs.

Because the U.S.S. *Alden* was in such sad shape, badly crippled from the past storm, and her stanchions on the second deck damaged much more than those on the *Barker* and there being no way to know to what extent her inner structure had been damaged, the senior officer present, Lt. Comdr. Leland Lovett, commanding officer of the U.S.S. *Barker,* deemed it was not feasible for the U.S.S. *Alden,* because of the still heavy seas, to try to make a run to her home port in the Philippines and the Olongapo Navy Yard. So he decided that the U.S.S. *Alden* should remain with the *Hoover* until the rest of its cargo could be salvaged and the seas calm enough for her to make a run for her home port in Manila.

About a week later, with the storm having subsided quite a bit and the seas much calmer, the captain of the U.S.S. *Barker* bid farewell to the captains of the U.S.S. *Alden* and the S.S. *President Hoover* and we headed for the Olongapo Naval Yard as ordered. Although the U.S.S. *Barker* was in very bad shape from the beating she took those past eight days, she made the trip home in grand style. In about a week to ten days, after the *Barker* had left for Olongapo, the rough seas had subsided enough to allow the U.S.S. *Alden* to make a run for the Philippines, where upon her arrival, she was immediately ordered to the Olongapo Navy Yard to undergo her much needed repairs.

13. The Sinking of the U.S.S. *Panay* and Attack on H.M.S. *Ladybird*

While enroute to the Olongapo Naval Yard for our much needed repairs, we received word from Washington, D.C. that on 12 December 1937, during the time that the U.S.S. *Barker* and the U.S.S. *Alden* were being tossed around like toy boats in that terrible typhoon in the China Seas, and before we had arrived at Formosa, that the United States Navy ship the U.S.S.

Panay and His Majesty's ship, the *Ladybird,* a British man-of-war had been attacked by the Japanese, and the U.S.S. *Panay* had been sunk.

Upon hearing this news, it immediately struck me smack in the face the reason we were treated so badly upon our arrival at Formosa. The Japanese didn't know what the United States and England were going to do in retaliation. This accounted for the big battle ships continually circling us and keeping us beyond the twelve-mile limit, thinking they would have two U.S. destroyers in their clutches should there be any retaliation on the part of the United States. What do you think the United States and England did? Yes, you guessed it. We accepted their "so sorry please," as the Japanese knew we would, in our weak position.

We were further told that out of a clear sky on Sunday, 12 December 1937 at 1:30 P.M., while the crew of the *Panay* were observing their usual Sunday routine, Colonel Hashimoto ordered his planes to attack and bomb a convoy of ships carrying refugees. The convoy consisted of three Socony-Vacuum oil tankers and the United States gunboat U.S.S. *Panay* and His Majesty's gunboat the H.M.S. *Ladybird*. The British gunboat had the British Union Jack painted on her decks and the U.S.S. *Panay,* likewise, had two large American flags clearly painted on her decks and very visible from the air. They attacked both ships anyway.

The *Panay* was mortally wounded. She had her engines knocked out, her three-inch guns disabled, her pilot house, sick bay, and radio shack completely demolished; the ship was absolutely beyond repair. The *Ladybird* was hit hard with repeated attacks, one officer was killed on the *Ladybird,* and most of her officers and many of the enlisted personnel were critically wounded. The captain of the U.S.S. *Panay* was put out of action with a hipful of shrapnel. With the captain down, the executive officer assumed command. Within seconds after assuming command, the executive officer was hit in the throat with a piece of shrapnel and, unable to speak, he gave orders by writing notes on a paper pad. What courageous men this country had then and still have. If only we would give them a fighting chance by giving them the tools to protect themselves with. We must remember, heroism is no help without the necessary tools to do the job.

Strong protest was sent to Japan, by President Roosevelt himself. But the Japanese, as in the past, said it was mistaken identity and they were so sorry. Was it mistaken identity? What do you think? At about 2:00 P.M., the executive officer scribbled orders to abandon ship, because all of the *Panay*'s officers and nearly every member of the crew were badly wounded and the ship was sinking fast.

While the wounded were being placed in lifeboats to be taken ashore, the Japanese came back. This time, they didn't bomb or strafe the ship; instead, they circled overhead and waited till the lifeboats were fully loaded. As the boats, loaded with wounded men, started to head out for the shore, the Japanese headed straight for the lifeboats, making several runs on them, strafing the wounded and dying in the lifeboats as they were trying to make the shore. Yes, such nice people; tell me about it. When they stopped strafing and were gone, the results were: two Americans killed, one dying, and fourteen critically wounded. The lifeboats had the Stars and Stripes flying in plain view, as was also the case in the bombing of the U.S.S. *Panay*.

This was not a case of mistaken identity. The *Panay*'s lifeboats were strafed when they were loaded with wounded and dying men and their lifeboats flying the U.S. colors. The Japanese, circling overhead, watched them load the boats before attacking them. I often wondered, after considering all the acts by the Japanese military from early 1932 to 1941, whether we were really at peace or Japan had secretly declared war on the United States and Great Britain.

The British and the Americans accepted their apologies. Japan knew they could sink our ship and kill our men and nothing would come of it. Their "so sorry please" would be accepted, as always. I heard many officers and enlisted personnel say, "When in the hell are we going to stop accepting their apologies and do something about it?" We who were serving on the Asiatic station were getting fed up with this "so sorry please" crap. We kept asking ourselves why we have to accept their apologies. Why? Are we that weak? God help us if we ever allow our cheating and knaving politicians to put us in that position again. They sure are working at it at this very moment. Wake up, America. Watch who you put in office at election time.

14. The Sinking of the U.S.S. *Panay* Erupts Emperor's Timetable

A newly activated Japanese reserve colonel, Hashimoto, singlehandedly torpedoed the emperor's plans to attack Canton and Hong Kong. By his ordering the shelling of the boat loaded with British refugees and bombing and strafing the British gunboat, the H.M.S. *Ladybird,* and the American gunboat, the U.S.S. *Panay,* he, thereby, instigated an international incident, and thus, upset the plans of Emperor Hirohito, forcing him to move his plans for the conquest of China and the rest of the East, back for almost a year. The emperor had massed 30,000 Japanese troops, embarked on transports in harbors near Taiwan, poised for an attack on the Chinese mainland. Hashimoto's attacks forced the emperor to unload the troops; it would be too dangerous to proceed as planned. There was fear of retaliation by the United States and Great Britain.

At the same time that the personnel of the U.S.S. *Panay* and H.M.S. *Ladybird* were being massacred, the "rape of Nanking" was taking place. Seeing no retaliation from the United States and the ready acceptance of their apologies by Great Britain, the Japanese went out of their way to further humiliate us. While they were raping Nanking and knowing that we were not in a position to do anything about it, they were tearing down the American flags and the British Union Jacks and burning and trampling them underfoot. They went so far as to either kill any American they could find or push them off into the gutters when they met as they were walking down the streets in Nanking.

In the raping of Nanking, they broke into homes and, after looting them, set them on fire, even though they were clearly marked as Western neutral property. Japanese Colonel Hashimoto, who was responsible for the sinking of the U.S.S. *Panay* in the Yangtze River, was highly decorated and made a hero for antagonizing the two great powers without retaliation by either. The Japanese knew they could get away with whack after whack at us by using three simple words, "So sorry please." What could we do in our deplorable unfit condition? Nothing. And the Japanese knew it.

It was sickening, yes, sickening for us on the Asiatic station to sit and watch this going on. It showed that the Japanese had no regard for life and certainly hated the Americans. They surely knew they could start a war with the United States and England by their unprovoked attacks. In fact, by their actions, they dared us to fight back. They knew we didn't have the resources to wage war at that time. They knew it from past experience and their intelligence agents. And it was true. We accepted their apologies and allowed them to get away with machine-gunning lifeboats full of wounded American and British naval personnel, and sinking our ships, with killing Americans and trampling our colors under their feet, looting our embassies in China, and the list goes on.

Will it happen again? We are surely heading in that direction. I hope and pray the American public will not allow our Congress to put the United States, this great, peace-loving nation on such a low level as that again.

Yes, we love peace, but not to the extent that we are to be trampled under-foot, as we were in those prewar days. Where was our intelligence people? Why couldn't they have seen what was going on? Nothing was ever done by either the United States or England. Instead of our beefing up our armed forces, we did just the opposite. We kept depleting our military strength. The United States took more than fifty American destroyers and sold them to the Gillette company for razor blades. They were cut up for scrap metal in the Philadelphia navy yard. I watched them doing it. Scraping ship after ship made matters worse. Japan was very happy watching us reduce our fighting power, and the same thing is happening today. *When will we wake up?*

I think Congress should have listened to Ogden Nash, who, after ana-lyzing the Japanese as far back as 1927, wrote in 1932 the following, as best as I can remember:

How courteous is the Japanese;
He always says, "Excuse it, pleeze"
He climbs into his neighbor's garden,
And smiles and says. "I beg your pardon."
He bows and grins a friendly grin
While he's calling his hungry family in;
He grins, and bows a friendly bow,
Then adds, *to his neighbor,*
"So sorry, pleeze, this, my garden now."

Even though Odgen Nash, back in those days, was just expressing his own feelings, those same feelings were on the minds of not only Odgen Nash, but on the minds of the majority of the American population in 1932. Japan used the phrase, "So sorry please" or "Excuse it please," so many times, it became sickening. But they just kept on with their plan to conquer the East so they would be a position to take on the West.

Whenever Congress needed money, whether it was to raise their own pay or for some pet hobby, they always ran to the defense department's budget to cut something to get the funds they needed, and they are still do-ing it today. *How stupid! How stupid!* is all that I can say, for the voter to just sit back and let them do those things, to continuously elect the same people to run our government, election after election.

America and England must have known that the Japanese couldn't be trusted, because as far back as 1932, their deeds didn't match their words, their "excuse it please" apologies went on and on. They just kept on raping and slaughtering the Chinese.

15. Italian Hospital Ship Carrying Arms Visits Peking

In the spring of 1938, the U.S.S. *Barker* and the U.S.S. *Alden* were ordered to Chin-huang-Tao, China, by ComDesRon AF to qualify their crews on the rifle range and for rest and relaxation and a chance for every man to go to Peking, the capital of China, for a ten-day visit. This visit was to help compensate for the terrible ordeal the crews of these two ships had gone through a couple of months earlier with the steamship, *President Hoover,* incident.

In the afternoon of the second day after our arrival at Chin- huang-Tao, half the crew were sent to qualify on the rifle range. At about 1:30 in the afternoon, the officer of the day was informed that an Italian naval hospital ship had steamed into the harbor and was moored to the dock. Upon being moored to the dock, the ship's crew proceeded immediately to unload its cargo. The cargo being unloaded from the hospital ship looked very suspicious to the officer of the deck on the U.S.S. *Barker*, who was watching the operation through binoculars.

After watching the operation for several minutes, the officer of deck called for a motor launch to stand by while he requested permission from the commanding officer to be allowed to go over to the docks to investigate the hospital ship's cargo more closely.

Upon receiving permission from the captain, the officer of the deck proceeded in the motor launch to the dock where the Italian hospital ship was busy unloading its cargo. After about an hour or so of investigating and seeing for himself firsthand what was being unloaded from the Italian hospital ship, the officer of the deck returned to the U.S.S. *Barker* to resume his duties and to make his report to the commanding officer. Upon completion of the report to the captain, he made the following entry in the ship's log:

1130 Regular routine. Anchored off Chin-huang-Tao.
1200 Regular routine. Ship's crew piped to dinner.
1300 Part of ship's crew left ship to go to the rifle range.
1305 An Italian hospital ship stood into port.

1325 Hospital ship docked and started to unload passengers and suspicious-looking cargo.

1340 The officer of the deck requested and was granted permission by the commanding officer to go over to the docks for a closer investigation to ascertain and find what type of cargo was being unloaded from the Italian hospital ship.

1345 The officer of the deck left the ship for the docks, where the Italian hospital ship was moored.

1428 The officer of the deck completed his examination of the unloading of the Italian hospital ship and returned to the U.S.S. *Barker*. He proceeded immediately to the captain's cabin to make a report of his findings.

1430 The officer of the deck made the following report to the commanding officer of his findings about the Italian hospital ship and its cargo. "Upon close examination it was found to be unloading Japanese soldiers, field guns, small arms and ammunition."

2150 Italian hospital ship completed unloading its passengers and cargo and stood out to sea.

This proved that Italy was aiding and abetting Japan as far back as 1938, while Japan was at war with China. It was helping by carrying arms, ammunition, and replacements for the Japanese army and using a *hospital* ship for this purpose to boot, in direct violation of the Geneva Convention to which Italy and Japan were both signers.

As ordered by ComDesRon AF, while the crews of the U.S.S. *Barker* and the U.S.S. *Alden* were being qualified on the rifle range, half of the personnel of each ship's complement was given a ten-day leave of absence to go up to Peking, now Beijing, for rest and relaxation, or R&R, which was badly needed by all hands. I went with the first group from the *Barker* up to Peking for the first ten-day visit to the capital of China.

We rode all day by train and most of the night, continuously climbing the rugged terrain of the mountains from the ocean below. It was a rough ride. The trains in China at that time were of the narrow-gauge type; they were not as wide as those here in the States, which made it a rough and rattling ride. The territory that we passed through that day while riding on the train was the first part of China that had been invaded by the Japanese on July 7, 1937, who consequently, had complete control of all the roads in that part of China. All the trains carried heavily armed Japanese soldiers as guards.

As we sat and gazed out the windows of the train while traveling that day, we couldn't help but notice, while passing through the countryside, that the highways were heavily congested with Japanese soldiers. We also noticed that all the railway stations where we stopped were all heavily clustered with armed Japanese soldiers. They all carried rifles with bayonets attached, and side arms attached to their belts. Just about noon, several of my buddies and I started to feel a bit hungry, so we decided to go back to the dining car to see what the invaders had to offer in the way of nourishment.

The Japanese had infiltrated the Chinese countryside with what they called Japanese occupation money. It was just green paper and was worthless on the open market, and not worth the paper it was printed on, as far as I was concerned. The Japanese themselves wouldn't accept it, so why would we. Their theory was that by taking all the American and Chinese currency out of the country, they would ruin the Chinese economically. Knowing this, we decided to hold onto our American money. They could keep their green money, as the Chinese called it; we didn't want it. Some of our buddies who had already had lunch in the dining car told us they wanted only the coin of the realm (meaning good old American currency). So we finished lunch and got ready to go back to our seats.

"I'll go and pay for the lunch. They are not going to get my American money, they'll take their own Japanese green money or they get nothing from me," I said to my buddies.

After having rounded up all the green money from my pals, I picked up the lunch tab and went to the cashier to pay the bill. Although I had American and Chinese currency with me, I offered to pay the bill in Japanese green money only, but the cashier refused to take the Japanese green money from me.

"From you American," she said, "me take only American dollar. Japanese and Chinese money no good from American." They would take only American currency wherever possible, because they needed the American dollars badly. They knew, as I said before, that their green money wasn't worth the paper it was printed on.

To this end, I knew if there were any change coming, it would be in the form of Japanese occupation (green) money. When she refused to take the occupation money, I offered to pay the bill in Chinese currency, which she also refused, saying, "American money only." She wouldn't take Chinese money either. I became stubborn and, although I had American money with me, I flatly refused to pay for the lunch in good old U.S.A. cur-

58

rency. I told the cashier that I didn't have any American money with me, but that it was in my bags in the next car, and I would go and get it.

When I failed to return to pay the bill, after quite a spell, the cashier, a little anxious, sent Japanese armed guards to look for me. However, I was one step ahead of her. Sensing this would happen I hid in about three cars back, so I was nowhere to be found. All that day, the Japanese soldiers kept going through the cars in which the Americans were riding. They were looking for me, and I wasn't going to let them get me if I could help it, and they never did find me. If I wanted something, my buddies would go and get it for me. My buddies also refused to give them American cash and paid only in Chinese currency. The Japanese, seeing that they were not doing so well with the Americans, finally capitulated and started to take Chinese money from anyone who presented it to them.

We arrived in Peking at about 2200 hours that night, after a hard day's ride in those rattling cars, and were all very tired and a bit shaken up. When we arrived at our destination in the capital city of China, a group of U.S. Marines met us at the train and transported us, along with our baggage, to the marine compound, where we were bedded down and squared away for the night. All the time we were in Peking, the Japanese tried to force their occupation money on us. Seeing this, we flatly refused to have any dealings whatsoever with Japanese merchants. We did all our business with the Chinese people or in the U.S. Marine's noncommissioned officer's club, in the U.S. compound. We were quartered in the main barracks in the U.S. compound all during our stay in Peking.

We had a grand time during our stay in the capital. The U.S. Marines stationed there saw to that. They took us to see and photograph everything worth while seeing or photographing. We visited the Summer Palace, the Forbidden City, saw the Marble Boat, which represented the Chinese navy, jade pagodas, and more. There were wonderful and strange things one might find in that ancient capital. The Great Wall of China was the biggest attraction of all and one of the seven ancient wonders of the world. One of the strangest things about the Great Wall, which borders the city on one side, was that it was built by slave labor. It was built to keep the Mongolians out of their country. It took many years to build the Great Wall of China. They used several hundred thousand Chinese prisoners, who were mere slaves; they were ill-fed and made to work until they dropped dead. Life was very cheap in those days, and is still cheap to this day in some parts of the world. In book stores and in the library are many fine books written on this beautiful, ancient city, which holds enchantment. Should one ever get to China, they should not fail to include Peking, or Beijing, on their must-see list.

It's a challenge to try to climb the Wall. Some people climb all the way to the top, but a vast number of visitors try and don't make it. As my object in view is to tell of the war and how we were treated as "GUESTS of his Majesty the Emperor of Japan." That is what I used to tell the guards while I was a prisoner in Japan. I always reminded the guards that I was a "guest of the Emperor," and that they should treat me accordingly. If they tried to make me do something which I didn't have to do being the head *honcho*. I would merely say, "Remember I am here as a guest of your emperor." As the head honcho of the American prisoners of war in Sacrajima Prison Camp No. Two in Osaka, Japan they didn't dare touch me. This was an order from headquarters in Tokyo.

After spending ten beautiful days sightseeing and enjoying my visit to Peking, that ancient and capital city of China, I returned to the U.S.S. *Barker,* which was still anchored in the harbor of Chin-huang-Tao. Upon my return to the ship, I was given a ten-day course of instruction on the rifle range by the good old U.S. Marines. When the ship's complements of both the *Barker* and the *Alden* had visited Peking and everyone had completed the course of instruction on the rifle range, the ships were ordered back to their home ports in the Philippines.

16. Japanese Foul Our Firing Range

While in our home port in Manila P.I. one December morning in 1939, the Thirteenth Destroyer division of the Asiatic Fleet, which included the U.S.S. *Barker,* received orders from ComDesRon AF that at 0800 on the sixth day of July to proceed out to sea and to remain within the territorial waters of the Philippine Islands for the sole purpose of holding night and day gun battle practice. When we received this message, my commanding officer was a little confused, noting that, heretofore, we always held these practices anywhere in the China Sea. We were never restricted to any one place. So this order set him back a bit as he wondered why this order was given; that is, to remain in the territorial waters of the Philippines.

However, he didn't have to wait long for the answer, because the commander in chief of the destroyers squadron of the Asiatic Fleet, better known as ComDesRon AF, issued correspondence explaining that the commander in chief of the Asiatic Fleet was the one who issued that order which forbade us to hold actual firing runs in Chinese waters any longer. Whether this was because the Japanese were involved in a war with China, or whether the commander in chief of the Asiatic Fleet did not want to antagonize the Japanese, or just for security reasons, we never did find out the answer.

ComDesRon AF sent out warning notices several weeks in advance, which was the usual custom in notifying all ships of all nationalities concerned, especially the Japanese government and all the ships at sea, that certain areas must be kept cleared as actual firing runs were to be held on such and such a day in such and such area, during which time, we would be utilizing live ammunition. That notification was broadcast to all ships at sea and all the governments who had any interest in that part of the world. The notices gave the exact Greenwich time and the longitude and latitude of the area where actual live ammunition and torpedoes were to be fired. This was done to avoid any accidents. Should any occur with the serving of these notices, the United States would be in the clear, and no country would be able to say we fired on them intentionally.

However, there always seemed to be a Japanese freighter out there taking pictures, even after they had been notified of the day we were to hold these firing runs. A Japanese fishing boat or freighter was always there, whether in the China Seas or off the coast of the United States or Hawaii, to take pictures and foul up our course. On the day we were to practice, just as the warning had been sent out, telling the world that we would be using live ammunition on our firing runs, we were coming on the range full speed ahead and closing in fast, ready to make our first firing run, when sure enough, what should appear. Yep, a Japanese oil tanker right there on our range, fouling it up.

The captain was mad as hell and issued the order to abort the run. Message after message was sent requesting the Japanese oil tanker to clear the range. However, from past experience, we knew it wouldn't do any good. This had been happening to the U.S. Navy for years in the Continental waters, as well as out here. It wasn't new to us. We always had to warn them again and again. However, on this particular day, our division commander, getting madder by the moment, called the radioman up to the bridge.

"This is it, I've had it, tell those sons of bitches to clear the range, the next run will be a live ammunition firing run." After the captain cooled down a bit, he instructed the radioman to send the following message:

"The next run will be a firing run with live ammunition, you are warned to clear the range."

The captain, after waiting a few minutes longer, told the signalman to hoist the firing-run pennant. He immediately gave orders to come on course and head down the range and to make it a firing run.

The Japanese oil tanker skipper got the message. They knew our captain was not fooling, they could see with their field glasses that our guns were trained on the target and we were traveling at a high rate of speed. The commanding officer of the Japanese freighter, realizing that we weren't playing games any longer, started to clear the range. You should have seen the smoke come out of her stacks as she hightailed it out of there. I really don't know which was moving the fastest, the cameras clicking, which they all had, or the ship's engines. However, our division commander got the range cleared that day in a hurry. You should have heard the ship's crew let off steam when they saw the skipper clear the range. Where has such bravery that we had then gone? Our captain was Lt. Comdr. Leland Lovett, U.S.N.

In those days, an officer in the field was given authority to do things. It isn't like that today. The civilians run the wars sitting behind a desk in Washington. It was wonderful to see General (Stormin') Norman Schwarzkopf have a free hand in running the war in Saudi Arabia, and he got the job done in a hurry with very little loss of life. That's the way a war should be run, with the people in the field having the authority to do the job he was sent there to do. Why in the hell do we spend so much money training our officers in the war colleges and academies if civilians, sitting on their duffs in Washington, smoking twenty- five-dollar Havana cigars, call the shots.

If President Truman had given General MacArthur a free hand in Korea, the world would be a better place to live in today. There would never have been a Vietnam, neither would the North Koreans been bold enough to challenge and capture an American man-of-war, as they did, nor would they be a thorn in our side by building the nuclear bomb as they are doing today. Nor would they have been bold enough to shoot down an American helicopter as they did, killing one warrant officer and holding the other captive.

President Truman should have allowed General MacArthur to cross over the Yellow Sea into China and bomb the Chinese bases. The Chinese had a safe haven to go to refuel and arm their planes, then go back over the border and bomb and strafe the Americans in South Korea. If MacArthur had been left to fight the war as he had been taught and not have had his hands tied by a civilian, it would have been a different story in Korea. When the Americans were not allowed to cross the Yellow Sea and bomb the Chinese base, that changed everything. We immediately became known as a "Paper Tiger," afraid of China. The senate and the civilians running things in Washington said that they were afraid of dragging China into the war. What war? China was already engaged in bombing our troops in South Korea. When China started to bomb our troops in South Korea, that was war, whether declared or not, *it's war* with the United States. Our boys were being killed by the Chinese who were coming from across their border.

17. Ordered to Cavite Navy Yard for Duty

Upon the completion of the battle practice, the destroyers were ordered to return to Manila. While at sea, enroute to the Philippines, I received a set of orders via my commanding officer, the captain of the U.S.S. *Barker* from the commander in chief of the Asiatic station, ordering me to report to the commandant of the naval district for assignment to duty. Upon reporting to the commandant, I was further ordered to report to the captain of the Cavite Navy Yard, Commander R. T. Whitney, for duty. This proved to be one of the best assignments I had ever received since I started serving in the navy.

Commander Whitney was a fine naval officer and a gentleman. He had received his commission in the First World War, after becoming a hero. When the Second World War hit the Philippines, Commander Whitney once again proved himself to be deserving of the term, "hero." Having been severely wounded in the first run of the bombing of the yard, all that afternoon while the Japanese were bombing the Cavite Naval Yard, Commander Whitney remained at his station. Not seeking safety for his own life, he remained on duty, with Japanese bombs falling all around him, and continually carried on his work of saving government property until he was finally struck down by a second piece of shrapnel.

He was removed to the Canacao Naval Hospital across the bay from the Cavite Navy Yard, over by Sangley Point. After serving a couple of years in the captain of the yard's office under my good friend, Commander Whitney, on about the first part of November 1941, Captain Albert H. Rooks, commanding officer of the U.S.S. *Houston,* which had just relieved the U.S.S. *Augusta,* the flagship of the Asiatic Fleet, came over to see me at

63

the Cavite Navy Yard and asked me if I would like to set sail with him.

I had served under him about seven years earlier, back in 1932, when he was the commanding officer of the U.S.S. *Northampton.* Our home port was Hampton Roads, Virginia, at that time. Later that year, we were transferred with all of the east coast fleet to the west coast, and our home port changed to Long Beach, California. He was a wonderful officer, well liked by everyone who ever served under his command. Anyone would have been proud to serve under him. It was deemed an honor for me just his asking me to set sail again under his command.

Captain Rooks told me that it looked like war was inevitable with Japan. If this were to happen, since Japan was already allied with Germany, it would more than likely draw us into a war with Germany as well.

"I certainly would like to have you on board with me if and when a war breaks out," he said.

I told him that I have a duty in the navy yard; however, I would be pleased to serve under him. I told him I would ask my boss, Commander Whitney, the captain of the yard for his permission. Commander Whitney flatly refused.

"No smoke, Paul, I can't let you go. I need your services here."

I was saddened at the time because Captain Rooks put so much trust in me. But there wasn't anything I could do other than inform Captain Rooks what Commander Whitney said. They were both fine officers, and it was a pleasure to serve under either of them.

As it turned out, it proved lucky for me when Commander Whitney refused to let me transfer and set sail on the U.S.S. *Houston.* The good Lord was watching over me, because within a few months, a very courageous Captain Rooks went down with his ship, the U.S.S. *Houston,* in the Java Sea, while fighting against heavy odds. In fact, the U.S.S. *Houston* was the last ship in that group to go down fighting in the Java Sea battle, against heavy Japanese odds. More about Captain Rooks later.

Part Two

War Is Declared

18. The Condition of the Asiatic Fleet at the Outbreak of War

When the bombing of Pearl Harbor took place on 7 December 1941, it found Admiral Thomas C. Hart, commander in chief of the Asiatic Fleet, on board the U.S.S. *Houston,* his flagship. The *Houston* had just relieved the U.S.S. *Augusta,* her sister ship, a couple of months earlier. Both of these ships were 10,000-ton heavy duty cruisers of the CV class, built approximately in 1932. The U.S.S. *Houston* was a well-equipped ship with the latest technology and only about eight years old, with my good friend Captain Albert H. Rooks, commanding.

The Asiatic Fleet (better known as the "Suicide Fleet" or "the expendables") under Admiral Hart, at the outbreak of the war, comprised the ships mentioned earlier plus six modern patrol torpedo boats (PT boats). The six very modern PT boats had a very brave naval officer, Lt. John D. Buckeley, as their commander (NOTR).

The Yangtze River patrol, which comprised four light gun boats and four river boats had to be destroyed, because it was deemed by the CINCAF to be so old and obsolete, there was no way they could survive the long voyage in the rough China Seas, which they surely would encounter while enroute to the Philippines to join the rest of the fleet. So rather than allow them to fall into enemy hands, they were ordered by the commander in chief of the Asiatic Fleet to be destroyed off the coast of China in the China Seas in an undisclosed area.

All of the above Yangtze River ships of the Asiatic Fleet were very old and obsolete, all built before 1910. The only decent fighting ships we had on the China station at the outbreak of the war were the U.S.S. *Houston,* a squadron of V-type submarines, which had just arrived for duty on the China station, just before the outbreak of war in the Philippines, and the six patrol torpedo boats (PT boats). So there you have it. However, I must say here that the destroyer crews of those very old and obsolete ships were well trained; I know, I was one of them, having served on the U.S.S. *Babbitt* in the States, and the U.S.S. *Barker* (213), on the Asiatic station. The many long days and nights we went through training on the open seas paid off, because those Asian-based, obsolete, four-stack destroyers of the vintage-200 class proved themselves when called upon to do so, by engaging the Japanese navy in the battle of the Sea of Java and elsewhere against very heavy odds. More about that later.

19. Japan Makes Sneak Attack on Pearl Harbor

When Japan made her sneak attack on Pearl Harbor on the seventh of December 1941, which was the eighth of December in the Philippines. I was living in Caridad, P.I. and was assigned to duty as the assistant to the captain of the Cavite Navy Yard, Commander Roul T. Whitney, U.S.N. Caridad was the next town from the town of Cavite, and about two miles from the Cavite Navy Yard.

Earl ("Joe") B. Hunter, a retired U.S. Navy Chief Quartermaster had transferred to the Fleet Reserve, after having served on active duty for twenty years, had just been recalled to duty. He was staying with me until he could find suitable quarters and get situated in the Philippines. Joe had been living in Shanghai since his retirement. He had married a White Russian gal and was in business in Shanghai until his recall to active duty in July 1941, just prior to the outbreak of war with Japan.

On that fateful morning in December 1941 when Japan attacked Pearl Harbor, I was awakened by my friend Joe. I had been out on the town and had gotten to bed about 4:30 A.M., and passed out into the arms of Morpheus, and was dead to the world. When I finally came to, I saw Joe standing over me. He was shaking me.

"Wake up, Ski," he was saying, "it's here, Ski, it's here! Wake up." I put out my hand expecting a Bloody Mary or a gin fizz or something for that big head of mine. Joe looked at me and said, "Come on, Ski, get up. We got a job to do. It's here, for sure." I looked up.

"What the hell is here? What the hell are you talking about, Joe? Just let me have a nip for an eye-opener, and then we'll do this job, whatever it is."

"Ski, you don't understand," Joe said.

"Come on, Joe, give me that eye-opener, then maybe I'll be able to understand what the hell you are talking about. What don't I understand."

"The Japs did it," Joe said, "they bombed Honolulu this morning."

"Aw, nuts, Joe, go back to bed, you're about as bad off as I am. You need a drink." He kept raving on and on. I finally said, "Hey Joe, give me a shot out of the bottle you've been getting this stuff from. Honolulu! They couldn't get within one thousand miles of that place."

"If you don't believe me," Joe said, "get up and turn on the radio and hear it for yourself. The Japs sank most of our ships in Hawaii."

"Now you're pouring it on pretty thick, Joe," I said, then I repeated, "sunk most of our ships in Pearl. What a bunch of bull. You're plain nuts. I'm not falling for that line of bull. You had better feed me another line, Joe."

He still kept trying to convince me as I still lay in bed while he was getting dressed. After a while, still not believing him, I started singing, "Pass around the bottle, and we'll all have a drink."

"Ski, please believe me," Joe said, "I'm not kidding. It's serious. Get up and get your damn clothes on. If you don't get dressed, I'm not going to hang around and wait for you. Ski, we got a job to do. Let's get some breakfast and get going."

After awhile, Joe went over and turned on the radio, and I heard the radio announcer speaking in an excited voice.

"Japanese planes, in a sneak attack, bombed Honolulu at 7:00 A.M. this Sunday morning. Damage not obtainable at this time. All servicemen report to your stations immediately."

That woke me up in a hurry. And it wasn't until late December 1945, after I was returned to the United States, that I got that eye- opener I had been begging Joe for.

The radio announcer continued, "President Roosevelt has declared that a state of war exists between the United States and Japan as of 0700 on the seventh day of December 1941, and he expects everyone to do his duty."

It didn't take me long to get out of bed and dressed. Joe and I skipped breakfast and immediately headed for the Cavite Navy Yard. I went to my office and reported to Commander Whitney to find out if he had any special instructions for me to pass along. Joe headed for his duty station, Section P, a large warehouse that stored all the food provisions for the navy. It was from where all the shore stations and all the ships at sea invoiced their food provision. Joe was in charge of Section P.

As soon as word came to the Philippines that the Japanese had bombed Pearl Harbor, in Hawaii, Admiral Thomas C. Hart, commander in chief of all naval forces on the Asiatic station issued alert orders to all departments under his command, which included the naval air force base at Sangley Point. Immediately, the naval aviation department went on alert, keeping a squadron of planes in the air constantly. The captain of the yard, Commander Whitney, immediately informed me to stand by to transfer all pertinent records to a place which would be designated later by Admiral Rockwell, commandant of the Twelfth Naval District, which would be somewhere out in town, far from the navy yard, where they would be safe from destruction.

After causing all that havoc on the naval fleet in Hawaii during their sneak attack, the Japanese immediately started to give their full attention to the Philippines by deciding to eradicate General MacArthur's Far Eastern air force everywhere in the Philippines as their first priority. This would stop all interference from the air and allow them to get ready for an all-out amphibious invasion on Lingayen Gulf and elsewhere on Luzon Province, such as the Cavite Navy Yard, and elsewhere, which was left intact so they could give it their fullest attention in due time without any competition.

According to Lt. John D. Buckeley, U.S.N. Commander of the Motor Patrol Boats, Admiral Rockwell had sent him a two-hour warning that the Japanese were coming from Formosa and heading in our direction across northern Luzon. However, we in the captain of the yard's office never got any information of that sort. If we had, we would have notified the air base. But he claims he was notified out in the bay to keep an eye out for them. On their way from Formosa, they surprised Clark Field, the army air base in northern Luzon, and the other bases in that area. After demolishing the air bases of Clark and the surrounding army air fields, they headed our way, giving us no time to get our heads together and a chance to recover from the shock of Pearl Harbor being destroyed.

The Philippine Islands are exactly twenty-four hours behind the United States. Japan made their sneak attack on the U.S. Fleet in Pearl Harbor on 7 December 1941, which made it the 8th of December in the Philippines. On 10 December 1941 the much dreaded war had finally come to us on Luzon in the Philippines with the destruction of the Cavite Navy Yard. That day, I had a luncheon engagement with four other naval personnel to discuss what to do in their departments about the war. They were Joe Hunter, Castle, Dutch Haag, and Rebel Lord, all retired navy chief petty officers who had been recalled to duty by the navy department and were the heads of various departments.

I left the yard at about 12:00 noon to meet with them. Luckily, where we met for lunch was just outside the gate at Slat Crawford's bar and grill. While we were having lunch, at about 12:20, the air raid siren in the navy yard sounded off as soon as the Jap planes were spotted. Upon hearing the sirens, we all went outside of Slat Crawford's cafe to see what was going on. We found out in a hurry.

Looking up, we saw coming toward us a beautiful V formation of Japanese bombers (they looked like a flock of geese in formation). We counted fifty-four bombers, and several groups of fighter planes, which they soon found out they didn't need. After attacking the air fields north of Cavite, which were Iba, Nielsen, all of which were reduced to rubble, they headed straight for the Manila area, bombing the shipping in the harbor as they passed over, but their bombs didn't do much damage to the shipping, just one or two hits.

As they came in, a group of about nine bombers broke off and headed for Sangley Point, our naval base for the PBYs. The balance turned and started to bomb Nichols Air Force Base, just across the bay from Cavite Navy Yard. Our air force obeyed Admiral Thomas C. Hart's orders to a tee. Our naval aviation department went on the alert, keeping the squadron of planes in the air constantly. However, about noon on the tenth, the planes landed to refuel and get a bite of chow. Just about the time they landed, the fifty-four enemy bombers roared down across the bay, escorted by several fighter planes for protection. It surprised the hell out of all of us. They came without a bit of warning of any kind, right out of the clouds; no one even heard the drone of the engines. But there they were, right out of the blue.

Our naval air force, which consisted of one squadron of PBYs, was based at Sangley Point near the Canacao Naval Hospital, just across from the Cavite Navy Yard. The naval air base had shops and living quarters for the air force personnel who were stationed there. With the naval squadron on the ground for refueling and lunch at that precise moment, our small naval air force of PBYs were caught on the ground.

After a couple of runs on the naval base and the oil depot over at Sangley Point, yes, they were destroyed, with the exception of one. For us, not knowing what had happened at Nichols Field and Sangley Point, standing there looking up at the Japanese formation overhead, it was hard to comprehend why not even one of our fighter planes had risen to engage the Japanese. Everyone was saying the same thing—where the hell are our fighters? Why in hell aren't they up there?—not a single one of our fighter planes ever showed up to engage the Japanese fighters, to our amazement.

I was astonished, to say the least, that they were getting no opposition from our planes and so, not needing fighter protection for their bombers. The fighter planes headed out over the harbor to look for more shipping.

71

Not finding any, they headed straight for our PT boats. But Lieutenant Buckeley kept his little fleet of six PT boats zigzagging, and the Japanese, I'm happy to say, didn't get a direct hit on a single one of them. However, those little PT boats blasted three of the six Japanese fighters out of the sky. If we only had the tools to work with on the islands, we would have given them hell. We had the men with the guts to fight, but nothing to fight with.

While we were still standing in the street outside Slat Crawford's saloon watching the bombing going on over Nichols Field, Christina, my lady friend, with two of her girlfriends drove up in a public utilities car. They were very frightened, and one girl was crying. I told them not to be scared of those Japanese planes, they couldn't get within fifty miles of Cavite or the navy yard.

"You fool," Christina exclaimed, looking straight at me, "fifty miles, my dear, are you blind? Look! Manila isn't even half that far, and they are dropping bombs on it."

"Well, Honey, they can't come here, anyway," I said, adding under my breath, "I certainly hope they don't."

"Let's find a safe spot for the girls in case they do come here," Joe said, and winked at me.

So we picked out several good spots for them, one in particular was just across the street from Slat Crawford's place, where we had lunch. It was the archway of the municipal building. I told Christina to take the girls and go over there and stay in the archway should the planes start for Cavite. About one of the safest places to be was in an arch or doorway during an air raid. And we soon got the girls squared away.

In about fifteen minutes after bombing Nichols Air Field and the naval base at Sangley Point, all the planes regrouped. What a shock I got when I saw them heading across the bay heading straight for the navy yard. The four of us left Slat Crawford's place in a hurry and started running toward the navy yard gate, which was just around the corner from Slat Crawford's. The marine guard at the gate saw us and yelled.

"Come on in, fellows if you're coming, because I'm shutting this gate pronto." As soon as we got in, he slammed the gate shut behind us. I made a beeline for the base exchange building to take shelter, which was just inside the gate.

20. The Devastation of the Cavite Navy Yard and Cavite City

When they first were spotted, they were flying at about 25,000 feet as they neared Manila Bay, then dropped down to about 20,000 feet. Seeing that they were not getting any opposition from us in the air, they dropped down to about 15,000 feet. What a mistake. Our motor torpedo boats shot down three or four of their big bombers with their twin fifty-caliber slugs. Lieutenant Buckeley said afterwards, "It sure amazed me to see my men in the MTBs shoot down those planes. If I didn't see it with my own eyes, I would never believe that an MTB could shoot down a plane." It sure surprised the navy bigwigs, too. This was one for the history books.

Before the Japanese planes that had destroyed Nichols Air Base arrived over the Cavite Navy Yard, we began to see several bombs going off down around the torpedo and battery shops in the lower part of the navy yard. Since the enemy had not yet started to drop their bombs, I realized that we hadn't neutralized all the bombs that had been planted in the navy yard and that those blasts were coming from bombs that had been placed in strategic spots around the navy yard for just this occasion by Japanese sympathizers, ("ganaps"), and now they were having their heyday.

Out of the 7,000 some odd civilians workers in the Cavite Navy Yard, there were only about four hundred ganaps employed in the yard. Although we had all the ganaps listed, we were forced to leave them on their jobs, because the majority of them held key positions. Our work load was tremendous at that time, so although we knew who they were and had them recorded in our files, we couldn't afford to charge them or fire them. We had to keep them on the job, as we needed to get certain work done for the fleet before the war broke out.

I had given Commander Whitney a complete list of names of all the ganaps who were working in the navy yard. However, the commandant and the captain of the yard felt it was better to not antagonize them by letting them know we knew who they were, as we wanted them to keep working and also to let them think they were pulling the wool over our eyes. Our intentions in the captain of the yard's office was to have them picked up as soon as their work was completed and, if possible, before the war hit the navy yard. It didn't happen. So they were able to get their licks in by detonating the bombs they had secretly planted before anything could be done.

73

We had located and neutralized several of their bomb emplacements prior to the war. The bombs that we did find were made impotent and left where they were so they would not know that we had found them. But they had some planted which we never found; how many, we will never know. However, the Japanese planes did most of the job for them anyway. Maybe we would have been able to salvage some batteries and torpedo warheads had we been successful in locating all they had planted. But that is just a guess. As it turned out, we were able to get more for our money by letting them stay and play their game—the work that we were able to get done to get the ships repaired and out on the open seas outweighed the amount of damage they were able to inflict on the yard by our not exposing them and letting them stay on their jobs.

Within a few minutes, they began giving their full attention to demolishing the Cavite Navy Yard, as had been planned. As I was running to the base exchange building for shelter, I noticed some of the men running for the lumber yard. Remembering what had happened in the First World War, I yelled at them, telling them not to go there, that they had better find a safer place. I knew that if a shell hit a lumber pile, it would send timber splinters flying everywhere, like it did in the First World War.

Before the First World War, we never heard of dropping bombs from the air, consequently, the wooden decks were not removed when the ships went into action. With the advent of the planes dropping bombs, they played havoc with the ships' wooden decks. The bombs, in ripping up the decks of the ships, sent splinters flying everywhere, cutting many of the crewmen in half who were in its path. The men took my advice, turned, and went to another spot. Sure enough, on about the third run, a bomb found the lumber yard, sending lumber flying through the air in all directions. Because there was no one around, there were no casualties from flying timber. Those guys couldn't thank me enough for warning them.

When the bombs started to fall, I hugged old mother earth, and if I could have, I would have burrowed deep into the ground. It was a horrifying ordeal, with the run lasting several minutes and seeming like hours. It was sickening to watch our antiaircraft shells bursting below the enemy's planes. The first run hit the docks where the U.S.S. *Sea Lion,* one of the modern V-class submarines, and a couple of other ships were tied up, undergoing repairs. The U.S.S. *Sea Lion* was fatally crippled. The docks where she was tied up were completely demolished with the exception of one small portion of about thirty feet, which didn't receive any damage and was still standing.

Lt. John D. Buckeley U.S. Navy, commanding officer of the motor patrol torpedo (MPT) boats immediately ordered all six MPT boats that were under his command rushed to that portion of the dock that was still standing for loading the wounded and taking them over to the Canacao Naval Hospital, which was located over at Sangley Point just across the bay, about five miles from the navy yard. Those six MPT boats did a magnificent job and Lieutenant Buckeley's quick thinking and those boys in the MPT boats saved many lives and all should be commended for their courageous actions that day. What bravery, what heroes those boys were in those MPT boats. They worked out in the open regardless of the danger to their own lives.

They were not only being bombed, but the fighter planes were making runs on them and continually shooting and strafing them. Their only thoughts were of their fallen shipmates who were wounded and dying, and of getting them to the hospital as soon as possible. Ironically not a Japanese bullet found its mark, and no one was hit. They say God works in mysterious ways. Well, I believe that any atheist who was out there watching this became a believer. Lt. John D. Buckeley was presented with the Congressional Medal of Honor for his actions. However, I believe every man in that yard that day deserved the same citation; they were all heroes.

This first run caught everyone off their guard. Sailors rushed to the docks with axes and chopped the lines of the ships that were moored to the docks, so they could get underway. Bombs were dropping everywhere. The lower part of the navy yard was completely destroyed. What damage the enemy didn't do with their bombs from the air, the Filipino ganaps did with their bombs planted in the ground. But those brave sailors carried on, chopping lines and setting the ships free. Some ships left with one boiler lit off, towing others who had no boilers to light off because their boilers were under repair.

Again we were lucky that only two of the ships were damaged. All the ships were moved to safety with the exception of the submarine, the U.S.S. *Sea Lion*. She was damaged so badly that our people towed her out to sea and blew her up in order to keep her out of enemy hands, thus denying them any useful information from her. The *Sea Lion* was one of the latest and most modern submarines the U.S. Navy had in service at that time. The officers and enlisted personnel of those ships and the civilians deserve the highest credit. They stayed there working on the ships and on the docks trying to get those ships underway and to get the U.S.S. *Sea Lion* towed out to sea while the bombs were falling and hitting the docks alongside the ships they were working on. But like the crews of the PT boats and the medics, they just kept on working with no regard for their own safety.

When the first run was over, those who were hurt and were able to, went to the dispensary, which served as our first aid station in the navy yard prior to the war. They were all standing in line, awaiting their turn, when the Japanese bombers came over to make their second run. When the bombs hit the ground, flying shrapnel severed legs and cut bodies in half of those standing. It was so bad that legs, arms, heads, and torsos of everyone in that line were blown all over the yard. Later, when I went down there, I saw the most horrifying scene I have ever seen in my life—pieces of the bodies of young men whom we had known, who were our buddies and shipmates, strewn all over the place. I don't think there was a dry eye among us. Later, one of the medics, who was working in the dispensary at the time, told me that he had seen over three hundred or more standing in that line cut to bits while waiting to get into the dispensary for treatment.

No one had ever instructed the military or the civilian population, for that matter, what to do in a case like this. The civilian and the military population should have had been informed that they should lie flat on the ground, as low as possible, in the event of being caught in a bombing raid. It was never explained to us that the bombs upon explosion would send shrapnel about two to four feet above the ground, thus cutting through anything in its path. Had it been explained and people knew what to do, many lives would have been saved.

The main dispensary was hit on the second run, blowing most of it to kingdom come, killing everyone in or near the dispensary with the exception of a couple of the hospital corps personnel and one doctor. There was a lieutenant commander who was on the operating table, badly wounded in the first run and being worked on at the time of that second run. He was blown to bits on this run, along with the rest in the wing of that building, with the exception of the two corpsmen and the doctor. It was another miracle that they were spared so that they could save others. The doctor and the two hospital corpsmen immediately went over to the wing of the dispensary that was still standing, but burning fiercely, again not thinking of their own safety, and went right to work in that blazing building, tending to the injured. They just kept tending to the wounded as if nothing was happening. Jimmy Bent, who was a retired chief boatswain's mate, held two positions. He was the police and fire chief of the Cavite Navy Yard. Jimmy rushed his crew of firemen over to the dispensary and started pouring water on the burning part of the building; the other half had been blown away.

There were parts of bodies strewn all about them, but Jimmy kept his crew working, trying to save that part of the dispensary. Thank God, we had doctors and hospital corpsmen and men like Jimmy Bent who were dedicated to duty. Jimmy Bent's firemen, under his direction, finally put out the fire, and the hospital crew stayed there working all the time. That doctor and his two corpsmen saved a lot of lives that day. They treated several hundred naval personnel and Filipino workmen. Some had minor cuts and bruises. Then, there were others who were in a very bad shape. The more serious cases were taken by Lieutenant Buckeley's PT boats, being employed as sea ambulances.

All during this time, bombs were falling from the sky, as if it was raining. Such bravery. I shall never forget that scene; it will never be erased from my mind. The Japanese knew they were as safe up there as being on the ground at their home base. After finding out they weren't getting any opposition, they flew as low as 15,000 feet above the yard. They knew more about us and our fighting power than I did. They knew that the anti-aircraft guns that we had at the time couldn't reach them, therefore they could pick their targets without any worry. We were helpless. It was devastating, to say the least. The Japanese just flew over at their ease, dropping their bombs; they even left their fighter protection at home. I and many others certainly got a rude awakening that day. I thought we had everything that one needed to fight a war with should one ever come to the Philippines. I never believed all this talk about the Asiatic Fleet being a "suicide fleet." I thought that was just a bunch of bull. I thought we were well protected, at least with the air force.

In just a few minutes that day, we all found out just how impotent we really were. We found out that we were not only the "expendables" or the "suicide fleet" at sea, but also on land. In just about five minutes or so after the first run, I heard someone say, "Here comes another load." I heard a sound coming that I shall never forget, that of bombs falling. They sounded like a freight train being hurtled through the air; as they were getting closer to the ground, they sounded like railroad boxcars *choo-choo-choo*. It didn't take long for us on the ground to find out that they had released their bombs a few minutes earlier, which was quite a distance from the target, so when the bombers reached the point directly over your head, where you were kissing mother earth, you knew that they had already dropped their load. I heard that sound constantly for the next five months.

When I saw the Japanese heading in our direction to start their third run, I hit the deck and kissed good old mother earth as that hissing sound

77

came nearer and nearer; it seemed like it was going to strike the very spot where I was digging and wishing I was a mole or something so I could burrow straight down. Well, I started digging that hole, or at least was trying to, when I discovered I was lying on concrete.

When that run was over, Joe and the rest of the fellows whom I went to lunch with came over to where I was, and I asked, "When in the hell are they going to stop?" He didn't answer me. In about five or ten minutes after the third run was over we could see another batch of planes heading our way. Joe and the boys took shelter, and within a few seconds the fourth run started to hit. The exchange building where I was staying during the air raids was completely surrounded by a wall made of adobe brick and concrete about four feet thick and ten feet high. These buildings were old Spanish forts built to protect the city of Cavite; they even had gun emplacements. They were built by the Spaniards before Admiral Dewey captured the navy yard from them during the Spanish-American War in 1898.

It was in this building that you would have found yours truly. If during that run you had dropped in to get a peek at me, you would have found me trying to make a new door through those four feet of concrete, just lying there, digging and praying, I don't know which I did the hardest, but you can bet I was doing both pretty good. When each run was over, I would rush outside to aid whoever I could. However, it seemed that only a few minutes passed before I could hear the drone of the Japanese planes as they came nearer and nearer to the yard for their fifth run. This was the run that was meant for the part of the yard where yours truly was dug in. It was the upper part of the yard, which contained, among other buildings, the ammunition depot, the baseball diamond and the grandstand, the ship's service store, which was where I took refuge, and of course, the lumber yard—in short, all buildings that were still standing and lining the fence adjacent to the city of Cavite. The rest of the navy yard was in flames and almost completely demolished.

Closer and closer the planes came. Then came that terrible hissing sound of bombs coming down, the sound of falling boxcars as they were getting closer and closer to the ground. I was lying as flat as I could in the darkness of that lonely room. No human being was near. I prayed as I dug at the walls with my bare hands, which were starting to bleed. Then came the crash. The bombs had landed. The Japanese had overshot their mark. That string landed in the city of Cavite. When that run was over, the enemy planes headed out to sea toward Corregidor. It was then, I suddenly realized, that with the exception of my God, who was watching over me, I was alone. I would have given anything just to be able to talk to one of my buddies or just have some of them nearby.

I ran out of the building and saw Joe and a few of the boys heading my way. Among them was Dutch Haag, a retired chief electrician's mate. He had been recalled to duty from the Fleet Naval Reserve just before the outbreak of the war, along with my buddy Joe Hunter. Dutch was in charge of the battery charging station.

"My place is on fire," Dutch said when he got near us. "I must go down and try to put it out before it hits the torpedo warhead lockers. I can't let that happen, because if it does, watch out, all hell will break loose."

Looking in the direction of the battery charging and warhead lockers, we saw a mess. Big billows of smoke rising in the air; that part of the yard was completely blackened and dense with smoke. Every second or so, you could see large flames shooting from 100 to 500 feet in the air. I turned to Dutch.

"Dutch, please don't go down there now, it's foolhardy for anyone to go down in that fiery furnace, you can't do a thing at this time without the proper fire apparatus and enough men to man them. Please, let's wait until the damn Japanese have had their fun and are done bombing, and we'll all go and help you." But Dutch wouldn't listen.

"Fellows," he just said, "that's my duty station, and it's what Uncle Sammy pays me for. I must go down and put out those fires."

He took off and just started running for the torpedo warhead locker.

We all kept yelling and trying to stop him. He wouldn't stop. He felt it was his duty and nothing was going to stop him from performing that duty. He just kept on going, heading for the waterfront where the torpedo locker was located, and as he was running, the large clouds of fire and smoke were getting so bad in that part of the navy yard that the waterfront was in complete darkness. It was almost like nighttime. About the time it took Dutch to get down there to the battery charger lockers, the inevitable happened. From the darkened Cavite Navy Yard, we heard the torpedo warheads beginning to explode one after another; it went on for over thirty minutes, the smoke clouds with high balls of fire were getting bigger and bigger, shooting into the sky. I am very sad to say none of us ever saw Dutch again.

There was a young Filipino lady running around in the navy yard, clothes ripped off by a Japanese bomb. She was screaming in her native tongue. All she had on were sandals on her feet. She had gone completely berserk. She had no blood on her, so it was obvious she wasn't wounded, so no one paid any attention to her. We were too busy taking care of the wounded. I never did find out where she came from or even how she got into the navy yard, but there she was, running and screaming with no clothes on. A couple of marines were trying to catch her to give her a blanket to cover herself with, but as far as I know, they never did catch up to her. The last I saw of her was when she got lost in the dense smoke in the yard.

We didn't hear any more explosions from the torpedo warheads for about thirty minutes.

"Let's go, Ski," my pal Joe Hunter said, "and look for Dutch. He may be in trouble."

As we started for the torpedo warhead lockers to look for Dutch, a naval lieutenant came running up.

"Fellows, he said, "I need your help. I need somebody to go over to Porta Vargo, near the Dreamland Cabaret. Chief Boatswain Boyd is over there all alone with an antiaircraft gun. He needs help to man it."

Joe turned to me.

"Do you think we should continue looking for Dutch or not?" he asked. "Which do you think we should do?"

"Joe," I said, "we're not certain about Dutch. I really don't give him much hope. It's very bad down there where he went. I think it would better for us to go and help the chief, don't you?" He agreed.

We immediately changed course and headed for Porta Vargo to relieve Chief Boatswain Boyd. There was a hero if there ever was one. He was out there all alone, manning an antiaircraft gun for several hours with the Japs bombing and strafing all around him.

21. Off to the Aid of Chief Boatswain Boyd, U.S.N.

The Japanese overshot their mark on that fifth run, and instead of hitting the upper part of the yard, as intended, they hit the city of Cavite, devastating it completely. Buildings were left half-standing and burning furiously. Electric wires and poles were down all over the streets. Slat Crawford's bar and grill, our old hangout, where just about an hour or so ago, I and my friends had enjoyed a delicious lunch, was completely demolished. There are no words that could describe the beating and devastation that the city of Cavite and the navy yard took that day. When the Japanese got through with us, it was worse than one could even imagine.

We had just witnessed war at its worst. We gave the Japanese no competition, thereby, a free hand to bomb and strafe as their hearts desired. There were over two thousand lives lost in the destruction of the Cavite Navy Yard that fateful day, 10 December 1941, Asiatic time or 9 December U.S. time.

Joe and I decided that in order to get to aid Chief Boatswain Boyd at Porta Vargo, we would have go straight through the ruins of the city of Cavite, even though it was all in flames, just like the navy yard, which was still burning fiercely. In making our way to reach Chief Boatswain Boyd, we had to pass over hot electric wires lying all over the ground. If one touched them, he could be electrocuted right on the spot. We stood there for a moment looking over the situation.

"Just think," I said to Joe, "a few short moments ago, this was the beautiful city of Cavite."

"Ski," Joe said, "I served in the army during World War One overseas, and I never saw anything that could match this much destruction in such a short time." Then he went on to say, "Hell, we just ate lunch here, less that two hours ago."

"That guy that said 'war is hell' sure knew what he was talking about," I replied. "I agree with him one hundred percent. Hell, I had arrived to that conclusion in less than two hours, watching those Jap planes dropping their bombs on us." I had witnessed all the war I ever want to see again.

Dreamland Cabaret, where Chief Boatswain Boyd was holed up with his antiaircraft gun, was about two miles from the center of what was the city of Cavite. So Joe and I started down through the ruins, fighting every foot of the way, climbing over burning timbers, piles of concrete, brick, twisted iron and steel, and fallen electric lines. We were extra cautious regarding the electric lines that were down on the ground, for fear of them being hot, and we gave them a wide berth, which at times was hard to do. We were just about a quarter of the way through the city, when I heard my girlfriend Christina yelling.

"Get us down, you damn fools."

I turned and saw Christina and her two girlfriends with whom she had driven from Manila over to Slat Crawford's place to have lunch with me. But they didn't get any lunch. Instead they arrived just in time to see the Japanese bombing Nichols Air Force Base across the bay. Her two girlfriends had never been to Cavite. Christina had told them so much about it, they decided that this was the day that they would drive over and see

Cavite for themselves. They saw it all right, for their first and last time, or before and after. One of the girls told me afterward that it was like seeing a magician at work—now you see it, and bingo, now you don't. They at least had a sense of humor through it all.

Christina and her two girlfriends had stayed in the passageway and under the archway of the municipal building, as Joe and I had instructed them to do, all during the bombings of the navy yard. The last run of the Nips had hit the municipal building, killing everyone there with the exception of these three young ladies, because they stayed there as we had instructed them to do. Also, they were half scared to death, which also accounted for them not leaving the archway cover. The building was a wreck, it was left half-standing and in flames. The girls had miraculously climbed up a blank wall where there were no stairs. How they got there, neither Joe nor I nor they themselves could understand, but there they were, on top of that building amidst the debris, with fire creeping in on them.

Joe looked about and found an old two-by-six beam that had more than likely been blown from that same building. We set it up at an angle alongside the building and told the girls to quickly slide down, that we would hold the beam and catch them as they came down. The building was on fire, and we were afraid it would collapse. Christina and one of the other girls came down immediately. The other girl was shy and refused to come down. She was crying.

"I'm not dressed properly," she kept saying. She was scantily clad and didn't have any undergarments on. I yelled to her.

"Baby, this is no time for modesty! Joe and I are over twenty-one, and we can't be shocked." I made as if I was leaving her.

"Please don't go," she said. "If you don't look up, I'll slide down."

"For God's sake, lady, snap out of it," I yelled. Just then her clothing caught fire.

It didn't matter if everyone was watching her or not, down she came. Yes, sir, that fire brought her down. When she hit the ground, her dress was all in flames. We grabbed her and rolled her on the ground. Christina took off her dress and threw it over her, and put the fire out. Miraculously, she didn't get burned very badly. We took Christina and her two girlfriends to a first aid station that had been set up at the Dreamland Cabaret. After getting the young lady's burns taken care of and getting the gals squared away, Joe and I went on our way to assist Chief Boatswain Boyd. His gun emplacement was just around the corner from the cabaret.

The Dreamland Cabaret was considered at that time to be the second largest dance hall in the world. It was built in 1922 and was immense. I and my shipmates spent many happy nights there. It became a custom for me and my navy buddies that I hung out with to go there almost every night to dance and drink beer, but the best thing of all was to pick up a senorita. We knew all the gals by name. We had a routine that we followed pretty closely. We would first go to Slat Crawford's bar and grill about 9:00 P.M. or so, down a few beers, and then wander out to the Dreamland Cabaret, which was about two or three miles out in the sticks, so to speak, the boon-docks. The cabaret closed at midnight, in compliance with the orders of the commandant of the Cavite Navy Yard. We just took our time. We didn't want to arrive there before 10:30 or so. This gave us time to get some dancing in or whatever. If we got there too early, we would have to buy drinks for the ladies. We let the other guys do that.

When we arrived where Chief Boatswain Boyd was manning the machine gun, we told him we came to spell him for a while so he could get some rest. He welcomed us with open arms. After we were there about two hours or so, we decided that the Japanese had gone back to their base for the night and were not coming back to pay us a visit again that day. So we secured the battery for the night. Joe said he was going to the navy yard to see how his section P had fared in the bombing that day and to check over the buildings he was responsible for. I told him that I would stay there at the cabaret to help out in anyway I could, and I would also check on the girls to make sure that they were okay.

"Okay, Ski, you do that, I'll see you later at Castle's house," Joe said.

He left, and I headed over to the Dreamland Cabaret to see what I could do to help out over there and to check on Christina and her two friends.

22. The Bravery of the Naval Medical Corps

Upon going inside the cabaret, I immediately looked up Christina and her two friends. All three of the young ladies had chipped in and were working like beavers helping the doctors and corpsmen in aiding the wounded and trying to do their best to comfort those who were dying. The naval doctors and hospital corpsmen worked feverishly in trying to save as many lives as possible in this makeshift hospital. They worked on mangled bodies, some with scalps, legs, and arms blown off; there were bodies almost severed in

83

two—it was a horrible, horrible scene. I was sick to my stomach. I never want to witness anything like that again in my life. One thing for sure, I will never be able to erase from my mind what I had seen that day.

The natives and the military personnel were going around the towns of Caridad and Cavite searching through the ruins of the drug stores, hotels, etcetera, bringing in beds, medicines, food, and whatever supplies they could find for the doctor's use. So I chipped in to aid the doctors and hospital corpsmen in any way I could. While I was outside, helping with the wounded, some fellow put on his gas mask. One of the natives, seeing this, started to yell.

"Gas! gas! Those Jap sons of bitches have gassed us."

There were about four hundred natives in the area. Others started to pick up the cry, yelling and screaming.

"We have no gas masks. We have no gas masks."

I yelled as loud and as hard as I could to the natives.

"No gas, Joe, believe me, Joe, there is *no* gas. The Japanese are afraid to use gas. They know we have more gas than they have and that ours is much more deadly than what they have." Holding my gas mask in the air so they all could see it, I said, "See, Joe, here is my gas mask, I don't put it on." I went over to a fellow and grabbed on his gas mask and told him to remove it immediately. I said, "No gas, Joe, no gas."

When he removed it and the natives saw this, they quieted right down. Whew, I wasn't so sure there wasn't gas in that area myself; it sure smelt like it. I guess it was due to the large amount of acidity in the area at that time from all the bombings, fires, and destruction of property. But no matter how I felt about gas being used, I didn't dare put on my gas mask after making this other fellow remove his to quiet down the natives. A few minutes after they had settled down, I felt relieved to see that we were still conscious. But I was still a bit apprehensive.

It was a good thing that no one else put on his gas mask at that time. If so, it would have caused a disaster, because if that crowd, especially those who were not injured but were just shell- shocked and shivering in their boots, should get out of control, that was all that was needed for some damn fool to again holler "gas." If those with gas masks started putting them on, all hell would have broken loose. The crowd consisted mainly of natives who were either wounded or were there trying to find a loved one who was being worked on by the doctors or corpsmen. I was glad I happened to be there right then.

The doctors and hospital corpsmen just kept going from one body to another, not stopping for a breath of air, just for a drink of water now and then. They sure deserve a lot of praise. It's a good thing that the enemy planes had called it a day. It gave us a chance to survey the damage and get things quieted down, as everyone was in shock. I was not so sure I myself was not in shock. I don't know what kept me going, but I just kept on going from here to there, working wherever I could help. Yes, I and many others who were there and had witnessed the bombings and had a chance to watch those medics work, felt that every man in that unit deserved the Congressional Medal of Honor, the highest honor our nation can bestow on heroes like them. That medal should have been given to this group of medical officers and hospital corpsmen for their bravery that day, under the worst possible conditions, with bombs dropping everywhere, people being strafed, buildings blowing up and ablaze, etcetera.

People were running around screaming in their native tongue. Most of the time, the doctors or the hospital corpsmen didn't know what they were trying to say or tell them. Still, under those conditions, the medical corps did not stop working; they just stayed, helping the wounded and dying with not a thought about their own safety. Two more air raid medical stations were going full blast, one in the Cavite Navy Yard main dispensary in the part that was still standing and the other one under the naval prison, which was also located in the navy yard.

Here was another dedicated group of medical personnel, doctors and corpsmen. They were not fully recovered from the shock of the first two runs, having their main dispensary half blown to bits and in flames and with many of their best friends killed on the spot. There they were, still running around, the bombs still dropping, aiding the wounded and carrying them to the first-aid station that was still intact. They had a job to do, and they did it without hesitation.

These were dedicated men. These were heroes in the strongest sense of the word. They worked on the mangled bodies all that night and into the early hours of the morning, with no rest or sleep and most of them with nothing to eat. They worked on civilians as well as military. It didn't matter, officer, enlisted, civilian, or whoever, they did what was within their power. There are a lot of people to this very day who can thank God the navy had such finely trained medical personnel. I don't think that any one of them could be singled out as the most outstanding; they were all outstanding in discharging their duties under the most horrifying conditions one could imagine.

There was a young naval medical officer, a lieutenant (JG), who found a bicycle and rode all around town, going through damaged store buildings, drug stores and the like, gathering up all the medical supplies he could find. He was still doing this late into the night. Early the next morning, I found him back on the job, doing the same thing. He had set up a hospital in the Catholic church near the Dreamland dance hall, a job in itself, which took a lot of guts. Later on, I had a chance to chat with him.

"Doc," I said to him, "you certainly deserve a helluva lot credit. I am very proud to have known you."

"Hell, this is only my duty to humanity, and thank God, I can do it," he said, smiling. "We need all the medicines we can muster up."

Yes, those are the unsung heroes, forgotten forever. What brave men. They showed not only how brave they were then, but continuously throughout the war and even in the prison camps, later, in Japan. Dr. Nardini, a lieutenant (senior grade), in the United States navy was one of those. He served with us in the prison camp in Osaka and in Ackanobe. Enough cannot be said about this doctor. May God bless him, wherever he is.

23. Return to the Burning Cavite Navy Yard

As dusk was starting to set in, I felt that I was at the point of not being much help to the medical staff, and I decided to go to Castle's home for the night. It had been a long, hard, and devastating day for me. As I was about to leave, a young Filipino officer came to me.

"Sir," he said, "it don't look like they are coming back any more today. Don't you think we should round up some men and try to save as much food as we can from the yard? All the buildings in Cavite are still burning, and the winds are blowing the flames in the direction of the navy yard. I am told that the navy yard is still being destroyed by fire and the torpedo warheads are still being detonated?"

As tired as I was, I couldn't turn him down.

"Yes," I said, "I think that's a very good idea. Let's do it."

I got him to help me round up all the Filipino naval personnel who were not required to help the medics to go with me into the navy yard to help save as much canned foods and other supplies that we possibly could by moving them to a safe area, if one could be found, or at least, out of the buildings that more than likely might be blown up the next day by the re-

86

turning Japs. As I and the Filipino officer started to go out to round up some help, I noticed an empty bus over by the cabaret and recognized the bus driver. I went over and told him that I needed transportation to take a group of workers to the navy yard. I asked him if he could take us.

"Let's go, Ski," he said, "I'm ready."

I told him that a Filipino officer was rounding up some help, and as soon as they got here we would take off. I explained to the driver that I had been told that the street by the marine barracks had been cleared, and we could get to the navy yard by going around that way. The young Filipino army officer and I then started to round up Filipinos. However, the Filipinos were a bit reluctant to go back into the yard; most all of them had their families and little children with them, their homes having been destroyed. So naturally I could hardly blame them for not wanting to leave their families at this stage of the game. The shock of the last six or seven hours had not worn off yet.

I assured them that we would bring them back to their families and get them bedded down in the Dreamland Cabaret. However, they still kept shaking their heads, telling me they wouldn't go with me. Nothing else to do, I simply broke out my forty-five.

"Let's go fellows," I said, "I'm through fooling around."

That did it. They, thinking I meant business, started to get on the bus. However, that was just an act on my part. I would never have used that forty-five—no way. I knew most of those boys, and they were good boys. I knew most of their parents also. However, here was a job that had to be done, and the only way to get it done was to pretend I would use force if necessary, and it worked. I got a busload of Filipinos in a hurry, and we took off for the navy yard.

Upon our arrival at the navy yard, we proceeded directly to Section P of the supply depot. It was here that I ran into Joe Hunter again. Section P was his baby before the war, and there he was, doing his duty. Joe had a group of men there already working frantically loading stores on yard trucks and taking them up to the baseball diamond at the far end of the yard, where they would be safe. So I had my gang chip in and help them.

All during the time we were working trying to save food from Section P, there were terrible blasts going on down by the receiving ship; they were explosions from the torpedo warheads. The fire had got to them, and those that were left were now starting to explode. I took off with Joe Hunter for a few minutes to survey the damage in the Cavite Navy Yard and Cavite city; they were both completely destroyed; both lay in ruins. There were great columns of rising smoke. It was like a blasting furnace with flames shooting high in the air. There were bodies and parts of bodies of many of our buddies strewn all over the place. One cannot imagine the horrifying scene the Japanese left, one had to be there to believe it. I myself cannot adequately describe it, and still can't shake it from my mind. In fact, many of the boys who were there and witnessed this nightmare refused to talk about it, saying they want to forget it. They never will. I know that I never will. In fact, it is only now, some fifty years later, that I am able write about the dropping of the first bombs on the Cavite Navy Yard, about 12:15 P.M. on the tenth of December 1941.

There was another very brave man, Jimmy Bent, working in the navy yard trying to put out fires, etcetera. Jimmy Bent was married to a real nice Filipino lady. Jimmy had three small children with her, and they made their home in Caridad, about five miles from the city of Cavite. Jimmy was a retired U.S. Navy Chief Boatswain's Mate. Upon his retirement, he was made the chief of police and the fire marshall in the Cavite Navy Yard.

Jimmy kept his fire department, consisting almost one hundred percent of Filipinos, working continuously on the buildings below us, trying desperately to put out the fires to stop them from getting to the buildings where we were working. Jimmy and his crew worked until daylight the next morning, some sixteen hours since the first bombing, without food or rest. Under Jimmy's supervision, his gang accomplished what they had set out to do, to save the buildings that contained the food and clothing that supplied the whole Asiatic station, including the ships and personnel stationed in China. Jimmy Bent's bravery by staying on the job allowed us to salvage and transfer food and clothing to Corregidor and the Bataan-Mariveles area. I am sorry to say that Jimmy never made it through the war; he was killed in one of the bombings a few days later.

We worked steady for several hours in the Cavite Navy Yard, moving the provisions to a safer place just in case the Japanese came back the next day, which they did. It was starting to get so dark, we could hardly see, with the electricity throughout the yard having been blown out.

"Let's quit," Joe said, "and go look for some chow and a place to bed down for the night." I agreed.

Just as we were about to leave to find shelter for the night, a naval officer from Admiral Rockwell's office came over.

"Clear the navy yard, fellows," he said, "the ammunition depot might blow anytime."

The fires from the town were slowly creeping toward the navy yard, and Admiral Rockwell issued orders to blow up the buildings near the navy yard gate that had not been destroyed by the bombing raids. This was to put a gap between the fire and the ammunition depot.

We cleared the navy yard in a hurry, to allow the admiral to put his plan into effect as fast as possible, which proved very successful. The admiral, by his stopping the fires from crossing into the navy yard, saved the ammunition depot from blowing up. If the ammunition depot had been allowed to blow up, it would have caused havoc beyond comprehension. We had gone through enough for one day, and we sure didn't want that to happen.

The ammunition depot was built mostly below ground. Although the door that gave entrance to it was built on the ground level, one had to look very hard to find the depot because of it being so heavily camouflaged. The depot was completed covered with dirt with huge trees growing on top of it. The foliage made it look like a densely thicketed forest. One, looking at the ammunition depot, would think it was just a mountain densely covered with big trees. It was one of the finest camouflage jobs one could find anywhere. The entrance and the inside of the ammunition depot was built so that a big semi could drive right inside, allowing it to load or unload the various munitions that were required by the ships of the entire Asiatic Fleet. Upon learning that the ammunition depot might go off at any time, I turned to the Filipinos who I had brought in with me on the truck.

"Fellows, quickly grab some canned fruit," I said, "vegetables, or anything else that is handy that you can carry to take it to your home, and then let's get the hell out of here."

I told Joe what I was planning on doing, and he said he would follow the bus and pick me up at the cabaret. The boys quickly grabbed burlap sacks and filled them with all the canned food that they could carry along with a few bags of rice and boarded the bus. In just a few minutes, the bus was loaded, so I told the bus driver to take us back to the Dreamland Cabaret, where we had left their families and Christina, and her two girlfriends. Joe followed us in his car. Joe's car was parked in the Cavite Navy Yard alongside Section P in Joe's usual parking spot, which he had used before the war. With all the devastation of the yard that took place that day, his car had been spared without a scratch.

After returning the Filipino boys to their families I made sure they all were well fed and that they had a place to stay in the Dreamland Cabaret for the night, as I had promised I would do. I also thanked the driver of the bus and made sure he was taken care in the way of food and a place to bed down. Making sure that Christina and her friends were bedded down and taken care of, I told her that I would see her in the morning and see to it that they got back to Manila.

I got into Joe's car, and we headed out to Castle's home for the night. Both of us were almost dead on our feet. Joe and I had just started to drive away when one of the fellows stopped us.

"Mr. Ski," he said, "tell me true, you don't use gun on us, do you if we don't go to navy yard with you?"

I looked at him for a few seconds and, with tears in my eyes, embraced him.

"Philip, my boy," I said, "I love you guys. Hell, no! I would have never, never use that gun. In fact, it wasn't loaded. I just tried to scare you guys. It was the only way I could get you to leave your families to help me." So after giving him a another big hug for assurance. I told him to tell the other fellows what I had told him.

Joe and I then took off, heading down the road for our good friend Castle's home and, possibly, a good night's sleep.

24. Destruction of the Naval Air Force at Sangley Point

On our way to Castle's house, we passed through the city of Caridad, where Big Ski lived. We decided to stop at Big Ski's home first, to get a beer or two. His home was about six miles or so from the Dreamland Cabaret. He met us out in the driveway.

"I had a hunch you guys would come here, and I have been waiting for you," he said. "I put a case of beer on ice, so let's have a drink."

"I thought you'd never ask," Joe said. After a couple of cold ones, Big Ski embraced his wife and kids and told them he was going with us. But first, he assured them that he would be back the next morning after he had found out the scoop of what was happening.

Well, we all got into the car again and went on to Novelleta, which was a few more miles down the road toward Manila and where Chief Machinist's Mate Castle lived with his pretty Filipino wife and their four little kids. Upon arrival at Castle's home, we had a couple of more cold ones and sat around and tried to figure what we should do the next day. In the meantime, his wife fixed us a very good dinner. After dinner, we went out and sat on the porch to relax a bit.

At about 9:30 that night while sitting there and reminiscing about what had happened during the day and trying to map out our plans for the next day, a Filipino boy came running up the driveway.

"Sir," he said, "there are a lot of American women down the road in the schoolhouse with no food. They need help. If you follow me, I show you."

"Here we go again," I said, "but we must go and see what we can do, if anything."

So we got into Castle's car and went down with the young Filipino boy to find the women. It was back in the province a little way. When we got there, we found that the group consisted of twenty-seven women. They were holed up in a schoolhouse, just as the Filipino boy had said. One of the women came out and met us as we approached the door, and took us inside to meet the rest of the women. They told us a marine had brought them there at about noontime, when the first wave of planes started to bomb the navy yard, and that they were afraid to stay there in the dark because there were a lot of ganaps (Japanese sympathizers) hanging around. We found out that some of these women were nurses and some were the wives of navy men who had left with their ships, leaving them stranded, their homes having been blown to bits in Cavite City limits. They begged us to stay with them.

We informed them that we would remain with them, that we were armed, and that Castle would go and get some kind of transportation to take them away from there to a place where they would at least be around other people and not isolated. We also assured them we would try to get them some food. With that, Castle left in his car to get help and arrange for some sort of transportation for them. The rest of us stayed to protect the gals.

Castle drove back to where the navy PBY squadron was located. There he ran into Doc Fraser, a chief pharmacist's mate who had been recalled to duty from the Fleet Reserve, where he had transferred after twenty years active service in the navy. Castle explained to him about the plight the women were in. Doc Fraser was able to secure a bus to allow us to transport them. Next, the fellows of the PBY squadron loaded food into Castle's car to take to the gals. When the food was loaded, Castle, with the bus following him, returned back to the schoolhouse where we were with the women.

Right after Castle had left, they told us they were hungry, that they didn't have a thing to eat all day. So when Castle arrived with all that food, it was a godsend. The women warmed up the food in the schoolhouse kitchen and chowed down. When they were finished eating their much appreciated meal, we loaded them onto the bus and took them to Caridad near the causeway, where the naval aviators of the PBY squadron were quartered, which we all felt would be good protection and with suitable housing for them. At least there they would be fed and looked after until they could be moved to Manila to better quarters in a day or two. We realized this wasn't a place for women; we were expecting the Nips back any time after dawn to blast us off the face of the earth.

But the personnel of the naval aviation department started the next day after the destruction of their base to immediately search for any parts that they could salvage from the wrecked and battered airplanes. These parts were loaded onto trucks and taken to Mariveles. When all the parts that could be found were loaded and taken to Mariveles, the aviation mechanics were taken to Mariveles to try to put the parts together and possibly come up with some planes that they could fly, to be used at a later date. I am pleased to say they made six planes out of the wreckage that they could fly.

While we were at the PBY aviation headquarters with the women, I overheard the naval aviation officers talking over what they were going to do with the one plane they had left, everything else being wiped out. They were pulling straws to see who was going to fly "Betty" that night.

"Look what brave souls we have here," I said to Hunter, "all wanting to go with one lone plane to challenge the whole imperial Japanese air force. What courage!" Then I thought all these aviators and only one plane, and they are just dying to get into the air.

By the time we deposited the women near the PBY's station, and got them bedded down, it was now the early hours of the morning.

We went back to Castle's home in Novelette to get some shut-eye. It was almost four o'clock in the morning before we got settled down for much needed rest, being weary and worn out from that first hectic day of war. Courageous men without weapons is what I kept saying to myself. While thinking, among other things, about those aviators, Chief Boatswain Boyd, Jimmy Bent, the medical personnel and still wondering about the fate of my good friend Dutch Haag, I fell off to sleep and was out for the night.

25. Parts of Dutch Haag's Body Found

It was almost ten o'clock the next morning when we woke up. Castle's wife had a hearty breakfast prepared for us. After breakfast, we again tried to comprehend just what had taken place the day before. The more we thought and talked about it, the more heartbreaking it became. Oh, we all knew that we were known as the Suicide Fleet, but I, for one, never believed it, not for one second. I had faith in my government and never for a moment did I ever think my Uncle Sam would write us off even before a war got started. I always laughed when they called us the Suicide Fleet.

However, seeing what took place that fateful day 10 December 1941, it didn't take me long to realize that it was true.

Yes, indeed, we were a "suicide fleet." I and my buddies started to get mad and cuss those in the halls of Congress and to think those rotten so and so's didn't even see fit to give us the proper weapons to allow us to make a decent showing when the chips were placed on the table. Their ears must have been ringing from the words that came out of our mouths about them that day.

I remembered that before the war, I used to tell the Filipinos when they would ask me how we were going to protect them against the nation they feared the most, the Japanese. Well, in all sincerity, I'd say "Joe, don't worry. You've got the greatest nation on the face of the earth behind you. We've got secret weapons here in the Philippines that should any Japanese try to come here, he would be blasted out of the sky. Have faith and stick to your good old Uncle Sam, he'll take care of you. He will never let you down," And to think that I myself believed all that bunk that I was telling them.

Hey! as I said, I myself believed that spiel. It had all been drilled into our heads; Uncle Sam had such high tech secret weapons out there, so secret that they could not be talked about. We were told to just keep your faith in your government. We did. What fools we were. Oh boy, what a rude awakening I and my buddies got when the Japanese did come. We found out that our dear old uncle couldn't even take care of the Americans out there, let alone the Filipinos, and had no intention to. This all came true on 10 December 1941.

That day shattered our faith in Uncle Sam, knowing now that we really had been let down. When those enemy planes flew over and the marines and sailors sent up those barrages of shells at the Japanese aircraft.

What a sight it was, the barrages completely covered the sky. But our shells couldn't reach the enemy's planes. They were flying at about fifteen thousand feet and our antiaircraft shells were exploding five to ten thousand feet below them.

The Japanese flew at ease, in a leisurely manner, and dropped their loads of bombs when they got ready. They had no competition. All they had to do was sit back, pick their teeth, and smoke a fine cigar, like one would do after having feasted on a great dinner. When they had showered us with all the eggs they had, they headed for home to get another load, knowing that we had nothing to stop them with. When the sun went down that night, many lay their heads down to rest, brokenhearted, trying to shake it off as a bad dream. I was one of them, and sometimes, to this day, I still feel it was a bad dream and never happened. Although we were brokenhearted and hurting inside after that terrible, rude awakening and finding ourselves in such a bad predicament, we were not broken in spirit, nothing could do that. We loved our country too much for that. We were true blue navy men, and as we had been taught, when the going gets tough, just "hang in there," and that is just what we did.

We had worked ourselves up to the point of being fighting mad at the senators and congressmen who had failed us. With all the frustration built up inside of us, we eventually got us the nickname, "The fighting bastards of Bataan," given to us by none other than Japanese General Homma, the officer in charge of the Japanese troops in the Philippines. General Homma, in his report to the emperor on losing so many men on the Bataan front, called us, "The fighting bastards of Bataan," more of which later.

The second day of the war in the Philippines, 11 December 1941, the day after the destruction of the navy yard, we enjoyed a nice breakfast cooked by Mrs. Castle.

After discussing the events of the day before, we found ourselves sitting there, trying to decide just what we could do to help the cause. So we decided to take a ride to have a look-see. But I asked them to go with me first to my office in the navy yard and help me try and find what records I could, if any. They consented. When we arrived there, I was shocked to find the building in which most of the records were kept was still standing after all those bombing raids. We were able to salvage most of our records, thereby allowing me to carry out the captain of the navy yard's orders by moving them to a safe place out in the province. When we finished moving all the records out in the province, which took almost all day, we decided to go to Novelette, the next town. We had heard that the military were all gathering there.

Well, when we arrived there, we found everything in a turmoil; no one had taken charge, people were lost, no one knowing what to do or where to go. They were all asking the same question, "What can I do to help?" Everything was in disarray. The strafings and bombings were still going on. There was not a soul to get advice from. It was every man for himself. It seemed that everyone, including the officers, were shocked to find the deplorable condition we now found ourselves in. If you ran into a high-ranking officer and asked him what you could do, the reply always was "Go into the hills. As soon as we get organized, we'll call you." I said to myself, "Go into the hills. No way. That wasn't the answer for me." I turned to my buddies, Joe Hunter, Castle, and Big Ski.

"I can't speak for you guys," I said, "but no way is this guy going into the hills. I'll find something to do. I wasn't trained to go hide in the hills with a war going on." Then I added, "I wasn't trained to fight a war on the beach either, I was trained to fight a ship." I made up my mind I wasn't going to sit around. I wasn't going into the hills. I'd find something to do.

They all agreed with me, and we decided to band ourselves together and go and find a job where we would be able to aid the cause.

"Fellows, before we go looking for a job," Joe Hunter said, "how about seeing what happened to Dutch Haag. Don't you think we should try to locate him?"

We had been inquiring around and couldn't seem to find anyone who had seen him since we had lunch at Slat Crawford's bar and grill just before the destruction of the navy yard. After many inquiries and not getting anywhere, we decided to take a ride to find gas for the car and then go over to the navy yard to look again for our buddy Dutch Haag.

Upon entering the yard, we went down to the torpedo warhead and battery lockers, which were Dutch's duty stations, before the war. After searching around a bit, Rebel came up with one of his legs, with his foot and shoe still intact. Then one of us found the shirt that he been wearing the day before. We kept searching, but that was all we could identify that belonged to Dutch. There were a lot of parts of bodies strewn around but we didn't know if any of them belonged to Dutch, so we just left them there. However, we notified Police Chief Jimmy Bent, who rounded up a group of Filipinos to clean up the yard of all the body parts they could find.

Jimmy knew that not only would the stench become unbearable in a couple of days, especially if they were left lying there in the hot sun, parts were already starting to bloat. But Jimmy also knew they could cause an epidemic if the body parts were not picked up and burned immediately. It was not an easy job for the police chief to round up men to do that kind of work. I didn't blame the natives for not wanting to do it, but it had to be done. I figured that there were at least two thousand bodies torn apart by the bombing the day before, the majority of them being Filipino yard workers.

It was a horrible job—a torso here, a leg there, a head here, and an arm there—so in order to get the Filipinos to do it, Jimmy filled them up with liquor. It was mostly straight alcohol, which he had salvaged from the navy yard dispensary. That got the job done. He had this group of Filipinos going around picking up arms, legs, and heads and putting them in one of the bomb craters. Before they put the body parts in, they covered the bottom of the crater with debris that was burnable and saturated it with gasoline. When all the body parts that could be found were placed in the crater, the natives then doused the pile with more gasoline and set it afire. Brother, you should have seen the fire that made. Joe and I were still looking for anything we could find belonging to Dutch up until the time they lit it off.

As there wasn't anybody working in the Cavite Navy Yard with the exception of Jimmy Bent's gang, and finding nothing to do at the moment in the navy yard, we drove out to Dutch Haag's home in the province of Caridad. We explained to his wife and little children that their daddy sensed his duty and did it. He went down like the hero he surely was and that they should be very proud of him. After consoling Dutch's wife the best we could, and after she had regained her composure, we helped her gather up and pack what clothing she could carry along with her and her little children in her car. Joe drove her car, seeing that she was too shook up to drive, and he followed Castle's car. We took her to their relations and friends farther back into the province, away from the war zone, where they would be safer. We figured that was the least we could do for our fallen shipmate. It was much better than having them stay in Caridad, where the Japs were dropping their bombs.

After we got Dutch's family squared away, we decided to go back to the Cavite Navy Yard and look around some more to see what we could do. Upon our arrival back in the navy yard, we found that they were loading food and ammunition in trucks to take to Manila, so we pitched in and helped until it started to get dark, which was about eight o'clock in the evening, at which time we quit for the night and proceeded out to Castle's house, which by now, was our headquarters, or meeting place.

As we were heading out of the yard, we ran into "Rebel Lord," a retired chief watertender in the U.S. Navy. Rebel was one the fellows we hung out with prior to the war. Upon completion of twenty-two years' service, he requested and was granted a transfer to the Fleet Reserve; he was called back to active duty about a year prior to the war and placed in charge of the oil depot at Sangley Point. He told us he had been working at the oil depot the past two days. We told him we were going out to Castle's home and asked him to come and join us.

He said, "Why not, I haven't anything else to do, and I'd love to work with you guys again," and with that, he got into his car and followed us.

Before returning to Castle's home, we decided to load as much canned food from Section P that we could carry in the car and take it to Castle's house to replenish his supply of food he had been giving us. Rebel filled his car also. As we headed back to Castle's home, while going through town, we stopped and searched through the rubbish of the stores that had been bombed for whatever we could find, such as clothing, medical supplies, or anything that could be used by Castle's family.

We were able to locate quite a bit of loot, especially medical supplies from the bombed-out drug stores. Upon our arrival back at Castle's home, as usual, his wonderful wife had dinner prepared for us. After enjoying a nice repast and downing a couple of cold beers, we laid our weary bodies down on the floor for some much needed sleep after these first two hectic days of war. By the time we got through bringing Rebel Lord up to date about what we had done the last two days, I glanced up at the clock and noticed the time.

"Fellows," I said, "would you believe that it is almost 2:30 in the morning? I'm going to get some shut-eye." They all agreed with me, and we all rolled over and went to sleep. I made a pillow out of my clothing, and as soon as my head hit it, I went completely into the arms of Morpheus.

26. Burying the Gas and Oil on the Beach

I guess we were in a semishocked condition and still all worked up from the events of the past two days, because none of us slept very long although we were dead tired. Consequently, we were up early the next morning and skipping breakfast, we were on the road at about 6:00 A.M. We were off again in Castle's car, this time to the Canacao Naval Hospital, where all the civilian workers from the navy yard and military personnel were gathering to await instructions and to get some breakfast, which was being brought out from the hospital. So we had breakfast there.

While eating breakfast, at about 8:00 A.M., a messenger came and told us that we must leave the area immediately, as the ammunition depot over in the navy yard had just been hit and might blow up momentarily, making the area we were in very dangerous. However, we didn't pay much attention to that report, the Japanese had made several direct hits on the ammunition depot in the past two days, but they were not able to penetrate it. It made us all happy to learn that this was one thing they could not destroy, it being so well fortified with the jungle of trees protecting it.

Prior to leaving the Sangley Point area, Joe Hunter went over and asked a navy commander if there was something we could do. The reply was the same as we had been getting from all the high brass, "We have no orders for you. Just go into the hills, and you will be notified when we need you." We were running out of jobs to find for ourselves.

"This crap is getting damn old and hard to take," I said. What a mess. This was no way to fight a war, but then, what else could we do with nothing to work with and no one taking control.

Scratching our heads and finding there was nothing else to do, we decided to go back to Castle's house to see if we couldn't map out some kind of strategy that would fit us into this war effort.

"There must be something, somewhere, some place where we are needed," I said, "especially four able-bodied men like us. There must be a job somewhere for us. If necessary let's create a job for ourselves. There has to be something out there that we can do. Let's get the hell out there and find it." We pondered all the rest of that day, just talking and thinking what we could do to help.

"Fellows," Joe Hunter said at about 6:30 that evening, "I suggest that we turn in early so that we can get a good start tomorrow and go to Manila over to MacArthur's headquarters and see if they can put us to work."

We all agreed, and so, after we had feasted on a good dinner that Castle's wife had fixed us, we immediately turned in for the night. The next morning, we were getting ready to go to Manila.

"Fellows," Rebel Lord, as he was affectionately called, said, "I've got a hell of a lot of fuel in the tanks over there at Sangley Point right next door to the Canacao Naval Hospital. You know, they have bombed that area several times, so I think I should go down and see what's happening. If possible, I'll get a crew together and start to barrel and move the oil and gas to safety, because I'd hate like hell to see it all blown up. It's all in those big tanks out in the open. Maybe I can save some of it."

Just about that time, we heard the drone of those big bombers, and within a few minutes, all hell broke loose over by the oil depot and the Canacao Naval Hospital. We told Rebel to wait a little longer, that as long as we were looking for something to do, we would love to help him barrel the gas and oil. But let's first wait until the Japanese stop bombing in that area. We all felt it was too dangerous at the present time, while the bombing was still going on down there.

"No," he said, "I think I'd better go now and see what I can do. They have a pattern, and they will not come back again for about two or three hours."

Before we could talk about it any further, Rebel left. He had been gone just about a half-hour, which was about the time for him to have reached Sangley Point, when we heard that familiar sound of the droning of the planes we had been hearing the last two days along with the sound like boxcars hurtling in the air. The Japanese were at it again over in the oil depot area.

"Rebel was wrong," I said, "they didn't wait two hours. They're at it again over there."

At first it seemed like they were coming down on top of us right where we were, so everybody hit the dust. But we soon found out, as the bombs started to rain down that explosions were going on everywhere over in the Sangley Point and the Canacao Naval Hospital area. We all started to talk about Rebel Lord and praying that something happened to make him miss that load of bombs. We just knew he had to be in that mess. However, we didn't give up hope. After it was all quiet for almost an hour or so, we decided to go and look for Rebel.

Just as we were about to leave and look for him, bingo, Rebel came driving up. We were so glad to see him that we rushed out to his car to hug him, to put our arms about him because he wasn't hurt and our prayers were answered. He was shivering and shaking so badly, I could hardly hold him. I also noticed that all his hair was singed, even his eyebrows were burnt. After Rebel quit shaking and had a cold beer in his hand, he began to tell us what happened.

"Well, fellows," he started out, "here is one guy who is going to see this war through, even if it lasts fifty years, after what I have just gone through. Nothing can stop me. Look at my hair and eyebrows, see how they are burnt. That's the closest I want to come to meeting my Maker.

Yes, fellows, after what I have just gone through over there, I am going live this war out." And he did. Thank God. He was still alive at war's end in 1945.

"Okay, Rebel," Castle said after he settled down, "tell us what happened. We are all ears." So Rebel began.

"Fellows, right after I got inside the naval hospital gate and about halfway between the naval hospital grounds and the fuel depot, the bastards let their load come down. I jumped into a crater that was made with one of their bombs on the first run, and thinking about that old cliché that lightening never strikes in the same place twice, I jumped into that hole." Then Rebel went on to say that he soon found out that bombs are not like lightening, because a bomb can hit the same hole twice. He then went on to tell us that the hole that he had sought refuge in was hit again on the second run. He said that it was in this hole that he was burnt as mentioned above, and it was this same hole he was tossed around like a piece of straw.

He also told us that the bomb had blown a car that was parked near the hole clean over him and far out into the field, rolling over and over. He was a lucky man, and the good Lord was watching over him is all that I can say. On that surprised second run, quite a few sailors and marines were killed, as they had left their foxholes to finish eating their lunch as soon as the first run was over and the sirens sounded all clear. They figured it was safe, because up until that time, the Japanese had never made a second run for at least two or three hours in the same area.

Chief Radioman Stevens, who was one of my best friends, was killed in that run. He had been retired in the Philippines for ten years or so. He was also a brother and one of the lights of the Masonic Lodge Bagong Buhay No. 17, in Caridad, the same lodge in which I had received my degrees, and of which I remained a member until 1946, when I affiliated with a lodge in San Francisco.

Rebel Lord told me that Brother Stevens was just going in the Canacao Naval Hospital gate with a load of Filipinos to help put out the fires, which were still burning fiercely from the first run the Japanese had made just a few moments before, and to help clear up the mess that occurs after a bombing. Rebel said a bomb made a direct hit on Brother Stevens's truckload of Filipinos. His body was never recovered. While we were sitting there, drinking beer, and listening to Rebel Lord tell us about his experiences of what had happened on the surprised second bombing run that he just encountered when he went down to check the oil depot, Castle's wife was busy preparing a nice lunch for us, which she served as soon as he was finished with his story.

"Fellows," Rebel finished with, "I should have taken your advice and waited awhile, but I am very happy that none of you were there with me in that fury of hell. You guys had enough of it a couple of days ago on over in the navy yard."

About an hour after we had finished lunch, Rebel said he was going to start moving the oil and burying it in the sand on the beach in fifty-five gallon drums. We begged him again to wait a few days, and we would all give him a hand. But he insisted and headed out to the oil depot. So we got in Castle's car and followed him. He didn't have any trouble rounding up a work crew consisting of military and native personnel to help fill the drums with gas and oil. He commandeered a Hugh tractor with a driver to go down to the beach and dig large trenches in several places to bury the filled drums, thinking it would be useful later in the war when the Americans returned to reclaim the islands from the Japanese.

Rebel asked us to go and chart the beach for him, which we did. We made several charts of the beach, so that after drums of oil and gasoline were buried, our troops would be able to locate them. In this way, we could preserve it, and it wouldn't fall into enemy hands for their use, which made the job twofold. Rebel and his crew worked all night long for several nights filling the barrels with gas and oil and taking them to the beach, where they were placed in the trenches and covered over. They worked in the dark, only dimly lit by the moon, burying hundreds of barrels of aviation gasoline and oil. Just as soon as it started to get daylight, they would quit for the day in order to keep the place of burial a secret from the Japanese. The enemy kept planes in the air all day long.

After the third night of working under cover of darkness, at exactly twelve noon on the fourth day, Japanese snipers came in flying low. They went right to the place and bombed and machine- gunned the area where Rebel had buried the gas and oil, blowing all the barrels up. It was heartbreaking for him and his crew; they had worked so hard for the past three nights burying it. It didn't seemed possible that the Japanese could know just where those barrels were buried. It was a big puzzle that no one seemed to be able to figure out. This work was performed while the moon was not bright and under a cloud of strict secrecy. The Japanese flew only in that area in the daylight hours, and Rebel only worked in the dark of the night.

How could they go to the exact place and find it? There had to be a leak somewhere. Each night, Rebel would bury the oil in a different locale far from where it was buried the night before. Sometimes he would bury the barrels as far as five miles further down the coast than the last ones he had buried. Rebel kept right on working in the dark, burying the drums. And every day thereafter, right on the dot, like clockwork at noon they went to the exact spot where Rebel had buried the gas the night before and bombed and strafed that area, blowing up the oil and gas. We were completely baffled and kept asking over and over how they could know where we worked the night before.

27. Tracking the Radio Signals of a Traitor

A radioman reported to Lieutenant Schofield, U.S.N.R., who had assumed the duties of captain of the yard in the absence of Comdr. Roul T. Whitney, U.S.N., who was in the Canacao Naval Hospital, having been wounded on 10 December. He told Lieutenant Schofield that he had picked up a signal he thought was guiding the Japanese. I was the assistant captain of the yard under Commander Whitney, so Lieutenant Schofield assigned me the job of tracing this signal. He told me to get this traitor at all costs: "kill that son of a bitch" were his exact words. I was further instructed not ask any questions, just silence that "son of a bitch." He pointed to the forty-five I was wearing on my belt and said to use that on that bastard, which meant only one thing to me—silence him forever.

I saluted him and said, "Yes, sir," then I left to try and locate Charlie, the radioman who had reported intercepting a signal he thought was guiding the Japanese. I went over to the radio shack and located Charlie and told him to get the necessary equipment for tracking and to report back to me as soon as possible. Within an hour, he was back with his tracking equipment, and I transferred his paraphernalia into my jeep.

"Let's go, Charlie," I said, "and locate this son of a bitch and silence him and his damned radio forever."

We hadn't driven more than a mile, when the radioman turned to me.

"We got him," he said, "I've picked up the signal. Let's get him."

I instructed my driver to follow the directions that Charlie gave him, so the driver turned the jeep around and, under Charlie's directions, we started to track the radio signal he had picked up. It was being transmitted in Japanese, and it was real close, and although Charlie couldn't understand it, he knew it was a guiding radio beam. While we were riding around in the area where it was coming from, three Japanese civilians came running out of a Filipino bamboo shack area.

"Stop," I yelled out loud from our jeep, but they kept on going. Once again I yelled, "Stop," and they didn't pay any attention, so I grabbed onto the forty-five that I was carrying. The driver, in the meantime, had swung the jeep around, and we got ahead of them. I jumped out of the jeep and stood right in front of them with the forty-five in my hand and again yelled, "Stop. Put your hands in the air. Now." They complied with my order.

Then one of the fellows started to put his hand inside his jacket as if he had a side arm there. My forty-five was about two feet from his face. I immediately pulled the trigger when he reached into his jacket. I thank God to this day that that gun didn't go off. I thank God that in my haste, I had not taken the safety off. Lucky for both of us, because just about the time I was trying to pull the trigger, he pulled out an identification card. It was a U.S. Army Intelligence card, all three of them had one.

I just stood there shaking and trembling. It was several minutes before I could make my mouth utter a sound; I was scared almost to death. To think I had almost killed an innocent man. To this day I shudder when I think about it. I feel it could have destroyed my life. I have thanked my Heavenly Father many times for not letting that gun fire.

After I had gained my composure, one of them told me in very broken English, so bad I could hardly understand that they were Japanese Americans from Hawaii and were working for the army and that they too had been assigned to find and silence the radio signal, the same one we were looking for. I explained, by using my hands and arms in gestures and in the best broken English I could muster, that we had located the signal and were tracking it now. I tried to explain to them in the best way that I could, using broken English, that they should never do that again. I told them how close their man had come to being killed and that they should *never, never* do that again. I explained to them if anyone tells you to put your hands up in the air, especially with a gun pointed at you, do it immediately, never ever reach inside your jacket for anything. You can always explain later.

Then I told them that as long as we had picked up the signal and were tracing it, they should report back to their headquarters. After all, we were only a few days into the war, and with such turmoil and everyone being utterly confused, it was hard to get word out to those working in the field. So I was not made aware of any Japanese Americans working out there. Later that day, I was informed that a few friendly Japanese Americans had been flown in from Hawaii within the past twenty-four hours and were working as interpreters for the U.S. Forces.

Yes, there were a lot of things happening that most of us were not made aware of for several days. Also, there were many things taking place that did not get out to the troops in the field. The navy had never been told about any Japanese working for us or about their identifying markings to allow us to identify them on sight as friendly Japanese.

In tracing the radio signal, our trail took us inside the civilian shipyard drydock. Just as the radioman and I entered the building where the signal was coming from, we heard a shot ring out in the far end of the hall. I raced over there and saw a U.S. Marine Corps lieutenant who had just shot a fellow in the back of the head.

"I just walked up behind the bastard and fired this forty-five into that son of a bitch," the marine officer said. "I asked no questions, just killed that dirty rat on the spot."

I introduced myself and the radioman who was with me to the marine lieutenant and told him that Charlie was the fellow who had first picked up the signal and had reported it to headquarters. I also told him that my orders were the same as his. I was to ask no questions. Just silence the dirty bastard for ever.

As I picked his head up by his hair to see his face, I recognized him immediately as being a retired chief radioman from the U.S. Navy. It was hard to believe that this damn traitor whom I identified to the marine lieutenant as a Chief Radioman C. E. Smith, U.S. Navy, whom we all knew as Smithy, was the man the marine lieutenant had just shot and killed on the spot. I could hardly bring myself to believe that of all people, it was a retired U.S. Navy Chief Petty Officer. Yes, he was an American traitor and still had his hand on the key sending signals and guiding the Japanese planes up until the time the marine lieutenant shot him in the back of the head. He got just what he deserved.

Smithy had served over twenty-five years in the U.S. Navy. How could he stoop so low as to accept a pension from Uncle Sam and also get a pay check from the Japanese for being a spy against his own country? We found out later that he had been working as a spy for the Japanese several years before he had retired from the navy. He had been recruited by the Japanese and had started working in a spying capacity while doing duty in Shanghai, where he was on duty as the chief radioman in the U.S. Embassy in China. A good place for the Japanese to recruit a spy.

Upon his retirement in 1938, Smithy, over a period of four years, had made several trips to Japan before the bombing of Hawaii by the Japanese. After returning from his second or third trip, he started to spend a lot of money; he even opened up a bar and grill in Manila. The bar was located right next to the navy landing docks in Manila. Of course, where else would a spy open a place.

His place was frequented by American sailors, who accounted for over ninety-five percent of his business. No one ever questioned him as to where all this money was coming from. We knew he had made several trips to Japan, but never in a million years would we suspect that this guy could be a traitor to the country to which he gave over twenty-five years of the best part of his life. It came as a shock to those of us who knew him and frequented his bar and grill when the truth came out that he had been spying for the Japanese all this time.

In reality, our naval intelligence should have figured it out, because each time after returning from Japan, he would spend money very freely, and to top it off, opening up the most likely business to eavesdrop; what better place to gather information to pass on than a barroom near a navy landing dock. The Japanese were known to open establishments that were always located near an army post or naval base, such as barber shops, bars, restaurants and any place that a military man would frequent when he was on shore leave, any place where they could eavesdrop and gather information to help their cause. These Japanese spy places could be found in China, the Philippines, as well as in the Hawaiian Islands. Yes, and some were even in the United States in the home ports of the naval fleets on the East and West Coasts. I remember a Japanese barber shop next door to the YMCA outside the Brooklyn navy yard gate on Sand Street, the main thoroughfare.

Several years before the war, a Japanese was considered undressed if seen without his camera in the United States. Today, they are practically buying whole cities in this country. Long before the war, the Japanese had ham radio stations near every military base. The one Smithy was operating was located just across from the Cavite Navy Yard. Don't think they won't do it again. Wake up, America.

The radio station where we caught up with Smithy, in the dry dock building, was not the only one in the Manila area; there were several more. In fact, the Balintawak Beer Brewery (BBB) in the Philippines, which was owned by the Japanese, was just a front. It was full of arms and ammunition. It was, in every sense of the word, an arsenal. It was even equipped

105

with a radio station, which was used to guide the Japanese bombers in the Manila area when they first entered the war.

The Japanese continued day after day, even after Smithy was taken out of the picture, to come over at noon to bomb and strafe the beach. Rebel Lord buried some oil in the same spot where they had bombed before and some in different places on the beach miles away; the enemy never located any buried gasoline or oil again. Gosh, how they tried. They were out there every day for weeks after, but to no avail. They, not knowing what happened to Smithy, probably thought he had quit them.

Now that Smithy was taken care of, I dropped Charlie back at the radio shack and then proceeded back to the captain of the yard's office. I reported to Lieutenant Schofield, the acting captain of the yard—Captain Whitney was still in the hospital—and supplied him with all the details about the marine lieutenant's gun silencing the man who was directing the Japanese and that he was retired navy chief petty officer, C. E. Smith. I inquired if he had any further orders for me to carry out, or should I go over with my friends to Manila and report to General MacArthur's headquarters for an assignment. He said he had nothing else at the time, but should something arise he would send for me. After giving him a brisk salute, I had the driver take me to Castle's home, Upon arrival, I told the driver to report back to the car pool with the jeep.

28. Introducing Another Hero, Naval Payclerk Hanson

Now that Rebel Lord was all squared away with his crew and getting the oil and gas buried without it being detected, and our seeing that he didn't need our gang any longer, we decided to go on to Manila and report in. Big Ski decided to stay and help Rebel Lord, saying that both of them would catch up with us when they had completed burying as much of the gas and oil that they had drums to put it in. We ran into two more fellows whom we knew from the Cavite Navy Yard. We told them that we were headed for Manila to report to General MacArthur's headquarters for duty. They said they would like to join up with us, and we told them we'd love to have them.

One fellow was Mike Sedan, a retired chief storekeeper, U.S.N., who had been recalled to active duty about a year before the war started. The other fellow was A. B. Lowell, a civilian navy yard worker who said he couldn't find anything to do, but would love to do something for his country if he possibly could. I assured them both we would find something and that they were more than welcome aboard.

So with Chief Quartermaster Joe Hunter, Chief Machinist Mate Castle, Chief Storekeeper Mike Sedan, civilian A. B. Lowell, and I headed once more down the road toward Manila. The road was jam- packed with traffic all heading toward the big city. I think we drove most of the time in low gear, hardly moving.

There were crowds of people, most of them natives, with their backs loaded down, some with caribou, laden with about everything they owned, and even driving livestock, such as pigs, goats, etcetera, jamming the highways; they numbered in the thousands. There were very few motor cars, mostly pushcarts and handcarts were employed. Some, with their babies piled on top of their belongings on a two- wheel cart with shafts, and they pulled it as a horse would. I felt so sorry for these poor folks. Their nepa shacks had been destroyed by the bombings, and they were carrying all their earthly possessions with them. Some were heading to the province, others to Manila. It was a pitiful sight. It reminded me of the people of France when they were forced out of their homes and took to the highways.

Also in this crowd were several hundred Americans and Filipinos from the U.S. Navy with no orders, nowhere to go, all eager to get in and do something, but where could they go? Where could they start? All were searching the same as we were for the answer. After several hours we finally reached the four corners of Novelette, where a lieutenant commander of the U.S. Navy was directing the great mobs of homeless, trying to steer them from going toward Manila, trying to get them to go into the province back in the hills, where they would be safe from the Japanese strafing and bombing raids.

We stopped, and I got out and went over to the lieutenant commander.

"Sir," I said, "three navy chief petty officers, a navy yard employee and I are in that car over there. What can we do? Where do you suggest we report? We're looking for a job."

As he looked at me, I could see sorrow in his eyes. After a moment or two, he finally answered.

"I'm sorry, I know how you feel, but I too am looking for a job. They are telling everyone to go into the hills, and if needed they would be called. I really don't know, I truly wish I had the answer, but I don't, Sorry, fellow, we are caught in one hell of a mess. Your guess is as good as mine." After talking with him awhile, I went back to the car and told the fellows what he had said.

"Hell," Joe said, "let's keep on going to Manila and see what they have to say over there."

One thing was certain, all five of us had made up our minds we were not going into the hills. There was a war going on, and we could not fight it in the hills. So we headed toward Manila. About a mile further down the road, we noticed a couple of navy cars hidden under the trees off the side of the road. We also noticed a bunch of naval personnel lying on the ground under the trees in a big field. So we stopped, and Joe and I climbed over the fence and asked who was in charge. Mr. Hanson, a navy warrant officer (payclerk) told us no one in particular, and no one seemed to know where to go.

"I'm taking it on my own," he then said, "to get together all the naval personnel I can. I am going to try to supply the ships that needs them with personnel."

"Where do you intend to make your headquarters?" I inquired of him.

"I'm going to try to make the navy club down by the navy landing in Manila," he replied. "We'll try and make it before daybreak. I really don't know where we will end up. We have a couple of cars and a bit of food, so you people might join us if you desire. The more the merrier."

We told him we had a place to stay about a mile down the road, at Castle's house. Also that we had our own transportation, so we would go to our friend's home to spend the night and go on to Manila in the morning and report in to see if we could get a job from someone in General MacArthur's headquarters.

Mr. Hanson could hit the road with his crowd of sailors only when it was all clear, which wasn't very often. The Japanese kept in the sky pretty much all that day, which made traveling very dangerous in the daylight with this group in military uniform. He told me that as soon as it got dusk, they would hit the road and hike until the early hours of the morning, and that he hoped he could make his destination before daybreak.

"I feel that it would be too dangerous to be on the road with this group after dawn."

So we shoved off and headed for Castle's house. It was too late in the afternoon to start out for Manila. We stopped on our way at Big Ski's to tell his wife that he was working with Rebel Lord at the oil depot at Sangley Point. She gave us a couple of cold beers after we had relaxed a bit, and after about an hour or two, we left and went to Castle's home to spend the night. Later on, Castle's wife made us a nice dinner. After dinner and after our plans were all mapped out for the next day, we sacked out for the night.

While at Castle's home, it seemed that the main topic of our conversation all that afternoon and night was about what a brave guy this navy payclerk Hanson was; it seemed really that that was all we talked about. We certainly were proud of him. It took a little payclerk like that to get up enough initiative to round up men to aid the skippers of ships that had lost some of their complement a couple of days before from the Japanese bombing and the destruction of the Cavite Navy Yard and their having to get underway too fast to get all their ship's complement on board. This little payclerk found something helpful to do, while all the senior officers told us to go into the hills.

That made us feel that all was not lost and we did have fighting men with spirit. I did not come into contact with all the officers and men, only a few. I am sure there were other men just like payclerk Hanson. We were proud of him then, in the first days of the war, and we had the opportunity to be proud of him later, in the first days of prison life, but more about that later. Wherever Mr. Hanson is, may God bless.

29. Heading to MacArthur's Headquarters in Manila

The next morning, bright and early, as soon as we had a hearty breakfast at Castle's home, our gang got together and, after bidding Castle's wife good-bye, we headed out toward Manila, as planned. We traveled with the same fellows all the time, namely: E. B. (Joe) Hunter, Castle, A. B. Lowell, Mike Sedan, Big Ski, and Rebel Lord, all of the U.S. Navy. However, Big Ski and Rebel Lord weren't with us at this time. We left them working at the Sangley Point oil depot a couple of days ago.

Upon arrival in Manila, we went down to the Marsman building, where General MacArthur, the supreme commander of the Asiatic station, had made his headquarters, now that Admiral Hart, commander in chief of the navy had departed for Australia. Just as we got there, the air raid siren went off, so we ducked in the doors and stayed in the lobby with the rest of the personnel who were there in the building. The outside of the building had been barricaded with sand bags which made it a fairly decent air raid shelter for the time being. No one was allowed to go upstairs during the air raid.

Joe found the commander in chief's secretary and told him our situation and how we had been told to go into the hills, that we would be called if needed at least a dozen times in the last two days.

"I served in the army during the first big war," Joe also told him as best as I can remember, "and our organization was disrupted many times, but we always regrouped immediately and were ready for the next eventuality. Believe me, sir, if I'm told once more to go to the hills, I'm heading straight for the army. There at least, I know I'll be wanted and won't be told to go into the hills until called for."

The flag secretary was a very fine officer. He reasoned with us and agreed that we were right in insisting on being able to find something to do. He told us that there was an ensign of the supply corps down at the navy cold storage plant, and if we could get some riot guns, it would be a good thing for us to go down and act as armed guards for the provision trucks carrying food to the boys at Olongapo, Mariveles, and other outlying stations.

"We know where we can plenty of guns," we told him, "but we need authority to get them from the ammunition depot in the Cavite Navy Yard; the marines are guarding the yard and may not let us through."

He gave us a pass that read that we were on a special mission for the commander in chief, General MacArthur, and to grant us passage and allow us to have as much arms and ammunition as needed to carry out our assignment, without questions. Before going back to Cavite for the guns, Whitey, a chief yeoman told us that we had better first go down to the navy club, where payclerk Hanson had set up headquarters, to inform him we were alive and not injured, and also that we had been assigned to ride shotgun. He was making up a roster, so headquarters would have an idea of who was alive and who was missing since the bombings of the last few days.

We headed down there immediately to report to payclerk Hanson. Arriving about 12:00 noon, we checked in just about the time they were having lunch, so we all went over to get a bite to eat, not having had a crumb since breakfast at Castle's home. Just as I had gotten everything on my plate, the old siren sounded. All hands ducked and went helter skelter in all directions, and so did my chow—it went flying. Everyone was yelling.

"Here they come, boys." I started to look for a shelter of some sort. I yelled over to a fellow to find out where they went for shelter during the air raids. "You're there, boy," he said. "Just lie on the ground and pray that your name is not on one of those babies." Just as I dropped to the ground, a fellow came over. "Secure," he said, "That was just the noon-hour siren whistle for Manila." I burst out into a big laugh.

"What the hell kind of outfit are we in now," I said. "They are using the same siren that they use for air raid warnings to tell us it's twelve o'clock."

We complained to Mr. Hanson, and he soon got that junk knocked off. No more twelve o'clock noon whistles for Manila. Mr. Hanson told us that from then on, when that siren started to wail, you had better seek cover, because it will be the real McCoy.

"Joe, let's get the hell out of here," I said to Hunter, "before we all go nuts with sirens going off all day long, and one doesn't know whether the bombs are about to fall or if it is just to announce the time of day." So we went to the gate to leave.

The officer of the day told us that his orders were that he was not to allow anyone to leave the compound, and that meant us. We then showed him the pass that had been given to Joe by General MacArthur's secretary.

"Stick around, all of you," was all he said.

"Come on, we'll just ease out the gate one at a time. If anyone says anything, we'll tell them we are going after our baggage in the car," Hunter said.

Each one of us in turn were asked where we were headed, and each said, "to get my luggage." It worked, and in about ten minutes, we were all out and we never went back inside that compound again. They can have their air raid sirens going off all the time. We drove directly to Cavite, which was about twenty-seven miles around the bay on bumpy and sometimes bombed-out roads.

On arriving at Porta Vargo, the entrance to the navy yard ammunition depot, Joe and the other fellows went in to get the guns and ammunition while I stayed outside to shoot the breeze with some of the marines on duty there. They said they would pick me up when they came out. Well, it seems that after they had secured the guns and ammunition we needed, they missed me on their way out of the gate on their way back to Manila to get the trucks. Not being able to locate me, they just continued on to Manila, which left me stranded there all night. I spent the night there at the gate with the marines. The next morning, I was still at the Cavite Navy Yard gate, waiting for Castle and the other fellows to return to get me so that we could help load the trucks with provisions for the outlying stations, and I would ride shotgun with them.

30. Riding Shotgun for the Provision Trucks

When they arrived, Castle and the others told me about a horrifying experience they encountered on their way back to Manila the night before. They told me that Hunter, Lowell, and Castle went in and, without any problem, picked up the guns and ammo they needed, and that they had told the officer in charge of the provisions they would be back in the morning with trucks to carry food to the outlying stations. They told him that we would be riding shotgun for them. He replied, "That would be just great, as they need food badly, especially down in Olongapo."

Then Lowell told me it was a good thing they had missed me by accident and that I wasn't along with them on the trip back, because on their way back to Manila, they were stopped by two marines on the road near Novelette who demanded to commandeer Castle's car. Castle showed them his U.S.N. shield to let them know his car was being used for official purposes, but they still insisted they wanted his car.

He then produced the letter from General MacArthur's secretary, saying they were on an important mission for that office and to give them speedy passage. The marines just ignored that and still demanded Castle's car. By this time, Castle noticed the boys had been drinking, so he started to drive off. The marines raised their rifles, which were Springfield .30 caliber, and emptied them in his car. The bullets went through the back of the car and rear window, and passed directly through the front window.

Why, they said, it was a good thing I wasn't there was because had I been in the car, someone would have been killed. As it were, with only three being in the car, it afforded them space to duck down low. The bullets being emptied into the car were all high and over their heads because they were able to duck down, hence, no one was hurt. But it was horrifying and really shook them up.

By the time they completed telling me about the night before, we had arrived down at section P, where some of the provisions were still stored. This was Joe Hunter's territory. He had all the keys to the buildings and opened them for us. And with the help that we enlisted from those standing around outside, we were able to get the trucks loaded with the necessary provisions in nothing flat. We made several trips to Olongapo, Mariveles, and Bataan before the roads were bombed out so badly that we couldn't get through any longer, but we had gotten one heck of a lot of food to those stations and also put a lot in storage in the Mariveles tunnels for later use.

31. General Homma Lands on Lingayen Gulf

General Homma of the Japanese imperial army was placed in charge of the Japanese expedition in the Philippines, but only after being given direct orders to follow the specific plans that were laid down for him and which had the prior approval of the chief of staff, none other than General Sugiyama. General Sugiyama disliked General Homma with a passion and didn't mind telling it to everyone. General Homma, who, with the consent of the emperor, was placed in charge of conquering the resistance of the Philippines, figured that the emperor had given him a free hand to get the job done and questioned General Sugiyama about some of his tactics in the plans he had given him and with which he was not in accord. He also said that the emperor had given him the authority to carry out orders at his own discretion.

For this, he was bluntly told by General Sugiyama that "if you don't like the plan I have laid down for you, I can relieve you, and I will give it to another." As was noted before, General Sugiyama disliked General Homma intensely and did not trust his judgment. But General Homma had the ear of the emperor, and the emperor himself had named General Homma for the job. So although it was against General Sugiyama's better judgment to give this job to General Homma, he did it to keep himself in the good graces of the emperor, who General Sugiyama dare not go against.

General MacArthur's family, his father, General Arthur MacArthur, and his children had all lived in the Philippines. They had dedicated themselves to study the Oriental mind and be ready to lead us in case of a war. Douglas MacArthur, as did his father, both graduated from West Point. Douglas served in the U.S. Army as a full lieutenant under his father, General Arthur MacArthur, in the Philippines, before World War One. Later, in World War One, while in Europe, he served as a lieutenant general, which rank he retired in 1935. Upon retirement, he immediately returned to his home in his beloved Philippines.

Upon General MacArthur's arrival in Australia, he was immediately advanced to the rank of five-star general and general of the army. Among the many medals that decorated his uniform was the Congressional Medal of Honor. His father, General Arthur MacArthur, before him, had also received the same medal. Few men in history have garnered as many honors as did General Douglas MacArthur in a lifetime of service to his country.

The Philippine government never had an army. They did have an outfit called the Filipino Scouts, and, I daresay, there has never been such a dedicated and fearless group in the world than the Filipino Scouts. They were a family tradition. As soon as a young man became of age, he immediately followed his father or brother into the Filipino Scouts.

Immediately upon retirement, in 1935, MacArthur was requested by President Manuel Quezon of the Philippines to form a Philippine army, a position that he accepted. He was given the rank of Field Marshal. He had the distinct honor of being the only military officer from another country to hold that rank. He served in that capacity until July 1941.

He recruited and trained Filipino recruits with wooden guns. The Philippine government couldn't afford real rifles at that time. So they had never been taught how to fire or use a real rifle before being thrust into battle with the Japanese.

However, they made General MacArthur very proud. When the chips were down, those boys turned out to be a formidable force against the Japanese on the fields of the Lingayen Gulf and again on Bataan. All during the war, they fought with valor, and they went down fighting as heroes, gaining the name of the Battling Bastards of Bataan, while fighting alongside their American comrades. Seeing the war clouds getting darker with the passing of each day, on 1 July 1941 MacArthur was recalled to active duty in the U.S. Army by President Roosevelt, in his retired rank of Lieutenant General.

He was given overall command of the ground forces on the Asiatic station, in which position he remained until March 1942, when he was ordered to Australia to take supreme command of all the allied forces, in the Far East. I've heard him called "Dugout Doug," but don't you believe it; I had the pleasure of serving under him, and we had to really fight to keep him away from the front lines. But he still went over there against our warnings. He even slept out in the open, with Japanese bombers flying overhead.

32. MacArthur's Strength and Strategy and General Wainwright

The full strength of General MacArthur's forces was about 145,000 troops. Of those, there were about 25,000 well-trained American troops and about 15,000 well-trained Filipino Scouts. The balance of about 105,000 were Filipino troops who had no training. The Filipino Scouts proved to be well-trained and very brave soldiers. In all, the 145,000 under MacArthur's charge had to defend all of the Philippine archipelago, which included Luzon, Mindanao, and the Visayans. The three largest islands in the chain were Mindanao and Visaya in the southern part of the Philippines, and Luzon in the northern part. Luzon was where the big battle took place.

There were many more smaller islands to defend. MacArthur gave General Sharp, in Mindanao, in the southern part of the Philippines, about 35,000 troops, which left about 110,000 troops for General Wainwright to defend all of the northern Philippines. Of the 110,000 troops turned over to General Wainwright, there were only about 30,000 well-trained troops, consisting of American and Filipino Scouts combined. They were combined with the rest of his troops, who were raw recruits.

A great majority of the Filipinos under General Wainwright's command had joined the army just a few days before they were put into battle, without even a day's training. They had not only not fired a gun, most of them had never seen a gun before in their lives. The rest of the Filipino troops had been recruited and were in training with wooden guns just a few months before the war broke out. However, all the Filipinos proved themselves to be a fearless fighting group of men on the front lines of Bataan. Wainwright put a few thousand seasoned troops in reserve at important road heads to the south. As mentioned before, most of his troop strength had just enlisted within the last forty-eight hours. They were mostly young men, seventeen to twenty years of age. They loved America as well as their own country, and so, seeing it as their duty to protect their homeland and America, the country that had given them so much freedom, they joined up and were sent into battle. Upon enlisting, they were given about two to three hours training in the handling of a rifle or machine gun, and that was it.

General MacArthur had made up his mind that he was not going to sacrifice his little army of some 30,000 highly trained fighters and the balance of about 115,000 raw recruits on an impossible mission under General Wainwright in the north to make a stand against the highly trained and well-fortified imperial troops of Japan on the plains of Lingayen Gulf, where they would be mostly out in the open fields with no air power; it would be plain slaughter.

General MacArthur spent many sleepless nights trying to map out the most feasible place on Luzon where he would have a fighting chance against such heavy odds the Japanese were throwing against his forces. In his studies of the Luzon peninsula in the northern Philippines, he felt that the Bataan-Mariveles province was the only logical place on Luzon where he would have a better chance to confront the enemy on a battlefield.

Those plans were not disclosed to even his closest friend or advisor. MacArthur kept them to himself to the very end, for fear of a leak to the enemy. He refused to tell his wife or even Manuel Quezon, the president of the Philippine Islands, about his plans. MacArthur, being made aware of the vast number of Japanese being landed on the Lingayen Gulf by General Homma, decided to put his plan into effect immediately.

This big buildup by the Japanese is what prompted MacArthur to send the message ordering General Wainwright, in charge of the troops fighting in the field on Lingayen Gulf, to fall back slowly toward Bataan. MacArthur's reasoning was that on the Bataan peninsula, by commingling his raw and seasoned troops, he would have a fair chance of inflicting a great amount of casualties on the enemy, which proved to be correct. MacArthur's troops did indeed inflict heavy losses on the Japanese while fighting later in the jungles of Bataan-Mariveles province.

The plans laid down by General Sugiyama called for General Homma to occupy the Philippines by late January 1942. He was to first destroy all the airfields, thereby putting our air force out of commission. With all resistance broken from the air, General Homma was to land on Lingayen Gulf in full force at the outbreak of hostilities on or about 12 December 1941.

So after breaking the back of our air force, General Homma started landing his troops; they were being landed from all directions, coming from the north, east, south,and west. They landed from over eighty to eighty-five transports. They came with no resistance, swarming onto the beaches at Lingayen Gulf, Albay, Altimonan and Batangas.

General Homma went about the plans given to him by General Sugiyama, not watching his right or left flanks. He thus allowed General Wainwright's guerrillas to steal away and form a force in the mountains—a grave mistake by General Homma, because it also allowed General Wainwright to carry out his plan, which was to fall back slowly, when possible, without being noticed and, again, when possible, to head south toward the Bataan peninsula.

General Wainwright carried out General MacArthur's orders to a tee without being detected by General Homma. The enemy was well aware of MacArthur's strength, through their spy system that they had set up in the United States, as well as in the Philippine Islands many years before the war. After all, this war was actually declared in 1853 but not literally or in earnest until 1906, when Admiral Dewey fueled and provisioned the Russian fleet in Manila while Russia and Japan were at war. (Proof of this was found in the Mariveles mountains, across from Corregidor island and will be explained later.) The fallback of General Wainwright's troops toward Manila and into Bataan went as planned, very slowly, without being challenged by the enemy.

General Wainwright had been slowly making his way around Manila and into Bataan by zigzagging through Pamapanga. General Homma was furious at the way Wainwright was getting his troops into Bataan. It was absolutely impossible for him to cut off Wainwright's troops due to their zigzagging operation. Wainwright kept deploying his troops and then attacking unexpectedly, then deploying, then attacking, thus keeping General Homma off guard and highly frustrated. The Japanese were so bewildered by these tactics, they were at a loss, not knowing what to do. It just kept fouling General Homma's plans that had taken days for him to map out.

On or about 15 December 1941 General MacArthur saw how the war was going and that his plan was taking effect. He knew we must move everything into Bataan if we were to entertain the Japanese long enough to allow the United States to get a foothold in Australia, which after all was the objective of the United States. The reasoning was that without Australia under our control, it might take years to defeat Japan. The United States needed that foothold in Australia as a jumping-off point.

Seeing that General Wainwright was making good headway against General Homma's troops, General MacArthur ordered the rest of his plan to be put into effect immediately, thus starting to move large amounts of food and ammunition into the Bataan-Mariveles area, which was a small peninsula about 400 square miles. Bataan and Mariveles controlled the land approaches to Corregidor Island. The Mariveles mountains were like one big rock, as like Corregidor was. It was known as the Mariveles Mountain Rock. The demolition crews had been blasting, digging, and honey-

117

combing huge tunnels in this massive rock, for several years in anticipation of the war that had been brewing between Japan and the West.

Most of the food and ammunition to supply the battlefront and this area were stored in the tunnels in the Mariveles mountains across from Corregidor, which, being near the seaway, made them easily accessible to Corregidor or the Bataan front lines. Corregidor's job was to defend the entrance to Manila Bay. Corregidor was a fortress consisting of artesian wells, disappearing guns, and concrete tunnels. It, too, was honeycombed with tunnels, at a very great expense. One of the tunnels (Malinta tunnel) housed a 300-bed hospital, complete with operating and X-ray rooms, etcetera. The hospital was outfitted better than some hospitals in the United States. It was equipped with the best technology of the times.

33. Admiral Hart Saves the Asiatic Fleet from Destruction

About the twentieth of December 1941 General MacArthur decided that the Asiatic Fleet should try to make a run for Australia, so he notified Admiral Hart to that effect. It should be noted here that Admiral Hart didn't see eye to eye with General MacArthur because MacArthur felt that he was the supreme commander of all the Asiatic station, including the navy. This was not the case. He was the commanding general in charge of the Philippines only.

Admiral Thomas C. Hart was the commander in chief of Asiatic Fleet, in all aspects considered an arm of the Pacific Fleet, and was therefore under the command of the Pacific Fleet and not under the command of General MacArthur. The Asiatic Fleet, under the command of Admiral Thomas C. Hart, U.S.N., was charged with a realm to protect, which consisted of not only the Philippines, but all of China and all of the countries of the Malay Barrier, which itself was quite a large territory to protect. And Admiral Hart resented MacArthur's trying to order him to do his bidding. So here we find an admiral and a general at odds as to who was boss. Clearly, MacArthur was in the wrong.

However, Admiral Hart, seeing the way things were going in the diplomatic field in Washington, D.C., and sensing that war was practically inevitable with Japan, in a very strategic maneuver, about the first of November 1941, about a month and a half prior to MacArthur's order, moved most of his ships to safer waters. He moved them down along the

Malayan Barrier, so that when the war came to Manila and the Philippines, the Japanese had very few naval targets to fire on.

Then on 8 December 1941, Admiral Hart, under the strictest secrecy, ordered the balance of the fleet still in the Manila area to proceed out to sea. When out on the open seas, he then ordered them to proceed toward Australia and await further orders, which would be forthcoming. With Admiral Hart's very intelligent move and quick thinking by ordering the main body of the Asiatic Fleet, about forty-two warships, out to sea, where they would have a better chance of protecting themselves, he saved the Asiatic Fleet from what would have been a terrible disaster had they remained in the port of Manila. In all probability, it would have been another Hawaii. With Admiral Hart's strategic move, the navy only lost the U.S.S. *Sea Lion* a V-type submarine, two navy yard tugs, a couple of hundred torpedoes with their war heads, and a small amount of spare parts for our motor torpedo boats. They were losses that couldn't be helped, as they were stored in the Cavite Navy Yard, which went up in smoke.

The Cavite Navy Yard was one of finest and best-equipped navy yard installations this country had at that time anywhere in the world. The reason for the loss of the one submarine, the U.S.S. *Sea Lion,* was that she was under repairs and moored alongside her mother ship the U.S.S. *Otus,* so she was unable to get underway, as her sister ships did. The mother ship, the U.S.S. *Otus,* was very badly damaged also; she was leaking water, etcetera. However, she was able to get underway under her own power and moved out to sea. The Japanese were really mad when they found out the only naval ships in and about the Philippines were those few under repair in the Cavite Navy Yard. Had the war come to the Philippines two weeks later, all the ships would have been gone, with the exception of the U.S.S. *Genessee,* a seagoing tug, and possibly the six PT boats, because they were all out on maneuvers.

34. Setting Up a Soup Kitchen at the Mango Inn

Seeing that our job was about to wind up in taking provisions to the outlying stations, due to the roads being bombed so badly and becoming almost an impossibility to travel over with loaded trucks, I decided to look up Lieutenant Schofield, U.S.N.R., the acting captain of the Cavite Navy Yard, to ascertain if he had a job for me. This information I communicated to Joe and the others who were riding shotgun with me. I told them that being I was the assistant captain of the yard under Commander Whitney, who was still in the Canacao Naval Hospital, maybe I should go over and see if there were something that Lieutenant Schofield would like me to do, and if not, he would at least know that I was still alive and kicking and that I was available for anything he might need me to do for him, now or in the future.

So I went to Lieutenant Schofield's office and reported to him, as assistant captain of the yard, that since the Cavite Navy Yard had been completely demolished, I had been working on various jobs with five chief petty officers who had been recalled from the Fleet Naval Reserve in whatever capacity our services were needed at that moment. That right now, we were working as armed guards for trucks that we had commandeered and were engaged in carrying provisions to the outlying stations. I went on to explain to him that now, due to the roads having been bombed so heavily, they were becoming an almost impossibility to travel on. Therefore, I told him, we were making ourselves available for whatever capacity he could use us.

"I certainly can use you," Lieutenant Schofield said. "In fact, I have been looking for you. I need someone to supervise the feeding of the military stragglers, women, and children, natives, etcetera. I feel that you are about the only one who could handle this kind of a job for me. What do you think? Can you handle it?"

"I'll sure give it a whirl, Captain," I said, "and with your permission, I'll get started right away and tackle the job. But first, I must go over and let my buddies know, so they don't wait for me. They have one last load to deliver."

I went back and told Joe Hunter and the other fellows that Lieutenant Schofield had been looking for me, that he wanted to assign me to a job of setting up a kitchen to feed the Filipino natives, the military, civilians, and their families. I told him I'd try and tackle it, and that I think I'll try and set it up at the Mango Inn, away from the bombing area. When I got done telling them about the new job I was going to start, Joe and the other chiefs said that as soon as they got back and were free, they'll get over there to give me a hand.

I told them I'd sure love that and will need all the help I can muster. They told me they would see me that night at Castle's home in Novelette, and after our so-longs, I went back to Lieutenant Schofield's office to report for duty.

While I was still there, Joe and the rest of the fellows got finished loading, and as they drove past, riding shotgun for the trucks carrying provisions to the outlying stations, they noticed me standing outside the office that Lieutenant Schofield had set up. They called over to me and yelled out.

"So long, Ski. See you tonight at Castle's house."

I waved back at them and watched as they went on down the road.

"There go a great bunch of guys," I said to the lieutenant.

Lieutenant Schofield asked me if I had in mind a suitable place that was sheltered where I could set up a kitchen, where we could cook and feed the hungry without drawing too much attention from the Japanese planes.

"Captain," I said, "since you first mentioned setting up a kitchen, I have been thinking about the Mango Inn. That place was bombed so bad it could never be used again, but all the cooking utensils, etcetera, are there for the taking." I told him that I knew Mr. Trinidad Ibanez), the owner, real well, that I used to hang out there quite a bit, and that I would go to his home and get his permission to salvage and utilize anything we could find in the debris.

"Go for it," he said. "I'm a hundred percent behind you. Whatever you need, let me know, and I'll try and secure it for you."

I then explained to the lieutenant, that before I could turn a hand, I needed suitable transportation.

"That's no big chore," he said. With that, he turned to his yeoman and told him to have a car and driver assigned over to me to use in any capacity I saw fit.

In a few minutes, the car and driver came up. I instructed the driver to take me to Trinidad's house over in Caridad; he lived about five or six miles from the Cavite Navy Yard. I told Trinidad what I had in mind and asked him for permission to use what utensils and other things I could find in the wreckage of the Mango Inn.

"The place is yours," he said. "Take what you need. You have my permission to take whatever you can find while ransacking through the debris of that mess out there, anything that will help you in carrying out your orders to set up a soup kitchen to help these needy people. I won't be able to set up shop out there for quite sometime, and it may be never again."

I thanked him and told him to come out and bring his family for food after I was all set up in a day or two, that I'd love to have them and that they were more than welcome, anytime. He assured me that he would be glad to.

The Mango Inn was a former restaurant and bar. It got its name from the four enormous mango trees that surrounded it. I mean they were *big trees, huge.* The natives told me they were several hundred years old. The Mango Inn, from the continuous bombing in that area by the Japanese, had been knocked completely out of business. The building was a mess; there was hardly a stick of lumber standing.

I went back and got a few Filipinos, and we started scouring around in the ruins. We located a lot of utensils that we could use—pots, pans, silverware, ladles, etcetera. The Mango Inn was ten miles from the Cavite Navy Yard area. I figured that we would be sheltered from view of the Japanese planes by setting up shop under those big Mango trees, making it about the safest place to work that I could think of. It seemed the Japanese had quit bombing in that area for a few days.

I reported back to Lieutenant Schofield and told him I had secured permission from the owner of the Mango Inn, my good friend Trinidad, to use whatever I could salvage from the debris.

"Wonderful," the lieutenant said. "You got a job to do. Let's get the show on the road and feed those hungry people out there."

The lieutenant also gave me the authority, a free hand, to round up all the chickens, turkeys, rabbits, pigs, caribou, or any other live, eatable animals we found. Also, all the vegetables that we located in the countryside, whether on vegetable farms or those which had been left in the gardens by the people who had fled their destroyed homes. In fact, I was given the authority to commandeer anything that was eatable, in order to enable me to accomplish the job of feeding all who came to the Mango Inn for food.

Lieutenant Schofield turned over two trucks with drivers to me to use in whatever capacity necessary to allow me to carry out his orders. I sent one of the trucks with a few Filipinos over to the Cavite Navy Yard to look for, and round up, any mess gear and all the cooking utensils they could find in the old mess hall. I also instructed them to go to all the restaurants that had been bombed in Cavite or Caridad and the surrounding areas and gather what cooking utensils and supplies they could find, such as seasonings, canned foods, or anything that was salvageable, and bring whatever they found to the Mango Inn, where I was going to set up headquarters for the soup kitchen.

I was able to secure the services of a few more Filipinos who I turned over to the driver of the second truck. I assigned him the duty of scouring the countryside to round up and bring to the Mango Inn, all the live stock they could find: rabbits, pigs, caribou, horses, poultry, or any other food stuffs they could find, even vegetables growing in any abandoned gardens.

After the trucks were on their way, Lieutenant Schofield told me to be sure to notify the bunch of naval aviation personnel and all the civilians who were working on salvaging fragments of our destroyed navy patrol bombers from the raid on Sangley Point when we were initiated into war in the Cavite Navy Yard. I was also instructed by the acting captain of the yard to see that everyone who came to the Mango Inn for food was taken care of regardless of who they were. I saluted and told him his orders would be carried out to the best of my ability, with what tools and help I could muster, and that he could count on me.

When the first truck returned to the Mango Inn that afternoon, I immediately sent it over to the Cavite Navy Yard, to Section P, to get bags of rice, sugar, canned goods, and anything else they found that we could use to carry out the task that I had been assigned to. I was able, with the help of the driver, to round up about twenty-five or thirty men who had worked in the Cavite Navy Yard prior to the war. After telling them that we were about to set up a galley on the old Mango Inn grounds to feed the natives and stragglers, I asked them to give me a hand to get things going. They were more than pleased to help.

Within a short time, as the day went on, that first batch of workers grew from the original twenty-five or thirty workers to over fifty. Before nightfall, I had all the help I needed and then some. It sure made me a happy man to get so much good help.

By luck, I ran into a good friend of mine who happened to be a Filipino commissary steward. After explaining to him what my intentions were, I asked him to get me about five or six good Filipino cooks and a few Filipino mess boys and bring them out to the old Mango Inn over in Caridad. I told him I could use as many as he could round up, which would help us in carrying out the duties of feeding those in need. That didn't take him long to do. He got the job done, and the men were on the job ready for work in less than two hours.

With the Mango Inn itself lying in ruins and unfit for us to use, we did the next best thing. We lost no time in getting a kitchen set up under the big mango trees in the Mango Inn Park area. This was a beautiful, spacious area with lawns and shrubs all over the place. It was a delightful place to set up a kitchen, and with those great big mango trees towering above, it would serve our purpose to a tee. A group of fellows moved parts of the kitchen, the stove, sinks, etcetera, and anything we could find in the building that we needed out in the yard under those big trees. As the stove and other kitchen parts were brought out of the building, another group started to set them up so they could be operative immediately.

I was very lucky, because in the group were a couple of navy electrician mates. They strung electric lines and did all the electrical jobs that were needed. There were plumbers to run pipes for running water to the sinks that we had moved out into the yard. They tied right into the lines of the Mango Inn, and we had electricity and running water in no time. They even got the hot water heater from the Mango Inn working, so we had hot water. There were several men from the construction and repair division of the navy yard whose talents were utilized in building pens for the livestock that the boys were bringing in.

It was wonderful. It seemed that the men were able to salvage from the Mango Inn almost everything required to get the job done, from electric lines to lumber, and what they couldn't get, such as tools, nails, gate hinges, they got from the bombed-out hardware stores in Cavite and the navy yard itself, and in a very short time we would be able to cook and feed the hungry. Everything worked out beautifully. Everyone was rushing around doing his assigned job of getting a "soup kitchen" ready to start cooking that afternoon. If I wasn't there, I would not have believed how fast we got set up and food cooking in the big vats.

After all, most of the natives were half-starved from not having a decent meal in several days. The carpenters did an outstanding job in getting the holding pens set up for the chickens, turkeys, geese, pigs, caribou, fighting cocks. Yes, we even had fighting cocks. This was a great sport for the Filipinos. They drew large crowds, and large sums of money was won and lost on those fighting cocks before the war. They were now being used for food and yes, to make soup; they made good chicken soup.

We found that some of the chickens were laying eggs each day. We singled out the laying hens and put them in pens by themselves so they wouldn't be killed by mistake; we needed the eggs. The eggs were reserved for the people who were helping in the cooking and preparation of the food, for those gathering the food, and for those keeping the place clean and as sanitary as possible. In short, the workers got the eggs as a little something extra. They sure deserved a little extra; they were working under the worst possible conditions one could imagine.

35. Feeding the Natives and Stragglers

I was more than delighted to report to Lieutenant Schofield that within a few hours after being assigned the job of feeding the natives and others, that they would in fact be fed that first night. I told him that I had run into a Filipino navy chief commissary steward, whom I had known, and I enlisted his help. He went out and rounded up a bunch of Filipino mess cooks to help him, and they were all set up and had fires going under three huge stainless steel one-hundred-gallon pots, or boilers, which we had salvaged from the navy yard. They were cooking rice and making chicken soup, and within a few hours, by nightfall, everyone in the area would be fed and sent home with a full stomach.

We fed over three hundred people within a few hours that first evening. Some of these people hadn't had anything hot to eat since the first bombing, four days ago. It was gratifying to watch those natives get something in their bodies, especially the little children. We made chicken and rice for the first meal with plenty of coffee and cocoa on the side. The word got around that the kitchen was open and in full swing, that we had started feeding the hungry. The next day, the wives and children of the men who had left for other parts of the Philippines or left with the naval ships and gone out to sea, and also Filipinos who had lost their homes, over several hundred, came to be fed. I guess we fed about 500 people that second day.

The number kept growing each day as word got around more and more. About the fourth day, the crowd of hungry folks had grown so big, I started to wonder what I was going to do. I needed help in controlling the crowd. Well, my prayers were answered, because just in time, in walked my pals Joe Hunter, Lowell, and Castle. They had finished their job of riding shotgun and had come and asked if they could help me. I grabbed and threw my arms around each one of them in turn like a long-lost brother.

"Are you guys kidding?" I said. "I'm just about to go crazy. This job has grown so big, it's almost out of hand. Do I need you guys?" I asked. "Do bees make honey?"

I immediately got Castle and Lowell to go with the trucks and commandeer whatever we needed to make this a successful operation, which it certainly turned out to be. Thanks to the more than fifty helpers who showed up and chipped in each day voluntarily to help me. I had my good pal Joe Hunter stay and help me in the camp. He became my second in command,

and I sure needed somebody like him to help me in handling the crowd, to see that they were being fed, and to keep things working smoothly.

Although this job grew so big, so enormous, within a few days, one almost felt it to be an impossibility to carry on. But Joe and I kept up the pace. We got four more navy chief petty officers to help us handle the feeding and seeing to it that everyone got some food to take home for their dinner. The Filipino chief commissary steward put more boilers on the line and cooked more and more food each day. I told Joe Hunter that "it is absolutely unbelievable what men can do when the chips are down." It was a tough challenge to feed everyone.

We would run out of food, due to not knowing how many would appear at each feeding. Each day, Joe would order more food prepared than he had ordered the day before, trying to keep up with the pace. Each day we fed more people than we did the day before. We would invariably run out of the planned menu for that day. But good old Joe Hunter. He saw to it that the chief steward had a substitute, a backup, handy for just such an occasion, which was every day. After a few days, it became routine to have a substitute to prop up the main menu.

Within a few days, all the beautiful grass lawn was gone because of so much traffic, and we found ourselves working on bare ground; our parklike setting had disappeared. Seeing this, Castle took his truck and his gang and went to a rug and carpet shop in Cavite and was able to salvage several rolls of carpet and a bunch of throw rugs. They laid these on the ground, which helped keep the dust down and made it a more sanitary working condition, better than working on bare ground, which generated a lot of dust, and which we certainly did not need around the food we were cooking. There was still a little dust, but not as bad.

On the fourth day, Rebel Lord, who had now finished with his work at the Sangley Point oil depot, came over to the Mango Inn to see if he could help me. I told him about the dust and that we could use a truck with a water tank for watering the area down. He told me he had just such an animal over at Sangley Point and that he would go and fetch it. Upon Rebel's return with the water truck, he assumed the job of keeping the dust down. He had his driver water the park area each night and morning. This was a blessing; now the dust was really gone.

It seemed everyone wanted to help me, and needless to say, I loved it. I made a report to Lieutenant Schofield about every two days. He was delighted the way things were going; after all, it was his brain child. He was taking his meals at the naval hospital, but he would come out and see us every two or three days.

Out kitchen staff was set up as follows: I was in overall charge. I put Joe Hunter in charge of the amount of food to prepare each day. And by using the number of people fed the day before, he would add enough beef, chicken, rabbit, and rice for about fifty more. My pal Castle was in charge of the slaughter house. He kept enough meat on hand ready to be cooked each day. So we had a good thing going in that department. I had the Filipino chief commissary steward in charge of the menu and the preparation and cooking of the food. The Filipino chief CSTD had twenty Filipino mess cooks preparing and cooking the food. *No one*, yes, *no one*, ever went away hungry. and they all were given food to take home to cook for their evening meal.

There were also about twenty-five to thirty Filipino volunteers who did whatever I needed to get done, such as cleaning up. When all was done and all had been fed and had gone home for the night, this gang would take over and clean up. Their number would vary. Some days a few would stay home with their families, but there would be others to take their place. There were always enough to get the place squared away for the next morning. I always rewarded them by giving them a little extra to take home when they were through, so I never had a shortage of workers.

It seemed that after about a week or so, with the stores coming in from Section P of the Cavite Navy Yard, we were getting an overabundance of canned food and other essentials, such as toothpaste, toothbrushes, and toiletries. Feeling that we would not be able to utilize all of it, I started thinking about the Japanese bombing us out one day, since they were moving in closer and closer each day to Manila. Not wanting all this food and provisions to fall into Japanese hands, I told all the military and nonmilitary Caucasian men who were married to Filipino women to move their families way back in the province and stash away as much canned goods and other essentials for their families to help tide them over during the war.

I had the Filipinos do likewise, but they being natives of the Philippines, the Japanese would spare them, so they didn't have to hide as did the Caucasians. However, I encouraged all of them to take as much canned food and medical supplies they could carry back to their homes each night for use at a later date. So they had been loading their cars and trucks each day since to store up supplies in their home in the province.

We would make breakfast at daylight, which consisted of two one hundred-gallon pots of steamed rice, fifty gallons of coffee, and another seventy-

127

five to one hundred gallons of Vienna sausages, and some tomatoes and other vegetables cut up small and made into a sauce for the rice. At noon we would boil chickens, ducks, or other fowl in one of the large stainless steel pots and serve it with steamed rice one day, and the next day, it would be pork or caribou with steamed rice. We would make soup by putting a few vegetables in the broth when we cooked chicken or other fowl.

One day Castle's truck driver spotted a rabbit farm. The owner had fled to the countryside. So the driver confiscated all the rabbits. He brought all the rabbits and their cages to the Mango Inn. There were about five hundred grown rabbits, many of them bearing young. This gave us a chance to put several rabbit dinners on our menu. We tried to give them something different each day as best as we could while the variety lasted. It was gratifying to see the natives come in for food. They would bring the whole family. There were mothers with seven and eight children, from tiny babies on up to teenagers. Hunter and I enjoyed every moment watching those kiddies eating such good nourishing food and to know that we were making this thing work.

In about a week or so, the Japanese got the word that we were feeding the hungry. They made it a point to come and pay us a visit every day after that. Sometimes even twice on the same day, we were visited by a group of nine bombers divided into groups of three, plus a few snipers. They would come over around noon at intervals of about every five minutes or so. They would drop their calling cards and then head home, unmolested by any of our planes—we had none. But thankfully, the bombs never found us; they dropped all around us, but the good Lord spared us. No one got hurt from those bombings.

However, it was starting to shatter our nerves a bit. We would try to feed all the people breakfast before the raids, which started every day at about 11:00 A.M. Therefore, we would begin feeding the people as close to eight in the morning as possible so that we could be all cleaned up and everyone out of the area by 10:00 A.M. Then we would all get back as soon as the raids were over, by 11:45 A.M., to get lunch and food for the natives to take home for their dinners. We accomplished this each day by 3:30 P.M., which allowed us time to clean up and prepare things for the next morning, also allowing time for the workers to get home to their families before dark, as some of them had many miles to go, most of them traveling on foot. A few had bicycles, and several had cars which they loaded up with friends.

Each day after the natives finished lunch, we would give them all a cup of raw rice and a small amount of meat of some kind, and maybe a can or two of something or other to take to their home or to a friend's house to prepare for their dinners. No fires were allowed after dark, so they had to prepare their evening meal while it was still daylight. It was a joy for us to know that the Filipino population was being fed, and that we were a part of it. I made every endeavor to see that no one went away hungry. If there was anything left that was perishable and couldn't keep to the next day, we fed it to the animals and to the cats and dogs that came around, which were many. All leftover soups went to the pigs. There wasn't a drop of food wasted. This was interesting work, but not what I was cut out to do in time of war. I could never have imagined, in my wildest dreams that if war came to America during my time in the service, I would be doing such things as slaughtering pigs and caribou, killing chickens and turkeys, cooking rice, running a food kitchen, feeding natives in the Philippine Islands. I never dreamt I would be on the ground in the Philippines or anywhere else, I was a Navy man and trained to fight a ship in time of war; that is where I expected to be, on a ship, not in a jungle feeding natives.

36. Christmas Eve 1941

Christmas Eve 1941 found me still on the job of feeding the hungry, and being bombed daily, the Japanese by now had stepped up their visits to our kitchen area to twice daily, and some days there would be a third visit. These raids were starting to tell on my helpers. Some of the natives quit, saying they couldn't take the bombings any longer. I didn't blame them, although they were good men and I hated to see them go.

On Christmas Eve, I ordered the chief commissary steward to give all the Filipinos and anyone else who came for food on the twenty- fourth of December enough food for their dinner that night and enough food for them on Christmas Day. I told him to make sure they all had enough meat, rice, and a can or two of something according to how many mouths they had to feed in their families, which they could take to their home or to their neighbor's or friend's house to cook themselves. I had everyone notified that we would be closed Christmas Day to allow the workers a chance to be with their friends and families, to be able to celebrate Christmas Day as best they possibly could under the circumstances.

After the usual bombings by the Japanese and everyone had been fed on Christmas Eve at about 3.30 in the afternoon, I told everyone to get the place cleaned up as soon as possible and to give the animals plenty of food because they wouldn't be fed for two days. I told them to also round up enough food to take home to last them over Christmas Day; we were not going to be open on the twenty-fifth.

I had been rounding up and hiding as much beer and hard liquor that I could find during the past two weeks, to be used as a little Christmas cheer for the workers on this festive occasion. So before the workers left to go home, I broke out my little surprise, and we had a little party. It helped to straighten my nerves as well as those of the helpers. After everyone had a little Christmas cheer along with some refreshments that I had the boys round up, I told them to all go home and have a good Christmas and I would see them on the twenty-sixth of December, the day after Christmas. We all wished one another a merry Christmas and departed for our homes, such as they were.

Even though the continuous bombings, by this time, were starting to tell on me also, I had to keep my cool. I couldn't allow the natives to know how I felt. I guess I had to act the clown, although I was hurting inside, I always had a smile on my face. We were scared out there, but we had a job to do, and we stayed to perform it. Sometimes we didn't get out on time and were there when the emperor's goons paid us a visit and dropped his calling card. So we took cover in whatever way we could. Sometimes I would just drop down by the big soup kettles, which was as good a place as any there. We would stay put while the Japanese were up there having their fun, and after they were gone and it was clear, we would all get up and go right back to work.

Castle, my partner in this humanitarian job of feeding the natives, went home to his wife and three small kids. I went over to my lady friend Christina's house. One of the girls, Lillian, who was with her during the bombing of Cavite was living there with her. She was the one who was afraid to come down the pole because of being scantily clad. She was about eighteen years old, very pretty, and a real nice girl.

Upon my arrival, I broke out some of the Christmas cheer that I brought along with me so that I could try and relax for a change. I had not been away from the soup kitchen for about six days, so I needed this rest and relaxation badly. As I said, those continuous bombings and strafings by the Japanese planes were starting to work on my nerves. I wasn't married and didn't have a family to worry about as did so many of my workers, and so, I allowed them all to go home to their families each night, while I stayed watch over the soup kitchen. Once in a while, I would take off and go to see Christina, my lady friend. Every night since the bombing of the navy yard, all lights that could be seen from the air were extinguished, so we who were working in the soup kitchen in the evening were likewise in the dark.

However, here I was, one guy who was going to have a real old-fashioned Christmas, come hell or high water, at my lady friend's home. I looked around and found a live wire and decided to hook up a radio and some lights to make Christmas Eve a little happier occasion than what we were having, but that was soon squashed by the girls, who outnumbered me two to one, so I was forced to give in. They said no lights, so there were no lights. They won.

I got the radio hooked up, though, but the girls also decided against the radio, saying the lights on it might be seen from the outside. Well, I had given up having the lights in the house, but no way was I going to give up my musica, as the Filipinos called it. So I merely threw a blanket over the radio so no light was visible, and we proceeded to drink our good cheer and make merry.

I had a big tom turkey that weighed in at about thirty-five pounds tied up in back of the Mango Inn for about two weeks. He was being saved along with the trimmings for a good old fashioned Christmas dinner for all the working crew. After having a little libation with the working crew, and in my haste to leave, I forgot all about old tom and left him tied up at the Mango Inn. After a couple more drinks of good cheer with the gals, Christina and Lillian and I jumped in the car and drove back to the Mango Inn to get old tom, my thirty-five-pound turkey, along with what trimmings I could find that I had been stashing away for this particular occasion.

When we got back to Christina's home, we tied Mr. Tom in her backyard with a rope around his leg for the night. I told her that in the morning I would get my crew and their families together for that long awaited old fashioned Christmas dinner I had promised them. But that never came to pass, and old Tom was spared and may be waiting still. Yes, I am sorry to report that the events that took place that night prevented him from becoming a Christmas feast and shattered all my expectations for that Christmas Day in 1941. Yes, it sure knocked the hell out of all my well-laid plans for a great Christmas evening with Christina and the big Christmas feast the next day with that gang of mine. I found out very shortly that General MacArthur had a different idea. At that moment, little did I know what fate had in store for me, and little did I dream that my next Christmas dinner would not come until five years later, Christmas Day, 1946.

Part Three

Christmas Day Enroute to Bataan

37. General MacArthur Declares Manila an Open City

On 24 December 1941 General MacArthur saw that the Japanese were moving very close to Manila, and did not want to see the ancient city of Manila along with its big, beautiful and magnificent cathedrals, which had been built hundreds of years ago, destroyed. Those ancient buildings had withstood the ravishment of time for centuries.

In order to preserve them and the city of Manila from being destroyed, General MacArthur had a message drafted and sent to the Japanese Supreme Commander General Homma, offering to trade the city of Manila and surrounding area for safe passage of his troops to the Bataan peninsula. If accepted, he would declare Manila an open city as of 11:00 A.M. Christmas Day, the twenty-fifth of December 1941, thus allowing General Homma's troops to take the city of Manila without a fight and saving the beautiful city of Manila from destruction and from the loss of many lives on both sides.

General MacArthur had in mind two very good reasons for making this proposal. One was to preserve the great city of Manila. The second was a way to get the rest of his troops and all their paraphernalia, their guns, ammunition, etcetera, intact to the Bataan peninsula, where he would be able to set up a line of defense, thus placing his troops in a better position to confront the enemy in battle. He had convinced himself that Bataan was the only place on Luzon where he could defend his troops and the Philippines which was held secretly in the back of his mind from day one, since the war began. General MacArthur reasoned with himself that if only he could get a line of defense set up in the Bataan-Mariveles province, he would be able to entertain the enemy on his own ground and on his own terms? And so, declaring Manila an open city, if accepted, would be the ticket he needed. MacArthur had spent many days and sleepless nights before the war to help him come to a decision should a war break out.

As mentioned before, he never said a word to any of his staff or to anyone else, not even his wife about his secret, for fear of its leaking out and getting in the wrong hands. He already had a great burden on his mind, just trying to run a war, knowing that no help of any kind, food, replacements, or ammunition, would be forthcoming. He must fight the war with what he had on hand. That in itself placed a huge burden on MacArthur's shoulders, worrying about his troops and trying to get them to a place where they would stand a chance. Yes, he spent many sleepless nights with all this on his mind, still trying to keep such a big decision all to himself, which he knew he must for fear of it leaking to the enemy.

General Homma, the supreme commander of the Japanese imperial army, in command of the enemy troops in the Philippines, accepted General MacArthur's offer. General Homma had been telling his superiors in Japan that with MacArthur bottled up on Bataan, would be just a big carp in a small pool ready to be fished out at any time? However, that big carp in the small pool proved not so easy to be caught. It cost General Homma one helluva lot of fish bait to fish us out.

General Homma's pledge to allow General MacArthur's troops and equipment safe passage to the Bataan peninsula, without any interference on his part, proved to be a big mistake for General Homma. Because in the very first battle on Bataan, which occurred shortly after the first of the new year, 1942, he not only lost 20,000 of his crack troops and the three field commanders whom he brought up from Singapore, it also cost him his own life as well at the war crime trials. If we "fighting bastards of Bataan," as General Homma called us, had been given just a little bit of help from the Congress of these United States, we would have never been fished out at all.

About midnight on the twenty-fourth of December 1941, a naval officer who was trying to round up all the naval personnel came to Christina's home and told me that an evacuation plan had been placed in effect by General MacArthur and that I should get my crew to the Bataan-Mariveles area as soon as possible. This being my first good night away from the soup kitchen and the bombings since the war began, I decided to wait until daylight to do anything about it. I needed some rest first and, to make matters worse, this was Christmas Eve, so I decided, come hell or high water, this guy was going to enjoy this night and get some decent shut-eye for a change.

Well, about 6:30 Christmas morning, I was awakened by one of my former yeoman, a Filipino, who came to tell me that he had just been discharged from his naval duties and that everything was in an uproar, that all hands had gone somewhere and he couldn't find them. Upon hearing what Jose, my former yeomen, had told me, I got a cup of coffee, grabbed a piece of fruit, and immediately got into the truck and drove over to Sangley Point to see what had happened and to see if I could find some of my buddies.

I was not successful in finding any of them. In fact, when we parted the day before at the Mango Inn, about 4:00 P.M., after our little party, that was the last time, to this day, that I saw, or heard of, the whereabouts of any of my traveling buddies in the Philippines, with the exception of Castle and Joe Hunter, who were with me in the Bataan-Mariveles area. I lost track of Castle and Joe Hunter, when I went over to Corregidor. I guess they both went into the hills with the Filipinos and joined up with the guerrillas. I never saw or heard of either of them since the fall of Bataan. I never was able to learn if they got through the war or not or what happened to them.

Upon arrival at Sangley Point, I met a naval captain sitting on a chair with a thing that looked like a bicycle air pump in his hand. I introduced myself and told him that I was in charge of feeding all the natives and stragglers out at the Mango Inn and asked him if he had any orders he would like me to carry out for him.

"All hands are ordered to the Bataan-Mariveles area," he said. "The last boat has left, but you can drive your car if you desire. You must hurry because, according to the army, all the roads and bridges leading to the Bataan Highway will be blown up shortly. The Japanese are moving in fast."

"Thank you, captain, for this info. I'll notify my people and just drive the car to Mariveles, but how about the food at Mango Inn? What shall I do?"

"You be the judge on that one," he said. "Do anything you want with it. As soon as the causeway is clear, I will blow up everything around here with this gadget," he said, pointing to the pump he was holding, "so you had better clear out fast."

Not waiting to hear any more, this kid got lost in a hurry. I immediately headed for the soup kitchen at Mango Inn. On my way, while I was passing through Caridad, I saw a lieutenant of the Philippine constabulary whom I knew. I told him about all the food that we were leaving behind. I told him there were about two hundred live chickens and ducks, many cages of rabbits, about fifty pigs, large and small, several caribou, and a few horses, all penned up, and several hundred cases of canned goods, and that he could have it all.

He thanked me very much and immediately sent a couple of guards out to watch the place. I asked him to give as much as possible to the na-

137

tives who had worked so hard in keeping the food kitchen going and would be coming in for work tomorrow, I even suggested that they could keep the kitchen open and still feed the Filipinos, although we would be gone. He said he'd take good care of them.

I went back to the Mango Inn and found Castle's truck driver and a couple of natives sitting in his truck. We loaded the truck with as much of the canned goods that we could in the back of the truck and headed for Castle's home to tell him what I had been told by the captain at the causeway and what I had done about the food kitchen. Castle was out in his backyard. When I arrived at his house, he was roasting a small pig over an open fire-pit, sort of barbecuing it. This was to be his family's Christmas dinner.

I immediately gave him all the information I had from the captain at Sangley Point. While having a bite of food, we discussed the situation we found ourselves in. I told Castle that I thought we should not hesitate, but get on the road to the Bataan-Mariveles area pronto. He agreed with me; it wouldn't be advisable for us to stick around. We should get on the road pronto.

While Castle was getting ready and his wife was rounding up some clothes for him, the driver of the truck and I unloaded a few cases of the canned goods for his family's use. His wife helped him gather up some more clothing and what gear he thought he would need, and we put everything into the truck. Castle and I both kissed his wife and kids good-bye, and with tears in our eyes, we drove off, not looking back. As it turned out, that was the last time we were to see his family again. That was a helluva Christmas present to give his family.

Upon leaving Castle's place, we took a few bottles of beer, a gallon of gin, a gallon of tomato juice, and some of that nice juicy pig that Castle had cut off from the one he was barbecuing, leaving the rest of the roasting pig to the girls. In this fashion, we started out for the Bataan-Mariveles area via Manila, because we wanted to stop at General MacArthur's headquarters in Manila to get up-to-date orders his office may have for us.

38. Christmas Day on a Dusty Road to Bataan

On our way to the Bataan-Mariveles province we stopped at Christina's home to bid her good-bye and to drop off the rest of canned goods we had taken from the soup kitchen. Upon arriving, we immediately informed her about what had taken place. The saddest part was that as much as I wanted to, I couldn't have dinner with her and Lillian. We had to hit the road and not linger any longer than absolutely necessary. Castle told her they had a suckling pig all roasted at his house, and he and his wife Florence would be delighted if she and Lillian, her girlfriend, would go over there and keep his wife and kids company this Christmas Day, as she, too, was very sad that we were leaving for Bataan, not knowing if we would ever come back.

"Maybe we can cheer one another up. We'll go over and stay a few days," she said.

So after gathering up my shaving gear and a few clothes, I turned to Christina and, with tears flowing from the both of us, I gave her a big hug and a good-bye kiss. I also gave Lillian a big kiss, then kissed Christina once more. Castle and I said good-bye to them and told them to keep their chin up and to keep the faith. Never did I dream this was truly a farewell kiss, and that I and my lovely ladyfriend, Christina, were destined to never meet again.

Old tom turkey was now Christina's bird. As we were leaving, she said she was going to share old tom with Florence, Castle's wife. Did he ever grace their table? That's a big question. I think old tom turkey was given a new lease on life, because I don't think the girls knew how to get tom ready to adorn their table. We left so fast on that Christmas day, there was no time to teach them how to butcher or dress old tom. I'll never know. I never saw or heard from Christina since I held her in my arms with tears streaming down both our cheeks as we kissed and said good-bye, on Christmas day in 1941. Before I left, I gave her the keys to the car and told her that she could do as she pleased with it. I gave her all the necessary papers she would need to prove the car belonged to her.

I got into the truck and told the driver to head toward Manila, which was to be our first stop enroute to Bataan, not knowing then if we would ever return. Castle and I and many thousands of others ate dust all day instead of that long-awaited Christmas dinner. After we left Castle's family and my wonderful Christina and were on the road to Manila, we each were wiping tears from our eyes for several miles. Writing these words now brings tears again to my eyes. One thing that we can be happy about is that we left them in good shape with plenty of food and essentials to see them through for quite a spell.

That day was one of the saddest in our lives, for Castle and me, and I guess, for many others as well who were forced under those circumstances to leave their loved ones, their families and friends, in such haste, perhaps to never see again. Especially it being Christmas Day, which was supposed to be a festive day, a day of rejoicing for the birth of our Savior, little Lord Jesus. Instead, it was turned into a very sad occasion, to be torn away from your loved ones, and to head out to war against such heavy odds, not knowing if we would ever meet again.

I never did get back to the Philippines. Most of us never did get to see again those happy faces that we once knew and which had been a great part of our lives. I have often wondered what happened to them? How they fared in the hands of the Japanese? Did they live through it? Were they able to get enough food to keep their bodies nourished? Were they raped? Were they left to starve to death? The questions go on and on. They will never be answered. I would have loved to see Christina again after the war, but I was in no condition to go back to the Philippines. I weighed only sixty-five pounds and was hospitalized for months after returning home, consequently, we lost track of one another.

The road to Manila that day was clustered with people all heading for Manila, Just as we arrived at the outskirts of Manila, the air raid sounded. We looked up and saw what seemed like hundreds of planes. Actually, there were only fifty-four heavy bombers, divided into six groups of nine, and a few fighter escort planes. However, that was one plane too many for little old Ski.

This old boy had seen all the Japanese bombers he wanted to see for the rest of his life on 10 December 1941, in the devastation of the Cavite Navy Yard, in the city of Cavite, and every day while working in the soup kitchen at the Mango Inn. However, this day those planes didn't drop any bombs. I figured they were either just getting a look-see, or they could have been out of bombs, having dropped them somewhere along the way and now going back after another load. They at least didn't drop any bombs on us on that trip, for which I thanked my Heavenly Father then, and still do now, every day of my life.

Upon arrival in Manila, we reported to General MacArthur's headquarters. While Castle and the driver waited I went inside and met with MacArthur's secretary, whom I knew. I told him I was heading for the Mariveles-Bataan area; however, I was at his disposal and would change my plans should there be something he needed me for. He said to "just carry on what you have set out to do. There is nothing for you to do here."

So we got back in the truck and continued on. After a few miles or so, we finally reached the outskirts of Manila, where we ran into a long train of heavy-laden trucks, tanks, ammo and whatever it takes to run a war. There were also thousands upon thousands of weary, worn-out soldiers walking, all heading down that long dusty one-lane road, along the mountainside, to the Bataan-Mariveles province to set up a line of defense as a last ditch effort to defend the Philippines. It will be a Christmas that I and thousands of others will never forget. That day will never be erased from our minds.

As I sit here and write, some fifty years later, I can still see the miles and miles of those worn-out, ill-fed soldiers, barely dragging their war-torn bodies, racked with pain and sweat. It was a very sad sight. Most of those boys were still in their teens, hardly any had reached adulthood. They were in filthy, dusty uniforms and half-starved. They were mostly half asleep, being on the battlefield fighting the Japanese for more than two weeks with hardly any food or rest and no place to bathe. Here they were, on that dusty, one-lane mountainside road, along with thousands of trucks loaded with their war paraphernalia. It looked like the exodus from France when the Germans were moving in, in the First World War. This long, one-lane dirty, dusty, and rocky road, built alongside a mountain was the most precarious road I have ever seen, but it was our only way to get to the Bataan-Mariveles area from Manila. It was a ledge, of a huge mountain, cut through a jungle and was about ten- to twelve-feet wide, and a helluva drop straight down the mountainside. How far down it was to the bottom, I really don't know, because of the trees blocking the view below down the mountainside. One could not imagine such a horrible road with no room to pass. If a truck broke down, it was just pushed over the mountainside so the others could pass and keep going. Luckily, there was only one truck lost in this fashion in that long day of travel.

The traffic was so heavy along that mountainside, it was bumper to bumper, which made the road just one big cloud of dust. One could hardly see a thing. The dust was so bad it made the air next to impossible to breathe. We had to cover our nose and mouth with our handkerchief. We didn't dare wet our handkerchiefs with what little water we had, but had to preserve it for any emergency that might arise, of which we had quite a few. Driving down that precarious, dusty, rocky road, the only route to Bataan, got so bad, that after an hour or so, the traffic slowed to a snail's pace. We had now nicknamed Bataan, "MacArthur's hideaway."

Our thoughts were always the same; of Christina and Lillian, Castle's wife and children, and the hard working Filipino boys who had helped me to feed the natives at the Mango Inn. We couldn't get our minds off those we had left behind. However, we both felt good in knowing we had taken care of them. We were certainly glad that I had given all that food to those fellows to take home to stash away when they were helping so generously at the Mango Inn. The Filipinos, as well as the Caucasians, now had plenty of food to supply their needs for quite some time to come. It was a wonderful feeling, as we were heading into Bataan, knowing that those boys and gals were left in such good shape.

It was a good thing we had taken Castle's truck and driver from the soup kitchen back at the Mango Inn to drive us to Mariveles, instead of taking my jeep. The truck came in handy. I had the driver stop from time to time to load the truck with as many of the foot soldiers that the truck could carry. Allowing them to take turns riding and walking in this fashion, enabled them to get a little much needed rest, a chance to get off their feet. Those boys had been on their feet most of the last fourteen days or more.

There was no place to stop and rest on the road either, and even if there were, we wouldn't have dared to stop. There was no way that one could pull off the road to allow others to pass. Also we had to get into Bataan as soon as possible. How those soldiers were able to carry on was a miracle. So, Castle and I would ride a bit, then walk a bit, but most of the time, Castle and I would walk to allow room for two more weary, worn-out foot soldiers, who had been fighting the Japanese forces on the front lines since 10 December, a long fourteen days ago, without rest or the benefit of any relief.

It was not bad enough eating the road dust, our slow pace gave us the jitters, especially with the Jap planes flying so low overhead. However, we kept plowing along slowly, continually moving toward our destination. The only time we would stop would be to unload and load the truck with foot soldiers. Every time we stopped, we would have a little nip of Bloody Mary, such as it was, followed by a little bite of dusty piggy. We shared the beer and the gallon of gin with the foot soldiers. It was ironic as we traveled all that day making our way to the Bataan-Mariveles peninsula that the Japs let us alone. There were many Japanese bombers and fighter planes flying overhead, watching us; they did not fire a shot. We were allowed to travel that long, one-lane, dirty, dusty, and rocky road along the mountainside unharmed. I said many a prayer that day and I am sure everyone else did, too. However, my prayers were answered as they had been so many times before, in that not a gun was fired, nor a bomb was dropped on us all that day.

After a few miles of this kind of traveling, our pig got pretty dusty. However, feeling that this would be our last meal for a day or so, we just wiped the dust off Mr. Piggy, and what we couldn't wipe off was washed off as we ate and drank our gin and tomato juice mixture. I had always been told when I was a small boy that "one had to eat a pound of dust in his lifetime." I told Castle that we were eating our allotted pound of dust right now.

What was foremost in our minds and kept us worrying was whether those planes flying overhead would renege on General Homma's promise and drop a single bomb on that first truck. It would be a catastrophe with the first truck stopped. The rest of us would be like sitting ducks. We wouldn't be able to move a foot on that road, and they could have simply machine-gunned us at their leisure. Not one of us could have gotten out of there alive. The mountainside was so steep, there would have been no way for us to even attempt to slide down should they decide to attack us.

"Ski, I bet those Japanese aviators who are flying above right now wish that General MacArthur and General Homma had not made that bargain," Castle said to me.

The bargain he was alluding to was that if General MacArthur declared Manila an open city, General Homma would in turn grant us safe passage into Bataan. To my knowledge, this was the only time in history that Japan had kept its word, and I thank my Heavenly Father that this was the time they did. I figured that those Japanese planes overhead were keeping General Homma informed of what was going on. However, General Homma must have ignored their reports. He told the emperor and his superiors not to worry, that as MacArthur had only twenty to thirty thousand seasoned troops, at the most, to fight with. He saw no great danger with such a small force digging in Bataan, which was only fourteen miles wide.

He reasoned that those few thousand seasoned troops along with those raw Filipino recruits, who he knew had little or no training, would never be a threat. He also knew the raw Filipino troops had never shot a gun before, that the only training they did have was with wooden rifles. General Homma figured MacArthur's troops had no chance of holding out under bayonet and amphibious charges along with steady bombardment for more than a week or so. General Homma had said so many times that he considered the Fil-American troops a drop in a bucket; they were like a carp in a large pool that could be fished out anytime. He had now convinced himself that time alone would force the Fil-American troops on Bataan to surrender from frustration and starvation. He even bragged to the emperor and his immediate superiors that he would take MacArthur and his men anytime at his leisure. What a dreamer.

However, I for one, was very glad that his thoughts led to his giving us free passage to the Bataan-Mariveles area that Christmas Day in 1941, or I wouldn't be here today writing this account of the war.

On that trip, the Japanese did nothing but scare us all half to death, leaving us all shivering in our boots all day until we finally arrived at our destination all in one piece. Yes, I can only say the good Lord was on our side watching over us every minute of that Christmas Day.

We arrived in Bataan very dusty, dirty, and tired. Thanks be to God that we actually arrived, although shaken and scared, all in one piece. I shall never forget that day as long as God allows me to live on this planet. That day shall linger in my mind, just as those Christmas Days when I was a little boy in an orphans' home. I spent many Christmas Days sitting in a corner, crying and holding my only Christmas gift, an orange, in my hands, and watching the other kids tearing at and opening packages sent to them by relatives, of which I had none. But this time, my life was at stake. I was either walking or riding in that truck scared half to death, watching enemy planes flying overhead. This time I didn't even have an orange to hold.

39. Arrival in Bataan-Mariveles Area

Two Great Heroes—Commander Harrison and Chief Boatswain Boyd

We arrived at about 8:00 P.M. on the twenty-fifth of December 1941 in the Mariveles area. After that hectic day of traveling, we were hungry, weary, and worn to a frazzle. We were completely covered with dust and dirt, our faces were so covered with the dust, they looked like masks. We were all a mess but glad to be alive. There was no place to clean up or get a shower, so we were forced to go to just lie down dusty and dirty where we were and try to get our much needed rest. What a day to remember.

Castle and I were just starting to make a bed to lay our weary bodies on, when lo and behold, along comes Joe Hunter.

"Joe," I said, "you sure are a sight for sore eyes. Sure am glad to lay my eyes on you again."

He then related to us the events of his day, and we talked about our day's events for about an hour or so.

"Let's get some shuteye," Joe said, "and see what tomorrow brings." None of us, including Joe Hunter, my buddy Castle, and me, got a thing to eat that night. My dreams of sitting down to a Christmas dinner, consisting of Mr. Tom Turkey didn't come true.

At about 9:30 that night, just as the three of us had lain down on our makeshift beds, it was discovered that the radio station in Manila had not been destroyed as planned. A call went out for a volunteer to go back into Manila and destroy it. Felix Skevaski, a retired navy chief radioman and a brother Freemason immediately volunteered for the mission. He was the one who gave me the application to enable me to take my degrees in Masonry. Felix knew full well that he could never get back again to our lines in Bataan. Not hesitating for one moment, Felix stepped up and volunteered for the mission. What a brave man he was. Where are those guys today?

Felix was married to a real nice Filipino lady. They had three little children and lived in the city of Caridad, a few miles straight down the road from the city of Cavite and the Cavite Navy Yard. As Felix was leaving, he came over to me to tell me good-bye and told me he didn't think he had a snowball's chance in hell of getting back to Mariveles through the Japanese lines. His thoughts were that after he had silenced the radio station, he would work his way back into the hills on the outskirts of Caridad where he taken his family at the outbreak of war. He figured they would certainly need a radio operator in the hills, and he could work as a guerilla and be safe there. So at about 10:00 that evening, after giving our good friend and brother a hardy hug, said our good-byes, wished him Godspeed and a safe return, Felix was on his way to Manila via a jungle route to carry out the mission for which he had volunteered.

After Felix left, we finally got to lay our weary bodies down on our makeshift beds on the hard ground. After a very strenuous day and being so tired and all worked up from the day's events, we hardly got any sleep that night. But when I did fall off to sleep, it seemed I did nothing but dream about old tom, that big turkey we left behind. I guess it was because we had all gone to bed very hungry.

Felix got to Manila and silenced the radio station; this we knew, because at about 9:25 the next morning it abruptly went off the air. Whether he made his way into the hills and found his wife and three small children, we shall never know, because neither I nor anyone else that I have talked to have ever seen or heard from him since that Christmas night of 1941. One must assume that Felix either was blown up with the station or was killed by the Japanese, trying to get back to the province with his family. These are the unsung heroes that you never hear about.

The next morning at about 6:30, Castle and Hunter and I were able to scrounge up some breakfast. After breakfast, Hunter said that the supply officer had a job for him and he would see us later. Castle and I got in the truck and set out to find a job for ourselves. We headed down toward the docks. In a short time, we ran into Lieutenant Commander Harrison, U.S.N.R., a swell fellow. I don't mind saying there was never a braver man than he, unless it was Chief Boatswain Boyd, U.S.N. More about these two later.

I told him we were looking for a job and inquired if he could use two good men. I also told him that I had brought a truck and driver with me from Manila. We asked him if he had any specific use for the truck and driver. Commander Harrison's reply was, "Do I ever." He told me to turn the truck and driver over to Castle. Commander Harrison assigned Castle and his driver immediately to a job of putting in a drainage system in the section base, which was needed badly, and he could use the truck very nicely on that job. He also gave him permission to round up enough help, as needed, to assist him in getting this job done as soon as possible. He then said that he could use me in and about the quarantine station.

Since there were no ships for the navy men to man, a few of the naval personnel were given the job of drilling holes near the entrances of the tunnels. The holes were drilled inside and outside the entrances to the tunnels, then filled with sticks of dynamite without the caps. If and when the Japanese broke through our lines we could cap and detonate them, closing off the entrances of the mountain tunnels to keep what little supplies we had left from falling into enemy hands. My job with Commander Harrison didn't pan out so hot. He never assigned me to a real job. I hung around for quite some time, hoping the commander would find something for me to do.

After a couple of weeks of this, I decided that my services were not needed under Commander Harrison and I should look elsewhere for a job. I ran into Captain Stoval, and he finally assigned me the job of getting supplies and ammo to the troops on the front lines.

Commander Harrison had assumed the job as dock officer and assigned Chief Boatswain Boyd as his assistant. They also took on the job of dispatching boats to Corregidor and around the bay. Commander Harrison and Chief Boatswain Boyd took on a very dangerous job. It consisted of standing on a nearby hill across from where the U.S.S. *Canopes* was tied up, completely out in the open, scanning the skies for Japanese planes, which would come down out of the blue without a moment's notice. Standing out there in the open made them perfect targets for bombing or strafing by enemy planes. Their job was to sound the air raid warning when planes were spotted. They also kept headquarters informed via the field telephone as to where the enemy planes were and how many. Then they would sound the siren again when it was all clear.

All during an air raid, they would remain out there in the open, perched on top of a hill, giving the dope over a loudspeaker or the telephone system to those who lived and worked in the huge tunnels cut in the rock far back under the mountains. They kept everyone warned at all times, day and night, throughout the fighting on Bataan, up until the day it fell, April 8, 1942. What brave men they both were. They carried on this work all the time the battle of Bataan was raging, which was well over four long months. Many times, bombs exploded within a few yards from their station, and some of the personnel by the tunnel entrances were hurt, but these two officers carried on, out in the open, never flinching or shirking the job they had undertaken to do. They just kept on the job of scanning the skies for enemy planes and also kept the traffic going to, and returning from, Corregidor.

After Bataan fell and we were all moved to Corregidor, they still did the same work on top of Malinta tunnel on Corregidor, scanning the skies for planes and sounding the siren for an air raid until the sixth of May 1942, at which time, the troops under the command of General Jonathan (Skinny) Wainwright, on Corregidor, the "Rock," were ordered to surrender. I don't believe there could ever be two more courageous men than those two officers. Five will get you ten that neither Lieutenant Commander Harrison or Chief Boatswain Boyd ever had medals displayed on their chests for a "job well done," beyond the call of duty, as, certainly, theirs must be classified as such. We had many such brave men. The works of these two brave men and the others will never be known.

There were many, many more unsung heroes out there, like Payclerk Hanson, Boatswain Oster, the many doctors and hospital corps personnel, Jimmy Bent, Felix Skevaski; yes, the list goes on and on. However, these two were outstanding.

Not all of our officers and men kept their wits about them. There were some who broke down to such an extent that after a month or so of this kind of warfare, we were forced to have them removed from the Mariveles area. They were sent down to Cebu, in the southern Philippines, where they wouldn't be a hindrance to those who were carrying on. It was enough to try and fight a war under the terrible conditions the Congress of the United States had left us, without being hindered by our own comrades who had broken down under the stress and strain.

We all know, all men are not alike, and we can't expect all men to be heroes. We had hundreds of very brave men looking for jobs, such as the naval personnel, aviators, deck hands, petty officers, commissioned officers, and civilians, but there were no ships for them to fight a war with. They were left out in the open day and night, living under damp, wet and generally miserable conditions, with hardly any food and just the clothes they had on their backs, which, after about five months, had started to get a little rancid. Looking into the faces of those young navy men, I thought to myself, *What is going on in their minds? They're smart men, who had been trained for many years to fight on the high seas, just as I had been taught to do. But here they find themselves stranded on the beach, with no help ever to reach them and no rescue in the foreseeable future.*

We all realized that Uncle Sam had left us with one of two choices: first, we must ultimately surrender or second, in lieu of surrender, turn the pistol we carried on our hip on ourselves. Take your choice. This was war at its worst. So it is no wonder that some of these fine men broke down, knowing what was in store for them. Some days there was food, some days there was none. Our kitchens would be blown away by the continual bombing and strafing. To top it off, we had no way to fight back or to protect ourselves, giving the Japanese a free hand. That was mental torture, and I, for one, can never condemn a person, be he an officer or an enlisted man, for breaking down under conditions such as we were living with.

For the life of me, thinking back, I can't comprehend how I myself was able to stand up under such conditions, not being able to do the things I was trained to do. If those officers and men had been on board a fighting ship or in a plane, I know, deep in my heart, it would have been a different story; they would be doing what they were trained to do. I know I would have been happy to have been either in the skies or on the high seas, fighting a ship for my beloved country. I kept saying to myself over and over, "Uncle, you put us here to do a job when war came. Where the hell are the tools to do it with?" Where were replacements for the boys on the front lines, a few planes, ammunition for their guns, medicine for those who were sick, clothes for their backs, food for their stomachs.

I am fully convinced that if given those tools mentioned above, we could have, and would have defeated the Japanese at that time. We proved this in the few months that our supplies lasted. Were we not named by the supreme Japanese commander of the Philippines, General Homma, the "Fighting Bastards of Bataan?" If those in Washington had *not* told us in no uncertain terms that we would *not* be given any supplies whatsoever, be it planes, manpower, or food, it would have been different for those men who reached the breaking point. After constantly being told by Washington that we weren't going to get any help, that we were to fight to the last breath, with nothing to look forward to but eventual torture, starvation, and ultimately death in the hands of the Japanese, one had to have a strong constitution to hold up. I can only thank God that, with his help, I never lost faith in Him or in my country, I knew that God would lead us to victory. With this strong belief I was able to survive that terrible nightmare of torture.

40. Those Rusty Old Tin Cans Prove Themselves in Battle

On or about the first of January 1942, seeing the way the war was going in the Orient, President Roosevelt ordered Admiral Thomas C. Hart, CINCAF, to proceed immediately to Java and assume command of all the Allied Navy via first available transportation. Admiral Hart arrived in Soerabaja, Java, aboard a submarine, the U.S.S. *Shark*, from the Philippines on January 7, 1942. Upon Admiral Hart's arrival, he immediately relieved Field Marshal Archibald Wavell of the Netherlands Navy, thereby assuming command of all the Allied nations' fighting ships located there, which included Dutch, Australian, British, and American men of war; this command was known as the ABDA command.

Within a few hours on 7 January 1942 after Admiral Hart's arrival, he was informed that the Japanese was making up a large Japanese invasion force in the Makassar Strait for an assault on Balikpapan, Borneo, a very rich oil area. Admiral Hart immediately ordered Admiral Glassford, who was on board the cruiser, U.S.S. *Marblehead,* to be assisted by a task force of destroyers, which consisted of the U.S.S. *Ford,* U.S.S. *Pope,* U.S.S. *John Paul Jones,* and the U.S.S. *Parrot,* all destroyers of the vintage type from the Asiatic Fleet, to go down there and entertain the enemy by breaking up their little game by stopping them from landing. The Allies just couldn't afford to allow the Japanese to take over this oil-rich territory.

Admiral Glassford ordered his task force to put out to sea immediately. As they approached Balikpapan, Admiral Glassford issued orders to the captain of the *Marblehead* to proceed and engage the enemy, but almost at that precise moment, the *Marblehead* was forced to retire from action due to its having fouled its bottom. So with the U.S.S. *Marblehead* out of action, with Admiral Glassford on board, the lot fell upon the shoulders of Commander Paul H. Talbot, of the Fifty-ninth Division, to go into battle alone.

This destroyer division that he commanded had just recently acquired the name, the "Fighting Fifty-ninth." It consisted of the four destroyers mentioned above. They were the ancient and rusty destroyers known as the "Expendables" from the Asiatic Fleet. All were of the 200-class of World War One vintage. I had the pleasure of serving under Commander Paul H. Talbot in an earlier day in the Philippines; he was a fine gentleman, none better. Commander Talbot was the commanding officer of the U.S.S. *Alden* who had refused to allow his ship to go out on the high seas without him at the conn. He is the one who dove out of an airplane and swam to his ship on the high seas as we were on our way to rescue the S.S. *President Hoover.* That's the kind of an officer he was.

As a former member of the Asiatic destroyer squadron, I am very proud to have known most of the crews of those four gallant destroyers. The twenty-third day of January 1941 was a great day in naval history. It was the day when Commander Talbot ordered his ships to engage the enemy against very heavy odds. It makes me very proud to know that my former shipmates who were manning the guns at their various battle stations on those *four* very old, rusted, and leaking destroyers of the Asiatic Fleet were the first American ships involved in naval warfare in the East. These same four destroyers were also the *first* to engage and sink an enemy ship in that part of the world since the duel encountered with the Spanish fleet at Manila Bay by Admiral Dewey back in 1898. Yes, sir, I feel very honored and proud to have known those guys and, more so, to call them "my shipmates."

During the battle, the U.S.S. *Ford,* carrying the division commander, Paul H. Talbot, all of a sudden found herself fighting alone, having lost sight of the other three destroyers. After weaving in and out among the transports and not being able to find any more targets to engage that were not destroyed or sinking, Commander Talbot gave the order to withdraw and head full speed to the south. They traveled as fast as the old destroyer could muster up speed. I was told that the old ship hit as high as thirty-two knots. Yes, that great night, the twenty-third day of January 1942, will go down in history, when Commander Paul H. Talbot of the Fighting Fifty-ninth Division, composed of four very old destroyers, while on board the U.S.S. *Ford,* in that dark of night, ordered his ships into battle against very heavy odds.

They distinguished themselves in a major victory by sinking four or five enemy transports. What a victory for those tin cans. Having sailed on destroyers for several years in the United States and in the Orient, I was always led to believe the expected life of a destroyer in night battle to be a matter of minutes. These destroyers must have had nine lives, because they fought gallantly, sinking and damaging the enemy ships with no loss of life or limb and suffering very little damage to their ships against a very heavy Japanese naval force. To think, all this was done in darkness.

A year or so earlier, when I was serving on the tin cans out in the Asiatics before being transferred to the Cavite Navy Yard for duty, we were out on maneuvers while proceeding at "flank speed," which is full speed ahead, the most we could travel at was about twenty-seven knots. So thirty-two was really pushing it, especially for those outdated, four-stacked destroyers. The builder of those old tin cans, William Cramp, owner of the Cramp Shipbuilding Yards, I just bet would have loved to have been aboard one of them that night to be able to watch his product perform in an actual duel to the death, and to see their accomplishments, especially of those destroyers that were rusted and leaking and had been in service all those years.

Again by his strategic actions and astute ability, Admiral Thomas C. Hart, U.S.N., should have been highly commended for moving his ships out of the Manila area to safer waters prior to the start of the war, thus saving them to engage the enemy on a later day. If it wasn't for his knowledge of warfare, we would have, in all probability, seen most of our fleet sunk or destroyed right in Manila Bay. It would have been another Pearl Harbor. About the end of February 1942, Admiral Thomas C. Hart, commander in chief of the Asiatic Fleet, returned to the States to go into retirement. However, before his retirement, he, too, exclaimed how proud he was of his little leaking destroyers engaging and destroying an enemy force against such heavy odds, and he said, "I can now go into retirement knowing my boys did such a magnificent job." The heavy training they received on the China Seas paid off.

41. Java Sea Battle—Captain Albert H. Rooks, U.S.N., Commanding the U.S.S. *Houston*

Upon the surrender of Singapore to the Japanese, and with the former senior naval officer, Admiral Thomas C. Hart, being returned to the United States, Admiral Doorman, of the Netherlands Navy, found himself to be the senior naval officer present. He immediately assumed command of what was left of the little fleet consisting of the American, British, Dutch, and Australian navies, the ABDA fleet.

On 26 February 1942 Admiral Doorman on board his flagship, the *De Ruyer,* of the Netherlands, steamed out of Soerabaja to search for, and break up, a huge task force that was bearing on Netherlands Java. This was the last hope held by the Netherlands in the East Indies. He had under his command the remains of the ABDA naval forces, which, in addition to his flagship, the *De Ruyer,* consisted of the Netherlands's cruiser, *Java;* the British heavy cruiser, *Exeter;* the Australian light cruiser, *Perth;* and the United States heavy cruiser, U.S.S. *Houston,* and ten destroyers from various countries.

In the darkness of night, the Japanese were sighted; they outnumbered and outgunned the Allied forces badly. The Japanese opened fire first, and the battle had begun from which there would be no retreat. The U.S.S. *Houston,* soon after leaving the Philippines, acquired the name of the "The Galloping Ghost of the Java Coast." A name given to her because the Japanese had reported her sunk so many times. But her gallant skipper and my friend, Captain Albert H. Rooks, U.S. Navy, kept her afloat in spite of these reports. He would show up when least expected by the Japanese and give them hell and then disappear. Hence the name, the Galloping Ghost.

After three and half days in this battle in the Java Strait, the U.S.S. *Houston* found herself alone as she watched the last ship in the convoy, the *Perth,* going down. All the rest of the fleet had either been sunk or were put out of action. Captain Rooks, seeing there was no hope for his ship, which had been so badly wounded and was almost out of fuel and ammunition from the last three days of intense fighting, picked up the loudspeaker and said, "We are going down, boys, but they are going to pay dearly for our lives and this gallant and beloved ship." He then ordered a course that took him directly into the heart of the Japanese convoy.

As the ship came on course, Captain Rooks again picked up the loudspeaker and said in a loud and clear voice, "Fight on, *Houston,* to the death with your colors flying high." With that, he ordered his men to open fire with everything they had left. The U.S.S. *Houston* obeyed Captain Rooks's last words to his crew. It went down fighting and with its colors flying high.

As the U.S.S. *Houston* was sinking, with all her fighting power destroyed, Captain Rooks came down off the bridge and was saying good-bye to several of his officers and men outside his cabin, when a Japanese shell exploded on the deck just a few feet from where he was standing, and he was mortally wounded. The mighty U.S.S. *Houston* was sinking rapidly. Men were jumping overboard, some getting into lifeboats, others, in the water, were just clinging onto anything they could grasp that was floating about them.

Captain Rooks's private cook, Buda, seeing the captain had been killed, refused to leave the ship. He just sat cross-legged outside the captain's cabin alongside the captain's body, rocking back and forth and continuously chanting, "Captain dead, *Houston* dead, me die, too," Buda ignored and refused to listen to the pleading of his shipmates to abandon ship. He admired Captain Rooks, as we all did, and went down with his ship and beloved and gallant skipper, Captain Albert H. Rooks, while still rocking back and forth and chanting, to Davy Jones's locker.

I was told that as the *Houston* went down to her grave, with the colors of this great country still firmly two-blocked on the main mast, the colors was the last to go under while still flying high as the water enveloped her. She did just as my dear and wonderful friend Captain Rooks had asked her to do in his last words to his crew, "Fight on, *Houston,* to the death with your colors flying high." (It is fitting and proper that I pause as I brush the tears from my eyes and say a prayer for my good friend and former shipmate Captain Rooks.) He was truly a brave man and a *hero* who loved his country and proved it.

I am very proud to have served under his command and to have had the chance to know him. May the good Lord let his soul rest in a well-deserved peace. I could have been on the U.S.S. *Houston* with Captain Rooks. I missed it only because Commander Whitney turned down my request to be transferred to the *Houston,* saying my services were more urgently needed with him in the captain of the Yard's office than on board the U.S.S. *Houston.* A few days later as I sat in my office watching the *Houston* heading out to sea with my good friend Captain Rooks at the conn, my thoughts were *Did I do right? or should I be on that cruiser heading out to sea? What fate lies ahead for her, with the war clouds brewing and getting darker as each moment passes?*

Yes, a lot of thoughts ran through my mind that day in November of 1941 as Captain Rooks took the U.S.S. *Houston* out past the breakwaters of Manila Bay with Admiral Thomas C. Hart, U.S.N., the commander in chief of the Asiatic Fleet on board. I was a little sad, as I liked Captain Rooks very much and it hurt me to have turned him down. But I guess it was fate that day. As we are not able to look into the future, we must put our faith and trust in God.

42. Strafed by Japanese Fighter Planes

On the twenty-sixth of December, the morning after our arrival, the cooks found a building that was standing out in the open field and turned it into a cook shack. Every morning, like clockwork, the cooks would be ready to serve breakfast at exactly 5:00 A.M. So every day at that time, we would line up outside the cook shack, waiting to go in for breakfast. This became a pattern, which the enemy soon found out. One morning along with about three hundred other soldiers, sailors, marines, and civilians, I found myself lined up at the usual time, waiting for breakfast.

All of a sudden, one fellow, seeing Japanese planes coming down at us, yelled, "Look out, here they come, boys. Japanese *snipers*—Japanese *snipers,*" and pointed toward the west. There, in the direction he was pointing, lo and behold, two Japanese fighter planes were coming in very low and heading straight for the cook shack. This was my first encounter with Japanese sniper fire power; other than being bombed during the destruction of the Cavite Navy Yard and being bombed two and three times a day while I was in charge of the soup kitchen at the Mango Inn in Caridad. I had never been attacked by Japanese snipers firing at me.

There was a grove of trees about 300 or 400 feet away from where we were standing in line at the cook shack, an area, I would guess, of about 80 to 100 feet in diameter. Without letting grass grow under our feet, we made a mad dash for that grove of trees for protection, and once there, we hit the ground. In just a few seconds, I could hear the machine guns rattling off bullets. I knew then that we were in God's hands. The two fighter planes were starting to strafe the grove of trees we were under. They made three runs over the treetops, flying very low, firing six-inch machine gun bullets at us. Unbelievably, not a person was hit. How they missed all three hundred or so of us, with no one even getting a scratch, just had to be a miracle. The good Lord was watching over us is all I can say. After that episode, I started to feel the same as Rebel Lord did when he was being bombed and machine-gunned at Sangley Point. I too, knew right then and there that God was on my side and I would live to see the end of the war. I knew right then that all I had to do was to keep the faith. I never lost that faith for the duration of the war and still have that faith to this day.

After the Japanese snipers finished making their third run over the grove of trees, probably thinking they had killed us all, they pulled up and started to go toward the hospital building. The hospital was clean across the field. Seeing where they were heading and fearing for the patients, I being the senior person in the group, commandeered a car from a marine gunnery sergeant. He didn't want to give it up, but in the end, I pulled rank and won out.

As soon I had the car for transportation, I asked for volunteers to go with me to the hospital to help, should there be any casualties there. Several men volunteered, so I loaded as many as I could in the car and the rest stood on the running boards; I think we had about eleven altogether, counting myself. As soon as they were loaded, I made a mad dash for the hospital (the heck with breakfast, we weren't hungry any longer). We had work to do. I felt that I had better get us over to the hospital pronto, because if they hit the hospital, I wanted to be there with this gang to help, in any way we could the sick and wounded.

The hospital was about half a mile away as the crow flies, just across from where the cook shack was located. However, to get to it, one had to travel about four miles on the road in a big circle. We were around the last bend in the road, which put us on the last stretch straight for the hospital gate. This part of the road was lined with large trees on either side. We were almost to the hospital gate, when one of the fellows who was standing on the running board yelled, "The snipers are bearing down on us, sir, get the hell off the road." He just kept yelling, "They are coming straight down the road toward us." Not taking any more chances, I took the ditch. The snipers went straight down the road with guns blazing right through the group of trees that lined the road.

When I left the road, the car turned over on its side in the ditch. All the men were thrown clear, and no one got hurt. One of the fellows said, "What the hell are you trying do to us, kill us?" However, I was too shook up to say a word. We were very lucky no one was hurt; this made the second

155

time we were under attack by snipers that morning, but again, their bullets never found one of us. Again our prayers were answered, and the good Lord was watching over us and still on our side. All I said was "Thank you, Lord, for letting us live this one out."

After we had gathered our wits together, we noticed a very large culvert that went directly under the road. It was about five feet in diameter and one could stand almost upright in it. It was about three feet from the spot where our car had turned over. So we all got into the culvert and just sat there until it was safe to come out. The Japanese snipers turned and made two more runs, strafing the car. We guessed they were probably thinking we were still in the car after their several runs, strafing the car and the surrounding area. They turned and headed out over the bay toward Manila.

As soon as the snipers were out of sight, we came out of the culvert and headed across the road to see how badly the car was damaged and if they had put it out of commission. We were flabbergasted when we crossed that road and saw it plastered with bullets about two inches round and six inches long; they looked as if they had been driven in the ground with a sledge hammer. They reminded me of the cornfields back home, with the corn about six or eight inches tall.

When we reached the car, we found that the top was almost cut off; it had been riddled with bullets so bad. We turned the car upright. I got in, and to my amazement, the motor started right up, and I was able to drive it back up on the road. Looking at the car and remembering that day in the Cavite Navy Yard and all those bombing raids on the soup kitchen I had set up, I turned to the men with me and said to them, "Fellows, we can all bet our bottom dollar that when this war is over, we'll be around to tell about it, because the Lord is on our side." I figured as long as they didn't get us on those last two deals, we were home free. We continued in the battered car to the hospital. We found everything okay there.

43. Our Six Planes Assembled from Wreckage—We Have a Heyday

The morning after our arrival in Mariveles, the naval aviation mechanics, letting no grass grow under their feet, immediately went to work in secret with the parts they had reclaimed from the battered PBYs. They immediately started to try to assemble a couple of planes from the remnants of what was left of the PBYs the Japanese destroyed at Sangley Point in their

156

bombing raid. Within a few weeks, unbelievably, that gang came up with six planes that could fly. This was kept a secret. No one other than the crews that worked on them knew this.

They waited until the dark of night to test them. They took them, one at a time, and flew them to make sure they were in the pink of condition. When they were satisfied they were ready, the planes were kept under cover in the jungle till the time would be ripe to use them and give those Japanese the surprise of their life and a taste of their own medicine.

Every day at about noon, twenty-seven Japanese planes, in three groups of nine, arrived to bomb us. At first, they had plenty of fighter planes with them for cover should they encounter any interference from our side. Like clockwork, they arrived each and every day at exactly the same time, almost to the minute. One could almost set his watch by their appearance in the sky. After a week or so with the Japanese continuously using this pattern, it gave us something to work with. But as long as they had fighter cover, we figured it would be foolish to unleash our makeshift planes, knowing that they wouldn't be a match for their fighters.

The Japanese, seeing that they had no competition from our side, figured that all our planes had been destroyed, since not a single plane came up to engage them in aerial combat, giving them complete control of the skies. After about a week of steady bombing each day at noon with no competition from our side, they got brazen and left the fighters home, sending the bombers over unprotected each day without fighter cover. The chance that we had been waiting for finally arrived. Our commander waited patiently for about ten or twelve days more of their flying over with no fighter protection. On about the twelfth day, he issued the order to unleash our planes. I remember his words well:

"Go up there, fellows, and give those sons of bitches the surprise of their lives. Knock those bastards out of the skies, boys. Good luck."

And *surprise* them, they did. The Japanese, thinking we were sitting ducks and that they didn't need fighter cover, got a helluva big surprise that day. Our boys had a heyday, knocking all twenty-seven Japanese bombers out of the skies with not a single loss to our side. That was a day for us to remember, seeing six makeshift U.S. planes shooting down those twenty-seven Japanese bombers. What a boost to our morale. You can bet they brought fighter protection after that.

It took the Japanese about three weeks of daily encounters and furious air battles with a great loss of their fighter planes and big bombers before they were able to regain superiority in the skies again. Every day for about

157

three weeks, up until we lost the last one of our six planes, we would stand out there, cheering, screaming, and yelling at the top of our lungs every time we saw a Japanese plane coming down. When it hit the ground, we rushed toward it and dragged a piece of it inside the tunnels. Why did we do it? I've asked that question of myself many times. I'll never know the answer. I guess, maybe just to touch a piece of a Japanese plane our boys had shot down.

It never occurred to any of us what danger we placed ourselves in by standing out there in the open with the fragments of the planes falling all around us. We were just a proud bunch of guys who had thrown caution to the wind to yell and cheer our boys on. It was a great sight for us to watch the planes coming down in flames near and about us. The enemy paid dearly during those three weeks for those six makeshift planes that our boys had put together. It cost the Japanese plenty not only in bombers but in fighter planes. I don't know how many Japanese planes our boys brought down, but they got quite a few before our planes gave up the ghost. By great good luck, we didn't lose a pilot; they all parachuted to safety.

Our boys up in the front lines on Bataan were kicking the hell out of the Japanese army, while our Naval aviators down here in Mariveles with their six battered PBYs were doing the same to their air force. Everyone of us who were in the Philippines engaging the Japanese in the Bataan-Mariveles province still insist to this day that if Congress had given us the tools to fight a war with, we would never have lost the Philippines to the Japanese. It was senseless to throw some 80,000 men to the wolves, even before the fight had begun. We proved to the world the Japanese couldn't fight worth a damn when they were confronted with well-trained troops from the United States. They thought because they had China on its knees, they were great warriors. The Chinese were no match for them; they didn't have the proper equipment or the proper training to fight a war.

44. Newscaster William Winters—a Thorn in the Side of the Emperor

About the latter part of December 1942, the Japanese had conquered Singapore with 30,000 of their best-trained and well-seasoned troops who had been fighting in China several years. The United States, fearing that as long as the Japanese were right next door to Australia, they would move those crack troops over and take Australia. It would have been a very easy task for them to take that country over, because Great Britain had moved almost every able-bodied man from Singapore and Australia to Europe to bolster their troops in fighting the war against Hitler's Germany, which was in full swing in Europe.

The United States, in order to stop Japan from taking over Australia, had no other alternative but to resort to a war of words. They must keep the news commentators throwing as many insults as possible at the enemy, with the hope of humiliating the Japanese to the extent that they would by-pass Australia and go after the Philippines. The thinking of the United States was that with the threat removed from Australia, they would be able to land their troops, thereby giving it a jumping-off place in that part of the world closer to Japan.

The United States had hopes of winning the war with Japan in a year or two. Without Australia, our plans would be set back several years. So for the above reason alone, the United States had to, at all cost, keep the Japanese away from Australia. But how was this to be accomplished without any of our air power or ships in that area, so early in the war? So they decided that the answer was to resort to the use of words.

They say that the pen is mightier than the sword, which proved true in this case. Only this time, the spoken word was mightier than the sword. Back in late 1930s and early 1940s, there was a news commentator, William Winters. I used to listen to his program every night before the war. He was a great commentator and put on a good program. Every evening and sometimes at noon, the troops not on the front lines in Bataan, Mariveles, Corregidor, and the southern Philippines, would listen to American commentators on the radio. Among them was "William Winters and the News," Edward R. Murrow, and Walter Winchell. These broadcasts were beamed from America to the people on the Asiatic station, their main target being the Japanese empire as a whole.

So in fearing the loss of Australia at the hands of the Japanese, who had just conquered Singapore, the United States got William Winters to put his radio program on the air several times daily for the benefit of the Japanese and the Oriental countries. He was to continually humiliate the Japanese emperor and his leading generals in any fashion he could. He would keep harping about the bravery of that little handful of Americans in the Philippines who were defying the mighty imperial Japanese army. Mr. Winters would go on to comment about how the mighty imperial emperor's army didn't stand a chance against a handful of Americans. Anything to arouse the emperor, to get him so frustrated, he would go after us in the

159

Philippines in a big way. His job was to make the emperor forget about Australia and to bypass it. And that the emperor did.

Every day, William Winters would be on the job, as follows:

"And that little group of Fil-Americans, known as General MacArthur's Magnificents, are still holding out against the great Japanese emperor's imperialistic nation's crack troops."

"Those brave Fil-Americans haven't got a single plane, hardly any fighting power, no food, and, to top it off, there is no relief in sight for those brave men."

"The Japanese are now showing their true face to the whole world as just a bunch of weaklings."

"If they don't take Bataan and Corregidor now, they will never get that chance again."

"The whole world is fast getting to know that the whole Japanese imperial army are weaklings and no match for that small band of brave Americans. Japan is the laughing stock of the whole world."

This went on day in and day out with no letup. Imagine being in the line of fire and hearing this several times a day. We would yell, "Shut up, you so-and-so." Every night or day he would praise us boys in the Philippines to the high heavens. Twice a day, the Japanese and the Filipino people, as well as the rest of the Orient were hearing these insults thrown at the emperor and his generals. The emperor and the Japanese high command got madder and madder as they listened to those humiliating radio programs. So the more Mr. Winters and Ed Murrow and others harassed the Japanese, the more the Japanese stepped up their attacks on the Philippines by bombing us around the clock, more determined than ever to crush our resistance in the Bataan-Mariveles peninsula to shut up those humiliating attacks on them.

William Winters and the other news commentators kept on calling us "MacArthur's Magnificents" with no letup. Two or three times a day, they would praise us end on end for defying that great imperialistic Japanese army. We in the Philippines, not knowing why they were doing this, cursed and booed each of them. We didn't know the score about Australia. We all thought, *Why are they doing this to us? Why are they bringing the whole Japanese empire down on us?*

The newscasters got the emperor and his imperial command so worked up over their insults that finally the emperor took the bait and issued orders to his commanders in the field to silence those insults and get those news broadcasters off his back.

In order to do so, the commanding general of the Japanese army issued orders to his commanders in the field to give the Philippines top priority, to move everything necessary, including the crack troops from Singapore, to the Philippines in order to crush Bataan. This, he felt, would stop the insults from the United States and would also put him in the good graces of his majesty the emperor.

William Winters kept right on boasting to the world several times a day, starting his program off by saying, "And that little contingent of Americans in the Philippines, without any help in sight, with their country's flag flying high, is still defying the whole weakling Japanese empire." Then he would go on to further antagonize the emperor and his generals by saying, "Yes, folks that great imperial army of his majesty the emperor can't even silence the guns of a small helpless bunch of American patriots in the Philippines."

It wasn't until the war was over that we found out the logic for all that harassment, the Japanese being there on the doorstep of Australia with over 30,000 of the best-seasoned and crack troops they could muster, of there being nothing in their way to stop them from taking over Australia, that it didn't stand a chance of holding off the Japanese. We needed Australia badly, and America was trying to get a five-hundred-ship convoy to Australia to set up a jumping-off place to fight Japan. Had Japan continued on her course and taken over Australia, the United States would have had to fight for every inch of land, which could have certainly changed the course of the war in Japan's favor.

But the Japanese, much to the delight of the United States, chose to listen to "William Winters and the News" and the other broadcasters. The Japanese showed they weren't very smart in taking the course they did. After capturing Singapore, they should have moved immediately against Australia in order to secure that part of the world for their emperor. What a mistake to leave Australia open for the Americans to land without a fight. This could very easily have been one of the turning points in the war, with a big plus for Japan.

45. The Loss of General Homma's Crack Troops

On New Year's Day of 1942, with the Japanese high command taking the bait, Japanese Lieutenant General Nara arrived with 30,000 seasoned veterans from Singapore and reported to General Homma, the supreme commander of the Japanese troops in the Philippines. Upon the arrival of Japanese Lieutenant General Nara with his seasoned veterans, General Homma immediately pressed them into service in Bataan against the Fil-American positions on the Bataan Abuccay line. He succeeded in forcing our troops back ten miles to their next position, the Bagac-orion line. General Homma lost no time in getting the troops he had on hand in position.

Within the course of the next couple of days after General Nara's arrival, General Homma moved in thousands of his best troops, which he had been saving for this special occasion, into the Bataan-Mariveles area. So, in reality, the battle didn't get started until about 5 January 1942, at which time, Homma had most of his troops in position on the battleline.

On 29 January 1942, just twenty-four days later, General Homma was forced to relate to his superiors and to the emperor of Japan that he had suffered a major humiliating defeat, fighting the Fil- American troops on Bataan. He reported that over fifty-six percent of his crack troops and three of his best battalion commanders who arrived from Singapore had been killed in action at the hands of those Fighting Bastards of Bataan. Hence the nickname was born and was to be carried by the boys of Bataan for the duration of the war.

He also related to the emperor that the remaining forty-four percent were incapacitated either by wounds, disease, or exhaustion. He said he couldn't carry on without at least 100,000 replacements. General Homma soon found out that General MacArthur's Fighting Bastards of Bataan were not "the carp in the pool" that he thought they were, "that could be fished out any time" he wanted to go fishing for them, as the general so often bragged to his superiors and to his troops in the field.

General Homma was very fortunate in that there were no replacements for General Wainwright's Fil-American troops on Bataan, whereas, on the other hand, he could get as many replacements that would be needed to break the backs of the Fighting Bastards of Bataan, which would eventually enable him to declare victory over the Philippines. Had our side been in a position to have gotten just a few replacements while the Japanese were building up during the lull in the fighting, a much different story would have come out of Bataan. The Battling Bastards of Bataan proved it with Homma's drastic defeat at that point in the war, in the air as well as on the ground.

General Homma made two fatal mistakes. Lingayen Gulf was his first mistake, allowing General Wainwright to withdraw his troops to the Bataan area. The second one was allowing MacArthur's troops, with his blessing, safe passage into the Bataan-Mariveles province that Christmas day in 1941. Those two mistakes backfired on General Homma. It cost the Japanese empire over 53,000 of its best troops, his own demotion, and the ruination of his career, then later, his life by a firing squad at the end of the war.

46. General Eisenhower Stops All Help to the Philippines

One day in January 1942, one of the news commentators, on a radio broadcast beamed all over the world and which we picked up in the Philippines while we were engaging the Japanese on Bataan, said, "America will produce 65,000 planes this year. Fifty of those, bombers, have already landed in Great Britain and more are on their way there." What an insult to us men who were fighting Japan on the other side of the world. Where were our planes? We had the pilots, plenty of them. Those pilots should have been in the air in a cockpit fighting and protecting us from the bombs that were being rained down on us and from the Japanese fighters who were strafing us from the air, instead of allowing us to be used as cannon fodder on the battlefield of Bataan.

Upon hearing of the fifty bombers sent to England and that more were on the way, the cry went up with "What about us out here in the Philippines? Are we not fighting your war out here against heavy odds? Please give us one shipment and we will defeat the Japanese out here." But we were told they could not get help to us until late in 1943, which would have been far too late. We needed help now, not in 1943 or 1944. We were fighting for our lives now against heavy odds. We also resented them telling the world on every broadcast, sometimes three and four times each day, about all the food being shipped to Europe, while in the Philippines, we were starving.

Why couldn't they send us food? Our boys on the front lines went as long as three days at a time without any nourishment whatsoever and very little water. It didn't make sense to us out in the Philippines; if they could get past all those German U-boats going to Europe with ships loaded with food and planes, why not send one load to The Fighting Bastards of Bataan in the Philippines? The logic of broadcasting to humiliate the Japanese empire by continuously making them look bad in not being able to defeat a small handful of Fil-Americans worked well for the United States. However, after the United States had landed on Australia, there was still no attempt or even the intention of coming to the aid of the Fil-American troops fighting in the Philippines, who by now were fighting without food or relief of any kind in the mosquito-ridden and disease-infested jungles in the Bataan-Mariveles province.

The broadcasts went on every day, bragging of the wonders the United States was doing in getting those shiploads of planes, food, ammunition, and replacements to Europe, but where the hell was ours? It was because General Dwight D. Eisenhower, who had served in the Philippines studying "dramatics" under General MacArthur, disliked General MacArthur's so called dramatics with a passion and didn't mind talking about it in public. During the time that Ike was getting his schooling under MacArthur, he complained that MacArthur was tough on him. Maybe this was his way of getting back.

But why take it out on us? Eisenhower didn't like MacArthur's methods and so, was not interested nor did he believe in the U.S. commitments in the Philippines. He was more impressed with Germany than imperialistic Japan or the 140,000 Fil-American troops he was leaving to die from lack of aid, which they could have gotten to us if they really wanted to. They proved that by General Doolittle's raid on Japan.

General Eisenhower had the ear of General George C. Marshall, who at the time was chief of staff in Washington, D.C. I often wondered why, because of a difference with MacArthur, should General Eisenhower take it out on us who were fighting and dying, giving that last ounce of blood for our country. Why let all those brave Fil-American troops go down in defeat at the hands of an enemy when it wasn't necessary. We proved we could beat them in the air as well on the battlefield. But we needed help to do it.

Eisenhower told General Marshall, "MacArthur's troops weren't worth sending food and supplies to." He told him that the boys in the Philippines were considered "expendables" by Congress, so he should leave it at that and let them be expendable. General Marshall listened to Eisenhower all too well and turned his back on us. They were sending ships as well as big cargo planes loaded with food and armaments across the Atlantic to Europe, also across the Pacific to Australia. Why not route one of those loads to the Philippines? But this could not be. General Marshall, on the advice of General Eisenhower, refused to send anything to the boys on Bataan. General Eisenhower also told General Marshall that in a report of studies he had made, he found that it was too late to help the Fighting Bastards of Bataan.

That was the farthest from the truth anyone could get; we were defeating the enemy on all fronts, so badly that even General Homma had admitted defeat to the emperor in late January 1942, at that same time we were being ignored. So with General Marshall believing General Eisenhower, no help was sent out to the boys in the Philippines; they left us to the wolves, so to speak.

General Marshall, after many days of receiving messages from MacArthur, the supreme commander of the Philippines, and General Wainwright, the commander in the field of battle on Bataan, and General Sharp, the commander of all the southern Philippines in Mindanao, finally sent a wire to General MacArthur, telling him to look for no help until late 1943, or possibly even later, for his troops on the Asiatic station and maybe not then. It depended entirely on the outcome of the war in Europe.

Thus, we were informed that no food, medical supplies, ammunition, planes, or troops would be sent to the boys of Bataan. That message sealed the fate of all of us in the Philippines, and the Fighting Bastards of Bataan were left to be slaughtered at the hands of a force we could have easily beaten if given the tools. Here we were, let down by our own country, over 110,000 strong on Bataan and about 30,000 under General Sharp in Cebu, on the southern tip of Mindanao. Shame on you, America.

General MacArthur noting that our supplies of food and water were so low, he offered bounties to the Fil-American guerrillas if they would brave getting to General Homma's hordes and bring in what they could. Several of them got through and brought in a great quantity of food supplies stolen from the Japanese. In fact, it go so bad that the Japanese issued a threatening warning that if any of the guerrillas were captured while smuggling, they would be shot on the spot. I am happy to say this never came to pass; the Filipinos were much too crafty for the Japanese and none of them were ever captured.

47. The Exposure of Japanese Caves in the Mariveles Mountains

One night in February 1942, a report came in to General MacArthur's headquarters from the patrol torpedo boats that they had spotted a small light that looked like someone smoking a cigarette high up in the Mariveles mountains, on the ocean side facing Corregidor Island. Upon scanning the mountainside with field glasses from Corregidor and from the PT boats in the waters below, not one, but several of these lights were noted.

General MacArthur ordered our Big Berthas on Corregidor to fire a round of shots into the mountainside. He also ordered that a battalion of the Philippine scouts be sent up there to ascertain what was going on and to report back to him as soon as possible. As the battalion of Philippine scouts were getting ready to obey General MacArthur's orders, Brother Wilson, a first class pharmacist mate in the United States Navy, seeing that there wasn't any doctor going with the scouts, volunteered to go with them into the jungles to take care of any sick or wounded if necessary.

Brother Wilson knew full well of the dangers that lay in the jungles they must pass through, also what was ahead of these men, even to the point that he himself might never return. Brother Wilson was well aware of the kind of terrain they would have to penetrate in order to get to the top of the Mariveles mountains and over to the ocean side, where the Japanese were apparently dug in. He knew that they would have to beat a path through a jungle that was full of wild animals and venomous snakes. After Brother Wilson got done explaining all this to the commander who was going to take the scouts into the jungle, his services were accepted by the commander, who was in charge, and he was allowed to go with them.

On the third day out, they ran into Japanese snipers. The Japanese had strapped snipers in the trees along the trail and various other spots in the jungle. As the Philippine scouts neared their goal, my good friend and brother was hit by the first shell fired from one of those tree snipers. He was killed instantly. Up until this time they had not met up with any resistance, neither had they encountered any of the Japanese forces along the trail. Brother Wilson was their first casualty. Although Brother Wilson knew the dangers of the task he had volunteered for, he also recognized his duty to be there to aid the wounded if and when needed. We lost a brave man, and I lost a wonderful friend and brother, one whom I shall never forget.

Brother Wilson took me through all three degrees. I had the honor of having him raise me to the sublime degree of a Master Mason in Bugong Buhay Masonic Lodge in the Philippine Islands. He was the senior warden of that lodge. Bugong Buhay in Filipino means "New Life." I am very glad to be able to say one of the Philippine scouts got Brother Wilson's sniper. As soon as Brother Wilson was killed and they found out there were snipers up in those trees, the commander ordered all his troops to stop and rest, where they remained until he was sure it was okay to continue on.

166

An advanced guard was sent ahead to search and destroy the snipers and to weed out any other resistance they ran into. The commander had the main body stay behind until the all-clear to advance was given. Each time an all-clear signal was received, the main body would advance to that point. The scouts did not meet with any large resistance with the exception of the snipers who had tied themselves up in the trees, but these were carefully weeded out and brought down by advanced guards.

After several days of hard work, beating the brush and winding their way up the mountainside through the jungle terrain by using their machetes to cut through the dense jungle, they not only had the jungle snakes, wild animals, and those pesky little mosquitos to contend with, they had the tree snipers to watch out for at every step of the way. Well, at about 5:00 P.M. on the fifth day of that treacherous ordeal, the Filipino scouts finally reached the top. They immediately headed for the ocean side of the mountain, where the lights had been sighted and where it was believed the Japanese were embedded.

The Japanese soldiers, upon seeing the Philippine scouts arriving, knew they had been exposed, and having been brain-washed into thinking it was a terrible disgrace for a Japanese to surrender, started to commit hari-kari, cutting themselves open, and jumping off the cliff into the ocean waters several hundred feet below.

Upon arrival on the ocean side of the mountain, the scouts found caves dug all along the mountainside for several miles. A great percentage of them were directly across from Corregidor Island. After about two hours of very carefully searching the caves and the surrounding mountainside, the commanding officer, surmising that all the Japanese, upon finding that their hiding place had been exposed, had committed hari-kari, called off the search.

The commanding officer, noting that the men were weary and worn out, to say the least, issued orders to have the troops fed and bedded down for the night. This was the best news these Philippine scouts had in the last five days, since they started out on that mission. The next morning at daybreak when the scouts woke up, they found the seas below were crimson with the blood from the 200 or more Japanese bodies floating in its waters.

As soon as the scouts were cleaned and washed up, they were fed a good hearty breakfast for a change, their first in five days. After breakfast they started to have a closer look at their surroundings, and upon close examination, they got the surprise of their lives. They found guns and ammunition wrapped in newspapers bearing the date of 1906, which was the year yours truly was born. They were all in metal boxes, all had layers of grease on them, and were wrapped first in newspaper and then burlap bagging and buried in the floors of the caves. Another discovery which amazed us was the finding of all sorts of dried fruit and other dried food, the likes of which we had never seen before. There were whole meals buried there. It looked as if this dried food had been there for years. So samples of the dried stuff were shipped back to the States. It was assumed that the Japanese had secretly landed on Mariveles and secured their positions in the already made caves before the outbreak of war in Hawaii. I learnt more about this when I was a prisoner of war in Osaka, Japan; more of which later.

Part Four

General MacArthur Arrives in Australia

48. General MacArthur Receives Direct Orders from the President

Twice General Douglas MacArthur was ordered to utilize the first available transportation to Australia to take supreme command of the Allied forces. Each time, he vehemently protested being ordered to leave his beloved Philippines and abandoning his half-starved troops to die; he utterly refused to leave them. However, on 11 March 1942 he received orders direct from the commander in chief himself, Franklin D. Roosevelt, the president of the United States, to proceed at once to Australia via the first available transportation and to assume command of all of the United Nation's forces in the southwest Pacific. The general, who had been repeatedly begging Generals Marshall and Eisenhower to send him some help for his brave and worn-out troops that were fighting against heavy odds, had recently been informed once again within the past month, that there would be no help forthcoming whatsoever to the Philippines.

With this heartbreaking news of no help to come, he was thinking this move would put him in a very good position to be able to help his courageous troops fighting on the front lines in the Bataan jungles, and who were winning the war with bullets but losing it for the lack of food and medicines to combat their various diseases, which was forcing them to fight a losing battle with the enemy. Also this was a direct command from his immediate superior the commander in chief of the U.S. Armed Forces. He felt that he could not ignore this order as he had the ones before.

So the general started the ball rolling to transfer his staff to Australia. He immediately sent for Lieutenant Buckeley, who was in command of the patrol torpedo boats. MacArthur told him to get all four of the PT boats ready, under a high priority of strict secrecy and as fast as possible, to transport his family and staff, and Manuel Quezon, the president of the Philippines, and his family and staff, and Admiral Rockwell, the commandant of the Twelfth Naval District, to the southern tip of Mindanao. This would be his first leg to Australia, in carrying out the president's orders.

49. MacArthur Makes a Mad Dash under Orders to Australia

The four PT boats were the only available transportation left to General MacArthur under his command. These accommodations were not the safest for his wife and family and the rest of his staff who were going with him to Australia. There were always submarines he could have ordered, which he did when he ordered the nurses to be taken off Corregidor Island a few weeks earlier. But he had other things in mind in making his escape from the jaws of the imperial Japanese army. There were some who said he used the PT boats for theatrical reasons, which was far from the truth. This was serious business, and the general had pondered various methods to get through the Japanese lines to Mindanao without detection.

It must be remembered that the Japanese ruled the sea with their ships and submarines, as well as the skies in that part of the world in which he must travel. The general knew that the waters off the coast of the Philippines would be highly infested with native fishing boats all along his route in that part of the islands. So what a brilliant idea to go as a native fishing boat. The general figured he had a better chance in the PT boats, going down south to Mindanao, figuring they would be passed off as native fishing boats. Especially if word leaked out to the Japanese that the big "carp" had swam away, heading for Australia. The enemy would be scanning the skies for his plane or the ocean route for a submarine, which they would be able to pick up very easily by sonar.

Several times on his trip south, the PT boats with their precious cargo were passed off as fishing boats, just as the general surmised they would be. Here is where his intuition and his long study of the Oriental mind paid off. However, regardless of the reason, whether it be theatrical or the best thought-out way to travel with his wife and little son, it proved to be quite an adventure for MacArthur and his little group in making their mad dash to Australia, and it proved to be the best route for him and his entourage. That was really a desperate attempt of a great man, the supreme commander in chief of the Asiatic Station, leaving his beloved Philippines, getting into those four little PT boats with his wife and four-year old son, Arthur, and with his key staff, to move thousands of miles through the Japanese lines to another war zone to open a new front and conduct a new assault on the enemy in obedience to his orders from his commander in chief, the president of the United States.

172

It was approximately six hundred miles from Corregidor at the northern tip of the Philippines, to Del Monte in Mindanao, the southern tip of the islands. MacArthur knew that they had to travel through some very rough country in those small PT boats, the part of the world controlled by the Japanese army on the land, by their navy on the high seas, and by their air force in the sky above. Anyone of those arms of service of the imperial headquarters would have loved to capture such a prize for their emperor, the catch of the war for the Japanese.

With MacArthur out of the war, it could also have very well spelled victory for Japan, as MacArthur was the only man who knew enough about the Oriental mind to know what to expect there and who had the experience in running a war in that part of the country. Which is the reason President Roosevelt was so anxious to have MacArthur there to run the war. If victory were ever to be achieved over Japan, MacArthur was the man to do it.

Watching the general as he was about to embark on the PT boat for his trip to Mindanao, one could hardly breathe because of the stench in the atmosphere from the dead fish and the filth that was all along the water's edge. I stood there, watching General MacArthur and the rest of his staff who was to accompany him to Australia embark on those four little PT boats, and admiring that great hero as he spent his last few moments on Corregidor. My thoughts were as he raised his hand in a good-bye salute, *Here truly is a great soldier and general,* and then I thought *What could be on his great mind* as I stood there watching and waiting for my chance to say my good-byes and shake the hand of this very brave soldier whom I had the pleasure of serving for a little while. It proved to be my last chance to shake his hand, as I was never to meet him again. Standing there, I was getting more nervous by the minute, thinking this sixty-two-year-old man would have about the same chance that a snowball would have in hell of ever making that 600-mile trip through the Japanese-infested waters to Mindanao, in those small, battle-scarred PT boats.

Yes, here was a very brave soldier doing his duty for his country. He was braver than I would have been. I overheard a marine sergeant say, when asked about MacArthur's chances of getting through, "Don't know, but that guy is lucky. Maybe one in five." I thought to myself, *I sure hope he's right, and he gets that one in five chance.* MacArthur saluted and then embraced General Wainwright.

"Skinny," he said in a very sad voice, "the first airplanes, foot soldiers, medicines, and food supplies that I can spare will be sent to help you get out of this mess that I am being forced to leave you in. I want you to always remember, Skinny, the blame for the mess we find ourselves in today, truly rests on the shoulders of those so-and-so sons of bitches serving in the halls of Congress back home, who call themselves true Americans."

"What I wouldn't do for just a few planes; we have plenty of pilots to fly them," Skinny said to MacArthur.

"Skinny," MacArthur said, "I'll give it my best shot in trying to get help to you. Until then, may God bless all of you." He again embraced Skinny, stepped back, and with a brisk salute to us all, he stepped into PT boat 41. He raised his hat in the air and said his now famous three words, *"I SHALL RETURN."* He then turned to Lieutenant Buckeley (referred to as "Buck" by the general in his memoirs) and said, "You may cast off, Buck, when you are ready." Those words marked the start of this brave and courageous man's daring attempt, with his entourage, to carry out his orders, in compliance with those of his superior officer, the president of the United States, to get to Australia.

So on 11 March 1942 at about six in the evening, we find a very saddened General MacArthur being forced to leave the besieged Corregidor and his beloved islands. Darkness had just about fallen as he stepped into PT boat-41, followed by his wife and their four-year-old son. I doubt if there was an eye that did not have a tear, including that of the general himself. It was in this fashion this great general and his entourage escaped the besieged enclave of Corregidor and Bataan.

MacArthur's little convoy of battered, battle-scarred PT boats consisted of PT-32, commanded by Lt. (JG) V. E. Schumacher, U.S.N.; PT-34 was commanded by Lt. R. G. Kelly, U.S.N.; PT-35 was commanded by Ens. A. B. Akers, U.S.N., and the PT-41, the one MacArthur chose to take with his family and part of his staff was under the command of Lt. John D. Buckeley, U.S.N., who was in overall command of the PT boats.

Lieutenant Buckeley was already declared a hero while making runs carrying the mangled bodies during the Japanese devastation of the Cavite Navy Yard, with bombs falling all around him, with no thought for himself whatsoever. Here we find him again in overall command of those four PT boats moving General MacArthur from Corregidor to the southern tip of Mindanao.

Note: following are accounts of the general's escape; some were taken from his memoirs and the rest is from what I learned by talking to others.

174

As prearranged, the tiny convoy rendezvoused at Turning Buoy, which was just outside the entrance to the mine fields. At eight sharp that evening, they roared through the mine field in single file, with Lieutenant Buckeley leading in PT-41 with General MacArthur on board, then with Admiral Rockwell on board the PT-34 commanded by Lieutenant Kelly, then the PT-32 next in line with Lieutenant Schumacher, and the PT-35 with Ensign Akers closing the gap. On the run to Cabra, many lights were sighted, which was the enemy's signal that a break was being attempted through the blockade. Although the noise of the engines had been heard, the Japanese couldn't tell it from the sound of a bomber, luckily, they both sounded alike. Many enemy ships passed, but the PT boats were not sighted. They were being tossed around in the high seas so badly that if the Japanese had sighted them, they probably would have just passed them off as Filipino fishing boats.

The seas were very rough, with water slashing against the little PT boats while all the time, visibility kept getting poorer and poorer as the night drew on. Now, along the Philippine coast line, the seas were very heavy, and they were constantly being pelted with rain squalls. These little PT boats would at times crash through waves as high as fifteen feet. But in answer to their prayers, the little boats stood the test in that typhoonlike weather. As they passed the Japanese blockading fleet, they were expecting a shell-burst overhead at any moment to make them identify themselves; however, the PT boats rode so low in the choppy seas, they were not spotted. Lieutenant Buckeley, very wisely zigzagging, took a course to the west and north of the Japanese blockade and so, slid by in the darkness without detection.

The weather kept deteriorating very badly. Over and over, this zigzag course was repeated, and their luck held out. Finally, it got so dark and stormy that each PT boat commander had to navigate on his own initiative. Lieutenant Buckeley had told the officer in charge of each boat beforehand that in the event they got lost or were forced to make it on their own, they were to rendezvous off the uninhabited Cuyo Island in the morning.

The storm was getting worse by the minute. Lieutenant Buckeley started to get the feeling that they might not be able to remain together and may be forced to separate. Finally, it got so bad, the four PT boats could no longer keep together. So about 3.30 A.M., they were forced to separate. Lieutenant Buckeley tried for several hours to get them back together, but to no avail, and now they were on their own. Just about dawn, Lieutenant Schumacher, commander of PT-32, saw what he thought was a Japanese destroyer bearing down on him at about thirty knots through the early morning fog. He immediately cleared his torpedo tubes for action and ordered his crew to dump overboard the 600-gallon gas emergency drums containing his much needed gas to complete the run south. He did this in order to be able to make a run for it if need be; however the onrushing destroyer turned out to be the PT-41, commanded by Lieutenant Buckeley carrying MacArthur and his group. All the PT boats rendezvoused at Cuyo Island on the morning of 12 March, as planned, with the exception of PT-35.

A submarine had been ordered to meet the PT boats at Cuyo, but failed to appear. They waited for several hours in the stifling heat, which became so intense, it was getting hard to bear; all during this time, they kept trying to stay as camouflaged as possible from detection by the Japanese planes flying overhead. With the intense heat bearing down on them and the Japanese planes constantly flying overhead, it got to the point where they could wait no longer. They had no contact with the submarine that was to meet them, it being long overdue, and they had no contact since they were separated the night before from Ensign Akers's PT-35, also long overdue.

For fear of being spotted by the Japanese planes, they decided it would be better not to wait any longer for either the PT-35 or the submarine and to move on as soon as possible. When the sun was going down and dusk was starting, General MacArthur gave the order to prepare to get underway. Prior to getting underway, in view of the fact that the PT-32 boat had tossed their fuel overboard in anticipation of an attack earlier, an inventory of the fuel supply of the PT-32 was taken. It was felt that her supply of fuel was too low to make the attempt to continue the trip with such a heavy load of passengers and their gear, so Lieutenant Buckeley ordered some shifting to be done. The staff along with their gear that were on board the PT-32 were transferred to the other two already overcrowded boats. When the transferring of personnel and their gear was completed at about 6:30 P.M., what was left of the little convoy, namely, the PT-41 and the PT-34, with their much overloaded and crowded cargo got underway and headed out to sea. Still no word from PT-35. (According to reports, the PT-35 arrived an hour or so after the PT-41 and PT-34 had left from the rendezvous point at Cuyo Island and were somewhere out on the high seas. Being that the other two PT boats had continued on their journey without them, the PT-32 and the PT-35 made their way into Cebu and reported to General Sharp for duty.)

176

On this last leg of their daring attempt, the PT-34 took the lead, with MacArthur's boat, the PT-41, following. As they cleared the rendezvous point at Cuyo Island, they found the seas still very rough and high. The rain had stopped, making the night very clear as they headed southward into the Mindanao Sea for Cagayan, which was on the northern coast. About ten minutes after they were underway in those rough seas, keeping about a couple of miles off shore, they sighted a large and hostile warship, which later turned out to be a Japanese heavy cruiser, of the 10,000-ton class.

Finding themselves in a position where they were too near to run and also too late to dodge, they did the next best thing, which was to shut off their engines instantly and get ready to clear their decks for action if need be. Then they just sat there rocking and rolling in the heavy seas, watching and waiting for the enemy warship to pass. As they sat there, the seconds turned into minutes, and no signal was flashed from the heavy cruiser as she steamed slowly by in a westward direction, right across their path. Once again they figured they had been taken for a fishing boat.

Now that their road to safety had been cleared, they again resumed their journey. They continued on in those heavy mountainous seas all that night and arrived at Cagayan about seven the next morning and, of all days, it was on Friday the thirteenth, March 1942. Although that horrible trip lasted only thirty-six hours, I was told later that it seemed like they would never reach Cagayan, their goal, in the terrible storm that they went through, also that it was about the worst beating that a sailor would ever want to experience. According to General MacArthur, "It was like taking a trip in a concrete mixer."

Immediately upon arrival, MacArthur had a message drafted and sent to the high command in Sydney, Australia, requesting that four B-17 planes be dispatched immediately to Mindanao to transport him and his staff along with their gear to Sidney. He received a reply from Sydney, informing him that the transportation requested by him would arrive the next day. While MacArthur was drafting his message requesting transportation and getting it sent to Australia, Lieutenant Buckeley went out to find the much needed food and lodging for those who traveled in the PT boats. MacArthur and the rest of his entourage were completely exhausted from the thirty-six hours on the angry seas without any sleep and very little food.

Lieutenant Buckeley had to be very careful in scouring for food and lodging; the precious cargo he was transporting had to be kept an ultra top secret. There could be no leaks anywhere. On the next day, the fourteenth of March, only one B-17 arrived from Australia. It was in very bad shape.

Among other things, it had faulty brakes, its turbo supercharges did not operate, and it was very battered as a result of three long months of bombing raids. When questioned as to the other three B-17s the general had ordered, it was learned that two of the other four planes that were sent for had to turn back due to engine trouble, and the fourth one had crashed into the ocean.

When the plight of the other three planes was made known to the general, and after taking a beating from the angry and storming seas for the past thirty-six hours on the PT boats, he refused to board the B-17. He sent some very angry messages to Washington and to Sydney, Australia, giving them a piece of his mind, telling them that he himself would not fly in that plane, neither would he suffer any of his staff to fly in that plane. He demanded that they send three of their best planes for him and his staff immediately. MacArthur kept the battered B-17 and its crew there to be escorted back to Sydney along with the planes he had sent for. Later that day, he was informed it would take a couple of days to get other transportation to him, so there was nothing to do but rest and wait.

While waiting for the new transportation to come, MacArthur called the crews of both PT boats.

"It gives me great pleasure and honor," he said to them in true Naval style, "to award the boat's crews the Silver Star for gallantry and for fortitude in the face of very heavy odds."

Two days later, on the sixteenth of March 1942, three B-17s arrived at Mindanao to take MacArthur and his group on the last leg of their journey to Australia. Upon the arrival of the B-17s from Australia, he dismissed the crews of the PT boats but not before shaking each man's hand briskly and again thanking them for a job well done. The crews then headed for General Sharp's headquarters to report for duty under his command.

The three B-17s that arrived to take MacArthur and his entourage to Australia were worth waiting for. They were a real honest-to-goodness fleet of three spanking, brand new B-17s, spick and span, to say the least. When the planes were loaded with their gear, MacArthur's party boarded and departed Mindanao. So on the sixteenth of March 1942, MacArthur and his party started on their final leg of their journey to Australia, where MacArthur had been ordered to take supreme command of the Allied forces in that part of the world.

They were flown 1,400 miles through enemy-controlled skies to Australia, arriving there on the morning of the seventeenth of March. The battered B-17 and its crew, flying on a wing and a prayer, went along with them so the other three planes could keep them in sight. This was done by the general's orders; it would put them in a position to try to rescue them or, at least, wire their position should they have a mishap getting back to Sydney. I am very glad to state they all arrived safely.

50. MacArthur Arrives Safely in Australia

Shortly after General MacArthur's arrival in Australia, he called a press conference, in which he is quoted as saying:

"It is a great pleasure to be in immediate cooperation with the Australian people. I know you well, due to my contact with your troops in the first world war, which I admired greatly."

Here he paused for a minute, and while pausing, MacArthur's only thought in mind, was that of his beloved Philippines and those brave, heroic men he was forced to leave behind with hardly anything to protect themselves with, let alone food or medicine. According to the general, as he talked, he was thinking, *what a disgrace for this nation to put men in the field to fight without the proper tools to do the job with.*

"I have every confidence," he continued, "in the ultimate success of our just cause, but success in modern war requires more than courage and willingness to die for your country; it requires careful preparation. This means furnishing sufficient troops and sufficient material to meet the known strength of the potential enemy. No general can make something from nothing. My success or failure will depend primarily upon the resources which our respective governments place at my disposal. My faith in them is complete. In any event, I shall do my best with what they give me. I shall keep the soldiers' faith."

The general did not make mention directly of those he had left behind in his beloved Philippines, but if one reads between the lines, one can see what he was talking about when he said, "No general can make something from nothing," and in the same breath, "My success or failure will depend primarily upon the resources which our respective governments place at my disposal." That was enough right there to understand what he was thinking.

The Japanese were not made aware that General MacArthur, the big carp, had swum out of the pool that they figured they had him trapped in. The Japanese high command did not for one moment under estimate the importance of the general's success of getting to Australia to lead the forces back to the Orient or what he was trying to accomplish. They knew

179

he understood the Oriental mind more than any other general the United States could put in the field of battle, and so, it was important that he be captured and not be allowed to escape from the trap he was caught in on Corregidor Island.

Shortly after MacArthur left Corregidor Island, I was transferred back to Mariveles and assigned to my old job, helping on the docks, dispatching boats to Corregidor, and other duties as assigned by Commander Harrison, U.S.N.R.

All during the time MacArthur was making his escape to Australia, Tokyo Rose, unaware that he was not still on Corregidor Island, kept right on bragging, in a cheerful manner, during her radio broadcast each day that when MacArthur was captured, as he surely will be, there would be no escape for him. She kept bragging that when that glorious day came to pass upon the surrender of the Philippines, there would be celebration in the streets in Japan, and the great and mighty Douglas MacArthur would be publicly hung on the imperial plaza grounds in Tokyo. It would be where the emperor's towers overlooked the traditional parade grounds of the emperor's guard division.

Little did she know that in three years on that very same spot where she had so dramatically predicted to the world in her broadcasts, General Douglas MacArthur would ultimately stand and accept the surrender of the whole imperial Japanese forces and the salute of the first parade review of the Occupation forces in his capacity as the supreme commander of the Allied powers on the Asiatic station. Also that it would be General Douglas MacArthur who would preside over the trials of the Japanese war criminals. Also, little did she know that her boss in the Philippines, Japanese General Homma, whom she was making all these predictions for, would three years later, be shot by a firing squad for the many atrocities committed by his men on the American prisoners of war, not only for those committed during the brutal death march out of Bataan, but also for the many other atrocities committed later on the prisoners from Corregidor and General Sharp's men upon their surrender and while they were being held captive in the prison camps in the southern Philippines.

Tokyo Rose was right, a general would be executed there in accordance with her predictions, but it would not be General Douglas MacArthur, it would be her own boss, General Homma, the commanding general of all the Japanese forces in the Philippines.

On or about the fourteenth of March 1942, General Homma ordered his troops to step up the bombardment of Corregidor Island, where it was known that General MacArthur maintained his headquarters. General Homma also issued an order that a report be made to him morning and night of each day, that he was to be kept well aware of what MacArthur was doing and of his every movement. This was to be accomplished by the spies they had stationed on the island long before the war started, as cooks, etcetera.

However, due to the high priority of the cloak of secrecy placed on MacArthur's movements, Japanese General Homma never knew Douglas MacArthur had left Corregidor, or the Philippines, for that matter, until he read it in the papers via a press release telling of MacArthur's landing in Australia. Upon reading the press release of MacArthur's escape, Homma was furious that the big carp had swum out of the pool, where he had bragged to his superiors that he would be fished out any time that he saw fit. I bet a few heads of the Japanese intelligence corps went flying for making that big blunder.

51. A Lull in the Fighting on Bataan

Waiting for General Homma's Reinforcements

As mentioned in an earlier chapter, by the end of January 1942, the Battling Bastards of Bataan had so severely beaten the Japanese imperial army that General Homma was forced to notify the emperor of his exact losses and to request replacements, of which he was in dire need if he was to carry on his mission of the capitulation of the Philippine Islands.

The Japanese took advantage of the lull, which they created during the months of February and March 1942, by bringing in fresh troops to replace those lost in the battle with the Fil-Americans, The Fighting Bastards of Bataan. During this time, General Homma's troops were brought up to full strength with seasoned crack troops that had been fighting in China and elsewhere. They came from Japan, Indochina, and China proper. His forces had been augmented by over 100,000 of the best troops that the Japanese imperial army had to offer. They even brought along their big field pieces. It was said that General Homma had enough fighting power to blast a hole in the Maginot Line.

All during this lull, of approximately thirty days, the boys on Bataan were forced to sit and wait for the enemy to build up their forces, and all the time wishing we too could get even a small token of supplies and replacements. What a boost that would have been to our boys on the front lines. But this was not to be; our good friends, General Eisenhower and General Marshall were taking care of that.

While the Japanese were reinforcing their troop strength, our men on the front lines in Bataan, due to shortage of food supplies, were allowed only one meal a day, and very scanty at that. Sometimes they went two days without even a bite to eat, and all during this time, were only barely able to catch a catnap now and then, as the enemy kept up a constant shelling on our front lines. I think they did that just to annoy our boys and wear them out, which they were doing.

General Wainwright, all during this lull in the fighting, knew that the Japanese were only biding their time to allow them to reinforce their troops. He also knew that his own troops were too weak and not in a position to take the war to the enemy. He must just sit there and wait for an enemy he had on the run to build up to get strong enough to wage an offensive, a pretty hard pill for any general to swallow. It made General Wainwright, who had been placed in overall command upon General MacArthur's leaving the islands for Australia, and General King, who was in command on the front lines in Bataan under Wainwright, furious, knowing that their troops were far too weak to wage an offensive, and with no help in sight. Just this alone was enough to make one throw up his hands in disgust. But they kept their cool.

We who were fighting against such heavy odds in the Philippines could not believe our great country was so weak that they couldn't send us help, even just a small token of help to brighten up the morale of the boys on the firing line. If they could send all those things to Europe through seas infested with German U-boats, it was very hard for us in the Philippines to comprehend why they couldn't get through the Japanese lines to the boys in the Philippines.

General King, serving on the front lines with the Fil-Americans fighting on Bataan in the field of battle, was less fortunate than the Japanese General Homma, in that, General King would receive nothing to reinforce his troops with. And all the time, starvation, dysentery, beriberi, malaria, dengue fever, and yellow jaundice were taking their toll on his beleaguered troops. We in the Philippines were left to the nonexistent mercy of Japan. I do not believe the word "mercy" was in the Japanese dictionary. There was none shown to the American prisoners of war, to which I can attest. Neither President Roosevelt nor General Marshall would lift a finger to help us in our distress. Nothing was done to help the Battling Bastards of Bataan.

Part Five

The Fall of Bataan

52. The One-Hundred-Mile Death March

On 11 March 1942 having received no help of any sort for his beloved Philippines, General MacArthur, under orders of the president of the United States, left the Philippines to assume supreme command of all the Allied forces in Australia. General Wainwright immediately took over as the supreme commander of the Philippines. General King then assumed the duties of commanding the Fighting Bastards of Bataan.

On Easter morning 2 April 1942 the Japanese forces, having been brought up to full strength, started their attack in northern Bataan, and with over 100,000 fresh troops against the Fil-American troops, who in their sickened condition were dying from starvation and various diseases that had set in, reached their objective days ahead of schedule, and the eastern half of the Fil-American line collapsed soon after the renewed fighting began.

Sickness and death had taken its toll. Most of the troops had bacillary dysentery, beriberi, and malaria fever-wracked bodies and should have been in a hospital, not on the front lines fighting their country's battles. They were a sick, listless, weary, and sleepy bunch of soldiers, with no food and no relief since the start of the war, approximately five months before. If one did get any sleep, it was right where he was standing. This is what General King's boys on the Bataan had been reduced to, and this is what he had to rely on for his fighting force. General King himself was a very tired and sick man. He too had been on the front lines with his men, without even one day's rest since that fateful Christmas Day when the troops moved into Bataan.

General King on 8 April 1942 after six hard days of fighting since the new offensive began on that Easter morning, seeing that the will to fight had about all gone from his starving, sleepless, and fever-ridden troops, decided that his men had had enough. The general felt that the men under his command on Bataan could no longer defend themselves and were no longer a fighting force. He figured that it would be utterly disastrous and worse still, extreme cruelty, to ask his troops to carry on, which of course they would have; they were prepared to fight to the death for their country.

So General King, rather then just let these great, courageous men be annihilated one by one to the last man, sent word to General Wainwright in the command headquarters on Corregidor Island, stating the condition of his troops and requested permission to surrender. General Wainwright refused to allow General King to surrender and ordered him to fight on until the last man had fallen.

The next day, 9 April 1942 at about 4:30 in the afternoon, our front lines finally broke on Bataan. The Japanese, having no regard for life, just kept wading in row after row, climbing over their dead, which in some places were more than ten deep. Finally our boys on the front lines deteriorated to the point of no return, finally collapsed. Realizing there was no possibility of inflicting any damage on the enemy and that it would be sheer nonsense to allow his troops to be annihilated by the Japanese, as he had been ordered to do by his superior officer General Wainwright, General King decided his men could fight no longer and therefore decided to disobey the orders of General Wainwright.

First he ordered that enough trucks be sent to the front, all fueled and ready, should they be called upon to transport his troops to a destination. General King, at the same time, ordered a jeep and driver to report to him. As soon as the trucks were ready and his transportation was in place General King drove through the enemy lines with a white flag flying high on either side of his jeep as token of truce. When General King reached the command post of the Japanese army, he requested and was given an audience with General Homma and the rest of the high command of the Japanese forces to try and work out an agreement to surrender his troops on Bataan and relieve the suffering if possible for those brave, heroic men under his command.

General King explained to the Japanese that his troops were in very bad shape from lack of food and sleep, that they were very sick with various jungle diseases, including bacillary dysentery, beriberi, malaria, dengue fever, and just plain weary and worn out. He requested that he be allowed to load them onto the U.S. trucks that were standing by fueled and ready for this occasion. General King also told them he would deliver his troops any place where the Japanese wanted to intern them. He further explained that due to the weakness of his men, it would be suicidal to move them in any other way.

The Japanese high command insisted that the surrender be unconditional. General Homma just would not listen to General King. General King then asked if the troops would be treated well and given medical attention, in view of the drastic condition of his troops. He was told by the Japanese in no uncertain terms that they were not barbarians. Then Japanese General Homma stood up and, shaking his finger almost in General King's face, screamed at him, saying "Do you think we are barbarians? We are not barbarians. Is that what you think we are?" I know exactly what was on General King's mind and what his answer would have been had he been in a position to express himself freely.

General King knew they were barbarians, and I and thousands of other prisoners under their jurisdiction can attest to that. Not being able to get anywhere with the Japanese and knowing his troops were in no condition to continue, he felt there was nothing else to do but place his troops to the mercy of a merciless general. So, with tears rolling down his face, General King stood at attention and handed over his side arms to the Japanese general as a token of his surrender. This after having been on the lines, fighting for over five months with hardly any food, no relief in sight, no planes, not enough tanks to wage a battle, sleep only when there was a lull in the fighting, which didn't come very often. They slept standing in their positions with their guns in their arms, and of course, got very little sleep, if any, on those last six days of intensive fighting. Those Fil-American boys were heroes; they fought like heroes and many went to their graves as heroes, but they didn't get a hero's burial, in fact hardly any burial.

As soon as General King's surrender was accepted, the Japanese moved in and our boys were forced out, via bayonet, not even allowed to bury their dead comrades. But then, for that matter, the Japanese didn't take care of their own dead either. There were dead Japanese piled ten deep when our boys left. The Japanese may have gone back later to bury their dead; however, from my experience with them, I doubt it very much. The United States should be very proud of our boys who served over there, and proud that they held out as long as they did under the circumstances. May every one of their souls rest in well-deserved peace.

The Filipinos were mostly boys; yes, I actually mean boys. They ranged in age from seventeen to nineteen years. Many told me they felt alone and forsaken by the country they loved and were fighting for. I was also told they were downright discouraged, in that they had been asked to give their lives if need be by the greatest country on earth, the United States of America, a country that could and did send help everywhere else in the world, but not to the boys on Bataan. They considered themselves as forgotten men. Remembering that milestone in my life and how I just sat down and wept on that fateful day, the ninth of April 1942, I again find myself with tear-filled eyes as I write about it.

That was another one of the saddest and shameful days for all Americans, having turned their backs on the boys in the Philippines. Not only those who bore the thick of battle, but every American regardless of where he was on that shameful day in the history of the United States should remember the date of 9 April 1942. The ninth day of April 1942 marked the first time that any general was forced to hand over his sword in token of surrender in such a shameful, disgraceful position as General King and his brave warriors were forced to do, and just because his country let him down. Shame on you America. Shame on you.

I asked myself over and over *why* couldn't they have sent just a token of help to raise the spirits of those brave boys on Bataan? They bragged about shipping to Europe, to Australia, they even sent four planes to the Philippines to get MacArthur a month before Bataan fell. Why not one planeload of medicines to Bataan?

When General King was surrendering his heroic troops and trying to get decent treatment for them, the question was asked of him by General Homma, "Do you think we are barbarians?" I ask you, what do you think? Here were approximately 70,000 troops, stricken with diseases, beriberi, bacillary dysentery, ridden with malaria fever, starving, and half asleep, fighting to stay awake, let alone to stay alive, and having had very little food for the past five months. Those gallant troops were being forced at bayonet point to march some one hundred miles, even after General King had informed General Homma that he had trucks all fueled and ready to carry the troops to any destination that he desired to take them for internment. The Japanese didn't give the boys any food or water whatsoever on the twelve-day march. They just ran a bayonet through their helpless bodies as they passed out and fell down. "Do you think we are barbarians?"

Was that a question? They proved to be worse then barbarians. On that same march, if you can call it that, as the prisoners fell one by one, they were bayoneted and left on the spot where they fell. The weary, worn-out prisoners were so hungry and thirsty that when they passed a coconut tree, they would rush over to get a bit of moisture or a blade of grass to eat. The Japanese, without batting an eye, would simply run their bayonets through their bodies, leaving them there to die. "Do you think we are barbarians?"

Did the Japanese General Homma say that? That walk later became known as the "Bataan Death March," and that it was, with several thousand lives lost while on that forced march, and many thousand more lost after arriving in the prison camp at O'Donnell from the effects of the Death March and lack of medical treatment, which they sorely needed. "Do you think we are barbarians?"

Those 70,000 prisoners from Bataan who surrendered with General King were forced to walk at the point of a bayonet, twelve long days and nights to the town of San Fernando, approximately one hundred miles, without being allowed to ride the trucks General King had provided for them or the benefit of a rest period, a drink of water, or a bite of food; they drank muddy water from the ditches and ate blades of grass or leaves from trees if any could be found.

While the Japanese guards themselves were relieved to get food and rest, they kept the prisoners on the go for the full twelve days. Those who brought up the rear witnessed the full horror of the Death March. They saw dead bodies with their intestines hanging out, draped on farm yard fences, blackened and bloated bodies from exposure to the blistering sun and covered with flies, some with their mouth wide open, lying in pools of water and mud in the roadside ditches. There were bodies with their heads removed, and so on. The rest is too horrible to mention. But wasn't General King asked, "Do you think we are barbarians?"

The bodies of the dead prisoners lying in the road, and in ditches and strung on fences was to show the Filipinos that the Americans were nothing, and *not* their liberators as they had led themselves to believe. However, as soon as word got around of what was taking place, that the prisoners were being forced to march without the benefit of food or water, Filipino women and children immediately lined the streets of the little barrios that they were to pass through, such as Lubo and San Fernando, carrying fruit, water, and other foods, along with ointment and bandages that was passed out to the marchers.

The Filipinos did everything in their power to get the attention of the Japanese away from the prisoners. They didn't dare give the prisoners anything if the Japanese guards were looking. This could only be accomplished when the guards were busy and could not see them aiding the Americans. After twelve days of this merciless torture, the boys of Bataan finally reached the gates of Camp O'Donnell.

This camp was built to house and train the Filipino army before the war. It was located about halfway between Manila and Lingayen Gulf. It consisted of palm-thatched barracks, which were in very bad shape; the roofs were all rotten, there were a few wind-torn puptents still standing, the ground was soggy, and the palm leaves that covered the barracks in the

191

camp were now just rotting away. There were very few places to draw water, which was badly needed in the blistering hot sun. The camp was completely fenced by barbed wire. The Japanese had the perimeter of the stockades ringed with machine guns and searchlights prior to moving the prisoners in.

As they marched into Camp O'Donnell every man was staggering from starvation and weakness of body. Most of them fell down on the ground from sheer exhaustion as soon as they got inside the gate. Many were on their feet only because they knew what would happen if they fell on the roadside, and only their supernormal power carried them inside the gate. The 70,000 that started out of Bataan twelve days earlier, on 9 April 1942, were cut down to only fifty-four thousand, a loss of over sixteen thousand men in twelve days. Every one of those losses was due to brutality on the part of the Japanese. If the men were given even a little bit of food and allowed to ride in those trucks that had been provided for them by General King, every one of those heroes' lives could have been saved.

All the time that the Japanese were biding for time while reinforcing their troop strength and our boys were standing idly by, General Marshall kept telling MacArthur that they couldn't get help to his troops in the Philippines. That was *a pack of lies.* Because we found out later that at that exact time, those very same moments, a task force carrying Jimmy Doolittle's group for the raid on Tokyo, consisting of the U.S.S. *Enterprise* serving as the flagship with Admiral Halsey on board, accompanied by two cruisers, the U.S.S. *Nashville* and the U.S.S. *Hornet,* four destroyers, and a fleet oil tanker, were sailing right past us as we were fighting for our lives under such heavy odds. They made it within striking distance of Japan without detection, and General Doolittle carried out the raid, as planned, on Tokyo.

America sure as hell could have sent us at least a small fraction of the planes, arms, ammunition, and food that was being dispatched to Europe and Australia every day. They proved they could penetrate the China Seas by sneaking all those ships, which had to navigate the waters right past the Philippines, with General Doolittle's boys to make their raid on Tokyo. That was done during the time we were starving and begging for help. What do you think? But we were "expendables."

Again, for the life of me, I can't comprehend that while we were busy entertaining the Japanese in the Philippines, how in the hell the United States High Command could get a convoy of ships within 668 miles off the coast of Japan to bomb Tokyo. They launched Colonel Doolittle's boys on a bombing raid of Japanese cities on the eighteenth day of April in 1942. That was the day that the boys from Bataan who survived the Death March reached the O'Donnell Prison Camp. Funny how fast the United States got within striking distance of bombing Tokyo as soon as Bataan had fallen. That raid took place a little over two weeks before the fall of Corregidor. And they have the guts to tell us that they couldn't get even a small token of help to bolster the spirits of their comrades who were kicking the hell out of the best that General Homma and the imperial army could throw at us. Why would they sacrifice some 70,000 brave boys like that on Bataan and another 30,000 or so in Cebu? Somebody please tell me why.

53. Blowing Up the Mountains

Evacuation to Corregidor Island

It was late afternoon when Commander Harrison received word on that fateful day, 9 April 1942, that the Japanese had broken through the front lines and Bataan had fallen. He immediately ordered the demolition plan put into effect. The commander first gave the order to cap, wire, and fuse the dynamite that had been placed in the drilled holes in the tunnels. He then ordered all hands of the demolition team to stand by for the order to detonate them. Next, he ordered all available boats to be assembled at the dock with full crews to man them and to start to transport everybody, with the exception of the Filipinos, over to Corregidor Island. He then called me and told me to make sure that the tunnel that housed the food and medical supplies was not blown up until all the Filipinos were given a chance to carry off all the supplies that they would be able to carry into the hills.

He also told me to inform the Filipinos that none of them would be taken to Corregidor Island for the following reason: since this was their country, the Filipinos, if they were captured on Corregidor, should it fall, they would suffer needlessly at the hands of the Japanese. So it was deemed better to release them on the mainland rather than have them taken prisoner. Also, by being free, they could be of great help when General MacArthur returned with our boys to the islands. So I was to be sure they had as much food and medical supplies they could carry into the hills. In the meantime, they were getting ready to blow up the mountains in

Mariveles in an endeavor to camouflage and also block the tunnels so that the Japanese wouldn't be able to find them.

At about 6:00 that evening, I reported to Commander Harrison that the dynamite in the tunnels had been fused and capped and was all set and ready. He immediately gave the order for everyone to stand clear and to start blowing up the mountains, with the exception of the tunnel that the Filipinos were getting supplies from to carry into the mountains. The tunnel where the medical supplies and food were stored was near the dock where the U.S.S. *Canopes* was tied up and being scuttled. Now that Bataan and Mariveles had fallen and would soon be in the hands of the enemy, several Americans decided to go into the hills along with their Filipino comrades, where they would be able to eventually engage in guerrilla warfare.

It seemed that everybody pitched in and helped the Filipinos load all the canned food stores, medical supplies, radio equipment and whatever other materials they could find to be taken into the hills that would be useful in their work in guerilla warfare against the enemy. They even took radio equipment. Those supplies were loaded onto trucks, wagons, or anything they could use in getting the supplies over the back roads and into the jungles without being detected by the Japanese, who were at that same time moving very quickly into the Bataan area.

Just about midnight, the Filipinos informed me that they had all the boxes of food and medicines and other materials that they could carry to safety that would be useful in their endeavor to work in the mountain jungles of Luzon and Mindanao province.

I notified Commander Harrison, and he gave the order to clear the area. When the area was clear, I reported back to Commander Harrison, and he then issued the order to detonate the dynamite and blow up the last mountain entrance that contained the rest of the food and medicines. We would have loved to save everything in that mountain.

However, time was running out for us, leaving us in no position to even think of saving anything but the troops. We had all that we could do to get the troops safely across to Corregidor Island before the enemy moved in. Now that my job was completed of squaring the Filipinos away, Commander Harrison told me to report to Boatswain Oster and help him load the boats. We were taking everyone who came along with the exception of the Filipinos for reasons stated above. Commander Harrison said he wanted all the troops moved and bedded down on Corregidor Island by daylight.

We worked all night until early morning, loading men into boats and sending them across the bay to Corregidor. The last boat load to leave Mariveles was a little after 5:00 A.M. It was just starting to get daylight. Commander Harrison, Boatswain Oster, and I were in the last boat. I was assigned to push the boat clear, so I was the last American to touch the beach of Mariveles, since I was the last one in the boat. At that time, I didn't give it a thought about having the last foot on the beach or anything else; my only thought was of getting the hell out of there and to a little safer place. All night long as we were busy loading the boats with men to send over to Corregidor, the mountains were being blown up around us, it was like the Fourth of July. Boulders as big as a house going up in the air along with big balls of fire. One can't begin to explain it.

Although it was in the dark of night, it was like daylight all around us. The continuous explosions and balls of fire lit up the area to the extent that we didn't need any lights to aid us in getting the boats loaded and off to Corregidor Island. The city of Manila was approximately twenty-seven miles directly across the water, where the Japanese had their headquarters. Incredibly, they didn't send a single plane over to see what was happening. This amazed us, because the loud noise of the blasting and the great balls of fire shooting up and lighting up the skies could be heard and seen for miles around. It was a better sight to witness than on the Fourth of July.

This went on all night until early dawn, and not a plane came over to have a look-see. But then again, I guess they didn't need to come over, because they had eyes and ears already planted on Corregidor, keeping them in touch as to what was happening; this we found out later. The officer in charge of bedding down the troops that we were shipping over boatload by boatload on the mountain side of Corregidor was aware that there had been a leak on the island for some time. He figured that the Japanese were getting information from someone on Corregidor, just as they had gotten information from Smithy, the retired U.S. Navy Chief Petty Officer, when the war first started. Smithy led the Japanese bombers each day to the place along the beach where Rebel Lord had buried the oil off Sangley Point the night before. We got him, but it seemed we just couldn't put a hand on the one that was informing the Japanese on Corregidor.

The army captain passed the word around openly, giving out the wrong info as to where the troops were to be bedded down, making sure it got into the hands of the traitor. However, he bedded them down in a place far removed from where he said they would be. Sure enough the informer got the word and passed it on to the Japanese in Manila, as was expected.

As soon as the last boat was unloaded and dawn was beginning to break and all the men had been bedded down in the place assigned to them, in a densely wooded section on a mountain side of Corregidor Island, the Japanese came over and went directly to the spot where they had been told the men were sleeping and started to strafe the area. But as they were given the wrong information by the traitor, our men were not harmed. The captain, by his sound judgment, outguessed the Japanese and saved hundreds of lives that day.

We later found out the leak on Corregidor was the chief cook on the island. Although he had enlisted in the army as a Chinese cache, he turned out to be a Japanese plant on the island. He had been working as the chief cook for many years on Corregidor prior to the war, when all the time he was a Japanese army officer informing the Japanese what they wanted to know. When the Japanese came on board Corregidor on 7 May 1942, they brought a Japanese uniform for him, and he took our surrender of Corregidor along with General Homma.

54. Corregidor and Its Immense Tunnels

Before the war, Corregidor Island was a junglelike rock fortress guarding the entrance to Manila Bay. It was a huge solid rock mountain completely covered with trees, and spread with beautiful bougainvillea and many other tropical flowers. There were various kinds of large trees; hundreds of palm trees, and banana and papaya trees. In all, it was a beautiful island. It was approximately four miles or so long and about two miles wide. Looking at it from the opposite shores or from the waters below as one sailed by, it could be taken for a sleepy, peaceful, rugged jungle. Corregidor had three levels, each level with tunnels built deep into the rock.

Those tunnels comprised offices for the headquarters, commissary, hospital, store rooms, etcetera. There were also a hundred or so barracks built for the housing of troops, to be used in peacetime. Corregidor was the largest of the three islands in her group. The other two were Fort Drum, known as the "concrete battleship," a man-made island, about two acres or so, sitting on a reef made of steel and concrete about fourteen to sixteen inches thick. Fort Hughes, a natural island, was a little bigger than Fort Drum.

With Japan showing her fangs toward China as early as 1927, it was decided to dress up Corregidor Island and make it a strong fortress, along with its two sister islands just in case Japan should have designs on the Philippines. The United States started immediately to fortify Corregidor Island, Fort Drum, and Fort Hughes, the most attention being given to Corregidor, since she was the biggest of the three, although all three were fortified heavily. On Corregidor, they installed huge twelve-inch disappearing guns, called "Big Berthas," because they could sink a ship cruising as far out as fifteen to sixteen miles in the China Sea, thus protect the entrance into Manila harbor from an approaching enemy.

They also installed several ten- and twelve-inch guns, which were also the disappearing type of gun, several batteries of eight- and twelve-inch long-range mortars, and several smaller type of movable batteries on wheels. There were many three-inch antiaircraft guns along with many searchlight and machine-gun batteries installed throughout the island and on her sister islands. The Filipino scouts on the islands were furnished several fifty-five millimeter guns along with their other firing artillery. So Corregidor and her sister islands were well fortified.

In early 1930, a demolition squad of about a hundred or so men started working on the Rock, drilling and blasting three huge tunnels from one end to the other to store equipment, etcetera. These tunnels were blasted right through the mountain, so one could enter from either end; they were mostly completed in 1932. The three original tunnels were built for the main purpose of storing guns, ammunition, and fuel.

However, with the way things were shaping in the diplomatic field between America and Japan, with the dark war clouds drifting overhead and getting darker as the months rolled by, the drilling and blasting began again in 1939. This time, it was for the purpose of cutting laterals in the tunnels, which would add housing for the general headquarters staff, a hospital, sleeping quarters for several hundred personnel, and room for bomb shelters. The original three tunnels blasted in the Rock in 1932 were now being completely honeycombed with tunnels, and lateral tunnels.

These tunnels were so deep into the mountain that one couldn't even start to imagine how immense they really were. One tunnel was set aside for the kitchen, or cook shack. The other two tunnels were set aside for the army and navy headquarters; they were named Malinta and Queens. Malinta tunnel was so wide that it was equipped with two sets of railroad tracks to allow box cars to go in and out to be unloaded. This tunnel was lateralled and cross-lateralled. The laterals were dug back in the sides of the original tunnels one hundred feet or more long and twenty to thirty feet wide. When the tunnels were finished, they were stashed with about a three or four months' supply of ammunition and medical and food supplies. This was accomplished at no small cost.

The Malinta tunnel was taken over by General MacArthur and his staff and used as follows: Some of the laterals were used for office space, others for sleeping quarters, others for galleys, and so on. One office served for General MacArthur's headquarters and his staff, and one office for each of the following: defense, finance, quartermaster, ordinance, signal corps, and so on. There were also quarters set aside for MacArthur his wife, son, and staff, Quarters for President Manuel Quezon of the Philippines and his family and cabinet, and quarters for High Commissioner Sayre and his staff.

The soldiers slept along the railroad tracks, in the alleyways, on the cement floors, some made their beds on the ammo boxes, and some were lucky enough to find a cot; they used any place they could find to lay their tired bodies down on. All night long, the ambulances would roll by as they slept in those conditions, but they were too exhausted for that noise to wake them up and just slept on. In this same Malinta tunnel, there was also a 300-bed hospital, which was so large, it had room for enough beds for the sick and wounded and was completely outfitted.

The hospital was superbly built and built way back in the mountain tunnels. The hospital was outfitted with the same or better equipment than one could find in a hospital anywhere in the world. It had over a dozen laterals containing operating rooms, quarters for the doctors, nurses, and women officer patients, medical ward, laboratory, dental and X-ray rooms—you name it, they had it. There was even a large mess hall for only the hospital patients; however, President Quezon and his family and Filipino cabinet and the United States Commissioner Sayre and his staff took their meals there also. General MacArthur, with his family and staff, had a special dining area built in the lateral where their quarters were located. It must have taken a mastermind to design and engineer the building of the Malinta tunnel. It was the largest and, indeed, the best laid-out and organized tunnel of them all.

Queens tunnel was turned over to Admiral Rockwell, the commandant of the Twelfth Naval District. So the navy and marines set up their headquarters there. It, too, had many laterals jogging off the main tunnel. They were used for Admiral Rockwell's quarters and office, the paymaster's office, officers' quarters, and sleeping quarters for the enlisted personnel. One lateral was set aside for a dining area. There were large laterals for storing arms and ammunition, but that was a scarce commodity in the

Philippines. When the going got tough and it was suicidal to try and sleep outside under the stars, the space for the ammo was used for inside extra sleeping quarters.

The walls of the Malinta and Queens tunnels were draped with pictures from clippings out of magazines (mostly pretty girls scantily dressed). However, there were some with their own personal pictures of their loved ones, their wives, children, and girlfriends they had left back home and were longing to see. As we looked at the pictures of our loved ones, we would dream about getting back home. Yes, we all had dreams. But those dreams of our loved ones were really what kept us all going. We all knew that with God's help, we would return to our homes in due time and be with them again. I went around telling everyone to keep his faith in God and country, and we all shall return to our homes. Knowing that there would be no replacement for our food. The food supplies were very carefully meted out and were just about exhausted at the time of the surrender of Corregidor. As food supplies were being used up and space became available in the storeroom, that space was utilized for sleeping purposes. The Rock was impervious to any type of bombing.

55. Corregidor Falls

Surrender of the Philippines

About 10 April, a couple days after the fall of Bataan, the Japanese, being well aware that we didn't have any air power, didn't waste any time getting their big guns in position along the banks of Mariveles. That morning, with field glasses, they were spotted setting up heavy artillery on the beach and in the fields over in Mariveles just across the bay from Corregidor. Later in the afternoon of that same day, as soon as they were set up, the Japanese immediately started to shell the island, and the Rock's commander obliged them by returning their fire.

This became quite a duel between the heavy American artillery and the Japanese heavy artillery that they had moved into the Mariveles area upon our evacuation from there. The Japanese artillery proved to be no match for the big ten-ton mortars, the Big Berthas, that had been emplaced very scientifically on the Rock prior to the war. The first week or so, the Rock had the upper hand in the duel because of the caliber of our guns.

The boys on the Rock kept knocking out the Japanese guns, but they just kept replacing them. However, as we didn't have airplanes, as did the enemy, to spot their positions or to challenge their spotter planes, they had a tremendous advantage over the Rock. So with their planes flying overhead uncontested, they were able to spot and report back to their command posts. With this disadvantage, just short of a month, by the third of May 1942, all of the Rock's guns were eventually silenced with the exception of two of our big twelve-inch, ten-ton mortars, which were still going strong. As soon as we were squared away on the Rock and the heavy artillery gun duel had commenced, on the tenth of April, our scouts were ordered to keep a close watch for any activity on the shores of Manila and Mariveles.

Along about the middle of April, we received a notice in headquarters that the Japanese were building rafts on the beaches of Mariveles and also in Manila. As had been surmised and was expected, they were getting ready for an assault on Corregidor Island. The island had been bombed constantly, every day and sometimes twice a day, since the fall of Bataan, and we were being shelled continually since the big artillery gun duel started. Each day, the Japanese would send over a wave of twenty-seven bombers, which were divided into three groups of nine. They took their time, no rush, and picked their targets at random. They didn't even bring fighter protection with them; they knew we were helpless and didn't have a thing to contest them with. They knew we had quite a few antiaircraft guns on the island, and they also knew the range of those guns. It was sickening to see our antiaircraft guns firing away at the planes overhead and our shells falling short, not being able to reach them. So the enemy just took their time and dropped their calling cards at leisure, knowing full well they were as safe as in their front room at home with their feet on a stool, smoking a good cigar, and listening to the radio.

In the early dawn on the fourth of May 1942, they started to intensify their bombing raids, sending over fifty-four bombers, divided into six groups of nine, about every two hours until about noontime, when they would intensify the bombings to a point where there was a constant flow of bombers overhead from then on. General Wainwright said that this intensification of the bombings and gunfire from the beach meant that they were trying to soften us up for the big push to invade the Rock. He therefore notified all commands to get set for such invasion, which he felt could happen at any time. The constant dropping of bombs continued from early morning 4 May 1942 through all that night and the all the next day, with no letup.

Just about 4:00 P.M. the next day, 5 May 1942, we received word in General Wainwright's headquarters that the enemy had started to load the rafts they had been building for the past month. We were told that the men were dressed in warfare clothing and that as each raft completed its loading, it pulled away from the docks to make room for another one to take its place. The rafts were being loaded from the docks in Manila as well as in Mariveles. General Wainwright, figuring it would be a long night, ordered the troops on the island to be fed as best as they could, after which, they were to get ready to defend the island by manning all battle stations as soon as possible. At approximately 7:30 P.M. on the fifth of May 1942 under cover of darkness, the rafts started to head out to sea toward the Rock from Manila and Mariveles. The army lit up the rafts and barges with their searchlights, and we saw that they were loaded with the enemy.

General Wainwright, before giving the word to commence firing, said, "The time has come for us to fight with what little we have, which I know will be used to good advantage. Good luck fellows, let's *Give them hell*. No matter what happens, *keep the faith*. Commence firing."

With that, the army started to fire their Big Berthas into the rafts heading toward Corregidor. The army kept getting direct hits, sinking and blowing up many of the rafts and barges; the enemy were being slaughtered. However, the Japanese couldn't be deterred. It seemed nothing could stop them. They just kept on coming toward the island from Manila and Mariveles. Finally, at about 9:30 that night, they reached the beach, and their foot soldiers started their land assault against the Rock. Their bombings in the air intensified to the extent that the bombs were raining down on us, simultaneous with the Japanese artillery's steady barrage of shells from their big guns from across the bay in Mariveles.

That was another night I shall not forget, and I am damn sure that not a soul who was on Corregidor Island that horrible night will ever forget either. There is nothing that can describe the pounding we took that night on the fifth of May 1942 with the Japanese infantry landing and the constant bombing from the planes overhead and the parade of shells being thrown at us from Mariveles. It was the fury of hell having indeed broken loose.

While the enemy were trying to get a foothold on the beach, they were met by our army, sailors, and marines, who took their toll of the Japanese by machine-gunning and knocking them down. However, again, this didn't stop them either; they kept coming toward the barbed wire that had been strung days before all along the shore. They continued coming and climbing over their dead and over the barbed wire, which didn't faze them a bit. They were being torn open from the barbed wire, trying to get through the entanglement, and the Japanese dead were piling up; the dead bodies were ten or more deep. It was a repeat of the last days on Bataan; they just fell on top of one another, as they did that day when our lines broke in Bataan, just climbing over the dead bodies and dropping right there on top of those already dead. Life meant nothing to them.

About three hours after their first landing, the Japanese landed a few small tanks, forcing our troops to retreat. I was really frightened while steaming on the U.S.S. *Barker* along with the U.S.S. *Alden,* when we had to go through that terrible typhoon to rescue the S.S. *President Hoover.* I, as with many of my shipmates, had never expected to see shore again. But that typhoon was nothing compared to what we were put through that fateful day and night of 5 May 1942. That night was by far the most frightful I had ever been through since the war started or, for that matter, in my whole life. I felt even worse than when as a little child in the orphan home I was being badly beaten.

I've witnessed many terrible things in my life before this night began, many more of them in the course of this war. Even down in the jungles of Nicaragua when I was serving with the U.S. Marines fighting Sandino back in the late 1920s and early 1930s, it was never as bad as that night of *hell* on Corregidor. It was, as I said, all hell had broken loose: bombs hitting the ground, shells from the shore batteries exploding so fast, continual blasting and no space between, no letup, just plain hell. The fighting with the ground forces continued all that night and into the dawn, and so did the continuous shelling from the beach and the bombing and strafing from the air.

Although General Homma had been given reinforcement of some 100,000 troops in April, most of them were killed or lost to disease while fighting on Bataan. However, he threw all his able-bodied men into this battle; less then three hundred made it onto the airfield, the rest were driven back or lost their lives trying to get ashore. All of a sudden, about 4:30 or 5:00 in the morning, the bombing and the blasting from the guns coming over from Mariveles beach abruptly ended. Peace and quiet. Not a Japanese plane was overhead. When the dawn broke on the sixth of May, there were hundreds and hundreds of Japanese bodies floating in the waters below.

When it got a little lighter and one could see over the vast terrain that morning, I couldn't believe my eyes. The Rock was devastated, not a tree standing, it looked like a desert or, as some put it, "a newly excavated rock quarry."

"They sure gave us a hair cut, didn't they?" I said to my buddy.

"A hair cut, did you say? I'd call it a scalping," he replied.

All our armament was destroyed. There was nothing left to fight with but our small arms and our hands. But then, what could one expect from the pounding we took for the past month, the round-the-clock bombardment from the beach and continual bombing and strafing from the air for the past sixty-five hours or so.

Just about daybreak the sixth of May, a marine sergeant came up to the command post of General Wainwright and, after a brisk salute, told the general that a group of approximately two hundred Japanese down on the airfield were waving a white flag as a token of truce. He requested orders from the general. Skinny told the marine sergeant to send someone down to the airfield under a flag of truce and to inform them to lower their flag and to wait with patience, that we would surrender to them before noon that day. Skinny (as he was affectionately called) Wainwright, after careful consideration from studying all the reports received from his commanders in the field and a meeting with his full staff, decided it would be foolhardy to try to hold out any longer. The general estimated that ninety-eight percent of the Rock's armament was reported destroyed. The troops were in a deplorable condition from lack of sleep and nourishment for the past three days.

Feeling that the Japanese would come back again that night and that it would be complete suicide for his disorganized, demoralized, and shell-shocked, deafened troops to try and defend themselves, he decided not to put his command through that type of torture any longer. Another thing on his mind was that everyone had been placed on one ration a day for some time, food was running out. With all this in mind, General Wainwright went back to his quarters and remained there for quite some time mulling over his decision.

When he came out, he said, "This will mark one of the saddest moments in my life." He sat down, wiped a tear from his eyes, and drafted a message to his commander in chief, President Franklin Delano Roosevelt, the president of the United States, telling him that all our fighting power had been destroyed, that his troops were exhausted, disorganized, half-starved, and demoralized from the knowledge of there being no relief in sight, and were unable to carry on. He requested permission to surrender.

He then ordered the same wire to be sent to General MacArthur in Australia.

It seemed that within minutes, General Wainwright received a reply from the president (I don't have the exact wording, but to the best of my knowledge and belief it read like this): "Skinny, anything you do will be acceptable in the eyes of the American public. You and your men have done an outstanding job in holding the enemy at bay these past six months with little or nothing to defend yourselves with. You have allowed us time to rebuild our fleet and to land a 500-ship convoy in Australia, which is the foothold we badly need if we are to win this terrible war that has been thrust upon us. You have given us that foothold and that hope. You and all your men are in our prayers. Whatever choice you make will be deemed honorable in the eyes of the American public and also by me. May God bless you and bring everyone of you home safely with Godspeed." It was signed, Franklin Delano Roosevelt.

Upon receipt of this message from his commander in chief, Skinny sent a message to General Homma requesting safe passage under a flag of truce through his lines to his command post to hold an audience with him. No news could have been better for General Homma; he was pleased beyond words, as he was just about to get off a wire to the imperial headquarters in Japan requesting replacements. General Homma had lost so many men, he himself could not carry on.

At the start of the invasion of Corregidor on the evening of 5 May 1942, General Homma had only about five thousand good troops that could be used in the invasion. The balance of his troop strength were either killed the last days of fighting on Bataan or sick with dysentery and other diseases they had contracted while fighting in the jungles on Bataan. Of those five thousand troops engaged in the invasion of Corregidor, approximately three thousand men lost their lives that night, leaving him with only about two thousand troops at his disposal.

Since his losses were so great in the battle that night, Homma was just drafting a message accounting for those losses, with a request for replacements. When he received the message from General Wainwright requesting safe passage through his lines under a flag of truce, the timing could not have been better. There could not have been greater news for Homma. He not only saved face, but he didn't have to tell about his losses, and now could claim a victory. Homma wasted no time; he gladly sent a wire back to General Wainwright, granting him safe passage to his headquarters.

So with two marine guards under a white flag of truce, General Wainwright proceeded immediately to meet General Homma to sue for an honorable surrender of some 6,500 troops on Corregidor. Homma refused to take General Wainwright's offer to surrender Corregidor alone. General Homma was still furious about General MacArthur's escape to Australia. He told Wainwright that with MacArthur gone, he was the commander in chief of all the U.S. troops in the Philippines, and he would settle for nothing less than an unconditional capitulation of all the Philippines Islands. General Homma further stated that he would not be satisfied until all of the 80,000 Fil-American troops, of which Wainwright was still the titular commander, had laid down their arms.

General Homma, in speaking of some 80,000 troops, was considering the approximately 40,000 troops now being held at Camp O'Donnell that had surrendered on Bataan under General King and who were considered to be hostages, not prisoners of war, and were dying at the rate of 150 to 200 a day. He was also considering the 30,000 troops under General Sharp in the Mindanao area, plus those on Corregidor. General Homma said the 6,500 troops on Corregidor would also be treated as hostages until the approximately 30,000 troops who were still free under General Sharp in Mindanao, in Samar, Mindoro, Leyte, and Panay, in the southern part of the Philippines, have laid down their arms.

As General Wainwright kept pleading and pleading for an honorable surrender of his troops, Homma, in a fit of rage, jumped up and, furiously screaming and waving a finger almost in the face of General Wainwright, as he did with General King when he tried to get an honorable surrender for the boys on Bataan, said that only when all the Philippines had capitulated, then, and only then, would a complete surrender be entertained by his government, and only then would the status of all prisoners be changed from "hostage" to "prisoners of war."

General Homma gave General Wainwright a matter of hours to study his offer (if I remember correctly, it was twelve hours). He also told him that if he did not strike the American colors within that time frame, which would signal a capitulation of all the Philippines, he was afraid to say what might happen to those already in his hands. He kept emphasizing that those prisoners in his hands were considered to be hostages and not prisoners of war and they would all be made to suffer and pay very dearly, even with their lives if General Wainwright did not surrender every inch of the Philippine Islands on schedule.

General Wainwright did not know the sad plight that General Homma himself was in. He wasn't aware that Homma himself couldn't continue the war until he had received replacements. Had he known, he might have stood up to General Homma and things might have been different.

56. General Sharp Refuses to Surrender

General Wainwright felt as if his hands were tied behind his back, so to speak. After several hours of deliberation, he found the situation to be hopeless. He couldn't do a thing other than to order General William Sharp and all the troops in the southern islands of the Philippines to lay down their arms, undefeated as they were, and become prisoners of war under the Japanese. General Wainwright knew this was an order that would be very difficult to enforce, with his only having approximately 6,500 troops under his direct command, while General Sharp had under his command over 30,000 troops down in Mindanao.

Although General Wainwright was still the overall supreme commander of the Philippines and General Sharp was under his command, should General Wainwright be killed or surrender in battle, then General Sharp would assume the supreme command of the Philippines in Wainwright's stead. General Wainwright was the senior officer present, MacArthur being in Australia. So Wainwright truly could order General Sharp to lay down his arms and surrender. However, he knew he was in no position to enforce it.

General Wainwright, after serious consideration, broadcast his decision from General Homma's headquarters on Luzon in the northern part of the islands to General Sharp down in Mindanao in the southern part of the islands. This was the darkest hour in the history of the United States, that of striking the colors of this great nation. It had never happened before. Nothing could be more humiliating for a general in the field of battle.

General MacArthur's headquarters in Australia intercepted Wainwright's message to Sharp, and upon receiving the broadcast that Wainwright had sent to General Sharp ordering him to surrender, General MacArthur immediately informed General Sharp to ignore Wainwright's broadcast, feeling it must have been obviously transmitted against his will and under great duress, and that Skinny was at the mercy of the enemy.

General Sharp, in Cebu, upon receiving this message from MacArthur in Australia, refused to surrender. He replied by saying, "As long as a drop of blood runs through my veins, I shall not surrender to these barbarians but will fight to the death if need be." He then added, "I now declare myself the commander in chief of all of the armed forces of the Philippines."

Japanese General Homma, upon receipt of Sharp's wire to Wainwright, was more furious then ever. He immediately declared all captured Americans under his control including those on Corregidor to be henceforth treated as hostages instead of POWs. He further stated that General Sharp had twenty days to surrender. If he didn't surrender by the twenty-sixth of May 1942, all the hostages under his control would be executed by machine-gun fire.

There is quite a difference between being a hostage and a POW. A hostage is not held under the laws of any treaty and can be disposed of by an enemy as he sees fit. A POW is held under the laws of the Geneva Convention, by which mostly all nations abide. Under the Geneva Convention, all prisoners must be treated in accordance with that treaty, of which the Japanese government was also a signer, but they didn't adhere to it. At least, not until 1945, when they had lost the war. At which time, they tried to show the whole world what great keepers of prisoners of war they were by immediately starting to treat us in accordance with the Geneva Convention, giving us medication, hospitalization, clothing, etcetera, necessities we had been denied as prisoners of war heretofore by the Japanese.

When Wainwright was given Sharp's reply, he immediately dispatched members of his staff to carry letters in his own handwriting to General Sharp and also to the commanders in the field under Sharp's charge. Under orders from General Homma, the American army officers were dispatched immediately along with several Japanese army officers to see that they got safely through the Japanese lines. They went via Japanese air transport. General Wainwright was then escorted through the enemy lines back to Corregidor.

During the time that General Wainwright was at Homma's command post, trying to sue for an honorable surrender of Corregidor Island, about one hundred Japanese troops had swum ashore and tried to occupy the entrances to the army tunnels, which included the Malinta tunnel, where the 300-bed hospital, the kitchens, and the general headquarters were located. However, our troops immediately surrounded and disarmed them.

57. Wainwright Forced to Strike His Country's Colors

Upon General Wainwright's return to the island, he gave orders that he was not to be disturbed. He went into his quarters in the Malinta tunnel and stayed there for sometime with just his wife and young son. I feel that they were praying together. He emerged from his room in thirty minutes or so, and trying very hard to stand erect and keep the tears back, he said the words that would break any soldier's heart. "Boys, strike the colors of our great country." With that command, not only the general, but I believe there wasn't a soul standing there that didn't burst into tears. I know I did (as even now as I write).

It was a most pitiful sight, I pray to God I will never have to witness again. As I stood there, I said to myself, "What a shame. Here is a great general and hero of the United States Army, who knowingly fought a losing battle over a period of six long months. He was the general in command at Lingayen Gulf on the day the Japanese first invaded and bombed and raped the Philippine Islands. He had little or nothing to fight with, just courage and prayers from the first day of that war. Now here he is, going down on his hands and knees with the flag, sobbing like a baby and kissing it and crunching it in his arms all the way down to the ground."

As I watched, I thought my heart would break as I, too, was crying very deeply as he finally let the tip of Old Glory touch the ground. The tip touched the ground for only a split second, but long enough to break a man's heart, especially under the conditions we were under. It was one of the saddest days of my life. As I stood there watching General Wainwright striking the colors, I and many others standing there vocally cussed the president of the United States, General Marshall, General Eisenhower, and the Congress of these United States for the disgraceful position they had put us in.

And what a disgrace; forcing General King and the boys on Bataan to undergo that terrible death march, to have this great soldier and hero, General Jonathan M. Wainwright be the first man in over two hundred years in the history of this great nation to be made beyond his control to touch the ground with his beloved country's flag in token of surrender, the country we all loved so much in those days.

It brings tears to my eyes to this very day, some fifty years later, as I write of this grave injustice brought upon those great generals and the thousands of men like me by those in power back home. If the Congress of the United States and the American people had provided our fighting forces with adequate arms and the necessary tools to fight a war, we would not have needed a "suicide fleet" or "expendables" (on the Asiatic station), terms applied to us long before the war.

I cannot understand how the Supreme Court allows people to burn and drag our flag on the ground, under the guise of "free speech." It shakes me up when I see this going on; it brings back the sight that I shall never forget of seeing a great general crying and sobbing as he knelt, kissing his country's flag that saddest day of all days, forced to strike the colors of this great nation.

Many millions of men since the days of the Revolutionary War have laid down their lives and shed their precious blood on battlefields, as well as on the high seas, defending that flag so that you and I and our loved ones could enjoy the freedom that we are enjoying today. Although Old Glory is only a piece of cloth, it is the symbol of a free and peace-loving nation. Why allow a few punks to destroy what so many died for?

Immediately upon striking the colors and gaining his composure, the general instructed the army and the navy to destroy all encoding and decoding machines and that all secret and top-secret documents be burned. He also ordered that the bolts and firing pins be taken from the rifles and thrown into the seas below, along with all small arms, such as hand guns, swords, etcetera. This order was carried out to a tee by the navy. However, the army in General Wainwright's headquarters were still sending and receiving messages from President Roosevelt when the Japanese entered the Malinta tunnel, therefore they did not have time to destroy the encoding and decoding machine that they were using, so the Japanese confiscated that machine intact. But the machine proved to be of no use to them, to the best of my knowledge and belief.

As the clock struck the eleventh hour on the sixth of May 1942, General Homma. and his staff arrived at the entrance of the Malinta tunnel, which was the agreed time for the surrender to take place between Generals Wainwright and Homma, General Wainwright handed over his sword to General Homma at that time. The Japanese couldn't believe their eyes when they arrived that morning and found over 6,500 troops still alive. They kept saying over and over "How can it be?" "I don't believe this." "It can't be possible." True, it was amazing that there was very little loss of life on our side, when one thinks of the thousands of Japanese lives lost that night in trying to get a foothold on Corregidor Island. My answer to that is the good Lord was with us.

When we first surrendered, several men raised guns to their heads and killed themselves rather than surrender. I tried to talk as many of my buddies out of wasting their lives by using their weapons on themselves. Later on, I did everything in my power to stop many of them from self-starvation. They just plain refused to eat anything but rice. I was told by many of my friends that no way were they going to live on a rice diet or take the torture the Japanese were inflicting on them. They said they would rather be dead. So many of my good buddies went by way of either using their weapons on themselves or just refusing to eat the rice and just starved themselves to death. All my begging and pleading was in vain. I remember one fellow in particular, Ginsberg, who refused to eat and was slowly dying, but he kept telling jokes and laughing right up until the end. I worked so hard pleading with him, but that was what he wanted to do, and no way would he listen to me. I kept telling him, as I did many others, that within two or three months, we would all be free, and so on. The funny thing was that I told it so many times, I started to believe it myself.

58. Saved from Being Marched into the Ocean Below

The Japanese stayed for about an hour or so in Malinta tunnel going through the surrender formalities. After they were completed, the Japanese finally came over to Queens tunnel, where the navy and marines were quartered. They were furious to see that the navy personnel had dismantled all the rifles and that some of the parts were missing. They started to beat anyone nearby with the butts of their rifles, and some of them were seriously hurt. The Japanese were yelling and screaming in their native tongue as they were beating the prisoners closest to them.

Finally an interpreter came into Queens tunnel and explained to us that they wanted to know where the bolts and firing pins were. Johnny Cox, a chief petty officer, figuring he might quiet them down and stop the beatings of his shipmates, took them outside and said, "The parts are down there," pointing down over the cliff to waters about four hundred feet below.

Upon being shown where we had disposed all the small arms and the bolts from the rifles, the Japanese became more furious and rushed back into Queens tunnel, ordering everybody outside by the cliff. They were screaming in Japanese, *"Kuda Kuda,"* and something like *"Hiyaka, Hiyaka."* No one among us spoke or understood Japanese, and this also made them mad as hell because they couldn't get through to us what they wanted us to do. They again started to beat us over our heads and bodies with their rifle butts and piercing us with their bayonets enough to draw blood. Several of the men were cut and bleeding badly. Some were a mess of blood almost head to foot, but that didn't faze the Japanese, and they kept on with their torture.

The Japanese interpreter came in again and explained to us that they wanted us all outside the tunnel in a hurry. Queens tunnel, where the navy and marines were quartered, was right on the rim, overlooking the ocean. The rim was about four hundred feet above the rocks below. Once outside the tunnel, the Japanese kept on prodding us with their rifles with bayonets attached; they were pushing, shoving, and screaming, *"Kuda, Kuda,"* again, as they did back in Queens tunnel, and just kept hitting and shoving until we were all in a large group. We didn't know what they wanted. We learned very fast not to shake our heads in trying to say we didn't understand. That was a fatal mistake, because if you did, you were knocked down with the butt of their rifle and beaten horribly. The Japanese thought when you shook your head, you were saying that you wouldn't do as you were told.

Finally, the interpreter came over and told us that they wanted us all to line up, twelve men abreast. When all the marines and navy men were out of Queens tunnel and lined up the way the Japanese wanted, we were forced via bayonet point to undress. After we were completely undressed, which didn't take long for us to do, because all that time they were still beating us and prodding us with their bayonets, we were ordered to put all our clothing, including our shoes, into one big pile. Can you imagine the clothing and shoes of about two thousand or more men just thrown into one big heap? It was a massive pile, and what a mess.

Next, we were ordered to line up as before, twelve abreast. It was foggy and cold, and standing with not a stitch of clothing on, above the ocean, we were all shivering. I don't know if we were shivering from the cold or from sheer fright. Next, they started to come through and take our rings, watches, neck chains, anything of value, and kept cramming them in their pockets. They even looked in our mouths to see if we had any gold teeth. I didn't see them do anything at that time to those who did. But just the same, I was glad I didn't have any, in case they had designs. Later on, when a prisoner died, they pulled all his gold teeth before the body was

211

tossed in the waterhole. After they had stripped us of our jewelry, they told us to start marching over the cliff onto the rocks in the ocean below. "Are we barbarians?" was asked of General King on Bataan.

Just as the first line of twelve men got about two feet from the edge of the cliff, a Japanese general emerged from the tunnel along with his staff. He appeared on the scene just in the nick of time; it couldn't have been timed any better. If that general's appearance had been just two seconds later, we would have lost at least the first two rows over the cliff. I was in the sixth row. The good Lord had a different idea about this jumping off the cliff business. Seeing what was about to happen, the Japanese general ordered us to put our clothes back on and go inside the tunnel.

It was an unimaginable mess, with everybody trying to get clothes and shoes to fit them in a hurry. However, this time, with the general there, we were not beaten and prodded with bayonets as we were grabbing clothes and shoes. The Japanese general had the men who were responsible for this slapped around right in front of us.

Here we were, about two thousand men in the raw, not a stitch of clothes on, more scared than a rabbit with a dog on his tail, trying to get his hands on any piece of clothing. I kept yelling, "Fellows, take anything you can grab, large or small. We'll swap around afterward. Let's get the hell out of here and back in the tunnel before something else happens." I laugh now about that ordeal and how we looked with the clothes we had grabbed and carried into the tunnel. But at that time it was very serious business, not knowing what was going to happen to us next.

We found out later that the Japanese who were going to march us off the cliff were Japanese naval officers. I figured that when the Japanese naval officers came into Queens tunnel and found us to be U.S. naval personnel, they despised us even more because we had surrendered and did not commit hari-kari as they are taught to do in lieu of surrender. The Japanese navy people made no bones about how they felt about us surrendering, and they told us, too. All through our POW days, they were mean as hell to all navy personnel. To them, anyone who surrenders is a coward.

In America, we are taught differently. We are taught that "he who fights and runs away lives to fight another day." After we had been returned to Queens tunnel, a Japanese staff officer came in with the interpreter, who told us to wait there and not leave the area. How could we, when both the entrances were now guarded by Japanese soldiers. So this gave us time to swap clothing with one another to get a decent fit. I don't think anyone got the same clothing they had on before we were ordered to disrobe a few minutes before. But we were happy to even get what we got.

59. Held on Corregidor Airfield as Hostages

After a couple of hours or so of waiting in Queens tunnel, the same staff officer and the interpreter came back in. We were placed in groups of about one hundred and fifty men to a group and marched down to the airfield on the lower level, known as the "bottomside," which was down by the water's edge. General Wainwright and the two highest ranking officers of his staff were taken to Manila. The doctors and the nurses and hospital corpsmen were allowed to remain up in the hospital in Malinta tunnel to attend the sick and wounded.

As we were going down the road to bottomside, it made one feel sick to see what had been left of Corregidor after the seventy-two hours of shelling and bombardment that we had just undergone. Even the foliage that covered the ground was completely gone, trees were either cut in half or ripped completely out of the ground. Destroyed vehicles, cars, trucks, armored tanks, among other things, were strewn all over the place, the gun emplacements were all destroyed; in short, the island was a catastrophe.

There were hundreds and hundreds of dead bodies of Americans and Japanese strewn all over, mostly Japanese. Some were starting to turn brown and bloating from the blistering hot sun in just that one day. It was grotesque, to say the least, the positions they were in. Some of them had been cut in half by shrapnel, others, from their positions, looked as if they were caught running, and so on. I heard someone say "this is the valley of death." That reminded me of General Sheridan's March in the American Civil War. I thought to myself, *Buddy, you sure are right.*

As we were getting closer to bottomside, we noticed that the Japanese were manning submachine guns, spaced about every ten feet on the rim overlooking the airfield. Seeing this, I said to my buddy, "Boy, with those machine guns being pointed at the airfield where they are taking us we could be walking into the valley of hell and into the jaws of death." As I learned in school, studying General Sheridan's march, there was a line something like "into the Valley of Death and into the Jaws of Hell rode the six hundred." Only we numbered 6,500.

213

When we finally reached bottomside, we all started to stake out a place for ourselves, but about every hour or so, another one hundred and fifty prisoners would arrive crowding us more and more. The airfield was large, but not large enough for this many people. As each new batch arrived, I kept thinking to myself, *I hope this one is the end.* We were gradually being crowded out of our space. Well, just about dusk, all the 6,500 prisoners were finally moved to bottomside. Our accommodations finally ended up being a parcel of concrete just about two feet by six feet per person, leaving us each just about enough space for one to lie down. It was crowded, and I mean crowded.

To make matters worse, all the water and electricity had been knocked out during the bombing and shelling the night before, hence no water or electricity. It got so hot on that concrete runway, prisoners were fainting. We all started yelling for water. They finally gave in and had water brought in from an artesian well on topside. The airfield was nestled in a valley. It had a bank of approximately fifty feet on either side, the two ends were about fifteen feet above the ocean. A fairly good-sized plane could land on Corregidor Island, anything that was built before the Second World War could land there. At least anything built before 1940.

As the sun was starting to set and all the prisoners were settled down on the airfield, at approximately eight o'clock that evening, a bugler sounded attention. Looking up to the top of the rim, we saw a Japanese colonel standing on a platform completely overlooking the airfield; it had been erected on the hilltop with a couple of loudspeakers for this specific occasion. The colonel informed us, through an interpreter, what our status was at that time. Also what to expect from the Japanese while in their charge.

We were told that we were considered hostages, not prisoners of war, and we would be treated as such until General Sharp in the southern Philippines had ordered his troops to lay down their arms in token of surrender. We were also informed that we should be aware that, as hostages, we could be shot at anytime. Then he went on to tell us that, as hostages, we were not protected by the Geneva Convention. Also that General Sharp had until the twenty-sixth day of May 1942, only twenty days, to change his mind and surrender. The colonel went on to say that if General Sharp didn't surrender all of the Philippines before the twenty days had expired, we would all be shot.

He then pointed toward the machine guns spaced about ten feet apart on the ridge of the hill and along the water's edge, each being manned by a

Japanese soldier. These were the machine guns that we noticed being emplaced as we were being moved down to bottomside. We were told to take a good look and to remember that if anyone tried to escape, he would be shot. Then to prove that they meant what they said, they grabbed six soldiers near them, lined them up, and shot them in cold blood.

Then the Japanese commander said, "Take heed this will happen to each and everyone of you. We mean business. Your General Sharp had better learn fast and surrender." Then he screamed, "Remember, each and everyone of you, what you have just witnessed. You will all suffer the same fate if you try to escape and if no surrender comes from the south before the set time limit."

The shooting of those six innocent soldiers, who did nothing wrong but were just unfortunate to be close enough for the Japanese to grab, was the first baptism that we were to witness of the cruelty of the Japanese toward the boys of Corregidor. I couldn't believe what I saw. I daresay we were all in a semishocked state, with just the thought of those trigger-happy Japanese manning those machine guns. We feared that they might open fire at any moment and mow us down. That alone made us cringe and keep us in a continual state of terror.

Although they showed their colors in conducting the Death March out of Bataan, we who were on Corregidor didn't know anything about the way the troops that surrendered on Bataan were treated. It wasn't until after we arrived in the prison camp at Cabanatuan and met up with some of the survivors that we were told about that horrible nightmare that they had undergone at the hands of their captors. On hearing about the way the boys of Bataan were treated, I just said, "What more cruelty can anyone inflict upon his fellowman?"

60. Trying to Make Us Decode an Intercepted Message

While standing there, the Japanese commander was handed a sheet of paper. After reading it, he told us, with the aid of the interpreter, that the names he was about to call should report to him immediately. He then read off four names, and my name was the third on that list. When he got finished reading the names, the interpreter said, "You four men have only five minutes to come forward and report to the commander." The four of us were terror-stricken and trembling in our boots. We were searching our brain, wondering what we could expect after the barbaric act that we had just been forced to witness in the shooting in cold blood of those six innocent prisoners.

As we were making our way up the rim to report to the commander, we kept asking one another, How in the hell did they get our names? What does he want us for? What is going to happen to us? Are we going to be shot? When all four of us reported to the commander, we were shaking and trembling, and scared almost to death. The Japanese general, seeing how badly we were shaking and how fearful we were of what was to take place, told us in a very calm voice through his interpreter, to relax, he didn't intend to harm us, but that he had a mission for us to perform, and if we did it well, we would be well compensated.

We were then loaded onto a jeep and taken back up to Malinta tunnel. Upon our arrival, we were taken to the lateral that had housed General Wainwright's office. We were shown the encoding and decoding machine that was captured from the army, which was useless to them because they couldn't get anyone to show them how to use it. As soon as we were shown the machine, I got the drift. It was then I realized that they had gotten our names through their intelligence operators, because they knew that we four had been schooled in the operation of this machine and therefore were the only ones who knew how to encode and decode messages on this type of machine.

To our surprise upon looking over the encoding and decoding machine, we found that the army had left it intact. It was then that we learned that the army had been caught with their pants down when the Japanese arrived. They were still sending and receiving messages from the States. The Japanese instructed us to decode some messages they had intercepted from the United States forces. We spent some time in trying to explain to the Japanese officer in command that it was absolutely impossible for anyone to decode or encode messages with that machine unless they had the decoding and encoding procedure for the particular date on which those messages were drafted and sent out over the air.

However, the Japanese officers would not believe us. We kept protesting vehemently, telling them that it was utterly an impossibility for anyone to decipher those messages without knowing the code of the day on which they were composed. This went on for several hours, but they just wouldn't believe us, and we couldn't get through to them that we were telling the truth. Since the hour was late, approximately 10:00 P.M., we were told they would wait until morning. The commander said that after we had a good night's rest, maybe we would be able to remember. *Rest!* That was the word we wanted to hear, after being up for over three days with hardly any food or sleep.

We were taken to the dining room, where they had dinner already prepared for us, which consisted of steaks and all the trimmings of a good meal, and wine saki. After we had finished eating, they gave us cigars and cigarettes and other goodies to put in our pockets. We were then taken to Queens tunnel. They made sure we were bedded down comfortably for the night. The next morning, we were awakened very early and allowed to take a shower. After we were cleaned up, we were escorted to the kitchen, and we sat down to an outstanding breakfast, the likes of which I hadn't seen in many months. After breakfast, we were taken back to Malinta tunnel to the room with the encoding and decoding machine and given two intercepted messages and told to decode them.

We still insisted that it was an impossibility, that we could not do as they wanted us to do and explained again the reason why. For several minutes they kept trying to make us decode the messages and we kept on telling them we didn't know how. They just stood there and looked at us for several minutes, probably thinking that kindness wasn't working, and they were not getting anywhere with us. Because all of a sudden they made a 180-degree turn and really started to get rough with us, slapping and beating us, but to no avail, They found this didn't work. After about an hour or so of their beating and yelling, and screaming at us, the officer in charge finally said, "All right, we do it differently."

So they separated us and worked on us one man at a time. I figured they were thinking we were holding out and, in this way, they could break us down. I guess they finally got the message, because after two days of beating on us, they finally gave up. We were kicked and beaten for approximately two days, and had no food or water. One bastard kicked me in the mouth and knocked out three of my upper front teeth. I was bleeding badly but that didn't mean anything to them. The other fellows fared about the same as I did.

We finally had them convinced that our codes were changed every twenty-four hours and sometimes sooner, that the United States had enough code changes to last many years. If one didn't know the code that was used for that particular day, it was impossible for anyone to use those machines. We were ordered returned down to the airfield to await what was in store for us. Luckily, we had a few cans of chow stashed away down there, because we were half-starved.

61. General Sharp Surrenders

Status Changed to POW

On 10 May 1942 the officers who carried General Wainwright's hand-written messages to General Sharp arrived in Cebu and delivered the papers to him. The staff officers' hand-carried the messages was to assure him that General Wainwright did indeed write those messages without being under duress of any sort and that General Wainwright's fervent prayer was for the well being of his troops, who had fought gallantly. They deserved nothing but the best.

He told General Sharp in those messages that he was pleading for the safety of his heroic troops, who were now being held hostage on Corregidor, and for those who had survived the Death March out of Bataan, and could be shot at any given moment. General Wainwright's messages said, in part, to General Sharp, "These brave boys deserve more than being put in such a helpless manner. They do not deserve to be just mowed down with machine guns at the hands of their captors. Their lives are now placed in your hands. You and only you, can save them from being slaughtered, as surely they shall be if you do not surrender in the time frame provided."

After reading General Wainwright's messages and seeing the look of sincerity on the faces of the staff officers themselves. General Sharp was convinced that General Wainwright was not under duress by the Japanese in ordering him to surrender the troops under his command in the southern Philippines. General Sharp, in reading these letters, understood that it was General Wainwright's own personal plea to save the approximately 60,000 brave and heroic troops who fought until they could no longer stand on their feet. The 60,000 troops included those who had survived the Death March out of Bataan and were imprisoned at Camp O'Donnell. They, too, were being treated as hostages, and he feared for their lives as well.

General William Sharp was doing a magnificent job on the enemy down in Mindanao and the outlying islands in keeping the Japanese off guard. So he really didn't need to surrender. His troops were faring well, living off the fruits of the land. General Sharp pondered over the messages from General Wainwright along with what he had been told, giving the matter his gravest consideration for quite some time. He was further armed with the knowledge he had of the history of the treatment of other hostages taken by our Japanese captors. Knowing how they had treated the boys from Bataan on the Death March, he knew that *life* meant nothing to those Japanese who were in charge and that the prisoners could be annihilated at any moment. He was well aware that they did not adhere to or have any regard for the rules of the Geneva Convention, of which they were a signer.

So General Sharp decided that the 60,000 or so Americans now being held on Corregidor and those from Bataan who were dying like flies at Camp O'Donnell, all classified as hostages, must be saved. General Sharp also figured that the lives of these noble men and comrades being held as hostages accounted for much, much more than the damage he could inflict militarily on the enemy in his position. So by having this keen knowledge of their attitude toward the lives of those they held as hostages, in order to save the lives of the troops up north, who in his heart he knew would be slaughtered he had to lay down his arms in surrender. In fact I am not sure that they would have loved to have him hold out just for the chance to mow us all down.

General Sharp went into seclusion for quite some time, and after weighing all of the above, he decided to surrender, and he notified all units under his command to lay down their arms. General Sharp immediately notified General Wainwright of his actions via the Japanese high command of the Philippine Islands in Manila. Again the good Lord answered our prayers, because on the eighth of May 1941 at 6:00 A.M. General William Sharp, with much sadness in his heart, ordered all the commanders and their troops who were scattered helter-skelter in Mindanao and in the southern islands of the Philippines under his command to lay down their arms and surrender.

Prior to General Sharp's order to his troops to lay down their arms, he encouraged anyone who knew the terrain and had the talents of guerrilla warfare and wanted to take on the precarious status of spying as guerrillas in the jungles, rather than surrender, were free to do so. Knowing that many men up north, went into the hills when Bataan fell, quite a few under General Sharp decided to do the same. They proved themselves a great help in guerrilla warfare. In a short time, the guerrillas from up north in the mountains of Luzon linked up with the guerrillas in the Mindanao mountains down from the south. They were able to communicate by runners, as well as with radios, and thus were a great help in keeping the enemy off balance in all parts of the Philippines. They also provided invaluable information to the U.S. High Command in Australia and to ships at sea, via radio communications and other means that they had at their disposal.

219

The Fil-Americans who had elected to go into the hills on 9 April 1942 upon the fall of the Bataan-Mariveles province were doing a magnificent job. They kept the American submarines and our ships at sea well informed of the areas where the prisoners were interned and of the strength and whereabouts of the Japanese in the various areas. The guerrillas from the north and south succeeded in maintaining a spy network throughout the jungle area, keeping the outside world informed of what was taking place on the islands throughout the war.

They even, through a Filipino lady we called, "hip-pockets," a great gal, succeeded in securing and radioing a list of all the prisoners back to the United States who were being held in the Canbanatuan prison camps, as well as all the other places where the prisoners were interned throughout the islands. To top it off, they were a great help and saved many lives by helping MacArthur's forces in finding landing spots, where they would encounter little or no opposition upon MacArthur's return to the Philippines. Those Fil-American guerrillas were also successful in capturing many Japanese, to the extent that they had to set up prison camps for them, which they maintained all during the war.

Those Japanese prisoners were turned over to the legal authorities of the United States forces upon their return to the islands and the successful occupation of the Philippines had been completed.

As soon as General Homma received the notification of General Sharp's surrender of all the troops in Mindanao and the rest of outer islands down south under his command, he immediately issued an order changing our status from hostages to that of prisoners of war, as he promised he would do. Upon having our status changed to prisoner of war, the machine guns that the Japanese had surrounded us with on the rim of the airfield were removed. Without reprisals, we then were given our first bit of food, which we had been without for three days since being held as hostages on the airfield. A few of us were lucky that we had a few cans of rations with us, which we had passed around as far as they went during those three days.

With the removal of the machine guns from the rim of the airfield, everyone could now breathe a sigh of relief, knowing that at least one part of our nightmare was over. The Japanese meant business and surely, those Japanese would have used those guns on us if General Sharp had not surrendered. The place where we were quartered on the airfield on the water's edge turned out to be the place where the Japanese were able to come ashore and land on Corregidor the night before. The dead bodies had not been removed, and the stench was getting to the point where one could hardly breathe.

The third morning after being moved to the airfield, two Japanese army men came down and got a working party together of about one hundred men. I happened to be one of unfortunate ones. They took us up to topside and made us pick up the dead bodies, American and Japanese. Surprisingly, most of them were very young Japanese. There were very few American bodies among them. The stench in the air was unbearable. Those bodies had been lying there with the blistering hot sun beating down on them for the past three days. Not only was the stench unbearable, but it was a grotesque sight. The bodies lay in the same position in which they had fallen, and it would be hard to describe some of their positions. There were parts of bodies strewn everywhere, all burnt black from the rays of the blistering sun and bloated so badly that some of the bodies had burst open. Our captors didn't remove their own dead.

They gave some of the prisoners of war a large blade, called a bolo. The Filipinos used these bolos to cut bamboo and to make their way in the jungles. They had the prisoners going about finding the Japanese bodies and removing an arm or a leg. That was done only to the Japanese bodies. They also had them remove the dog tag from the body and tie it on the part removed for identification and toss it on a truck. I was sure glad I wasn't picked for that job of cutting off a part of the body for identification. Some of the men got so sick, they had to be removed from the area. I don't know how I stood it, but I did. Those parts from the Japanese dead were then cremated, and the dog tag was put in a can with the ashes and shipped to Japan to be given to their relatives.

The rest of us prisoners were made to round up all the body parts, regardless of whether they were American or Japanese, and place them in a heap, and when there were a hundred or so bodies, they would pour gasoline on them and set them on fire. The stench was so bad, the prisoners and the guards covered their nose and face with handkerchiefs or their undershirts, I took off my undershirt and wrapped it around my face to cover my nose and mouth. The handkerchiefs also helped to keep the flies away.

The flies were so bad, they piled themselves on one another all over the eyes and mouth of the dead. They even attacked our bodies. The Japanese wore gas masks, as the stench from the bodies lying on the ground and those being cremated was so bad, it was getting beyond endurance. Horrible was not the word, it was far beyond that. Many of the prisoners couldn't take it and got sick. The Japanese had no pity for them. They simply beat them and forced them to continue working. However, this job had to be done for fear of epidemic disease. Even now it makes me sick to think about it. I could never get over the odor of the dead bodies, let alone the stench from the burning flesh, never, as long as I live.

Part Six

The Fall of the Philippines

62. The March of Shame to Bilibid Prison

One morning about a week after General Sharp's surrender, for our break-fast, we were given a ration of rice mixed with something that I think was horse meat. About 9:30 that morning, we were told to get prepared to move out. We were made up into groups of one hundred and taken up to the storehouse tunnel, which was one of the laterals in Queens tunnel. On making our way up to the storeroom, we passed the area where the dead bodies had lain. The stench lingering in the air was still unbearable. Even though all the dead bodies had been removed and burned, the stench re-mained.

Upon our arrival at the entrance of Queens tunnel, each one of us was given a large burlap sack and told to take as much food and canned goods that we could carry from the storeroom. This surprised me. First, there wasn't much canned goods left, and second, the Japs needed the food themselves. When they were satisfied that we had all the canned goods we could carry, we were taken through Monkey Point tunnel down to the wa-terfront.

We were loaded on a large barge that was moored to the dock. Look-ing out over the waters, I could see several flat barges anchored out there. As one barge was packed, and I mean packed, with as many as it could hold, it would move away from the dock and drop anchor. Then one of the barges that had been anchored in the seaway would come in and replace it. When it was loaded with prisoners, it too would move out and drop its an-chor. This went on for a couple hours. When the last barge was loaded, we headed for Manila, which was about twenty-seven miles across the bay.

When we were close to the shore we were ordered off the boat, via bayonet, into the water. I was lucky because I could stand up in the water. It came up to about my chin. Some poor fellows who were small were com-pletely submerged under the water. I don't know if any prisoners drowned that day or not; there was no time to look back to see, because the Japanese were using their bayonets to move us along. One didn't falter, if possible, under those conditions, especially being prodded with a tip of a bayonet that without a blink of any eye would be run through your body. I just kept

225

wading, trying to get to the beach as fast as possible to get the hell out of that water and away from those bayonet-crazy Japanese. Many of the fellows were bleeding from the cuts they received from the bayonets.

When we arrived up on the road, a road named, of all names, "MacArthur Boulevard," and in a way, we were MacArthur's men. We were ordered to line up in rows twelve abreast. After about an hour or so, with everybody lined up on the street, we were ordered to start marching. We marched in the blazing hot sun, which was well over one hundred degrees with our clothes still soaking wet. However, when we first started out we welcomed the wet clothes because they helped to cool us off.

However, as we progressed toward Manila, the blazing sun bearing down on us heated the water that was left in our clothes, and it started to get unbearably hot, making things very miserable for us. Once again our Father above was watching over us, because just about that time there was a little breeze while we were still marching along the waterfront, and then it rained a little. That was a Godsend. It cooled us off. We were marching in the midafternoon, which was usually the hottest part of the day. But it still was well over one hundred degrees. They called this the "march of shame."

Our Japanese captors were in their glory as they prodded us along with their bayonets for all to see. The reason it was called the march of shame was to show the Filipino population that their Americans heroes had been defeated by the superior imperial Japanese army. The Japanese also wanted to show the Filipino population that we were not the great American protectors that they thought we were. They wanted them to see us being disgraced in their midst. To show them that we couldn't even save ourselves, how could we save them. We were all clad in our wet, filthy dirty clothes that we had slept in for the last week or two. Our faces and bodies were dirty from lack of a place to wash or take a bath. In was in this fashion that we were paraded some twenty miles down MacArthur Boulevard into the downtown streets of Manila enroute to Bilibid prison for all the Filipinos to witness.

The Japanese were especially happy to have the little children see this show of their American heroes in this disgraceful position, having been defeated by the mighty imperial Japanese army. The Japanese guards all carried a long heavy stick, and to try and make the Filipino people see that we were pure dirt under their feet, for no reason at all, they would beat those they could reach with their staff, or as they called it their walking stick. I was glad that I was in the center row and they couldn't reach me with their staff. The staff was heavy enough to kill with just one blow. They would start to beat the prisoners whenever we were passing a group of kids.

The Japanese had dumped piles of stones all along the route for the little children as well as the adults to stone us with. They kept putting stones in the hands of the children and trying to make them throw them at us. However, they refused, and instead, the little children kept putting their hands over their heads or sticking their little fingers out from behind their backs, each time making a V sign. The Japanese were furious and kept hitting the little guys unmercifully. Those bastards just laughed. It didn't bother them to hit a small child or even kill him, which in fact, they did to a few, as well as some older people who refused to throw stones at us.

"What do you think we are, barbarians?" said General Homma to General King upon his surrender. If hitting little children and even killing some is not barbaric treatment, then please tell me what you call it. However, all the beatings of the prisoners and civilians didn't stop the children or some of the older folks from making the V sign. This helped our spirits a lot, although it hurt us to see those little kids being beat up. But they just kept making the V sign, with their little fingers and made the Japanese all the more furious.

As we were being prodded along, we noticed that all the Filipinos had big smiles on their faces, which made us proud, and instead of just straggling along, it seemed we all were marching as if in a victory parade, with our heads held high. The Filipinos were all shouting "Victory Joe" or "Long live the Americano." The Japanese just didn't know how to handle this turn of events, so they started to step up their beatings on the prisoners. Seeing this, some of the Filipinos started to throw the rocks at the Japanese guards. Then the Japanese turned on the Filipinos and started all over again, hitting the women, as well as the children and men. And it still didn't stop them. They continued giving us the victory sign and shouting "Viva Americano, Viva MacArthur, he come back."

Instead of us being made out to be the beaten American slobs that the Japanese wanted to have the Filipinos think we were, it backfired, and they became the slobs, not the heroes they would have liked the Filipino population to believe. The Japanese had been telling the Filipinos that they were their friends and were only there to free them from the clutches of the American capitalistic pigs. The Japanese cry in those day was "Asia for the Asiatic!" What a laugh. The Filipinos never had it so good as they did under the United States since being made a commonwealth after having been removed from under the rule of the king of Spain, where they had been for

227

over three hundred years. The Filipino population knew this too well. However, with this march, the Filipino population were being shown the true Japanese colors.

As we got closer into the heart of Manila, the rain stopped and the sun came out. There were still a great number of people lining the streets as we passed by. They also were giving us the V sign. They were throwing bananas, fruit, rice balls, cakes, brown pony sugar, loaves of bread, and the list goes on. This infuriated the Japanese, who now started to use their bayonets on the population. Some women and small kids were bayoneted because they couldn't get away fast enough. It didn't matter to the Japanese who they killed. Again, they showed the world that life meant nothing to them. Again, how can anyone be so barbarous? General Homma asked of General King, "Do you think we are barbarians?"

Later in the day, as it was just getting dark, we arrived at the old Bilibid Prison and were marched inside in two lines. The International Red Cross was there taking moving pictures as we entered the doorway. They weren't allowed to take pictures while we were on the street, for fear of them seeing the piles of stones placed along the highway for the natives to stone us with or the Japanese beatings of the Filipinos as well as the prisoners. That would be bad publicity. The Japanese wanted to show the world how well the American prisoners were being treated and what others could expect if they would only lay down their arms in surrender.

They had piles of new clothing that the International Red Cross had brought in. There were also about twenty carcasses of uncooked caribou and about the same number of pigs. The caribou and pigs were all cleaned and hanging in a row, just as one would see in a slaughterhouse in the States. Then I noticed there were several large iron vats, like the ones I had at the Mango Inn when I was feeding the natives. They were all filled with cooked rice. Boy, did those vats of rice and uncooked pigs and caribou look good, they sure made our mouths water, we who had been half-starved the past few months.

As we filed past the Red Cross cameras, each prisoner was given several pieces of clothing and a tray with empty dishes, with the exception of one bowl filled with the cooked rice, no meat; the meat was just a show to let the world think we were being well fed. They told the International Red Cross that they would have loved to give us some of the meat, but they didn't have time to cook it for us at that time, but we were to get it later. That was a lie. They had all day to cook the meat. The meat hanging in the background as the Japanese were handing out clothing to us and dishing out the rice made a good picture for the cameras of the International Red Cross, which were clicking away. The Japanese were feeding this publicity to the world, and the International Red Cross was eating it up.

Just as soon as we entered the next room and were out of sight of the Red Cross cameras, they took the clothing and rice away from us. The rice was put back into a big kettle. We were then made to strip off all our clothes, and when naked, we were told to pick up our clothes and form six lines. There were three guards at the head of each line. They came down the line and took our clothes and searched the pockets and relieved us of any sharp instruments, such as razors, knives, can openers, etcetera that we had on our person, as well as any jewelry that the other guards missed when they searched us on Corregidor. As soon as each of us were searched, we were allowed to put our clothes back on. Did I say clothes? Well, later on, I would have been glad to call them clothes, because after a year or so in the prison camps, all that we had to cover our bodies with were rags.

The Japanese then backed up trucks to the back door and had about ten or twelve of the prisoners load the big kettles of rice and all the carcasses of the pigs and caribou into the trucks. These were sent to the various Japanese garrisons throughout the area, to be used in feeding the Japanese military personnel. In about an hour, they gave each of us a small sardine can full of just plain rice, nothing else, no meat, nothing. We were told when we were done eating (what a laugh), to get some sleep, that they were going to move us out sometime during the night. Those four or five tablespoons of plain rice was the only food that we had for the past twenty-four hours. Not much, especially after a hard day of walking in the sun. We had the canned goods that we had carried all day in burlap sacks on our shoulders, but we had no way of opening them; the Japanese had relieved us of all can openers and knives.

63. Another Long March—Cabanatuan Prison

We were awakened by being prodded via the point of a bayonet at 2.30 A.M. and ordered to line up outside in the courtyard. When we were lined up, they marched us about two miles to a railroad station. At 4:00 A.M., we were loaded, or should I say packed, into freight cars, again with bayonets to get the job done. At any rate, we were jammed into the freight cars to the point of there being hardly breathing space left. We were starting to think that the Japanese didn't know a damn thing except to prod and cut us with those damned bayonets. We all were wishing they had them jammed somewhere else, if you know what I mean. We rode that way, packed like sardines, standing up in the freight cars until about 7:00 A.M.

The guards opened the boxcar doors and told us to come out and line up by the railroad tracks, twelve abreast. It took quite a while for us to unfold in trying to emerge from the freight cars after being jammed in one position for three hours or so. The Japanese guards got a big laugh seeing us trying to get our bodies back in shape after being cramped in those box cars for so long. Surprisingly, they relaxed with their bayonet-prodding while we were trying to unfold. They mostly just stood there and laughed as we got untangled and were able to line up alongside the railroad tracks as we had been ordered to do.

We were then taken to a very large open field not far from the railroad depot. This place must have been prepared in advance for our arrival, because they already had several strands of barbed wire strung completely around the perimeter of the field we were to be caged in. As we walked inside the barbed-wire area we were dismissed, they told us to sit on the ground and *yashamay,* which we later found out meant "rest."

Consequently, eleven prisoners died from being in such a cramped position while on the train ride, brought on by being so weak, not only from the lack of food and water, but also the constant worry while we were being held on the airfield on Corregidor. Also worried and thinking whether at any moment they were going to open fire with those damn machine guns which they had trained on us. Several more men died while in the penned up area where they kept us. We were out in the open with the sun beating down and the temperature rising so high, the sun started to take its toll on the weaker among us.

While sitting there after a few minutes, one of the prisoners broke out a deck of pinochle cards, and four of us started to play cut- throat pinochle. A guard seeing us playing cards came over jibber- jabbering in Japanese and ran a bayonet through the soldier who had the cards in his hands. He made us give him the cards, then started to scream, *"kuda, kuda,"* then another one starting yelling, *"hiyaka, hiyaka,"* at us. None of us could understand what he meant. We just sat there, shaking our heads back and forth, trying to tell him we didn't understand what he wanted us to do. The guard, thinking we were saying no we wouldn't do what he wanted, proceeded to beat the rest of us with the butt of his gun.

One of the interpreters came running over and stopped him. The interpreter then explained to us that the guard wanted us to stand up, which we immediately did. Then he proceeded to tell us that we should never shake our head when a guard talks to us, especially if he is ordering us to do something. He explained that the guard doesn't understand that you don't know what he is saying, "so when you shake your head, gesturing that you don't understand him, he thinks you are saying no and are disobeying him, and so he will get mad and maybe strike you." It was also explained to us by the interpreter that the Japanese frowned on gambling. He said, "When they see you playing with cards, they think you are gambling, and they get furious." He told us to destroy any playing cards that we had in our possession to avoid any trouble in the future. One of the fellows took the cards and hid them in his duffle bag. He said he wasn't about to destroy them.

After about two hours in the fenced area, I guess it was about 9:30 A.M., four large trucks arrived on the scene, and of course, we all thought they were bringing us some breakfast. However, we were all fooled—there was no food. We all had expected the Japanese to give us some food because the last time we were given anything to eat was the little sardine can of rice at Bilibid Prison about 6:00 P.M. the night before. Several of the prisoners were dying, as this was our third day with practically no food and hardly any sleep; we were almost all dead on our feet. I started to think that as we had all that canned food with us, maybe, they thought we would eat some of it if we got hungry. However, we had no way of opening the cans.

Instead of being given food, we were ordered to line up again in lines of twelve abreast, then taken out to the road. When we were all out on the road, we started our walk to the Cabanatuan Prison Camp No. 3, which was a part of the old Filipino army training camp. I guess that was what the long delay was all about; they must have been waiting for the trucks to arrive, because as soon as they arrived, they had us on our feet, ready to march to our next destination. The four trucks took up the rear, followed us, and picked up those who passed out—weakness, the extreme heat, and the lack of nourishment, made it impossible for some to carry on. They just couldn't make it any further.

I saw several men pass out and fall to the ground, and surprisingly, the Japanese didn't run bayonets through them, as they did on the Death March the month before, out of Bataan. They simply had us load the fellows who passed out, along with their gear, on the trucks, which then carried them into camp. I was really surprised to see that they acted humanely on this march, which they called the "march of shame." I fully expected that half of us would have a bayonet run through us before we reached our destination, wherever it was. Well, glad to say it wasn't a repeat perform-

231

ance of the way they acted while taking the "fighting bastards of Bataan" to the prison camp at Camp O'Donnell, for which we thanked our Heavenly Father. Of the 70,000 or so Fil-Americans who surrendered with General King on Bataan, approximately one-third did not arrive at Camp O'Donnell. They either dropped and were left to die on the spot, or the Japanese used them for bayonet practice, which they did quite often.

We would straggle along for about ten minutes, and then the Japanese would yell, *"Yashamay,"* which we were all soon to learn meant "rest." We would stop, and they let us relax for about five minutes, this went on all day until we reached our destination, which we later found out was Cabanatuan Prison Camp No. 3. The trucks became pretty full with prisoners by the time they reached the camp. We lost only a couple more on the march. I don't know how any of us made it in that unbearable heat that day, being that we were so weak, unless it was sheer fright that kept us going. However, as weak as I was, I was able to walk all the way. My strong faith in God was the only reason I made it.

After a few miles, I spotted a lot of bamboo barracks just ahead, and I thought, *Oh, boy! This is it. I made it,* but we kept on going right past them. A little later I saw some more of those bamboo barracks ahead, and I thought this must be it, but no, they kept prodding us along past them.

However, after a couple of more miles, we finally made it. I was told later that the other two camps we passed was Cabanatuan Prison Camps, Nos. 1 and 2, and that we were in Cabanatuan Prison Camp No. 3. It was a about a twenty-five-mile or so hike from the railroad station to the Cabanatuan Prison Camp No. 3. It took, us in the condition that we were in, from about 9:30 A.M. to about 6.30 P.M., almost ten hours; they let us *yashamay* for a five-minute period about every mile or so. They didn't want to lose any more of us.

64. Made to Dig Our Own Graves

As we entered the prison gates, the Japanese separated the army personnel from the navy and marine personnel, the army prisoners going to the right and the navy and marines to the left. The three Cabanatuan prison camps were a complex of several hundred barracks situated on approximately three hundred acres (that is my guess). These were former Filipino army bases built prior to the war to house General MacArthur's newly formed Filipino army. Cabanatuan Prison Camp No. 3, the one we were in, covered an area of about one hundred acres, I would say. The prison camp was completely surrounded by two metal wire fences about fifteen feet high strung with three strains of barbed wire on top. There was a walkway of about twenty feet separating them, to be used by the Japanese guards. There were guard houses, built on stilts, overlooking the prison area all along the outer fence about every five hundred feet. There was a walkway about ten feet wide all along the inner fence, which was patrolled by the prisoners twenty-four hours a day. That was considered no-man's-land. It was absolutely forbidden for anyone to enter that walkway unless he was there on patrol. If a prisoner got caught trespassing in that area, the sentence was death by a firing squad, and they meant it, too. I witnessed several prisoners being shot on the spot for wandering onto no-man's-land. Cabanatuan prison camps consisted of three hospital barracks, but no medical supplies, for the hundred or so doctors who were in the prison camp to administer to the sick and dying. There was a food kitchen, but no food, for the cooks; storehouses, but no stores. There were also barracks, for officers and enlisted personnel. There was a large parade and maneuvering ground. They even had a rifle range. I don't know why the Filipinos had a rifle range, because they didn't have any real guns, just wooden ones to train with. Maybe it was a way to tell the Filipinos that real shooting guns would be furnished in the future. However, real guns and ammunition did indeed arrive a few days before the war started. Although the Filipino army were trained with wooden rifles, they did a helluva job on the Japanese in Bataan.

Cabanatuan Prison Camp No. 3, where I was interned along with the other 6,500 officers and men taken on Corregidor, was to be our home until we could be moved to Japan. The camp had over a hundred barracks to house the prisoners. One hundred men were assigned to each barrack. The barrack was tied together with rattan strips or Manila hemp. They were made from bamboo poles. The buildings were about sixty-five feet long and about sixteen feet wide, and about fifteen feet high. There was a four-foot dirt passageway down the middle. This allowed for a badly needed breezeway.

On each side of the passageway, there was a raised platform built of bamboo slats about one foot above the dirt. There was a second platform built about seven feet above the first platform. The roofs, with a very high pitch, were thatched with big, broad banana leaves. The top half of the sides were woven with bamboo slats, and they were tied on with rattan strips so that they could be lowered or propped open. The sides could be let down about halfway at night or completely open in the daytime the full length of the building, for fresh air to flow in. The bottom sides of the barracks were attached solid with bamboo rattan strips.

The upper and lower decks were used for sleeping quarters. They were divided into what was called bays. Each bay consisted of a ten-foot wide by seven-foot long space. There were four prisoners to a bay, which allotted each one a space seven feet long by about two and a half feet wide, and which gave each of us space to store what few belongings we possessed, which were very few indeed, mostly nothing. We had a mattress made of straw, which was about one-half-inch thick. We slept in our underwear while in the Philippines, because of the heat, and used the rest of our clothing for a pillow. In Japan, it was a different story, because it was so cold there, that even by keeping the rags on, which we called clothes, we could hardly keep warm in the fall and winter months.

A Japanese colonel was assigned as our camp commander. The next morning the first order he gave was for all of us to again strip down and lay out all that we had carried into the camp on the ground in front of us. A Japanese officer, an interpreter, and several Japanese non-commissioned officers came along and searched what little we had, but there was hardly a thing to be found, as we had been through this search just the day before at Bilibid prison.

While we were being searched outside, other guards were searching our barracks. Several fellows had decks of cards, but they hid them and the Japanese didn't find them. They came in handy later on. After the search, which we called the shakedown, had been completed we were given about thirty minutes to get dressed. Then the order was given for everyone to come as fast as possible to the old Filipino maneuvering grounds, better known as the "grinder," because this was where the troops were drilled. The grinder was located at the far end of the prison grounds. The land was flat with the exception of a little knoll about twenty-five feet long and ten feet wide on the far end; it resembled a small mesa.

When we were all assembled, we were ordered to face the mesa and to take strict heed of what we were about to witness. Again, for the second time, without warning, the Japanese guards grabbed six men nearby and took them to the top of the mesa, just as they did that first day of my capture when they grabbed the first six men they could get their hands on and shot them in cold blood just to prove a point. Each was given a shovel and told to start digging. It was a good thing the ground was soft and easy to dig. While the men were digging, the Japanese commander told us to *yashamay*

234

(rest), a word that we all started to get familiar with in a hurry and a word we all loved to hear, especially after a hard day's work—*yashamay*.

In approximately one hour and a half, when the men had completed their digging, we were ordered to stand up and were told that the camp commander had a very important message for us. We were ordered to stand at attention and to take heed in the strictest form of what we were about to see and be told. As the Japanese commander started to talk, the Japanese interpreter told us what he was saying. He said we should pay strict attention to the six Americans who had just completed digging the holes on top of the mesa. The camp commander then said, "I want you all to take note. You will be placed in groups of ten. Each man will be responsible for the others in his group. If one escapes from your group, then each one of you will suffer the same fate as your comrades who are standing before you on this hill."

The six men were then placed in front of the hole each had dug. Looking up at the holes, I saw them to be shaped like graves. They were about six feet long, two feet wide, and very deep. By now, I started to realize, but I thought it was impossible, these six men had been forced to dig their own graves? *No! No!* I said to myself, *tell me this isn't true.* But it was. In less that five minutes, it happened. I was to witness this act of extreme cruelty on the part of the Japanese.

WIth the prisoners standing at the head of the graves they had just dug, the guards gave each one a small bowl of rice to eat. In a few minutes, they were all given a cigarette, which the guards lit for them. When all the cigarettes were lit, they were blindfolded. The command was given and they were shot by a firing squad. Each man fell into the grave he had just dug. Then some of the prisoners were ordered to cover them with dirt. While that was going on, the camp commander said over a loudspeaker, "This will happen to you. Understand, I mean business. There will be no escapes made from this camp."

We were then dismissed and told to return to the barracks that we had just been assigned to. Seeing that those men who were standing nearby were always grabbed and shot when they wanted to prove a point, I learned right then and there to stand clear of them and not get too close. It didn't take me long to realize that I must never stand in front of the group, that I should always endeavor to get in the middle of the crowd if I wanted to live out this horrible nightmare. Oh, yes, one learns fast when his life is at stake.

The next morning, we were all placed in groups of ten, and our names were taken and turned over to the camp commander. We were then told that we must watch one another, because if one of our group escaped, the remaining nine would be treated as were the six men the day before. We were told, what you witnessed yesterday, let it be a warning. You are all responsible for one another. That in itself erased from our minds for the time being any thoughts of trying to escape. After hearing what we had just heard and having witnessed the shootings in cold blood the day before, I made up my mind that I was not going to do anything foolish; this guy was going home in one piece if at all possible.

However, the group that I was in got together, and we made a pact that we would all go together if the opportunity came our way. If we found an opening, we would take it, but that none of us would jeopardize the lives of any of his buddies. It was all or none. We kept a sharp lookout for an opportunity, but none ever came; we were too closely guarded.

We were free to roam about the camp ground and visit one another. Some men took their mess kits and etched designs on them. Several made wristbands from their canteens and etched their name, service number, home address, and other things on them. I made a wristband out of my mess plate, and I still have it to this day. How I ever kept it during all those shakedowns in the Philippines and while in Japan, I'll never know.

65. Farmer Jones and I Ordered to Start a Farm

The next day, all the prisoners were handed a questionnaire and told they must be filled out immediately and turned in by noon that day. Well, after the usual questions, as to name rank or rate, home address, etcetera, the next question was "What was your occupation in civilian life?" Well this was one time I wasn't going to be called a dumb Polack. I wrote down that I was a farmer, with only one thought in mind, food, food, and more food. Yes, sir, I wrote down "farmer" because I wanted to be on a farm if they had one. I wasn't going to starve if I could help it. I figured I could get a little extra to eat while working on a farm. The rest of the questionnaire dealt with what part of the United States did you live in. What did your parents do for a living, and all about your health prior to becoming a prisoner, and so on.

In a couple of days, I and an army sergeant, Jones, were called over to the Japanese headquarters. We were told that as we were farmers in America, we would be placed in charge of operating a farm to feed the prisoners. We were told that we would be placed in charge of the work force on the farm. I was to handle the navy and marines and my sidekick, Jones, was to handle the army. They then took us in a jeep to a large area consisting of about fifteen hundred acres, adjacent to the prison camp to the north. The camp commander told us through the interpreter, "Here is the land for farm." It was sandy soil and full of tall grass and weeds. "What do you think?"

I told him it wasn't a bad piece of land, but that it would take some doing to clear it and get it ready for planting. But with the proper tools, we could do it. He assured us that he would give us all the tools required to enable us to raise enough food to feed the prisoners. While we were being driven around the tract of land, I noticed a running stream of water running along the perimeter of the farm on the west side, which was the far backside of the land that was being proposed for the farm. We were finally taken back to camp and were given three days to have a detailed plan of what we proposed to do and bring it to the camp commander's headquarters.

Well, Sergeant Jones and I put our heads together and decided how best to work the ground with as little effort as possible, and what tools would be needed, along with plenty of seed and water to accomplish what the Japanese had in mind for us to do. On the third day, Sergeant Jones and I went over to the camp commander's headquarters and told him what we had planned and gave him a list of equipment and seeds that would be needed to do the job. We told him that we would also need a few tractors to work the ground. When I mentioned the word "tractor," that was it. I never saw a Japanese get so mad in so short a time than the camp commander upon the mention of the word "tractor." He flew into a rage and screamed right in my face. "You work by hand. No tractors. Prisoners work ground. Better for them than just laying around."

Two days later, a large truck appeared, loaded with the tools we had requested. The truck pulled into the southern gate of the farm area. Sergeant Jones and I and about twenty other prisoners were called out where the truck was, and we were directed to unload it. The truck carried several thousand shovels, hoes, rakes, and bags of seed. There was also a large metal prefabricated shed. We got a group of army engineers to put the building together. When the building was completed, it was a twenty-by forty-foot building with large sliding doors. We put all the tools and seed in there out of the sun and also away from field mice and other varmints that might come around. This was all accomplished in five days.

The camp commander then told Jones and me to get the land ready for planting. We were told to have a working party ready by seven each morning and that we could stop work in the heat of the day, about two in the afternoon. We told the Japanese that we needed about four thousand workers for the first day, which they gave us. Each day, it changed in accordance with what kind of work had to be performed. Jones and I were soon given nicknames by our fellow prisoners as follows: My sidekick, the sergeant, was "Farmer Jones." I was plain "Ski," although some of the fellows called me "Farmer Ski." I didn't mind it a bit, as long as we had our minds occupied rather than sitting around and worrying about what was going to happen to us. And we had the exercise, and it was great knowing that we were going to raise food to feed ourselves.

Every night, we would notify the camp commander how many workers were required for the working party the next day. As the workers came out of the gate each morning, they were put in groups of twenty. The highest ranking person in each group was made the boss of that group. We told him what we wanted his group to do, and he, in turn, took them over to get the tools for the job they had been told to do, after which, they proceeded out to the farm land and commenced work.

At first, there was a lot of dissension in the groups because the colonels and other officers didn't like taking orders from Jones and me, saying they outranked us. Well, it was true, the army colonels did outrank us, but I explained to them that they all had a chance for the job, also that rank went out the window when we became POWs of the Japanese. I also told them to quit bitching, that it was a darn sight better to raise food to feed ourselves than to just sit all day in the camp going crazy worrying or starving to death. Also, that we all needed the exercise.

After a few days, most of the dissension faded away. Within a week or so, it was completely gone, and we started working the ground together. Lucky for us the ground was sandy and it wasn't in such bad shape. After the weeds were eradicated by hoeing and raking the ground, the work became easy. In about two weeks, we had the ground in perfect shape, ready for planting. We had the men pile up the dirt in beds about eight inches high, each bed fifty feet long by about four feet wide. When the seed beds were all made and ready for planting, I informed the camp commander that we were ready to plant, but that it would be senseless to plant seeds without water. I explained to him that the closest water that could be found was the running creek on the west side of the farm. He told me to just *yashamay* until I heard from him.

66. The Hassle to Get Water to the Farm

While I was waiting to be called by the camp commander, I got a couple of U.S. army engineers from the prison camp to draw up plans that would enable us to pipe water right to the seed beds. When the plans were completed, I took them over and showed them to the Japanese camp commander. I told him that we would need several thousand feet of two- or three-inch pipe and a ten- to twenty-horsepower pump, and as soon as we got the pump set up, we could start planting immediately. Upon the mentioning of the word "pump," the camp commander jumped to his feet and again became as furious as before when I mentioned the word "tractor." He started to yell and scream loud in a high-pitched voice.

The interpreter explained to me that he was saying, "There will be no pump or pipe. Prisoners carry water, it will be much better for the prisoners to carry the water to keep healthy." I tried to explain as best that I could that the creek was too far away to keep the plants watered properly in that sandy soil, and that there was no way he could expect us to grow any produce without plenty of water. The Japanese commander said that will be taken care of, you shall have plenty of water. So I returned to my barracks and waited, thinking I had won and was going to get the pump and pipe that was required.

In a couple days, a big truckload of five-gallon, square aluminum coffee cans arrived in the prison camp to be used to carry water to the seed beds that we had prepared. After figuring out what the hell the cans were for, I sent my sidekick, "Farmer Jones," over to the camp commander's office to explain that we were in need of several hundred feet of one-inch doweling material, several boxes of two by one-eighth-inch big head screws with washers and several hundred feet of heavy cord. The prisoners could then carry water in the coffee cans, which had just been delivered to us for that purpose. When the sergeant came back, he told me that the camp commander sort of smiled at him and said that he would order the material immediately. I guess the commander thought he had won out on that one, and that we were going to get along without the pump.

While we were waiting for the doweling material and heavy cord to arrive, I was able to round up several carpenters from the army section of

239

the prison camp to aid me in getting the cans ready. I told them that the camp commander was securing doweling and cord and that I needed them to make handles and a harness to carry the cans with. So they went to work getting the five-gallon aluminum coffee cans ready so they could put the doweling spacer and cord on them as soon as the material we ordered had arrived.

The doweling and cord arrived in camp two days later. The carpenters were all set up and immediately started to make the handles. They sawed the doweling in lengths to fit inside the top of the cans and secured them by using the large screws. Then they cut the cord and fastened each end to the doweling. The cord made a shoulder harness, making it much easier for the prisoners to carry the water, that is, by using their shoulders and backs, instead of their arms to carry that heavy water.

Seeing that we were about to have water on its way to the seed beds, we immediately started to plant the seed beds with pumpkins, sweet potatoes, okra, corn, tomatoes, cantaloupe, and beans. As soon as the beds were all seeded and the carrying harness for the water cans was completed, the guards brought out three thousand prisoners for the water detail. Each prisoner was given two cans with the shoulder harness attached. They were taken under guard down to the river. Upon reaching the river they filled their cans almost full and immediately the guards headed them to the seed beds to where the water was needed.

All this was done in a straight line. It was just one continuous circle, about two miles round. The watering was done at night, after the heat of the day. This job entailed the usage of three and sometimes four thousand prisoners. Just imagine several thousand men with a pole across their backs, with two five-gallon cans of water suspended from it, on a moonlit night, walking in a huge circle on top of a ridge that was over a mile long. It looked in silhouette like one would see on film in a motion picture theater.

The prisoners would spill the water on purpose as they walked on the ridge, for two reasons. First, it made their load much lighter, and second, when they arrived where the water was needed on the seed beds, the cans were just about half full, so there was less water for the beds. The prisoners would wait until the Japanese guard was not looking or was not around, then dumped most of the water in the walkways or on places other than on the seed beds. That was done in order to keep the plants from growing from lack of water and to make the camp commander give in and pump the water rather than having the prisoners carry it. Also it would enable them to get more sleep at night instead of being out there working. Especially so for those who worked in the blistering hot sun half the day, and at night would find themselves on the watering detail.

Well, after about a week, it paid off. The Japanese guards were convinced that we couldn't keep enough water on the plants. Farmer Jones and I notified the camp commander that the plants that had come up were wilting and dying in the blistering hot sun, that we couldn't carry water fast enough to keep the other seeds wet and get them to grow. After listening to us, the camp commander finally gave in. He furnished us the pump and pipe that we had requested at the start of the project.

The engineers didn't allow any grass to grow under their feet in building a water line to pump the water wherever it was needed. So within a few days, we had the plants watered. What a relief to the prisoners, not having to carry water. They could now get a good night's sleep, which they badly needed, after working in the hot sun on the farm all day. With all the water reaching the plants, they took off like a shot out of hell, and in no time started to produce a good crop.

This made the camp commander very happy. He would come out to the farm every day to watched the vines and plants as they started to produce. It made him so happy that he gave us a Red Cross parcel, one for every six men. He also gave us the mail that had arrived for us from home, which he had been holding out.

67. Japanese Take All the Harvest

Bring POWs from Camp O'Donnell

When we got ready to harvest the crop, we had mountains of food, but the Japanese took all the tomatoes, sweet potatoes, pumpkins, corn, okra, string beans, in fact, everything that was eatable. They took the produce by the truckloads out of the camp and shipped them to their army posts throughout the Philippines. The prisoners received only the sweet potato vines, to make soup with. Even though we were half-starved, most of us couldn't eat the soup, it was so bitter.

When the prisoners saw that the crops they had worked so hard to grow, hoeing and watering out there in the blistering sun were being taken to feed the Japanese armed forces, they rebelled. They had been told when they started the farm that the produce was for their own use. They immediately started to sabotage the rest of the crops on the farm. The pump kept breaking down, the pipes kept springing leaks, etcetera, causing the plants to die from lack of water.

The camp commander knowing that the prisoners were sabotaging the rest of the crops in the field, issued orders to leave some of the crops in the camp, but the guards left very little. With the knowledge that we were working to feed the Japanese army, we quit. Oh, they tried to force us, but that didn't work either. Once bitten, twice shy was our attitude. The guards would beat the prisoners but to no avail. They had decided they weren't going to work in that blistering sun to feed the Japanese army.

They killed a few men in trying to force them to work, but they knew they couldn't kill us all, as they needed man power in Japan to make up for the loss of their able-bodied men who were out of their country fighting a war. The Japanese guards knocked Jones, my sidekick, and me around a bit, and issued some harsh, threatening words to the rest of the prisoners, but it didn't work. We were not about to slave in the hot sun to raise food for the Japanese army. We all had enough, so the farm went kaput.

By now, the fifty some-odd thousand "battling bastards of Bataan" who had made it to Camp O'Donnell upon the surrender, in accordance with the orders of their beloved General King, had now dwindled down to less than half, by way of bayoneting, torture, and shootings at the hands of the Japanese. Then starvation and disease: malaria, beriberi, scurvy, dengue fever, diphtheria, tuberculosis, and elephantiasis also took their toll. In addition, the prisoners were not only being beaten and starved, the Japanese decimated them in ceremonial executions by taking every fifth man. One never knew when he would be breathing his last breath while he was a prisoner under the barbaric treatment of his captor.

General Tojo, serving as prime minister and the head of the Japanese high command in Tokyo, was made aware that there were hundreds and hundreds of the American prisoners of war at Camp O'Donnell in the Philippines succumbing needlessly to death at the rapid rate of 250 to 300 or more a day. General Tojo knew that Japan proper needed men to work their factories and shipyards, and so, to this end, he didn't dare let them all die, or he might lose his own head. He immediately held a conference with the high command to inform them of what was happening, and that he had decided to transfer all Caucasians to the Cabanatuan Prison Camp No. 3 to which they all agreed.

Most of the survivors that were still alive from the Death March were Filipinos. There were only about 4,500 Americans still holding on to dear

242

life in Camp O'Donnell. General Tojo, after getting approval from the emperor, immediately issued an order to relocate all the Caucasian prisoners from Camp O'Donnell to the Cabanatuan Prison Camp No. 3, the camp that I was imprisoned in. The transfer took place on the tenth of June 1942, approximately seventy days after the fall of Bataan. The American prisoners of war were moved into our camp, and the Filipinos were mostly turned loose by the Japanese. I never was able to find out what really happened to them.

There were several reasons that prompted General Tojo to close down Camp O'Donnell: First, we, who surrendered with General Wainwright on Corregidor Island were faring quite a bit better in the death rate column than those who surrendered on Bataan. This was mostly because we came under the Japanese wing about a month later, the shame and torture of the Death March forced on those brave boys of Bataan were still fresh in their minds. So we were treated much better on our marches; second, the boys from Bataan had gone many days without food or water on their Death March, and prior to their surrender, they were almost starved from lack of any help from the United States, in the way of food or medicines; third, the boys from Corregidor were allowed to carry as much canned goods that one could carry upon leaving the island, whereas the boys on Bataan went away with nothing; fourth, because the boys from Corregidor had such outstanding men, like Teddy Brownell, a first-class yeoman in the United States Navy, who mustered several of his gang together and got them to carry all the medical supplies they could carry instead of taking food. Teddy told them to let the rest of the prisoners take the food, that they should take the medical supplies, which they did.

A lot of us owe our lives to Teddy and his gang. The survivors of Bataan at Camp Adenyl were without any medical attention whatsoever. There was no one there to comfort them, not even one doctor or a minister, priest, or rabbi. They were alone. Whereas, we from Corregidor had a large medical corps; we didn't have much medical supplies, however, they kept our courage up by talking to us and trying to keep our minds on other things. I must say it worked, too. We also had several of the clergy of all dominations; consequently, the daily losses of our group from Corregidor were at the rate of about fifty to seventy-five a day, which was quite less than the losses at Camp O'Donnell, where the death rate had grown to over three hundred a day.

The Japanese immediately moved the forty-five hundred American prisoners from Camp O'Donnell into our camp, all of whom were sick, and heavy with diseases, and intestinal parasites; every one of them was suffering from some kind of a disease. The medical corps had used up all the medicines Teddy and his boys had smuggled into the camp by the time the Battling Bastards of Bataan had been transferred from O'Donnell. The only medicine we had in the camp when they arrived was quinine and salversand plus a small amount of aspirin and some good doctorly advice. Within three months after the boys from Camp O'Donnell were moved into our camp, the diseases they brought with them spread through our ranks, making our death rate to climb rapidly.

With the boys from Bataan getting healing and counseling from the clergy and doctors, their death rate started to fall while the death rate of those from Corregidor started to rise due to the many diseases brought in by the boys of Bataan. So the death rate now was at about two hundred and fifty a day. However, it was dropping slowly. The doctors in the prison camp begged and begged for medicines to stop the flow of bodies being taken to the water hole for burial, but their pleas fell on deaf ears. Their pleas were flatly refused by our captors.

However, we had some very fine doctors, who worked wonders and saved a lot of lives by just using their skills, instead of medicines, they started to work on our minds, and good, sound medical advice, thereby keeping our hopes up and turning our minds to other things. We had quite a few chaplains in camp, and they were a great help in giving spiritual advice and counseling, along with holding church services.

Each day, the Japanese guards would go over to the death house and feel the pulse of each man, so weak he couldn't get up. If they couldn't feel a pulse, they would order the bodies stripped of their clothing which was mostly rags by this time. They would then order them dumped in a big crater made by a Japanese bomb when they were bombing in that area at the outbreak of the war. The hole was full of water during the rainy season.

We were forced to keep pushing the naked bodies under the water, with big bamboo poles, until they stayed down, which took hours sometimes. We would hold one body under the dirty water for several minutes, and before we could get to another one, the other would bounce to the top again. The Japanese would continue to beat on us and keep screaming and yelling in Japanese, which we couldn't understand anyway. I guess they were furious because we couldn't keep the bodies under the water.

However, they didn't use their bayonets on us at this time, because they were ordered to save lives, not kill anymore. The emperor had issued orders to ship all able-bodied prisoners to the homeland to work in the shipyards and elsewhere. One fellow, L. B. Barricklo, a chief commissary steward, U.S. Navy, from Stockton, California, was pulled out of the water three different times in the course of one month; once he twitched his eye; another time, his fingers moved; the third time, his head shook just a tiny bit, but enough to be noticed. His naked body was dragged out of the water, and he survived and returned home with the rest of us surviving prisoners. The last time I saw him was about twenty-five years ago in Lakeport, California. He was still going strong.

One must stop to wonder, how many other good men were drowned, cremated, or buried alive. The epitaph for those men buried in those bomb holes should read "Drowned or Buried Alive," or words to that effect. To my knowledge, there were a few thousand brave men buried in those water holes. How many would still be alive to return home to their loved ones if they had been properly checked by the American doctors, instead of having been thrown in the water hole and held under until they stayed down? It's a horrible thought.

To make matters worse there were over a hundred American medical doctors in the prison camp; however, the Japanese, for some reason or other, would not allow an American medical doctor to examine the bodies to see if they were actually dead before they were taken out to the water hole. That, we could never understand.

68. General Doolittle's Raid on Tokyo

Following is a brief history of the daring raid on Tokyo by Colonel Doolittle and his very courageous men. Jimmy was later promoted to the rank of brigadier general in the United States Air Force. Early in 1942, hardly had the war begun, when Admiral Ernest J. King, chief of naval operations, with his operations officer, decided that the citizens of the United States needed a shot in the arm after all the catastrophes that they and the Allied nations had witnessed in the past few months. So they decided to lift the morale of the Allies and the citizenry of the United States by giving them the shot in the arm, and also give Japan some of their own medicine by putting a group of our planes over Japan in a sneak attack on Tokyo. This would break the morale of the Japanese population by showing them they were vulnerable to attack anytime America desired.

They called in General H. H. (Hap) Arnold, who was the commanding general of the United States Army Air Force, and told him about their plans. General Arnold thought it was a good idea and agreed that they go ahead with their venture. It was decided immediately to get the ball rolling to send a task force with sixteen B-25 Mitchells within striking distance of Japan and bomb Tokyo in a sneak attack, in the same fashion the Japanese did on 7 December 1941 on Pearl Harbor.

A select few of the higher ranking army officers were told about the plan, and after receiving General Hap Arnold's blessing to go full steam ahead, the plan was put into effect. A very courageous army officer, Colonel James (Jimmy) A. Doolittle immediately volunteered to head such a group. Jimmy's offer was accepted, and he was immediately named as commanding officer and was assigned the duties of getting such a group together for this daring attempt. The task force was to be known as Task Force Sixteen.

In view that the raid must be made from ships several hundred miles from the mainland off Japan, the question of fuel had to be focused on. Fearing that the planes would not be able to carry enough fuel to fly to Tokyo and return to their ships, arrangements were made with General Chiang Kai-shek for the bombers to land on Chinese territory after they had completed their mission over Tokyo. This was an extremely dangerous undertaking not only in regard to fuel, but because it also had to be done from a distance very far out to sea. Then there was the matter of the Japanese patrol boats and search planes operating continuously in the same area from which they must launch their planes.

The job had to be done under the strictest secrecy so that Tokyo would not be alerted. However, with all the risks involved, Colonel Jimmy Doolittle mustered some 200 officers and men under his command, who eagerly accepted, whatever their fate, to get this job done. They amassed sixteen B-25 Mitchells and took them to the U.S. Army Air Base at Elgin Field in Florida for a month's training in practice take-off and landings on a strip of land marked on the airfield that resembled the flight deck of a navy aircraft carrier. Upon completion of their training in Florida, the planes were outfitted with special gear needed for such a venture.

When the outfitting was completed, they were flown to San Francisco, where they were put aboard the U.S.S. *Hornet,* commanded by Captain Marc A. Mitscher, U.S. Navy. On 2 April 1942, the *Hornet* met up with the rest of Task Force Sixteen, with Admiral Halsey on board the U.S.S. *Enterprise,* which served as his flagship. The balance of the task force consisted of two cruisers, the U.S.S. *Nashville* and the U.S.S. *Vincennes,* four destroyers and a naval fleet oiler.

When they were all on station, Admiral Halsey gave the order to immediately get underway for their destination, with the U.S.S. *Enterprise* providing air cover. The ocean was very rough, but Task Force Sixteen kept plowing on in those heavy seas, with every man eager to get this job done and give the Japanese a taste of the U.S. Army air power on their own territory. The task force had to travel some 700 miles out to sea from Tokyo, considerably farther than anticipated. This was done in order to not be detected by the Japanese patrol boats operating in the area where it had been originally planned to start their maneuvers.

On 18 April 1942, the U.S.S. *Hornet,* from which Colonel Doolittle was to make his daring attempt to bomb various spots in Japan, was spotted by a Japanese picket boat, which was immediately sunk by gunfire from the U.S.S. *Nashville.* Vice Admiral Bill Halsey, upon being notified about the picket boat, fearing that Tokyo had been alerted, although the picket boat had been sunk, lost no time in deciding that rather then scrub the planned attack on Japan, to go ahead immediately with the daring attempt. With this turn of events, Admiral Halsey found that his fleet of ships were approximately 150 miles farther away from the targets than had been planned. Since they were a much greater distance out to sea than had been originally planned, Admiral Halsey left it up to Colonel Doolittle to make his own decision.

Colonel Doolittle's men were all worked up, and their morale was at its highest pitch. So the colonel elected to have his fleet of sixteen B-25 Mitchells and his own plane launched as soon as possible, before Tokyo knew what it was all about. So very early on 18 of April 1942 on a windy and stormy day, the planes were launched on their long-awaited mission with the blessing of Admiral Halsey, commander of Task Force Sixteen.

When they got to a prearranged position out at sea, just off the coast of Japan, the planes broke position, as planned. Each plane flew individually, on their own. They crossed into Japan at sixteen different points, covering a stretch of more than 200 miles of coastline. It certainly did take the enemy by surprise. Thirteen planes did a job on Tokyo, while the other three flew on to blast targets in the Osaka, Kobe, and Nagoya areas. Ironically, the Japanese high command was conducting a mock air attack on the same day that Doolittle's planes arrived, which made it much easier for them to carry out their mission without being detected.

The American fliers successfully completed their job in bombing the targets that had been assigned to them. They were all able to fly away from Japan proper without being spotted and without any mishaps. But, sad to say, after the planned attack was successfully completed, they were not able to arrive at their prearranged destination as originally planned. The original plan was that upon completion of the raid, they were to fly to China in accordance with a set arrangement made with General Chiang Kai-shek, for them to land on Chinese soil. However, they had a fuel problem, having been forced to launch about 150 miles or so farther away from their targets than had been planned.

Upon completion of their mission, with their fuel running low, some of the B-25s crashed in the ocean. However, the majority of the eighty-five men made it to the Chinese mainland. Some were forced to bail out of their planes over the Chinese province of Chekiang, and they made it on foot into Chungking. Some of the planes landed on Russian soil. Russia had not entered the war with Japan and was, therefore, neutral, so the American crewmen were held by the Russians as prisoners. The Japanese got their hands on eight of Jimmy's daring fliers. They were plucked out of the ocean when they crash-landed. In all, only eleven of the original eighty-five who started out were unaccounted for. It was assumed that some of the fliers who landed in the ocean lost their lives by drowning due to the rough seas.

69. "No Work—No Food" Order Placed in Effect

Twenty-eight April 1942, the imperial headquarters wanted to make an example of the prisoners captured at sea from the Doolittle raid by publicly executing them in the town square in Tokyo. However, General Shigenori Tojo, the prime minister at the time, considered it to be barbaric treatment and would have no part of it. In order to have his will in this matter, he must first satisfy the imperial headquarters by offering a reprisal that would satisfy Emperor Hirohito. He came up with the idea of "no work—no food" for the prisoners. This represented a great change in the treatment of the prisoners of war.

Prime Minister General Shigenori Tojo, knowing the need of manpower in Japan in the work force, due to all of Japan's able-bodied men having been called off to war, told the emperor that all able- bodied prisoners should be made to earn their keep. He explained that this was the Japanese motto and order of the day for the Japanese population, so why not put the prisoners of war in the same category of "no work—no food." If the emperor would sanction this, everyone under Japanese jurisdiction, including prisoners of war, would be forced to work, whether sick or not, in order to receive a ration of food for that day.

The emperor agreed with the general. However, Japanese Lieutenant General Uemura Seitaro, who was the chief in charge of the prisoners of war, vehemently objected, arguing that it was strictly against the rules of the Geneva Convention, of which Japan was a signer, which stated in part that: (1) A prisoner of war should not be required to perform any labor other than for their own good health and well being. (2) They should not be required to perform any labor that would aid their captors. (3) They should also be paid a decent wage for any work done on the outside of their camp.

That was a big laugh. What pay? We were required to work in shipyards and elsewhere, which was not for our own good health or well being. All our work was for the benefit of the Japanese war effort. We were building ships and mining copper ore, and so forth, for which we were not only not paid any *decent* wage, *we were not paid any wage at all,* which the Geneva Convention calls for and which Japan was a signer.

General Seitaro, noting that not only were we working to benefit the Japanese on their shipyard and further, not being duly compensated, we were also being beaten and excessively tortured, again objected very strongly. He cited that his objections were that it conflicted with the Geneva Convention agreement as stated above. He again said that "no prisoner of war should be made to work unless it was for his own good, and not for the good of his captors." General Seitaro's objections were turned down by General Tojo. After quite a conflict of words among the warlords, General Tojo once more got his way, and after receiving the blessing of the emperor, the "no work—no food" plan was adopted and placed into effect immediately.

Now that Emperor Hirohito approved Tojo's decision, Japan immediately informed the world that they did not honor the Geneva Convention any longer in regard to the working of the prisoners, but they still would respect the humanitarian rights of all prisoners. (This makes me laugh even today as I write.)

What "humanitarian rights" was he talking about. There was no medicine, no hospitalization of prisoners. If one got sick, he worked until he dropped, without the benefit of medical care or hospitalization of any sort. The rest of my fellow prisoners were forced to work under the threat of a bayonet pointed at us in the shipyards, in the copper mines, or unloading ships on the docks, and so on. Most of the time we were forced to perform this work without food and with very little or no rest for weeks at a

249

time. Many prisoners dropped on the spot while working at forced labor, due to their weakness from the lack of nourishment, medical care, or adequate rest.

The Japanese-American citizens who were interned in California under the Americans, on the other hand, fared differently, immeasurably better. They were given good food and medical attention, and they were not required to perform any work whatsoever while being held throughout the war; and yet each of them was ultimately paid $20,000, for doing nothing. Where was our decent wage they talked about? What compensation did either the Japanese or, for that matter, America give the American prisoners held by Japan? Nothing.

We, to this day, some fifty years later, who were required to perform slave labor at the point of a bayonet haven't received a penny for our labor in the shipyards or in the mines. What an insult to us who really suffered as prisoners of war. Just having to aid the enemy in their war effort was cruelty enough in itself.

General Tojo's concept of "No work—No food" having the approval of the emperor, was placed in effect immediately. General Tojo issued an order to provide food and medical supplies to the prisoners in Cabanatuan so that we could regain our strength and be made fit for work in Japan, in their shipyards, and wherever we could be used to aid their war effort. In accordance with his order, the prisoners of war were given several loads of rice and the bones, heads, and feet from the caribou which they slaughtered for their troops to make soup. To the doctors, they gave quinine tablets and a token supply of a few other medicines: salvosand, mercury, aspirin, and some others. The food or medical supplies were not what General Tojo had ordered, but whatever we got was welcome.

Although it was just a drop in the bucket, what we did get helped to save some lives, which in turn made our death rate fall off considerably. They also allowed the doctors to have sick call each day, to treat the sick and afflicted. Most of the time, the doctor could only give advice, as there were no medicines for many of the diseases and illnesses that the prisoners suffered from. With General Tojo's decision, the approximate 6,000 prisoners still alive in Cabanatuan out of the approximately 20,000 Americans who had surrendered on Bataan or Corregidor in the northern part of the Philippines started to grow stronger. The rest had died from the beatings, bayonet practice, and the many diseases already mentioned, but mostly from starvation.

70. Getting Examined for Japan's Work Force

Several times during the years of 1942 and 1943 while I was held in the Philippines at Cabanatuan, the Japanese would order all hands to the drill grounds to be examined by a group of Japanese medical doctors. Although there were several dozen American medical doctors in Cabanatuan, they were not allowed to function at any of these examinations. This examination was for the explicit purpose of ascertaining our fitness to be transported to perform slave labor in Japan.

They used this examination for a two-fold purpose. The first was to again to humiliate the Americans by showing the Filipino people that their great American hero was nothing, at the hands of the imperial Japanese army. In order to do this, they had us strip off all our clothing out in an open field; we weren't allowed to even have anything on our feet. Here we were, completely nude, walking around for approximately four hours in the blistering hot sun, in plain view of the passing natives on the highway. This was to show the Filipinos that the mighty imperial Japanese were our superiors and that we were reduced to slaves. The second was to pick out the prisoners to be transported to Japan for slave labor.

The "examination" meant that each one of us had to be examined five times, which meant going through five different lines and being examined by five different Japanese doctors. Each doctor had a different area and different characteristics to look for to ascertain our body's ability to perform the work that would be required of us when we reached Japan. While these examinations were taking place, the Japanese doctors made sure they were under cover and not out in the hot sun. They were in tents set up for this purpose, while we were kept out in the open and in the nude. Several prisoners passed out from the heat. The Japanese, probably thinking that they were trying to get out of going to Japan, had other prisoners throw a bucket of water on them, and those who passed out were made to go through the examinations as soon as they came around.

After each Japanese doctor got through with his examination, he would put a mark with paint on our bodies. Then we went to a sixth doctor, who after looking at all the marks we had received from the other doctors, gave us the final mark. This final mark indicated whether you went to Japan or stayed in the Philippines. The final marks were as follows: A *green* mark meant "ship to Japan." A *red* mark meant "too weak, stay in camp," a *yellow* mark meant "go to Japan only if needed to fill the quota." There was

251

a special mark, in *purple,* for those whose services were needed in the camp: the American doctors, chaplains, cooks, hospital corpsmen, Farmer Jones and me.

Right after the farm had been shut down, they called for another group to go to Japan. Heretofore, because Farmer Jones and I were in charge of the farm, we were always given a purple mark. However, when the farm was shut down, on my next examination, they gave me a green mark, which meant "Ship to Japan."

I sure didn't want to go to Japan if I could help it. I had to get rid of that green mark, pronto. So I went to my *hancho* and asked him to get the mark changed to red.

"You sure you want I change it to red?" he asked. I told him, by all means, I wanted it changed to red. He said "Okay, I change it for you."

He went immediately and got it changed. When he came back, I thanked him and told him how happy I was and blew a little smoke by telling him what a great guy he was, etcetera. Of course I didn't mean a damn word I said, but he believed me and patted me on the back.

"I hope you happy now," he said.

In the past, a lot of the guys had their *hancho* change their mark to red if they were slated to go to Japan. The camp commander had found out about this practice, so this time he pulled a fast one. When the examinations were completed, he announced that all prisoners with red marks prepare immediately to move out, to board a ship in Manila for Japan, and all prisoners with green marks stay in camp. What a spot I was in by changing my mark to red. It sure made me sick. I quickly went to my *hancho* and told him that I had made a mistake, I wanted to remain with him in the Philippines.

"I tell doctor, before you get looked at to give you green mark," he said, "so you stay with me in Philippines. But you insisted that you wanted red, so I get change for you, now you must go, too late, no change back."

Part Seven

Nagasaki, Japan

71. Enroute to Japan on a Cattle Boat

At about 6:00 that evening, the camp commander ordered all prisoners with the red marks to line up on the drill field. There were 1,500 of us earmarked for Japan that night. We were taken by bus to the docks in Manila Bay, where we were loaded on to a cattle boat that had just arrived from Singapore with a load of cattle and horses for the Philippines. The group consisted of 1,000 navy men and 500 army men. We were put on the same cattle boat. I never did get to see the name of the boat. The boat had three large cargo holes that the cattle and horses had been removed from.

We climbed down a big ladder into the hole below. It was about eighteen feet down into the hole. The Japanese put 500 men in each hole, which made for standing room only. The prisoners were loaded on. They just put down enough new straw to cover the cattle dung without having cleaned the manure from the holes. We were being treated just like cattle. We were put right down where the cattle had been for the past two weeks and immersed in their dung. What a stench. One could hardly breathe from the stench of the urine from the cattle. The ship got underway later that night.

The next day, about noon, according to my watch, which they had allowed me to keep, they lowered buckets of rice and water into the hole, with a long rope. This was repeated again about seven o'clock at night just before dusk. Can you possibly imagine it. Five hundred starving men with standing room only, and those starving prisoners trying to pass a rice bucket over their heads so each man could get a handful. The water was passed the same way, each one trying to get at least a swallow. It was disastrous, to say the least. A great amount of the much-needed rice and most of the water were spilt on the already soaked straw from the urine of the cattle. Many received very little food, including me.

The hole in the deck where the rice and water were lowered from, was about twelve feet square. It was also the only opening for air. They lowered a three-inch hose, about four feet down into the opening, which was attached to a motor that forced air down in the hole to us, which was badly needed. Between the stifling heat and the stench, let alone being so

crowded, had we not had air forced down to us, we would have all suffo-
cated.

There were about 200 or so prisoners who died in the hole I was in
while we were enroute to Japan. Each morning, the guards would haul the
dead up with a rope and, I guess, just pushed them overboard, as their bodies were never seen again. I looked for them, as several of my buddies were
among them, but nothing was ever heard about them after their bodies left
the hole in that ship. Although it was very sad for us each day as the bodies were removed from the hole, it allowed us more room to stretch out,
and later we could actually sit down. The filth of the horse and cattle
dung and the wet straw from their urine and the spill of all that drinking
water and rice as the buckets were being passed, I can only say it was one
hell of a misery.

It might seem terrible to think of one sitting in wet manure, but after
two or three days standing up, with little or no food and being in the condition we were in, we welcomed that chance. For our toilet facilities, they
placed in each corner, a large bucket about the size of a thirty-gallon trash
can that had been cut in half to be used as a toilet. Each day, they were
hauled up, emptied, and returned. However, as the men got weaker, some
didn't make the bucket, which made the stench worse. How any of us made
it, I'll never know. I can only say we had a friend up there who was watching over those of us who made it. Did General Homma say, "Do you think
we are barbarians?"

We lost almost half of the prisoners, who died from either starvation,
thirst, or being just plain worn out. Many more prisoners died in the other
two holes; only about half in each hole survived the trip. When we were all
unloaded from the ship, the count was 711 men out of the original 1,500
who started out from Manila. At that rate, the hole I was in fared much better by only losing 214. They had allowed me to keep my watch, but it had
long stopped, which left us unable to tell the time of day.

We docked just about midnight in Nagasaki, Japan. I don't know how
many days we were in that hole on the ship, but it was a helluva long time, I
would think, about twenty-nine days, judging by the time it would take to
go from Manila, PI. to Nagasaki, Japan, during wartime with the zigzagging and what not. To me, it was a lifetime. It was good thing for me
that the trip was over. Another day or two, I would not have made it, I was
getting so weak. If it hadn't been for my faith in the Supreme Being, I
would have never made it. To this day, not a night passes that I don't thank
my Heavenly Father for watching over me.

72. Arrival in Nagasaki—Moved to Osaka Prison Camp

As soon as the ship was moored to the dock at Nagasaki, and much to our delight and amazement, the Japanese lost no time in unloading the prisoners. The Japanese probably figured that if they wanted to save the rest of us, they had better not waste any time in getting us out in the fresh air, and getting water and rice in our bodies. So before anything else was done, they started to disembark the prisoners, and not a moment too soon. Upon getting out of the hole and getting fresh air into my lungs, I remember saying "Boy, what a relief." Yes, what a relief to be able to breathe fresh air again.

There was a truck parked alongside the dock. It had several big vats of rice and pans of small fish. As soon as we were lined up on the dock, they handed each one of us a small dish filled with rice and fish, and a glass of water. They must have figured they had better get some water and food into us immediately, or they would lose a lot more of us. When we were through eating, we were ordered to line up and *tinko* (count off). There were only 540 U.S. Navy men left out of the original 1,000 who had left Manila on that cattle boat.

When we got off that ship in Nagasaki, we could hardly stand ourselves, we stunk from that wet straw with the cattle dung and urine that we had sat in for more than two weeks. I guess the Japanese couldn't stand our odor either, because as soon as we were unloaded and given some long-awaited nourishment, we were put in a large vat of water and given some soap to allow us to wash ourselves with. When we were done, they provided us with different clothing. Our clothing was placed in a pile to be burned. We all were very happy about it. Just to get out of those filthy, stinking clothes would have been enough. We never dreamed that we would be allowed to bathe.

It was a horrible, horrible trip. How differently my government treated the Japanese who were interned in Tulelake, California, in Modoc County, for the duration of the war. They were treated well, good food, hospitalization if needed, clothing, shoes, etcetera. We in Japan went barefoot and very ill-clad in the winter months when snow was on the ground, without food most of the time, no medication of any kind, and being forced to work till we dropped in the shipyards, and no compensation at all from either country. The Congress of these United States even now deny us any compensation in our old age, It makes me sick to think about it. They even returned the millions of Japanese yen they had in this country back to the Japanese, with no thought of us who had suffered under their charge.

When we were through bathing and fully dressed, it was in the very early hours of the morning. The Japanese commander called us to attention. We were then ordered to *"tinko,"* after which, the Japanese officer in charge, through his interpreter, informed us that we were now in Nippon, and they were Nipponese. He stressed that we were not in Japan, and they were not to be called Japanese. He told us that if he heard anyone even utter the word Japan or Japanese, he would be shot on the spot. Then to show him that we understood what he had said, the interpreter had us yell out, loud, "Nippon, Nipponese." We were made to do this several times, and each time, we were told to yell louder. He had us almost screaming our lungs out. Then he said, "Now you know, Nippon, Nipponese."

I don't know why they were so adamant about us being in Nippon. I thought maybe they were ashamed of the way they had tortured the prisoners in the Philippines and in other parts of the world where they had taken prisoners, and they didn't want the Japanese race to have to account for their actions. However, I guess that is how they got the name of "Nips" during the war. When the commander was satisfied that we knew we were in Nippon, he ordered that we were to be divided into groups of one hundred, to be transported to different prison camps throughout Nippon. After we were in the specified groups, we were now in a position to be moved. He then ordered the Nipponese *hanchos* to move us out.

Seeing that I was the senior member present in the contingent of the naval prisoners that was being transported to Osaka, I was made the *"hancho"* (leader, or chief). So with one hundred naval personnel under the charge of four Japanese guards, we were taken by truck to Sacrajima Prison Camp No. 2 in Osaka, arriving there just at daybreak. Upon our arrival, we found one hundred British soldiers from the Royal Naval Shipyard in Hong Kong and one hundred Australians from the Royal Naval Shipyard in Singapore were already in the camp. They had arrived just ahead of us that night.

After being assigned to barracks, we were told to *yashamay* (rest). The camp consisted of nine barracks of various sizes. They were as follows: a cook shack, a sick bay, a hospital or infirmary, a main office, a washroom, a bath house, and a lockup, or jail as we know it. Although we were already in jail, so to speak, they still locked up prisoners for punish-

258

ment. The other three barracks were for the prisoners' quarters. They were eighty feet long by twenty-five feet wide.

They were built almost identical to those that we were housed in at the Cabanatuan prison camp in the Philippines, except that the walkway down the middle was about eight feet, leaving us only about eight and half feet for our bedding platforms; in the Philippines, our platforms were ten feet, because in the Philippines, we didn't need space for a fire pit to keep the barracks warm. In Japan, the sides of the barracks were completely covered with several layers of Manila hemp to keep the cold out. The winters in Japan were very cold, however, not too much snow, but we only had scant clothing to keep ourselves warm. The barracks were built on the ground with cement floors; they were all closed in.

Our accommodations were laid out about the same as in the Philippines, with the exception that here we were placed three to a bay which allowed each prisoner a four-foot space to sleep in, whereas, in Cabanatuan, we slept four to a bay. There was a loft overhead just like in the Philippines. Each building housed one hundred prisoners, fifty to a side, twenty-five on the lower deck, and same amount on topside. There were three large concrete tubs, about six feet in diameter, located in the walkway resting on the cement floor. Two were placed a few feet from either end, and the third in the middle of the barracks. In the winter they would bring in large pieces of tree trunks and build a fire in those tubs to try to keep the barracks warm. This was hard to do, as the roofs were thatched and the sides were bamboo and Manila hemp.

Our bedding consisted of a very thin piece of woven straw, about one inch thick, and was laid over a thin piece of plywood. We had only a sheet for covering; therefore, in order to keep warm, we slept in the same clothes we worked in all day—they never came off our bodies except to bathe, which was not too often. We didn't have a pillow, most of us didn't need a pillow anyway. Several of us, including me, had to sit up all night for fear of drowning ourselves, our bodies were so full of water. Dr. Nardini got me a board about three feet long and eighteen inches wide, which I used to prop myself up with. The doctor was afraid that I might drown myself with all the fluids in my body.

The bathhouse was about fifty by thirty feet with a huge concrete bathtub down the middle. The tub was about forty feet long, fifteen feet wide, and two feet deep. It was built about two and a half feet above the ground. This allowed for a fire to be built underneath it.

The day after our arrival at the Sacrajima prison camp in Osaka, they transferred a naval doctor, J. E. Nardini, M.D., a navy lieutenant (j.g.) to our camp, but they gave him very little medicine to use. However, he turned out to be a Godsend. I and many others, including the British and Australian prisoners, would have never made it home if it weren't for Dr. Nardini. He was one of the bravest men I have had the privilege to know, and I knew many brave and heroic men.

I was now the camp *hancho,* in charge of all the prisoners and I made an Australian warrant officer (sergeant) D. A. Buckingham the *hancho* in charge of the British and Australians. Dr. Nardini took charge of the sick bay or, if you will, the infirmary.

None of the prisoners could speak or understand the Japanese language, at least, that is what the Japanese thought. The next morning after our arrival in the Osaka Prison Camp, the camp commander ordered Dr. Nardini, the British master sergeant and me to be placed in a small room with a book, *Learn to Speak Japanese in 36 Easy Lessons.* The commander did not know that Dr. Nardini was a Japanese language student in the United States and knew how to read as well as talk the Japanese language fluently. The camp commander gave an order that we were not to receive any food or drink until we learned the basics of the Japanese language.

I am glad to say, we didn't have to forego our ration of chow, a sardine can full of rice, for very long, because with Dr. Nardini's knowledge of their lingo, he whipped us into shape in a hurry. We had to learn only enough of the basics of the Japanese language, just enough to be able to understand and explain to the prisoners what was required of them by the Japanese who couldn't speak or understand English.

We learned words such as *whachamaru san* ("I don't understand") *shigoto* ("work") *yashamay* ("rest") and *tinko* ("count off"), etcetera. In about twenty-four hours, we were ready for the Japanese translator to test us. With Doc's teaching, we passed with flying colors. It really amazed the camp commander that we learned so fast. He keep saying to us, "You very smart fellah." We just laughed it off. The Japanese never found out that Doc could read and understood the Japanese language until the war's end. As soon as we had passed the test, all hands were ordered out to the parade grounds and told to *tinko* (we had taught the men, the night before, to count in Nipponese).

It was very easy to learn, as the Japanese only count to ten; after that, it is a repeat up to any number. Such as *itchey, ne, san, yuan, go, roko, sitchey, hatchey, ku, ju.* Then from there, it was *ju itchey , ju ne, ju san, ju yuan, ju go,* etcetera. You just took the first number and added it to the second one. When you reached twenty, you put the second and last together and got *ne ju,* then it was a repeat *ne ju itchy* for twenty-one etcetera. One hundred was *yaku* (pronounced "hoc-ko").

The learning of the basics of their language was very necessary for us. It put us in a position to protect the prisoners by speaking for them when they were being hit and kicked by the guards or when called upon to interpret what was required of the prisoner. With the camp commander satisfied that the doctor, the British warrant officer, and I were fluent enough in the Japanese language, he issued the order that we were ready for work.

73. Bathing and Toilet Facilities in Japan

Later in the day, we were lined up, and each one was assigned a number to carry with him throughout his captivity. My number was two hundred forty-four—*ne yaku yuan ju yuan.* We were taken outside the prison camp, and after walking a few blocks, we were loaded into street (trolley) cars that had been waiting to take us to the place where we were going to work. The camp commander wanted to show us what kind of work we would be required to perform to earn our keep, according to the words of the interpreter. After about twenty minutes on the street cars, we were taken off and marched inside a large gate, which I recognized immediately as a shipbuilding yard.

When we were all inside the gate and lined up, the guard told us that this "factory" was to be our workplace. It was at that moment that the realization came to me that the reason we were placed in the Sacrajima Prison Camp at Osaka was that all of us, including the British and the Australians were naval personnel, the Japanese thought we knew all about building ships, and we were brought here to build ships for them in the Osaka shipyards. As we rode on the trolley car that took us to the shipyard, we found that they had bathtubs with the same arrangement as in the prison camp in several places around and about Osaka for civilian usage.

They were community baths, and everyone for blocks around, women, men, girls, and boys bathed together. There was no modesty in Japan. The women went about town completely naked from the waist up, some had a baby strapped to their backs. This practice was used even in the dead of winter. Even the children went about bare from their waist up. The Japanese figured it made them strong and healthy to be exposed to the cold.

They may have had something there, because there wasn't much sign of the flu among them or, for that matter, among the prisoners either.

About once a week they would have the prisoners pull large logs under the bathtub by the use of heavy ropes. The logs were presoaked with kerosene before their being pulled under the bathtub. When they were in place, they were lit to heat the water for the bath. When the water was hot, a horn would sound, which notified everyone in the immediate area, and outside the prison camp as well, that the bath was ready. After we were in Nippon a couple of months, things started to get bad for the Nipponese, and in order to save fuel, they didn't heat the water under the bathtubs in the immediate area outside the prison gates, so the civilians on the outside would be allowed to use our bath.

When the signal sounded that the bath was ready, the civilians would all come running; men, women and kids all jumped into the tub. They would get in right alongside the prisoners, sometimes just crowding us over. They would all be naked, regardless of sex; modesty didn't exist. This was an embarrassing situation for us prisoners. We were not used to this. The Nipponese guards would just laugh at us while they fondled the breasts of the young ladies while in the water. They would beckon to us prisoners, making gestures for us to do the same. However, I cautioned the prisoners to keep as far away from the women as they could so as not to give them a reason for any charges against the prisoners.

The Nip guards and the civilians were full of lice. The water was so full of lice that we would come out of the water in a worse condition than when we went in. So I myself refused to get into the bathtub. I felt that there was no use taking a bath, since after we bathed, we put back on the same lice-ridden clothes. We weren't allowed to have any type of a razor, consequently, we all had big beards. Our beards and the rest of the hair on our bodies were full of lice. We would spend every nonworking hour picking lice off one another. Just when we were about free of those pesky, biting insects, it would be time for a bath again, so I restrained myself and passed it by. I figured it was better to be a little dirty than to be eaten up by lice. However, I was a little bit better off than the rest of the prisoners, in that I was the camp *hancho*. I was allowed to used the washroom in the off hours, at which time I was able to sneak in a sponge bath, but most of the time I had no soap. Once in a while, not too often, I was able to get a small piece of soap the Nips left lying around. Sometimes, I would get a small piece of soap from my *hancho*.

With Japan being such a hilly country, most of the level ground was utilized for factories, shops, and living areas for its large population. The mountainous hillsides were all terraced in two-foot-deep plots, which is where they planted their gardens. Most of their food crops were raised in that fashion. There wasn't any land that could be spared for pastures for the raising of cattle or sheep, hence no manure to fertilize their gardens, forcing them to depend on the excretion from the human body for fertilizer.

The toilet facilities were something else. They had the prisoners dig a pit about fifteen feet long by about eighteen inches wide and about six to eight feet deep. Then they placed a twenty-four–foot two-by-twelve-inch plank on either side, spaced about eight inches apart. This was their toilet, "straddle trench." All the straddle trenches were built out in the open. They had no cover or privacy whatsoever. They were found everywhere in Japan. I don't know which were worse, the flies or the terrible stench of the straddle trench itself. When nature called, one would find a straddle trench and squat down and let nature take care of itself. Again, not being used to this, it was very embarrassing for us. Once again, there was no modesty. One would be squatting over a straddle trench and a lady would come and squat right in front of you. How embarrassing to us, but it didn't faze the Nips a bit. Eventually, I guess, some of the prisoners got used to it. I never did get used to it. It was their way of life, and we were forced to do likewise.

When a trench started to fill up, the Nips would have a prisoner detail clean out the trench. This was accomplished by taking a fifty-five–gallon drum, cut in half, with two long, four-inch–round poles as carrying handles. They were run through holes made in the bucket on either side. The poles were about twelve feet long. It took four men to a carry the bucket, two in the front and two in the back. The bucket was called a "honey bucket." The men assigned to this job were known as the "honey bucket detail." Every once in a while, I was ordered to assign prisoners to the honey bucket detail. The prisoners would remove the straddle trench planks. Then they would dip out the excretion with a small bucket fastened on the end of a long pole and dump it into the big round half-barrel bucket until it was about half full. They were then made to carry it to the garden plots.

When the half-filled bucket with human excretion reached its destination, it was then filled with water, leaving enough room so that it could be mixed with a hand paddle by the prisoners. The contents were then dipped out with the bucket on the end of a long pole and poured around the plants.

Why the name, the "honey bucket detail," I'll never know; to me, it was the nastiest job that one could be assigned to. Having to detail men for this chore was about the worst job that I as a *hancho* was called upon to do. When I was ordered to call out a honey bucket detail, I wanted to really tell those bastards off. I was taught to never ask a person to do something I wouldn't do myself. But there comes a time when it must happen, and that was one of those times, when it was forced upon me.

74. Working in the Shipyards

But You Had Better Call it a Factory

The next day, after we had gotten all squared away and were now ready to go to work, we were ordered to line up for our first venture out of the prison compound to really go to work. We were lined up in front of the commander's office and ordered to count off to make sure everyone was present and accounted for. Upon completion of *tinko,* and the camp commander was satisfied that all the prisoners were present, he informed us, through the interpreter, that the workplace where we had been taken the day before was known as a "factory." When talking about our workplace, we should never mention the word "shipyard." It was a "factory." That was its name and that was what we must call it.

He then went on and told us in no uncertain terms that if anyone disobeyed, he would be very sorry for violating that order. However, regardless of what one called it, it was still a shipyard, not a factory, as the Japanese would have us believe. The commander had the interpreter again inform us that we should always remember what we were told upon first setting our feet on Nipponese soil. This was not Japan. We were in Nippon, and they were Nipponese, and we were again cautioned to refrain from using the words Japan or Japanese or shipyard. If they heard any of those words coming from the mouth of any prisoner, he would be killed instantly. So it was imperative to always remember—we were in *Nippon,* not Japan; and that they were *Nipponese,* not Japanese; we worked at a *factory,* not a shipyard.

After the camp commander had completed his talk, we were marched out the prison gates and down the street for about two blocks, where we were crowded, or rather, jammed, onto a street car, with standing room

264

only. One could hardly move his arms, we were so tightly jammed in those street cars. I felt sorry for the babies strapped to the women's backs and being jammed up as they were. This went on every day and lasted about twenty minutes in going to the shipyard in the morning and the same on our return back to our camp in the evening. What torture.

There were many young women on board, going to work, all naked from the waist up, the custom in those days in Japan. Some of them had a baby strapped to their back. The Japanese must have gotten a kick out of trying to torture us prisoners, because the guards would fondle the women's breasts, just as they did in the bathtub, and invite us to do the same. It was mighty tempting, especially if you had one of those sweet young things pushing tight against your body. But again, I immediately cautioned the prisoners not to touch the women. The prisoners listened to me and in no way ever attempted to touch the women for fear of the consequences. Sex was the last thing on my mind at that particular time, because, although we were not on the battlefield any longer, we were still fighting for our lives as a prisoner under the control of the ruthless and barbaric Japanese.

After about twenty minutes or so, we finally reached our destination and were again taken into the factory, as they called it. Upon our arrival at the shipyard, the prisoners were split up into several groups, according to their condition of health and their size. For instance, those who were weak were utilized in making dust out of large chunks of soft coal, using chipping hammers. The healthier ones were placed in a group of about sixty prisoners, who were utilized in forging the hot metal into shaping the keel, etcetera. After the prisoners had been placed in groups, they were turned over to a civilian Japanese *hancho,* who was to teach them the various tasks required in building a ship, Japanese style.

The way the Japanese built ships and the vast amount of men it required was a big laugh. They were at least fifty to seventy-five years behind the United States and the rest of the world, their work so outmoded in their various shops, so antiquated with no modern equipment for the construction of ships, it was pitiful. Everything that was required of us in the preparation and building of the ships were the same methods used in other parts of the world some fifty to seventy-five years ago. This was in 1943, which took them back into the 1800s.

75. Making the Rivets and Forming the Keel, Japanese Style

For instance, they had large pieces of soft coal, some as big as a bushel basket, which had to be pulverized almost into dust so that it could be used in the blowers for making rivets, etcetera. The prisoners who were given chipping hammers were placed in a sitting position in circles of five to a group. Several large chunks of soft coal were placed in the circle of each group. Then the prisoners would chip away at it until it was pulverized almost to dust. The coal dust was then taken to the shop where the outdated forges were. They would light the forges with a gas jet, then put little pieces of soft coal on the flame.

In a few seconds, after the little pieces caught fire, they would cover the fire with the pulverized soft coal. Then two prisoners were stationed on either side of the forge with a large fanlike blower made with a rubber sack and two clapboards. It looked like the smoke blowers we used on the farm when the bees were swarming. The prisoners would push the handles together and open them fast, open and close, open and close, thereby forcing air into the forges, getting the coals red-hot.

Then several little two-inch pieces of iron rod were placed in the red-hot coals. When they were red-hot, they were picked up one at a time, using large tongs, and dropped in a hole that had been drilled in a chunk of iron with about a half inch sticking out. The little piece of rod was then hit with a very heavy iron maul by a prisoner, squashing it down. This was how a rivet to be used in riveting the ships was fashioned. It took the services of one man to keep putting the rivet material into the hot coals as another man took them out when they were red-hot.

When a certain size rivet was needed, they took the rod for that size and cut it by hand with a hacksaw. They had several prisoners saw the rods to the desired lengths. The rods were then placed into the hot coals with old-fashioned tongs, and the whole process of making a rivet began again.

The manpower it took to make this little rivet was incredible. It took one to pulverize the soft coal, one to push the blower handles, two to fan the coals, one to put the rivets into the fire, another to take them out and put them into a hole drilled in a plate of iron, and another to form the rivet by hitting it with a setting maul. Not to mention how many it took to melt the iron and fashion the twenty-foot-long rods of various sizes used for making the rivets.

I never did see them make the various sized rods that they used in making the rivets. I can only guess those rods must have been bought from America or another country. When we first went into the rivet building, they had piles and piles of iron rod about twenty feet long. I would have loved to have seen them make some rods, for sure, it would have been a mind-boggling deal, according to the way they did other things.

There was another shop that also needed the pulverized soft coal. It was the shop that formed the keel for the ship. That iron also had to be red-hot in order to get it ready to form the keel. To shape the iron, they build a long tunnel, about forty feet long. In it they would build a fire, using the pulverized soft coal, and the prisoners would again be required to fan the coals by using blowers in the same way as they did in making the rivets, by clapping the two boards together, thereby forcing air into the tunnel to get the coals red-hot; due to the tunnels being so long, it took several men using the clapboards to fan the coals.

Seeing this, I finally convinced my *hancho* to get some big fans like the ones they had on the ship blowing down in the hole where we were prisoners. This he did. We placed them on either end of the tunnel. This latter method got the coals hotter in half the time and saved a lot of labor on the part of the prisoners. When the coals were red-hot, they would have about twenty prisoners pull a long piece of flat iron on the bed of hot coals by the use of heavy chains. The flat iron was of various sizes according the part of the keel they were working on.

When the iron in the tunnel got red-hot, twenty more prisoners on the opposite end were assigned the task of pulling it out onto a piece of sheet iron that covered a concrete slab. The keel was formed in a very crude fashion. As soon as the red-hot iron was pulled out of the fire onto the slab, a Japanese *hancho,* with a long, slender iron rod about six feet long, would stand back and tap a spot on the red-hot iron. Two prisoners with heavy iron mauls would take turns in hitting the spot that had been tapped by the *hancho*'s rod. The *hancho* would keep pointing, and the prisoners would keep hitting, until the iron needed to be reheated. Then the twenty prisoners on the other end would pull it back onto the red-hot coals again. As soon as it got red-hot, they would pull it back out on the floor, and two prisoners would again start hitting it with a heavy iron maul where it was being tapped by the *hancho*.

This went on and on until the iron was shaped for the keel plates and other parts. This operation took weeks and weeks to complete a keel for one ship. How long it took depended on the size of the ship we were building. After it was beat into shape, it had to be drilled for the size rivets that were required. Some of the bigger keels would take more than a month of repeated shaping and heating before it was ready for drilling.

The dimensions of the iron for the keel varied according to the ship being built; sometimes it was big and long and sometimes much shorter. The thickness of the metal also depended on the size of the ship being built. Sometimes while I was working in the Osaka naval shipyards, we were building small submarine chasers, so the keel plates we were working on were about two inches thick, fifteen feet long, and about six to eight feet wide. It took several of these plates to form the keel of one ship.

In manpower, it took sixty men to form one plate of the keel for a ship: Twenty to pull it onto the hot coals and back out on the concrete when it was red-hot; ten more to handle the sledgehammers in shaping the keel; twenty more on the other end to pull it back fast onto the coals to get it red-hot again for more shaping; and another ten (prior to my suggestion of getting electric fans) on each end of the tunnel to keep the blowers going and add more coals on the fire in order to keep the coals red-hot.

They had to work fast to keep the iron hot while working and shaping the keel. Many prisoners passed out from the hard work and the intense heat the red-hot iron threw off. This was a hard job, especially so for the prisoners not being in shape to do this kind of work due to lack of food and a proper place to sleep to get their much needed rest. When a prisoner passed out while working in this intense heat, he was allowed to rest, but not for long, and then continued on.

At this time of our imprisonment, a ration of food for a prisoner was twenty-five silkworms one day and twenty-five mulberry leaves the next day. That was all the food we were given in a twenty-four-hour period to live and work on. We were forced to work seven days a week with no days off for months at time. It was no wonder that so many prisoners passed out from being starved and overworked.

The British prisoners knew how to use a rivet gun because they worked in the navy yard in Hong Kong; whereas, the Americans didn't know the first thing about a rivet, let alone, using a rivet gun. I tried to tell the camp commander that we sailed the ships, we didn't build them. But my pleas fell on deaf ears. He just kept telling me, "You are navy men. You know how to build ship."

I guess they were finally convinced that the American prisoners did not know how to use a rivet gun, because on the third morning when we arrived in the shipyard, the camp commander had two large pieces of iron propped up by the yard gate. They were both about twelve by twelve feet square. They had holes drilled in them to hold the various-sized rivets. The commander had about fifty rivet guns nearby. The British prisoners were then instructed to teach the Americans how to use a rivet gun.

As I said before, Japan was fifty to seventy-five years or more behind the United States in mostly everything. They were still doing things the way we did back in 1860 and 1870, and riveting on a ship was no exception. It took two men working together to do one rivet, one would be inside the ship and the other would be outside; one would hold his rivet gun solid while the other did the riveting.

The British and Aussies were crackerjack riveters. Before the war, they worked in the Royal Naval shipyard in Hong Kong and Singapore, so they were well trained and knew what they were doing. When the British boys taught the Americans how to rivet, they showed them how to hold a rivet gun on a very slight slant, thus putting a slight crimp in the rivet so it would not set square, and thus make a minute hole alongside the rivet. After a few days of instruction in how to use a rivet gun, the Americans were ready for the real thing. The Japanese put them to work on a new keel.

All during the time we were working on the keel, I couldn't get the Nipponese *hancho* or even, for that matter, Little Caesar, our camp commander, to come down under the ship. Many times I wanted to show the Nipponese *hanchos* something, but they all flatly refused to come under the keel. They were all afraid and wouldn't dare to even come near the ship that the prisoners were working on. When I wanted them to come down and see something, they would say, "No, you lookee, you fixee anything. I trustee you." After a while, it appeared to me that they were afraid we might do something.

Well, we continued to build the shell for the ships, and when it was completed, I would notify the guards the hull was ready for launching.

Now things were different. They took control. The keel was launched with a Nipponese ceremony, which we were not allowed to see. There were ceremonies that would start immediately at the sound of the noon whistle. All the prisoners were crowded together and put behind a large fence during the launching ceremonies. They kept their launching ceremonies very secret. All we heard were Japanese screaming and yelling and the setting off of firecrackers, and generally having a gay old time. The ceremonies lasted all afternoon up until it was time to take the prisoners back to camp. Most of the guards got to feeling no pain from the *sake*. In fact, some got pretty drunk and very nasty. However, some of them who could carry their liquor remained calm and shielded the prisoners from those who were getting nasty.

76. Saving the Prisoners from Beatings

It was a good thing the Nips had insisted that the doctor, the British sergeant, and I learn to speak and understand their language, because our job was to aid the men under our charge. When a Japanese would tell a prisoner to do something and he shook his head, meaning he didn't understand, the guard, thinking the man was refusing to do as he had been ordered, would start to beat the prisoner. It was our job to run over and get between them to find out what the Japanese wanted the prisoner to do.

After separating them by jumping between them, I would say *"Whachamur san?"* ("What do you want him to do?") Then I would tell the guard as best I could that the prisoner doesn't understand what he wants him to do. This got the job done. Due to my being the prisoners' head *hancho* at the Osaka Sacrajima Prison Camp No. 3, the camp commander issued orders to the Japanese that I was to be respected and they were not to lay a hand on the British sergeant or me when we would knock them apart. And we made sure to knock them apart; that is, we got between the Nipponese guard and the prisoner.

We always pushed the Nip away—we never touched the prisoner. In this way, we would be always facing the Nip, and it made them mad, sometimes, to where they would have loved to batter us around a bit. But they didn't dare for fear of the consequences should one of us tell the camp commander. By learning to speak Japanese, the British sergeant and I saved a lot of beatings and many lives of our fellow prisoners. The Japanese were ruthless. They had no regard for life. They would laugh as they ran a bayonet through a man as if it was nothing.

They hated the Americans. But the English fared a little better. After all, it was the Americans who had humiliated the Japanese back in 1853, and again by Admiral Dewey in the Philippines during the Sino-Japanese war with Russia, when he aided and abetted the Russians by refueling and provisioning their fleet in Manila Bay.

We always knew when the Japanese had lost a decisive battle on any given day. If the Japanese had a bad day on the ocean or lost a battle somewhere, they would order all the prisoners out on the grinder regardless of the time, night or day. They had, beforehand, made up their minds as to how many prisoners they would torture in reprisal for their losses that day.

When we were all lined up on the grinder, we were ordered to *tinko,* count off. If the number picked by the Japanese was, say five for that night, right after we were done counting off, the camp commander would say, "all *go mie,*" meaning every fifth man was to step out. He would then say to the rest of us, *"yashamay,"* rest. If you happened to be that fifth man, it was your turn to be used for bayonet practice or whatever else they had in store for you that night. This was part of the extreme torture we were forced to live under from the first day of our capture when we were forced to watch as they grabbed six men and made them dig their own graves and shot them in cold blood. This torture lasted until our release in August 1945. This was truly the worst kind of torture to put a man through.

I ask you, what could be expected from such brave men who had proved themselves on the battlefield being put through this kind of torture for four long years? How can we condemn a man who breaks down and gives up after finding himself caught in the barbaric acts of the Japanese and what they were putting us through? Especially knowing that there was no help in sight. I can truly say that most of those men who broke down from the tortures were some of the bravest men fighting on the battlefield. May the good Lord watch over them and let them rest in peace, wherever they may be.

Consequently, there was hopelessness and debility among the prisoners, and this too accounted for a great loss of life in the prison camps, the prisoner having lost faith in their country and their Heavenly Father. My only strength, which carried me through, was my faith in my God, and second, my faith in my beloved United States of America, the country as I knew it then, not as I know it now. That is the only reason I am here today; by keeping my faith.

The Japanese were cunning. They wanted the world to think that they were abiding by the Geneva Convention, so they would, from time to time, have the International Red Cross take pictures of the prisoners, in their endeavor to show the world how well we were being treated. Several times, about fifteen or twenty prisoners would be taken out of the prison camp to a hotel in town and were dressed up beautifully.

During those occasions, we would be put in a room with beautiful surroundings and piles of clothing and various types of food in the background. They even gave us some food that we could eat while the cameras were clicking. We were not allowed to talk to the Red Cross people, so we would say to ourselves when they gave us something to eat, "keep those cameras clicking." In that way we got more food and sweets on the side.

Just as soon as the Red Cross left, we were returned to our usual prison barracks and were made to strip and put on our old rags, and the food and clothing were taken away. It reminded me of the treatment we got in Bilibid prison on our arrival there with the International Red Cross taking pictures. Well, I am sure the rest of the world knew better and could read between the lines. At least, we all hoped they did. The International Red Cross was never allowed to visit our work place.

They didn't know the Japanese were violating the Geneva Convention by putting us to work in the Osaka naval shipyards, building destroyer chasers for the Japanese, nor were they ever allowed to visit our prison camp to see the way we were living and under what conditions. In that way the Red Cross never did get to see the kind of rags we were dressed in, our being without shoes, our lack of food, or our condition of being just skin and bones. They never saw the true conditions under which we worked and lived.

The order of no work—no food, which had been put into effect by General Tojo while we were in the Philippines was still in effect in Japan. The order was that "one must report for work and remain on the job, whether he worked or not," or he was not to receive a ration of food for that day. Here's an example of how the no work— no food law really worked. One day, another fellow and I had pneumonia. We both had very high temperatures. The camp commander, a colonel in the Japanese army, better known as "Little Caesar" by not only the prisoners of war, but also by the Japanese guards, he was ruthless.

It was snowing hard that day and Little Caesar insisted that both of us must go to work, so they could collect the daily food ration for us. Our daily food ration was still twenty-five silkworms one day and twenty-five mulberry leaves the next day, and that was it. Dr. Nardini flatly refused to allow them to take either of us to the shipyard in our condition that day. He kept telling them we would die due to our high fevers and the present heavy snowstorm.

However, Little Caesar kept insisting, and kept roughing up the doctor by slapping him in the face. Dr. Nardini knew that when he confronted Little Caesar, he would get knocked around by the Japanese guards, so he prepared himself for it. This happened day after day, but he refused to give in; he just stood his ground for the sick. It had happened on numerous occasions before, when he would stand up to defend a prisoner who was

272

gravely ill. He was a brave and courageous man. He took many a beating for the sick.

Of course, Little Caesar won out as usual, and he ordered us out the gate with the rest of the troops. We were placed on stretchers and taken to the shipyard. They laid us both on the ground in the stretchers, where we stayed all day long. It snowed hard all day, and the temperature hung around thirty degrees or so. Although it was snowing and very cold, it didn't bother the Japanese a bit. They just laid us down there on the cement floor, with just a small piece of tarpaulin tied on a couple of poles and hung over us to keep the snow off. The other fellow died before nightfall.

Every day I would wander all over the yard, watching out for the prisoners to see that they were not in trouble with one of the Nipponese civilian workers or a Nipponese prison guard. Sometimes the camp commander would walk with me, or maybe a Nipponese guard would accompany me; most of the time, I was alone. Sometimes Dr. Nardini would come out to the shipyard to see what kind of work they were having the sick prisoners do. Those times I would accompany him about the yard, and sometimes I would go around the shipyard with the British sergeant.

One day as I was walking around the shipyard with the camp commander, he noticed a long vapor trail, the exhaust from a B-29, appearing in the sky. The camp commander pointed up toward it.

"B ne gee coo, erochy ney" (B-29, no good), he said.

"B ne gee coo!! Erochy erochy" (B-29 very good, very good), I replied in my broken, pigeon Nipponese. I kept on repeating it, and boy, did Little Caesar get mad. He got so mad that he raised his arm as if to strike me. I raised my hand to protect myself and said, "You better not, remember the rules. I'm off bounds. If you strike me, I'll report it."

He didn't say a thing, just looked at me and grinned in that certain Japanese style when they were really mad, as if to say "I'd like to kill you."

While strolling around the shipyard, watching out for the prisoners and making sure they were being treated right and there was no trouble, I was able to talk at great length with the camp commander, who was an army colonel. He and I would talk and compare various things in his country with those in the United States. We also talked about our childhood and what we did before the war. In this fashion, we both learned a lot about each other's country. To my surprise, many times when we were alone, Little Caesar would talk to me in plain English. However, it was different when we were in camp or in the company of others, he spoke only through an interpreter. Most of the time while on walks, he talked to me through an interpreter.

One day, while walking and talking about various subjects with the colonel, the subject of the Philippine Islands came up, and I had a chance to inquire about our findings in the Mariveles Mountains. I was more interested in learning what I could about the guns stored there in the 1906 newspapers. I was surprised to learn, through my conversation with him, that the Japanese high command had declared war on the United States when Commander Perry humiliated the emperor back in 1853 and when Admiral Dewey had fueled and provisioned the Russian Fleet in Manila Bay, thereby aiding them in their war with his country. This was so humiliating to Japan that they vowed to make the West pay for their humiliating acts to the emperor regardless of how long it took.

Time means nothing to the Oriental people. I was also told in no uncertain terms to always remember, "Japan never forgets." To this, I say, "Wake up, America." Japan hasn't and will not forget the humiliation they suffered under General Douglas MacArthur at the signing of the peace treaty to end the war with the United States back in 1945 on that magnificent ship, the U.S.S. *Missouri.* That day is embedded in their minds, and one day they will seek revenge.

I heard with my own ears, from their own mouths, many, many times while a prisoner of war in Japan that "Japan never forgets, even it takes one hundred years." If Japan never forgot Admiral Perry's entry into Japanese ports at gun point in 1853 or Admiral Dewey's actions with the Russians in Manila, at the turn of this century, how can they be expected to forget the humiliation they suffered from the United States, under General MacArthur, back in 1945 and during the Japanese war crime trials? That country is preparing at this very moment to avenge the West. Open your eyes, America, before it is too late. As goes the Boy Scouts' motto, "Be Prepared," so, America, you be prepared.

77. Being Questioned about the Masonic Order

One day a Nipponese general came in the camp to hold an inspection. He had a little dog, and the dog ran loose in the camp, but not for long, because the cooks got him, and before one could count to ten, that little dog was in the stewpot. I refused to partake of that particular meal. However, I was told later by one who did, that he made a nice stew for them. Although I was starving, I just couldn't eat some of the things that were laid before me, and this was one of them.

When the general started to leave, he called his dog, but there was no dog. So he had the prisoners start looking everywhere, but to no avail; there was no dog to be found. Finally, with some fast thinking, one of the prisoners told the general a little white lie, saying that he saw his dog run out the main gate and that was the last time they had seen him. This cleared the general's mind and spared a lot of punishment for the rest of us prisoners, because the general was getting madder by the moment, as was our camp commander. Well, the general went back to Tokyo minus one dog.

Another time, we were allowed to go into the backyard to exercise on the lawn. Did I say "lawn?" Well, it was a beautiful lawn when we were turned loose in there, but when we left a couple of hours later, it was just plain, bare ground; every blade of grass was pulled up and eaten. It was like turning loose a herd of cattle in a field of clover.

Our rations of food at this time was a small sardine can full of rice (about three tablespoons), once a week. The rest of the week, we would be given our usual twenty-five roasted silkworms one day, and twenty-five mulberry leaves the next. The Nips also had very little to eat. However, they did get two meals daily. I saw the guards' lunch that they carried with them each day. It consisted of about five or six large tablespoons of rice, which was topped off with a small piece of fish, and a piece of fruit of some kind, and there was always one cigarette packed in their lunch. We were lucky to get the silkworms, because some days we didn't even get that or the mulberry leaves. We got just plain nothing, but still had to go to work.

One day, when we were lined up, getting ready to go to work, and after we had counted off, the camp commander, speaking through the interpreter, said, "There are some members of the Masonic and Woodmen of the World orders among you. I know who you are, but I am going to give you a chance to identify yourself, so please step forward." No one stepped forward. He waited a few minutes, then he said, "I ask you once more, all affiliated Masons and Woodmen of the World step forward," and he screamed *"now."* Again no one stepped forward.

After a few minutes, he said, "I will count to five, if you don't come forward, great harm will come to you." No one stepped forward. So he said, very angrily, "Okay, you go *shigoto"* (to work). To this day, I can't figure out why they called members of the Woodmen of the World to step out or why they confused them with Masonry. Woodmen of the World, I am told is an insurance organization. Masonry is a fraternity that has been around for four thousand years before Christ. It was started with the building of King Solomon's temple. It consists of men banded together for fellowship and for the good of mankind. The doors are open to anyone to join who has attained the age of twenty-one, regardless of race, color, or creed, with the exception of those who do not believe in God or a future existence, that is, any man who has attained the age of twenty-one, except an atheist, a mad man, or a fool, can be accepted into Masonry.

There were six prisoners who were Masons in the Osaka Sacrajima Prison Camp No. 3, where I was interned. There were seven at one time, but a brother, Chief Commissary Steward Cox, U.S.N., had died a few months before. We all knew one another. So all that day during my rounds in the shipyard as head *honcho,* I made it a point to visit and consult with the other Masons in our camp to ascertain what they wanted to do. We decided to call the camp commander's bluff and not tell him who we were should he again call upon us to step out upon our return to camp from work that day.

That evening, upon our return to camp, and after we had held *tinko,* or count off, which was the regular routine upon leaving or returning to the prison to make sure we were all there and that none had escaped, the Nipponese commander again ordered, "all Masons and Woodmen of the World step forward." Upon our refusal, he said, "I warn you to take heed, you have five minutes to report to me. I know who you are. Don't tempt me, or you will be very sorry." He waited a few seconds, then yelled out very loudly in a seemingly angry tone, *"Yashamay, Yashamay."* He had always said that just once and in a very soft voice, but this day it was very different. He acted like he was really mad. It really set me to thinking.

When I got into the barracks, I saw my thin bedding, such as it was, all slashed with a knife and everything in my area disarranged. Looking around the barracks, I found, to my dismay, that it was only my bedding that had been slashed. This really put me to fright, as I was the only accent free and accepted Mason in the American group. I went immediately over to the British and Australians' barracks to see the other brother Masons, and to tell them what had happened to my bedding and also to see if the same had happened to them. To my amazement, they were in the same boat as I was. Everything was cut up. No other prisoners had anything disrupted, just we six Masons.

"This proves he knows what he is talking about," I said to them. "He certainly does know who we are. Let's get the hell out of here and report to him before he sends the guards after us."

276

So without any delay, we went out there and reported to the camp commander. I don't mind telling you that I and my buddies were shivering in our worn-out sandals we had on. We all knew our camp commander, or Little Caesar, was a rotten, no good son of a bitch, and there was no telling what he had in store for us, especially since we had disobeyed his orders three times in the morning before going to work in the shipyard, and again, upon our return that evening. We had steadfastly refused to step out when he had ordered us to do so, thereby disobeying his orders.

When we went out and reported to Little Caesar and told him that we indeed were the people he was looking for, instead of his going into a rage, as he often did in cases like this, he amazed us by giving us a little laugh.

"I fool you, hey," he said. "You didn't think I knew who you were, did you?" We were shaking too much to answer. We knew from past experience with the Japanese that they could look you in the face and laugh one moment, and the next, run a bayonet through you without batting an eye. Life meant nothing to them. I didn't quite know how the others felt at that time, but this little guy was too shocked to answer him. I just stood there in amazement, in disbelief, watching his actions toward us. I guess my other buddies were in the same condition as I was at that moment, because they too never uttered a sound. We all acted as though in shock, and I am not sure that I wasn't.

After a moment or two, the commander said, "Follow me, fellows." This amazed me also, as he never addressed us as fellows before, never in the two years since he had taken charge of us. The Nipponese all believed that only cowards who were afraid to commit hari-kari surrendered. So to them, anyone who surrendered was just scum and a coward. So his addressing us as "fellows" sure shocked the hell out of us. The camp commander, with the interpreter, took us over to his office. When we got inside, we were introduced to three high-ranking Nipponese army officers, who were sitting there waiting for us.

Looking around, I noticed a table covered with a nice, clean table-cloth, on which there were dishes of candies, cookies, Domino sugar cubes for coffee, assorted sandwiches, and a large pot of delicious coffee, and last, but not least a tray of various makes of cigars and cigarettes and a box of matches. What luxury! Could this be true, or were my eyes deceiving me? Should I pinch myself to see if I was alive, or had I died and was now in heaven? All that I could think as I gazed upon this arrangement was *what a sight for sore eyes* and *what torture to do this to us.* I felt like just diving in with both hands regardless of the consequences. We were all stunned for the moment, as none of us had seen anything like this since the war started in December 1941.

After our eyes had feasted on the spread before us for a few minutes, the ranking officer, through the interpreter, bid us to sit down and partake of the feast they had set before us. Did we wait for a second invitation? Hell, no. We all dove into that spread, leaving all our manners behind, and before we came up for air, it seemed we had cleaned almost everything from the table. The Nip officers just sat there and let us feast until the table was practically emptied. It seemed to me they were enjoying watching us while we were devouring the food almost as much as we enjoyed getting it.

When we were finished, each one of us was given a cup of coffee by Little Caesar himself. It almost knocked me off my feet. I would never in my life have expected to see the day when Little Caesar would serve me a cup of anything. Then we were told to help ourselves to the cigars and cigarettes. We all lit up a nice fresh cigar, my first in four years, and I did enjoy it, although I must admit it made me a little dizzy, but I didn't let that stop me, I just puffed on and on. I was in seventh heaven, and I guess, according to the expressions on the face of my fellow prisoners, they were too. After finishing that delicious spread and sitting there puffing away on that wonderful cigar, I was riding on cloud nine.

Finally, the senior Nipponese officer, who was a general, started to asked us questions concerning Masonry, by way of the interpreter. At first, we answered him freely. The questions we were asked were as follows: "Are all of you Masons?" "Where is your hometown?" "How long have you been Masons?" "Are you being treated well in Japan?" Then he asked, "I guess you are longing for the day to come so you can return to your homes and loved ones again," and more questions along the same line to which we could find no difficulty in answering, at least, I couldn't. The other two officers joined in the questioning. Little Caesar remained silent. After about fifteen or twenty minutes of that kind of questioning, the general, probably figuring we were well-loosened up, turned to the camp commander and told him and the interpreter to leave the room. He told Little Caesar that they wanted to be alone with us in his office.

When the camp commander was gone, the general opened his briefcase and pulled out the jewelry of the various officers of a Masonic lodge, and, in perfect English, asked us to describe them to him. This alone astonished the hell out of all of us, as no Japanese in uniform, let alone a high-ranking officer, a general, would talk to prisoners in their own tongue. They considered that to be an insult. However none of us volunteered to

278

tell him anything. He next brought out a deciphered book on Masonry, *King Solomon,* and passed it on to each of us. *King Solomon* can be read only by one who has taken the degrees in Masonry.

After allowing each of us a short time to examine the book, he requested that we read it to him, which we all refused to do. Each of us telling him in turn that we didn't know how to read the book. I told him it looked like it was printed in some foreign tongue. Upon our refusal to read *King Solomon* to him, he laid it down. Then one of the other officers jumped up and slapped each one of us one or two times. I told them that I was a new member in the Masonic lodge in the Philippines and didn't know much.

"Don't lie to us. We want the truth," the general said. And he immediately told me that I had been a Mason for over four years and was an officer in the Masonic lodge in the Philippines. I couldn't believe what I was hearing. I was puzzled. I thought where did they get all this information, every bit of which was true? The general went on to say "You all know how to read this book, and you will read this book before you leave this room, do you understand me?" However, we all steadfastly continued to refuse. After a bit more of face-slapping, the general set the book down. He couldn't get any one of us to read anything from the *King Solomon* to him. The general then turned to the British sergeant.

"You are the Master of your lodge in Hong Kong," he said to him point blank, "and you will tell me everything, and you will read this book to me." The sergeant flatly refused. The general started slapping his face very hard. The Sergeant's face started to get red from the slapping, but he still remained steadfast in his refusal to divulge anything to him. The other two officers got up and joined in hitting the rest of us. The British sergeant's face was now crimson.

"Go ahead and kill me," he yelled out. "That is what you want to do anyway. You guys are barking up the wrong tree. We won't tell you a thing. You can beat us all day and night, and you still won't get anything from us."

At this outburst, the general abruptly stopped slapping him, and he raised his hand and stopped the other two officers from hitting us. In a very low tone, as if nothing had taken place, the general stood up at attention.

"I salute you, gentlemen," he said. "You may take the rest of the things on the table with you and return to your barracks." With that, we gathered up what was left on the table, including the sugar cubes and cigars and cigarettes. Then he went on to say as we were leaving the office, "I personally assure you that no harm will ever come to any of you while you are being detained in this country as a prisoner." He apologized as we were leaving and shook the hand of each of us and said, "Good-bye, gentlemen, my wish for you is that you return to your homes and loved ones safely and very fast."

Each officer in turn shook our hand and each one said, "I apologize for my treatment to you this afternoon. Live in peace and have a safe trip home."

As we left that room, I was just as flabbergasted as I was when we first went in. I didn't know what to think, and after talking it over with my brother Masons upon our return to the barracks, I found them to be in the same quandary as I found myself, utterly bewildered. Deep in my heart, to this day, I still believe that the Japanese in that room were all Freemasons. My reasoning is that the Japanese general knew that the camp commander was not a Freemason. He allowed him to remain in the office while we were being asked questions about ourselves, but as the next line of questioning was to be on Masonry, the Japanese officers, equipped with the knowledge that Little Caesar was not a Mason, had him leave the room. We all figured that the general wanted a chance to test us under duress. We never found out one way or the other if it was true or not, but that will always be my belief. I still feel that they were from the Grand Lodge of Masonry in Japan.

78. Dr. Nardini Gets a Japanese Newspaper

The United States government had sent Japan, via the International Red Cross, thousands of food parcels and tons of clothing for the prisoners. We never received any of the clothing until the end of the war. However, about every three to six months, they would give us a Red Cross parcel to be divided among eight men. The contents of the parcel as best I can remember contained six packs of American cigarettes, a small box of macaroon cookies, three little packets of Domino sugar, a couple of Hershey chocolate bars, a small tin of butter, a can of Spam, a can of sardines, a small box of soda crackers, a pencil along with some writing paper and envelopes.

I would gather all the sugar and cigarettes and give them to our good friend Dr. Nardini. He used them to barter with the Nipponese on the outside. For instance, the Japanese would slip a Japanese language newspaper under the hospital tent each night, and the doctor would leave them a cigarette or a tablespoon full of sugar to pay for it. A tablespoon of sugar or an

American cigarette cost about five thousand yen in Japanese money in those days.

This made the Japanese laugh, as it was a big joke to them to get sugar and cigarettes for a newspaper written in Japanese, which they thought was of no use to the prisoners, because we couldn't read it anyway. That is what they thought. We let them keep on thinking that way. We were getting the last laugh. Until the day the war was over, we kept it a strict secret from the Nipponese guards about Dr. Nardini's ability to speak and read Japanese fluently.

So each day he received a daily paper, thus keeping all of us up to date on the war. Of course, he had to read between the lines, because most of what was in the papers were false propaganda for the benefit of the Japanese. They didn't dare tell the truth to their people on the street, because they didn't want them to know that they were losing the war. For instance, an item in the paper would say that a big battle was just won by the Nipponese, their losses were one ship or one airplane, while the enemy lost ten ships and seventy-five aircraft in a battle in a certain area in the South Pacific. They would also give the name of the area where the battle took place, knowing that their people at home had very little knowledge of geography and, therefore, didn't have any idea in what part of the world that particular battle took place anyway.

The American prisoners, knowing that part of the Pacific real well, also knew that the battles were coming closer and closer to the Philippines. We knew they were losing ground and, thereby, losing the war. Pretty soon, we were starting to see the big B-29 bombers coming over Japan more often now. This in itself was another giveaway that they were losing ground and the war. Another giveaway was that food was continually becoming scarcer and scarcer in Japan. There was hardly any rice for the native Japanese and none at all for the prisoners. They had reduced the feeding of the prisoners to only the usual silkworms and mulberry leaves. Deep in my heart I still feel they would have given us more rice, but their cupboards were getting bare. There was nothing else for them to feed us.

That was a big factor in keeping our hopes high, our knowing that it was due to the presence of the American naval forces that were operating in and controlling the seas off the Philippines and elsewhere in the Pacific; knowing that the Japanese were not able to get food to their homeland to feed their people because of the vast amount of Japanese shipping being lost at sea. That in itself was a very good sign and helped to keep our courage and hopes up.

It got so bad that the camp commander ordered Dr. Nardini to give us a one-hour talk each day, in which he was supposed to show us how to survive and still keep working with nothing to eat but the silkworms and mulberry leaves every other day. The Nipponese told him to explain to us to just pull our belts in another notch. So each day after we returned from the workplace, or "factory," just a plain shipyard, Dr. Nardini would take us into one of the barracks, where he would give us a talk, as ordered.

When we got inside the barracks, I would place a prisoner near each opening to make sure no Nipponese came in and get a chance to hear what the doctor was telling us. Should a Nipponese guard appear on the scene, the doctor would be warned, and he would immediately start to tell us how to keep healthy and work hard on our present allotment of twenty-five mulberry leaves one day and the like number of silkworms the next day. That we must tighten up our belts a notch, etcetera.

But when all was clear, Dr. Nardini would bring us up to date on what was happening in the war by his interpretation of what he had read in the Japanese newspaper that day. Dr. Nardini's daily talks kept up our spirits by keeping us informed about how close our forces were coming. This was the best medicine he could give us. It certainly kept many men alive who would have given up, hope gone, as many had done before we were getting this good news. Yes, the Nipponese guards laughed at our buying those Nipponese language newspapers that they thought we couldn't read. The prisoners were actually getting the last laugh, and many lives were being saved.

79. Easter Day in Japan and Shutdown of the Shipyard

During January, and February, we had been working seven days a week in the shipyard without a day of rest, so we decided to do something about it. Which we did. At several places about the campgrounds were large vats full of water and a dozen buckets to be used in case of fire. One night, some of the prisoners took a burning ember from the barracks fire and lit off the nepa roof of the guard house. The fire wasn't noticed by the guards until it got out of hand. They routed the prisoners out and had us carry water to the fire.

We set up a line and handed the buckets to the guys who were up on the roof where the fire had not yet reached. The guys on the roof would take the buckets of water and throw them over the roof to where it was not burning. Pretty soon it got out of hand and the whole thing burned to the ground. That was our excitement for a while. But we loved it. The Japs had to start the next day to rebuild their barracks. In the meantime, they pitched a tent.

Knowing that Easter was in March that year, I asked the camp commander to allow us to *yashamay* on Easter Sunday and if he would allow a Roman Catholic priest to come into the camp, as that was the most sacred day of the year for the Christian world. To my surprise, he agreed and allowed us to have Easter Sunday off and promised that he would do everything in his power to get us a priest for that day. The reason that I requested a Roman Catholic priest was that most of the Americans in our Sacrajima camp were Roman Catholics. Most of the British and the Australians and I were Episcopalians, which is very similar to the Catholic religion.

Little Caesar negotiated with the authorities in Tokyo, and they allowed a Roman Catholic priest to come into the prison camp on Easter Day. I told all the Americans, British, and Australians, regardless of their religion, to come to church Easter Sunday. Also, I encouraged those of the Roman Catholic faith to go to confession telling them it was a great opportunity for everyone. It was the first time since leaving the Cabanatuan Prison Camp in the Philippines to have had this chance, which was more than two years.

I had the men set up church in one of the barracks and a place for a confessional, as many had said they would like to go to confession. When everything was ready, the priest came over and told us he would hear confessions for those who wanted to be heard. But then he announced, "Before we begin, I want you all to know that my first faith is in my sun god (Shintoism). Your God comes second to my God." This we didn't need. We wanted a real honest-to-goodness Roman Catholic priest. Nobody went to confession that day. It was sad, as many had been waiting for this day for several weeks to go to confession and to have a real Christian Easter. However, we all went to church anyway. At least we got to sing and pray together. It all worked out, but not as well as we would have liked it to be, but it was a thousand times better then nothing. We were all very happy that we did get to go to church that Easter Sunday. The priest turned out to be a good Joe, which made our Easter Sunday even nicer. We were allowed to *yashamay* for two days.

I am glad to say we built only four ships for them. After they were launched, they wanted us to put the gun emplacements on them, but we re-

283

fused, saying it was against the Geneva Convention. Much to our surprise, they didn't quarrel with that. They simply called in some Japanese army and naval personnel to put the gun emplacements on. The ships we had launched started to seep water from the first day they hit the water. They had been forced to keep the pumps going in the bilges and keep pumping them out. However, the water kept seeping in very slowly. That went on all during the time they were installing the gun emplacements and engines on the ships.

One evening in early March in 1944 upon our return from the ship-yard where we had just started to lay the keel for the fifth submarine chaser, and were all lined up for *tinko,* as was the usual, to make sure that everyone was present and none had escaped, we were told by the inter-preter that immediately after *tinko,* Dr. Nardini, the sergeant, and I were to report to the camp commander's office.

Upon our arrival at the commander's office, we were greeted by some high-ranking officers from Tokyo, who started to question us as to why the ships we had built were seeping water. Dr. Nardini and myself told them that we had no explanation. But after a moment or two of silence, the Brit-ish sergeant spoke up.

"I'll tell what I think. Your country was buying shipload after ship-load of scrap iron from the United States of America for a such a long pe-riod of time prior to the war. The Americans are not fools, you know. They knew this iron was to be used by you for no other reason but in the prepara-tion for war and that you were going to build ships with the bloody iron and also use it in other ways in your war effort. So they sold you porous metal. That's what those American blokes did, they sold you porous metal."

This British sergeant had a great sense of humor, and I had a hard job to keep a straight face after hearing that one. I don't know if the Nips be-lieved him or not, however, they didn't learn a thing from us that day. The Japanese, being in a such a quandary themselves, and having no real an-swer as to the seepage of water by the ships we had built, issued orders to shut down the factory immediately. Within a day or two, the shipyard, or "factory," was shut tight.

The Nipponese immediately started to look for a place to put us to work in the Osaka area. However, they didn't have to look far, because within a few days, the high command in Tokyo received a warning from the United States military command ordering them to remove all prisoners from the Nagoya and Osaka areas immediately. They also told them that they would be held responsible for any loss of life of the prisoners in those

284

areas due to any aerial attack waged on that part of Japan by the United States.

80. Moved to the Ackanobe Copper-Mining Camp

At about six-thirty on the morning of 15 March 1944 the senior Nipponese guard, with the interpreter, came over to the barracks and told me that the camp commander had received orders to remove us from the Osaka area immediately, and I was to have the men pack all their belongings and be ready to move out in about one hour.

After he was gone, I laughed at the joke, "pack all our belongings." One could put everything we owned in one small paper bag. We had practically nothing but the rags on our backs, which were in shreds by this time. After informing the Americans to get ready, I went to see the British warrant officer and told him to get his men ready to move out, after which, I went to the infirmary and informed Dr. Nardini what was taking place.

About midmorning, the guard, with the interpreter, returned to the barracks. The interpreter told me to have everyone take their belongings and line up outside the camp commander's office as soon as possible, then added, "I'll give you five minutes to have all the prisoners, including the British and the Australians, lined up and ready to move out."

I repeated the orders that I had received to the American prisoners, and then went over to the British and Aussie's barracks and told them we had five minutes to move out. I then went back to the infirmary and informed the doctor to have the sick out on the grinder ready to move out. When we were outside and lined up with what little possessions we had, I reported to the camp commander that his orders had been carried out and that all the prisoners including the sick were ready to travel. The camp commander then had us *tinko* and, seeing that all were present and accounted for, ordered us to move out.

We were taken outside the gate and loaded on buses, which took us down to the railroad station. We were immediately jam-packed into boxcars. We traveled all that day packed in the boxcars like sardines in a can. We were taken up in the mountains to a copper- mining town, Ackanobe. We arrived there late that night. Upon our arrival, we were met at the railroad station with a complete new set of guards and, much to our surprise, a new colonel to be our new camp commander.

285

At the moment I met him, I knew we had a good Joe for our new commander just by the way he talked to us, via the interpreter. He had a smile on his face that was different from those in my dealings with this race of people, especially from that on the face of a Japanese officer. It took a big load off my back, knowing that my dealings with Little Caesar were over. Everyone in the camp was much relieved to get rid of the no-good son of a bitch, as was I. They, too, were in constant fear for their lives while under the command of Little Caesar. He was mean and became meaner as the days progressed, now that they were losing the war. I am glad to say that son of a bitch was well taken care of in the criminal war trials; he received thirty years at hard labor in prison. We found out fast that a Japanese can smile and even laugh with you, but eventually we got to be able to tell by their smile or laughter whether it was true or false. We found out fast that a Japanese could smile one moment and run a bayonet through you the next. Believe me that has happened many times, I have witnessed it with my own eyes in both the prison camps of the Philippines and in the Sacrajima Prison camp in Osaka. The Japanese guards and military were a tricky bunch of bastards. Beware.

When we were all lined up and clear of the railroad tracks we were loaded onto trucks, and taken to what was to be our new home, the Ackanobe Prison camp. The camp was about a mile up a narrow, rocky road from the town of Ackanobe, it was a steady climb all the way. The prison camp consisted of five buildings erected on the right- hand side of the road on a small hill. There were three large barracks built identical to those of the Sacrajima Prison camp in Osaka. Each of the barracks had a bottom and a loft overhead. Each barrack would house exactly one hundred prisoners. Toward the right as you came into camp was a cook shack. (For what? There was never anything to cook.) A little to the side of that was a smaller building for an infirmary to care for the sick. (For what? Doc had no medicines to administer to the sick), and we had a sick bay. Directly across the road were two nice-looking buildings: one for the camp commander's quarters and the other to house the prison guards.

As soon as the prisoners were all inside the prison compound, the camp commander had me assign the prisoners to their spaces in the barracks. I reserved the first barracks for the "Yankees," as the Americans were called by the British and Australians. It was the one nearest the gate. The British warrant officer took the second barracks for the British, leaving the Aussies the third one. As soon as we were all squared away in our new barracks, I was informed by the interpreter that we were all to line up on the grinder to await orders.

In a short while, the new camp commander came into the camp and introduced himself and told us, through the interpreter, what work we would be required to perform both in camp and in the copper mine. The mine, he explained, was about a quarter of a mile up a hill from the camp. He then told us that food was a scarcity at that time in Nippon due to the war, but he would do everything in his power to get food to us. He told us that we would be taken up to the mine the following day, where we would be able to see what work we would be required to perform, but in the meantime we should *yashamay*.

The reason I took the barracks nearest to the gate was because it was my duty to have a working party ready to go to work between five and six each morning, rain or shine, seven days a week. In order to carry out this mission, I had to send a messenger across the road every night to the Nipponese commander's office to ascertain how many prisoners would be required for the working party the next morning. The working party had to be up and ready no later than six o'clock each morning to move out of the camp and head for the mine.

Each night, I would check the list of names to be submitted to the camp commander for the next day's working party to Dr. Nardini. I wanted him to make the final decision as to which men were able to work. I did this to make sure no one was on the list who was not fit to go to the mine. Dr. Nardini, the British warrant officer, and I tried to give each man a break by giving him a day off now and then. We both went over the list before I finalized the working party for any particular day. Our new Japanese commander in the Ackanobe mining camp was a helluva fine man, I never thought I would ever see a Japanese who would look after the welfare of an American POW; however, this Joe did. He would not allow a sick prisoner to go to work in the mine, and if there was food to be had, everyone got a share, regardless if he worked or not.

81. Working in a Copper Mine at Ackanobe

The following day after our arrival in the prison camp at Ackanobe, about ten in the morning, we were taken by the camp commander on a leisurely walk up to the copper mine. We were told that we would be required to walk to and from the mine each day. The hill we had to walk up was sort of a gradual, lazy climb, not too bad. Upon our arrival at the entrance to the mine, the camp commander ordered the prisoners to be divided into groups of twenty to a group. I was then told to put the highest ranking prisoner in the group in charge as their *hancho*. He would serve under me, and I in turn was to serve under the leading Nipponese *hancho*.

In one year's time, the original prisoners that were sent to the Sacrajima Prison Camp No. 3 in Osaka had been reduced to 262. This reduction in ranks of the prisoners was due to loss of life from disease, bayonetting, or just plain giving up.

Seeing that there were always about eight to ten prisoners on the sick list, I could only make twelve groups of twenty prisoners, and one group of eight to work in the mine cart repair shop. That left the doctor in camp taking care of the sick, the British sergeant and me as *hanchos,* and two cooks to sort of clean up the barracks and count out the silkworms or the mulberry leaves to feed us when we returned to camp. So the *hanchos* for the thirteen groups were five chief petty officers and three first class petty officers from the American ranks, and five *hanchos* assigned by the British warrant officer, which made twelve groups of twenty to a group to work inside the mine, and one group of eight to work topside in the cart repair shop. When all thirteen groups were needed, it still allowed me to leave twelve prisoners on the sick list in camp. There were many days they needed only ten groups, which gave a bunch of the fellows a break.

Japan by this time, in 1945, had drained all the able-bodied men from Japan and pressed them into service in either the army or navy. All who were left in Japan were the very old or the very young to run their country, which was why they were very dependent on the prisoners for labor. My immediate superior, or *hancho,* was just a young lad, only about fourteen years old. There were about twenty-five older Japanese mine workers who were very efficient in the operations of the mine. They became the Nipponese *hanchos* for the prisoners working in the mines at the various levels.

The mine had eight levels, and all were working and producing copper ore. Most of the Japanese *hanchos* working down in the mine were men about sixty or seventy years old. The Japanese lad in charge of the mine cart repair shop was only about nine years of age. Our camp guards were regular army personnel, about thirty to forty years of age.

Japan had also imported Korean prisoners and used them for forced labor as well. The Koreans fared much better than we, because they were Oriental and also a neighbor of Japan. But they also were considered cowards and held in contempt as we and the British, because they, too, did not commit hari-kari, but, as the Japanese put it, used the cowardly way out and surrendered.

When the prisoners had all had been put in groups and were ready to go to work, an old timer from the copper mines was made the head *hancho* of that group with a prisoner of war *hancho* under him. The Nipponese *hancho* was responsible for teaching the prisoners how to mine the copper ore. The Japanese *hancho* took his group aside and explained what was expected of them. They were then loaded into mine cars and taken down to the mine level on which they would be working.

After they got down in the mines, the men were taught how to drill holes into the mine with a ten-foot-long drill bit. The holes were placed strategically in the bank of rock, and dynamite was poked into the holes. After each hole was packed, a fuse cap was then attached. When they were all capped and fused, a big, heavy metal chainlike blanket was placed over the area to be blasted to keep the rock from being blown all over. When the iron blanket was in place and all was ready, the prisoners were then taken out of the shaft to a safe position and the fuse was activated.

When the dust was cleared away and it was fit to go back into the blasted area, the prisoners went back and shoveled the ore onto the mine shaft carts and hauled it out to be crushed and the copper extracted from it. The tailings were dumped over the bank. This procedure was repeated over and over. The prisoners worked on all eight levels.

Every once in a while, when the rock was blasted away, they would find a large snake hibernating in the rock. The snake would fall out along with the blasted ore that had just come down. The snake was still asleep and all coiled up like a garden hose. Some of them were really big. When stretched out, they were seven or eight feet long and about three inches wide. They kept us all guessing and trying to figure out how they got there, but regardless of how, they were there. Snakes to the Nipponese were a delicacy, and the prisoners were instructed that all the snakes they found must be turned over to them.

One day the *hancho* did not go right in after the blast had been made, and a snake came down, all curled up with the rock. It was a smaller one, about a little over an inch wide and about three or four feet long. One of the prisoners retrieved the snake and put in inside his shirt and kept working. When he came up out of the mine to line up for *tinko,* as we did each night, and stood there, waiting to *tinko,* the snake crawled out of the prisoner's pant leg. After all, the snake had been inside the prisoner's shirt over two hours.

A Japanese army *hancho* saw the snake, crawling out of the prisoner's pants' leg. He went into a rage, and in a fit, he took his club and worked the poor guy over; he just kept beating him. Finally the camp commander arrived on the scene and stopped him. At the time, it was very serious, but after we got into camp and got to talking about how it crawled out of Joe's pants' leg and how the eyes of the guard lit up when he saw it, we all had a big laugh over it. However, the Nips didn't get all of the snakes. The prisoners were able to smuggle a few into camp without them knowing it. They made good soup. I never did find out what kind of snakes they were or how they possibly could get into the ore rock so far down in the ground. They were found as far down as the seventh level. I don't remember if any snakes were found on the eighth or not.

Each day, I would travel down into the mine in a mine cart and visit the prisoners on all levels to make sure the prisoners didn't get into trouble. But as I had just gotten over a bout with pneumonia, the doctor said I should stay in the fresh air as much as possible, so most of the time I left that chore to the senior member, who was the prisoner *hancho,* in each group. Therefore, I spent as much time that I possibly could with the men on topside in the ball-bearing shop, up and out of the mines in the fresh air.

Sometimes I would accompany the camp commander down to all levels when he was on his inspection tour, or if I heard of a prisoner in trouble, I would immediately go down in the mine to aid the prisoner. We used to have a little fun with the little Nipponese *hancho* who was in charge of the prisoners who worked in the bearing shop. Because he was only nine years old, I would spend quite a bit of time with him, trying to teach him English, while he in turn tried to teach me Japanese. He was a real nice boy. The prisoners got away with a lot with him; he was always smiling.

The bearing shop was on topside, and eight prisoners were assigned to work there. When a mine cart was returned to the mine, it went down directly to the lowest level, then made its way back to the top again, taking several weeks for a cart to reach the top. When an ore car worked its way to the top, it would go through the bearing shop to have the bearings oiled, greased, and changed if needed. They always needed changing; the prisoners saw to that. They would take a sledgehammer to get them out for checking and greasing, and in that way, they always got broken. If they didn't needed changing before, they certainly did when the prisoners got through working them over.

I told the boys who were working in the bearing shop to let a couple of carts every so often pass through and returned to the mines in order to not arouse too much suspicion. Also I wanted to protect our little *hancho*, who was so good to all of us. Also, when a big shot would visit the bearing shop, I had the prisoners take it easy and not damage the bearings in taking them off. They worked slower so as not to get too many cars repaired while the big shots were there. They didn't want too many carts going back into the mines. But as soon as they were gone, out came the sledgehammers to get the wheels off.

There was a fairly good-sized building adjoining the bearing shop. It was about fourteen by twenty-four feet with a fifteen-foot high ceiling. When we arrived in Ackanobe, that building was packed to the ceiling with boxes of bearings that had been purchased over the years from the United States and other countries and had been put in storage as part of their preparation for their war with the West. It was a grave mistake to allow the prisoners a free hand in the usage of these bearings, because within a very short time, the bearings were all used up. After they were used up, when the carts came up for a bearing check, it was simple; there were no bearings to fix them, hence, no carts to go back down into the mine, hence, no carts to handle the fresh ore that had been blasted.

Again, when a big shot was there in the shop, the prisoners would gently take the wheels off and grease the bearings and send those cars back into the mine. Or maybe we would take the good bearings off one cart and use them to fix another. That only happened when the big shots were watching. As the cars were useless without bearings, there was nothing left to do but to pile them up outside. Sometimes they would "accidentally" be run over the bank with the tailings from the mine. We got away with this because they had sent, as I said, all the able-bodied men off to fight the war. Also, we had this nine-year-old Nipponese boy as the *hancho* in the bearing shop.

He was the boss and a helluva good kid and a lot of fun. His lunch consisted of a sardine can filled with rice with a small fish about the size of a small herring, like the ones we used for bait back home, one cigarette, and once in a while, he got an orange or another kind of fruit. He felt sorry for us prisoners getting nothing to eat, so each day, he would give me his lunch and the one cigarette that was allotted to him daily. I would divide it among the eight workers in the bearing shop. We each got about two tea-spoonfuls of rice and a couple of puffs on the cigarette. He would also give us the apple or the orange from his lunch to share.

We never knew what was in store for us in the way of food each day when we returned from work. Which was nothing most of the time. Many times, after working hard in the mines all day, upon our return to camp, we received no food and were forced to go to bed without a thing to eat that night. Rice was a thing of the past for the prisoners. The *hancho*'s lunch, although just a mouthful, was truly a blessing, especially on the day he would give us his orange or other piece of fruit.

Each day when we arrived back in camp from the mine, I would go over to the cook shack to see if there was to be anything to feed the prisoners that night. Well, one day, upon returning to camp, I got the surprise of my life when I asked the cook if he had anything for us that night. He replied, "there sure is," and went over and took the lid off the big soup kettle. I got one look and immediately got sick and had to rush outside.

It seems that a horse had died or was killed by some means unknown to us. It was found up on a hill, starting to decay and was completely covered with maggots. The Japanese guards made some of the prisoners who had been left in camp because of being unfit for work in the mine that day to go up into the mountain and carry the carcass into the camp for the cooks to make soup for dinner for the prisoners that night. The pot was a mass of white maggots. It makes me sick even now to think of it. Well, I made the cooks get rid of it pronto. Not wanting to get the cooks in trouble, I immediately left there and went over across the road to the headquarters and told the camp commander about what I had done, expecting to take a beating for my actions. I explained to him that it would have made everyone in the camp sick even to look at it. Much to my surprise, the camp commander agreed with me. He got the guards that had the carcass brought into camp and punished them right on the spot. After he was through punishing them, he told them they themselves could not have any dinner that night, and that if the cooks hadn't got rid of that mess, he would have fed them some of the soup they had prepared for the prisoners. I was sure glad at that moment that we got rid of Little Caesar or it would have been different story. Nothing like that ever happened again, thanks to our new commander.

On 30 July 1945, while I was making my rounds, one of the Nipponese *hanchos* down in the third level broke out a picture and kept looking at it, and after a while he showed it me. It was a picture of a Hollywood movie star. He explained to me that this gal was going to be his new wife. I found out later that day that all the Nipponese had been given such pictures. They were told that they were all going to America to meet the girl whose picture each one had been given and that they would be married in the United States prior to bringing them back to their homeland.

292

Strange, but the Japanese had faith in their superiors; they believed everything they were told. One day, my little *hancho* told me that his boss had told him that due to not having enough food to feed their own population, let alone the prisoners, that all the elderly men, and all women, regardless of age, and all small children were going to be sacrificed to their God. They would be sent to meet their ancestors when the next full moon occurred on the twenty-first of August 1945, which happened to be my birthday.

They were also told that the reason that all the young men would be taken to America and be given new wives would be to repopulate their homeland after the war was over. Their wives would be the ones in the picture they had been given. They were told that the war would be over very shortly, that America was losing the war, because the Nipponese had landed on United States soil, and soon, America would be brought to its knees and surrender. It hurt me immensely to have these little fellows believe that line of junk that the elders were feeding them. And it hurt much more to know that they were believing every word of it.

All that day, our little *hancho* in the ball-bearing shop was so happy about getting this new wife in America that he never let the picture they had given him out of his hands. He kept looking at it all that day and saying, "I go America, your country. I get wife, see," and he would show us the picture of this beautiful girl that had been given to him. It was pitiful; he was such a fine boy, I wanted so much to tell him they were lying, your country is losing the war. But this, I could never do, for fear of breaking his little heart. He was such a good kid, and he told me he loved Americans.

Part Eight

The Atomic Bomb Ends the War

82. The Atomic Bomb Is Dropped on Hiroshima

After many months of meetings and deliberations with his advisors and those in the know about the power of a new weapon, the atom bomb, so secret that even our senators and congressman weren't aware of it, the president of the United States, Franklin Delano Roosevelt, had a terrible decision to make about this new bomb, how to use it and where.

Some wanted it to just burst in the air approximately twenty to twenty-five thousand feet over Tokyo. They felt that it would just be a demonstration to the Japanese war lords and not harm anyone, and hoped that Japan would sense its destructive power and come to its knees in surrender.

Others wanted to just drop it as they would any other bomb. It was thought that when the high-ranking Japanese generals and admirals saw the great clouds of fire and realized the havoc this bomb could impose upon their country, they would bring the war to a screaming halt. It was argued that if the bomb was set off above Tokyo, the United States would be able to say to the warlords of Japan. "Do you want to surrender or shall we use this bomb and blow your country off the map?"

There was another side who insisted that merely setting the bomb off over Tokyo would not work. They felt that the Japanese must be shown the power of the bomb, and it must be used on Japanese soil in order for them to accept an unconditional surrender.

All the discussion, which took place over a period of months late into the night, put a great responsibility on the shoulders of President Roosevelt. It was his responsibility to say where and when the bomb should be dropped. He wasn't convinced of how the bomb should be used or even where to use it, and it made quite a dilemma for him. President Roosevelt found himself alone. He was in a position where he could not discuss this topic with even his closest friends, not even with his own family. What a nightmare it must have been for him. He went night after night without sleep, the atomic bomb continuously on his mind. Enough to make anyone go berserk. The atomic bomb was so ultra-top secret, even the vice president was not made aware of it, and so, he couldn't even discuss it with the vice president, Harry Truman. Only the president and two or three of the inventors of the bomb were in on the know at the start. After so many sleepless nights the burden got too heavy to carry alone.

In his capacity as commander in chief of the armed forces, the president called in his chief of staff and, after swearing him to the strictest secrecy, enlightened him about the bomb. Upon the death of President Roosevelt, and only then, was the new president made aware of such a bomb being in existence.

Discussions started all over again with President Harry S. Truman at the helm. So after many weeks and listening to the pros and cons and of the destruction this bomb could produce, President Truman locked himself in seclusion. I feel he must have said many prayers for guidance from his Heavenly Father before making his final decision to drop the bomb on a target rather then just set it off over Tokyo, as was suggested, or whether to even use the bomb. This heavy burden on President Truman's shoulders and the worry that went with it also played havoc with Harry Truman's health, which was a great concern in Washington.

In the first week of August 1945, President Truman gave the secretary of defense authorization to order the armed forces to drop the bomb on a target. This authorization cleared the path for the ultimate dropping of the atomic bomb on Hiroshima that fateful day on 6 August 1945. Just three days later, a second atomic bomb was dropped, on Nagasaki. A third one was to be dropped on Osaka if the Nipponese didn't show any sign of surrendering.

All day long on the seventh of August, I could see a grave look on the faces of the guards, and even by the look on the camp commander's face, something was wrong. The camp commander talked to me every day while making his rounds up in the mine, but this day he came to the mine and did not even ask me how I felt. That was very strange. Our little *hancho* in the bearing shop was very quiet, not playful as he always was. The prisoners were all talking among themselves and wondering what the hell happened. Not even one guard would give us an inkling of why they looked so sad. We all knew by now something had happened, but what?

Neither the camp commander, the guards, nor the Nipponese civilians with whom we practically rubbed elbows with on the path each day going and coming from the copper mine uttered a sound about the devastation that had taken place the day before in Hiroshima. They just went quietly about their work as if nothing had happened. None of the little kids who were our *hanchos* in the mine said a word to me or anyone else about it.

298

About four days later, a Nipponese guard down in the mine was so happily showing me the picture of the lady in America who was to be his new wife, turned to me and said, "I go soon to your country and get my new wife," then he went on to say that Ohio, San Francisco, and Washington were no more; they had been bombed off the face of the earth like the Americans did to Hiroshima.

This struck me. I had never even heard a whisper about any city being blown off the map in Japan. This perked up my ears. It drew my attention fast. I immediately questioned him about what he had said about Hiroshima. He told me that on the sixth of August, the Americans dropped a big, big, big bomb on Hiroshima and wiped out the whole city, killing everyone, including the animals. Then he told me that yesterday, a second big bomb like the one dropped on Hiroshima was dropped on Nagasaki. He said that both cities were no more. This was the first I had heard about Hiroshima or Nagasaki being bombed or anything about such a big bomb as that Japanese guard had described. The rest of the guards never said a word to any of us.

I was flabbergasted.

"Wait a minute," I said to him, "did you say this happened on August sixth?"

"Yes," he said.

Then it all came to me. I knew why the camp commander and all the guards were so shaken up that day, just four days ago. Later, back in the camp, I told Dr. Nardini and some prisoners what I had been told. Then I went back to the barracks and told the rest of the prisoners what I had heard about Hiroshima and Nagasaki. They said, almost in unison, "It's a damn good thing that Little Caesar is not our boss now. He would have taken it out on us by using some of us for bayonet practice."

It set everyone to wondering how in heck they got the state of Ohio mixed up with the cities of San Francisco and Washington, D.C. Why Ohio? We couldn't figure it out. Later, when I questioned the guard who told me, he still insisted on saying Ohio, San Francisco and Washington were no more. I got to thinking that maybe the reason we prisoners in the Ackanobe mining camp had not heard about that "big bomb" having been dropped on Hiroshima was that probably the people were too shocked at having their towns destroyed in a flash.

299

83. The War Is Ended

The Terrible Nightmare Is Over

As mentioned before, every night it was my duty to send a messenger across the road to the camp commander's headquarters to find out how many men were needed for the next day's working party to go to the mines, as each day it changed according to what levels they would be working on. On the evening of 17 August 1945, I sent the messenger over to get the information on the working party for the next day. He was gone for quite some time, much more than usual. I started to get worried and was just about ready to go over myself to try and ascertain the reason for the delay when he returned.

The messenger was all shook up and very nervous and could hardly say a thing.

"Calm down, Carter, and tell me what happened," I said. He started to tell me, then he broke out in tears and started to stutter, which he never did before. He was really scared. "Carter, please, just calm down, and tell me what happened over there." I said again. He waited a few minutes.

"They are all drunk over there," he said, "and they are all acting very crazy. Ski, they are in a hell of a mess over there. It seems even the colonel is drunk. He keeps shouting along with the rest of the guards *'Oster, oster, yashamay. Yashamay. Shagoto ney. Shagoto ney.'*"

Yashamay (rest), *oster* (tomorrow), *shagoto* (work), and *ney* (no), together means No work tomorrow, no work tomorrow. By repeating it, they were saying, "There would be no work for many days."

Upon hearing this, I started to get very nervous and all worked up, as I knew what the consequences would be if I didn't have a working party out there the next morning. I figured that they were having a party and being all boozed up, they would not remember what they had said about no work, and I would find myself behind the eight ball. After awhile, I gathered my wits and, not taking any chances, went over to see Dr. Nardini in the hospital barracks and told him what was happening. I explained to Doc what my messenger had told me that they were all drunk and having a party across the road, that they were all shouting over and over, including the camp commander, "tomorrow tomorrow, rest rest." I told Dr. Nardini I was afraid that if I didn't have a working party ready to leave the camp by six in

300

the morning as usual, I would be in very serious trouble. In view of the fact that he understood the Japanese language better then I, I asked him to go over and try to get this thing straightened out.

Here at Ackanobe, the doctor didn't have the contact, and so, wasn't getting his newspapers every night as he did at Osaka, therefore wasn't as informed as before.

"I'll go over and see what gives over there," he said. "Come over with me if you would like to, Ski."

"No, I'd better not," I said. "It would be better for you to go alone, Doc. You can understand their lingo and that would put you in a better position to concentrate on what they are talking about. No, I had better stay here, Doc. You can get more done over there without me tagging along. I would only be in the way."

Doc went over to see the colonel. I stayed at the hospital barracks to wait for him to return. He was gone quite some time, about three quarters of an hour. When Doc returned, I noticed he had a Japanese newspaper in his hand, which he must have picked up at the camp commander's office. He told me that what the messenger had told me was true. There wouldn't be any work tomorrow for the men, so forget it, and get some sleep. He also told me that he would investigate it more thoroughly in the morning, at which time he hoped to be better informed and in position to enlighten me more about what was happening.

The next morning at about seven-thirty on 18 August 1945, the camp commander called me to his office and informed me that there would be no work for a few days and the prisoners would be given some much needed rest during the interim. He went on to say that I was to have the bathtub filled and heated so all of the prisoners could get a good hot bath. He gave me several bars of soap and about two dozen safety razors to pass out so that we could all shave off our beards and get rid of the lice.

Upon my return, I immediately went over and told Dr. Nardini what had taken place, so as to keep him informed. After giving him a couple of the razors and some soap for the sick, I told him as soon as the bath was hot enough, I'd have my messenger tell him. I then went back to my barracks to get a detail together to fill the bathtub and start the fire under it, and to get the bath ready as soon as possible.

As I was approaching the barracks, a Nipponese guard stopped me and said the camp commander wants me to send a detail of about thirty men over to get clean clothing for all the prisoners. While the detail was getting the clothing, I passed out the razors and the soap. I had a tough time containing the men, because things were moving too fast for any of us to comprehend. The men were almost going crazy at such a strange turn of events.

I then proceeded to pass the word around to let all the prisoners know what I had learned so far. I told them there would be no work for a few days, and they could get some of that much needed rest. I also told them that they we were getting the bath water hot so that everyone could get a hot bath, and they would be notified when the bath water was ready. But in the meantime they should all shave off their beards to rid themselves of the lice before getting into the nice fresh bath water. As the men were getting shaved, I told them that everyone would be given new clothes, which would be issued before their taking a bath. Boy, did I get a rousing cheer on that one. This was to be the first batch of clean clothes since we were taken prisoner on Corregidor in the Philippines, and did we need clothes badly? We were all in rags, and I mean rags.

While I was relating to my fellow prisoners the good news I had just received from the camp commander, a Japanese guard came in the barracks and told me to have about thirty men across the road in about five minutes to get an International Red Cross package for each man. I was overwhelmed and really had a hard time to catch my breath. After a minute or so, not believing what I had just heard him say, I inquired of the guard to tell me again.

"Did you say a Red Cross package for each prisoner?"

"That is what the camp commander sent me over to tell you," he replied.

I still couldn't make myself believe what I was hearing. However, I called for thirty volunteers, and when they found out what it was for, I had about fifty or more men wanting to go on that detail, It seemed like every person there volunteered; even those who were sick volunteered. I explained that each man would be given an International Red Cross package all to himself, that it was not to be divided with eight other prisoners as had always been required before. Did that go over big? I myself had a hard time trying to make myself believe all this was true. No work for several days, a hot bath, new clothing, and now one Red Cross parcel for each man.

No, this can't be true, it had to be a dream. I had one helluva time trying to contain the men, with all this news flying around so fast. Later in the morning, at about ten, the camp commander sent a guard over with the message for me to have all the men on the parade ground at eleven-thirty. He had a very important message for us. I went over to the hospital bar-

302

racks and told Doc. I told him all the good news I had received, and then I showed him the message the guard had just delivered to me. Doc didn't say a thing. He just stayed calm. I thought to myself, *Doc knows something and won't tell me.*

This was the first time since my arrival in Japan that I had a hard time trying to control the prisoners. They were as overwhelmed as I was. Things were happening too fast for any of us to comprehend. Yes, I think I was in shock. I was completely overwhelmed and could not for the life of me even come close to understand what the hell was taking place. So I decided to go over again to the hospital and see my good friend Dr. Nardini. I felt that, as he stayed calm through all I had told him on my last trip over to see him, he was holding back on me, and maybe he would tell me if I went over again.

I could hardly wait to get to the infirmary and ask the good doctor to help me in figuring out just what the hell was going on. I told him I was all shook up about the happenings for the past two hours: no work, getting all this clothing, baths, a Care package per person, yes, and even razors to shave with. And now the camp commander had something very important to tell us at 11:30 and wanted everyone on the parade ground at that time. I looked Doc straight in the eye.

"Please," I said, "if you know anything, please, tell me what the hell is happening, before we all go stark raving mad."

Doc put his hand on my shoulder.

"Yes, Ski," he said, "it is truly very important what the colonel is going to tell you, and we want to be sure everyone hears what the commander has to say. I will have all the sick out there, too. Please, Ski, bear with me for a little while longer. That is all I can tell you now."

From the tone of his voice, I knew there was something that he had learned from that Japanese newspaper he had gotten the night before from the commander's office and was not telling me at that time.

"Doc," I said, "last night when you came out of the camp commander's office, I noticed you had a Japanese newspaper under your arm. Please tell me if there was anything in that paper that caused the commander and the guards to all get drunk and party most of the night." I also inquired of him as to why we were being treated so kindly? "Please, Doc," I said, "tell me what you found out, if anything at all, in that newspaper?"

He just looked at me. "Ski," he said, "I'm sorry," and after a little pause, he repeated, "I'm truly very sorry is all I can say for now. Please wait a time, with patience, and listen to what the camp commander has to say at eleven-thirty this morning. I'm sorry, Ski, I wish I could tell you

303

more." Dr. Nardini told me he had very little sleep, as he had been studying the newspaper practically all night and morning to be able to interpret it to its fullest.

Now I noticed something in his face. Yes, he wanted to tell me something but was afraid. He was acting funny, unusually strange. It seemed he wanted very much to tell me something, but just couldn't. However, he kept what he knew to himself and never so much as uttered a peep to me or anyone, of what he had on his mind or what he read in that newspaper. We stood there in complete silence for about two minutes.

"Doc," I finally said, "I'm sure baffled and can't seem to find the right answer for this sudden turn around the Nipponese have made today. I have an idea, but it's too scary to even think about it. Do you think that the Nips have gotten a change of heart? Or that it has something to do with winding down the war?"

Doc just stood there staring at me, never saying a word. Looking straight into his eyes again, I could see he wanted to say something. After a moment or two, he spoke.

"Ski," he said, "you just showed me a note from the camp commander, saying that he was coming over in about an hour or so, and that he said he has a message he wants to convey to all of us. Let's wait and see what he has to say."

I was almost in tears as we were talking. I was frustrated about all that was happening and not being able to get to the bottom of it.

I went back to the barracks and told the fellows what Doc had told me, but they all kept questioning me, and all that I could say was, "Fellows, you all know as much as I do. It's all very strange and hard to comprehend. As soon as I find out what this is all about, I'll let you know."

At 11:00 A.M., all the prisoners were shaven and had a nice hot bath and were all dressed up in new clothing. I then told everyone to proceed out to the parade ground. In a short time, we were out there, including the sick. We were all milling around in the area, waiting for the camp commander to address us. We looked like a different bunch of guys. We hardly knew one another without our lice-ridden beards, shaved off for the first time in about four years. The Japanese had built a platform on a mound of dirt prior to our coming to Ackanobe. It was in front of this platform that we lined up each morning before going to work and again upon our return to *tinko*. Also, the camp commander would address us and tell us what we were expected to do.

304

I had all the prisoners, including those who were too weak to stand up, out there in front of the platform, as I was told to do by the camp commander. At exactly 11:30 that morning, the colonel came over and mounted the platform. He stood there for a while. He seemed to be a little bewildered as to how to begin or what to say to us. After a few seconds, through the interpreter, he finally spoke.

"Okay, please, all sit on the ground."

This took me by surprise, as never in the four years since I was under Japanese control had any Japanese said "please" to me. We were bewildered and wondering what the hell was the score. This was so strange, we all kept looking at one another. We were never allowed to sit down in the camp commander's presence. A prisoner was always made to stand at attention when a Japanese officer was present, especially so when we were being addressed.

After we were seated, the commander started talking in Japanese, and the interpreter, who was educated in the United States at Yale, was of course supposed to translate what he said. However, the interpreter was lying. He was not repeating, hardly a word, that the colonel was saying. With my almost four years as a prisoner under the Japanese, I understood quite a bit of the Japanese lingo. I understood the language much better than I could speak it. So I could understand some, but not all of what the commander was saying. It was nothing like what the interpreter was saying.

The interpreter told us the camp commander said, "We should rest for a few days, as America was begging for peace, and if America was not granted peace by the Japanese, we must go back and work hard in the mines, so we should get a lot of rest."

Dr. Nardini was standing right near the interpreter. I kept trying to get his attention, and after a few minutes, I was finally successful and got Doc's attention, and as the interpreter was talking, I kept shaking my head, signifying no, no, and moving my lips, and without a sound, I said, "Doc, this is all wrong what the interpreter is telling us. Stop him. Please stop him."

The doctor looked at me for a few seconds, and without warning, probably unable to stand those lies any longer, he jumped up on the platform and knocked the interpreter clean off the platform. He fell down among the prisoners, and a few of them were able to give him a punch or two, something they had wanted to do for the past four years. The Japanese guards started after the doctor with the bayonets drawn on their guns, but the commander stopped them. Then Dr. Nardini, in fluent Japanese, told

305

the camp commander that the interpreter was lying; he was not repeating correctly what he was telling the prisoners. Then Dr. Nardini asked the commander, in very good Japanese, for permission to speak to the prisoners. The camp commander stood there in amazement. He stood there looking at Dr. Nardini. You could easily see that the commander was stunned at hearing Dr. Nardini speak the language so fluently.

The camp commander, after getting over the shock of hearing a prisoner speaking so fluently in the Nipponese tongue, told him to go ahead and talk to the prisoners.

"Fellows," Dr. Nardini said, "I have some terrifying news to tell you, and when I am done I want you all to yell, scream, or cry as loud as you can at the top of your lungs, because I don't want any of you to have a stroke or heart attack this late in the game. You have suffered too damned long and too damned much these past four years at the hands of these bastards. My only prayer is that you all return safely to your home and loved ones. So listen carefully to what I am about to tell you." He hesitated a few seconds, probably thinking how best to put the news to us. Finally, after a few seconds, he brushed tears from his eyes and then went on.

"First, let me say this. That son of a bitch," pointing down at the interpreter, "is a lying bastard. He has been lying to you for the past four years. There were many times while he has been our interpreter, I found it hard to control myself while listening to that son of a bitch wrongly interpreting what our camp commander was actually saying to you. But I had to keep myself concealed, and not let them know I could speak their language and read their newspapers. Had they known, I would not have gotten hold of their newspapers, and I would not have been able to keep your hopes alive. A lot of you would not be around today to hear what I have to say if they had known for one minute that I could read their newspapers. Yes, although it hurt at times, listening to that son of a bitch lying, I was forced to swallow what that bastard was telling you, rather then expose myself.

"Fellows, it is the other way around, the Japanese are crawling on their hands and knees to Manila in the Philippines, begging for peace. At this very moment, fellows, the magnificent ship, the U.S.S. *Missouri,* with several U.S. battleships that are accompanying her, are steaming at full speed ahead toward Tokyo Bay to accept an unconditional surrender. I said unconditional surrender of the imperial Japanese armed forces.

"Okay, men, now get ready to scream, yell, do anything to avoid heart failure or a stroke. Here is the straight dope, fellows, *the war is over!*

306

"Your nightmare is over, and you will all be heading home in a few days. Good luck, fellows, you have weathered the storm."

As I write now, my eyes are full of tears, and I guess they always will be when I talk or even think of that time in my life. I can hardly control myself from crying out loud, just as I did that great day that the good Lord had set me free. I shall never forget that day as long as I live. This is some fifty years later. I am almost 91 years young, and I still choke up.

We all cried, yelled, and screamed at the top of our lungs for a considerable length of time. That celebration of screaming and yelling seemed as if it went on for more than an hour. But in truth, it probably lasted only fifteen or twenty minutes. I will never know. I only know I almost went crazy.

While the crying and screaming was going on, a British sailor broke out a British Union Jack that he had smuggled into the camp and had managed to keep it hidden throughout the war. I cannot, for the life of me, imagine, with the hundreds of shakedowns and inspections that we went through, how he kept it hidden.

Another British fellow, a bugler in the British army at the Royal Navy Yard, Hong Kong, China, went over to the camp commander's office and borrowed his bugle, and as they raised the Union Jack, the bugler played colors while the British sang "God save our king." Even we Americans joined in the singing along with the British and Australians. We Americans weren't as fortunate to have Old Glory handy to haul up to the top of the pole as our friends the British did. So I sent my messenger over to the Japanese camp commander's office and asked him to give us some cloth and some paint to make a flag with.

He returned with a piece of cloth that looked like a bed sheet, about eight feet long and five feet wide, and a can of red and a can of blue paint so that we could make a flag. The men painted a blue field on the upper corner of the cloth, and then a stripe of red paint four inches wide on the top and bottom, then divided the balance of the cloth to make eleven more stripes of six white and five red, and painted the other five red lines. It had thirteen stripes, seven red and six white. Now all that was needed to complete Old Glory were the stars.

The camp commander sent us over some more white cloth and about ten pairs of shears and some needles and thread, which we had requested. While the painting was being done, several fellows were making stars from the white cloth. Each man, no matter how weak he was, had his turn with a needle and thread to sew a star on the American flag we were mak-

307

ing. For those who were too weak to sew, we put a needle and thread in his hand and moved his hand so he could help make Old Glory. It made them very happy to think they had a part in the making of the Stars and Stripes, the flag of their country.

When Old Glory was completed with the stars on both sides, it was raised to top of the pole, with the bugler again playing colors. And the Americans were joined by the British and Aussies as we sang the American national anthem, "The Star-Spangled Banner," followed by "God Bless America." We also sang "America," (My country 'tis of thee . . . .) The British and Aussies sang along with us on that one. The tune is the same as their "God Save the King."

As we were raising Old Glory to the top of the pole, I happened to look over at the Japanese office across the road, and to my surprise, I saw the camp commander raising the Japanese flag the "Rising Sun" in front of his office at the same time. There were three or four Japanese guards standing there in a salute as he raised his country's flag.

As soon as I regained my composure and the ceremonies were over, I immediately had the men arrest all the Nip guards who had treated us barbarically. The camp commander aided us in this. He had the other guards who were good to us take their weapons away from them and turn them over to us. The Americans and the British took turns guarding them. They remained under guard until the arrival of the U.S. Armed Forces, at which time they were turned over to the U.S. Army personnel to be held for the war crimes trial.

The Japanese guards who we arrested were just plain mean and rotten. They all deserved to be punished for their cruelty against the prisoners. Some of the Nipponese guards treated the prisoners very humanely. The colonel, our camp commander, was a wonderful guy and treated everyone of us in a very civilized way, as human beings, while still letting us know that we were in his charge as prisoners of war. He was always fair and honest with us. Under him, there was no inhumane treatment such as bayoneting the prisoners, hitting and knocking the doctor around for protecting those unfit to work, and much more.

The commander at Ackanobe was a lot different than the one at Sacrajima in Osaka. Little Caesar was held for the war crimes trials and was sentenced to thirty years in prison at hard labor and deserved every bit of it. He was rotten to the core. He really should have been hung along with General Homma. Little Caesar was responsible for many of our buddies being killed, using the prisoners for bayonet practice every time the war news went against the Japanese. He is the one who always beat the doctor up for trying to protect the sick prisoners when the doctor was only doing his duty by looking out for them, trying to keep them from going to work when they should have been in a hospital.

When all the commotion was over, I went over to see Dr. Nardini, who was now back at the infirmary, and looked straight in his eyes.

"Doc," I said, "now I know why you were acting so differently this morning. You knew about the end of the war before the commander told us, didn't you?

"Yes, Ski," he said, "that's true, I did. But as much as I wanted to tell you, I couldn't say anything at that time, and I guess you know now it was for various reasons. Ski, right after you came to see me last night to tell me how scared you were about the Nipponese being drunk and having a big party across the road, and you asked me to go over there to ascertain whether they did or did not want a working party today, I went over there. And after I found out what you needed to know, as long as the Nips were drinking and weren't watching me, I politely picked up one of their newspapers and was about to leave, when the colonel walked over and offered me a drink, which I refused. And with the paper in my hand, I walked out and went back to the infirmary to learn what I could from the Japanese newspaper I had picked up." He told me that he had stayed up most of the night trying to digest what was in that newspaper, and that from his knowledge of the Japanese language, he learned a lot. After a few minutes, he went on to tell me that he didn't dare tell even me, for fear it would slip out and someone would have a heart attack if it wasn't presented in the right way. I told him that all along I could see something in his facial expression, that he knew something he wanted to tell me, so I just surmised that he knew something big. But I never in my wildest dreams, dreamt that the war was over.

That afternoon, the camp commander called me over to his office and told me he had received orders from the prisoner of war rescue party to have the prisoners paint an identifying mark on the ground for the planes to see, showing them where the prisoners of war camps were located so they would know where to drop food, clothing, etcetera for us. The camp commander had already called downtown in Ackanobe and had them send him more red and some white paint and several pieces of lumber one inch by four inches and about twenty feet long, which he had the guards carry into the prison compound. The camp commander now had the Japanese guards doing all the work, letting the prisoners rest.

309

The camp commander wanted to have the Japanese paint a big cross on the ground, but the Americans and British wanted to do it themselves. So about ten or fifteen of our guys went to the parade ground to paint a big cross, as directed, in the area where we lined up for working parties each morning before going to the copper mines. They first laid the boards on the ground a couple of feet apart forming a big cross. They painted the ground between the boards red, using a big scrub brush. Then they painted the boards with the white paint, which made a huge white border completely around it. Thus, it was a large red cross with a border of white. It looked very professional.

Our camp was located high in the mountains, about a mile or so above the center of the town of Ackanobe. The camp was completely surrounded by forest. We looked like a little bare spot in a forest. Within a few hours after we had completed painting the red cross, we could hear the drone of big transport planes coming closer and closer to the our area. Then all of a sudden as they neared our camp, they swooped way down and just about cleared the treetops, their bomb-bays opened and large boxes of food and clothing started to drop to the ground. I guess rather than take a chance with killing some of the prisoners, the planes in dropping the big nets which held the merchandise overshot the camp on purpose, and the nets all fell in the woods above us just outside the camp. So before leaving the camp to go out into the hills to retrieve the boxes that had been dropped, Dr. Nardini instructed us as follows.

"Fellows, listen to me very carefully. Please do not eat a thing that was dropped, not even a candy bar. It might cost you your life." He went on to say, "I am truly pleading with you, please bring everything into the camp. I don't know what they are giving us, so for your sake and mine, please let me look it over and tell you what you should and what you should not eat. Fellows, my body is in same shape as yours is in. Our bodies cannot tolerate rich food, so listen to my advice, and we will all return home safely."

I overheard several of the prisoners saying as they were about to leave that he just wants everything for himself, etcetera.

"Halt, stop right here," I said. Then I got up on a barrel, and standing there, I said, "Hey, fellows, you guys should be ashamed of yourself for even thinking of such a thing. Look, this doctor has gone through hell for us. He has taken many beatings in trying to keep us alive and as healthy as he could, and I, for one, think he has done an outstanding job these past two years since he has been assigned to us. Can't you understand he is on your side. Also, there will be more food and candies or what have you than we could possibly ever eat. I'm truly ashamed of you guys. Please, listen to Doc and do as he says, it may mean your going home or not. We've come this far, fellows, we endured all those tortures and beatings, we have endured a living hell. Let's do as the doc says. We have listened to him for over two years, why stop now?" Then I said, "Okay, fellows, let's go and do as Doc asked us to do."

Several of the fellows just didn't listen to Doc or me. They couldn't wait, they were so hungry. So the first candy bars they found, they opened and sat down and ate them. After eating three or four of those candy bars, that was all she wrote. They sat right there against a tree and died on the spot. We found several of the boys propped up against a tree with food clutched in their hands, mostly candy bars. They ate too much, which cost them their lives right there. It was a shame, after going through what we had been through, to die like this, especially now that they were free men. Dr. Nardini's advice and mine fell on deaf ears. Looking back now, I guess they should have distributed the food stuffs and candies to the camps directly to keep them out of the hands of the very sick and let the people in charge hand them out. However, they didn't know our condition. They only knew we were starving and were trying to get food and clothing to us as fast as possible.

One of the boxes contained long-awaited medicines, so our doctor was able to administer to the sick, including me. Several more got very ill, but the doctor now had medicine to give them. We lost about six or eight men from overeating. I don't know how many lost their lives in the other camps due to the same cause.

The day after we were told about the war's end, Dr. Nardini, the British sergeant and I were invited to a party in the town of Ackanobe which was given by the six families that ran Japan at that time. I was told later the party was their way of saying thanks to the prisoners for the work that they had performed. We were ushered into this large room with high ceilings. There about twenty-five or thirty well-dressed Japanese men already there standing in a line to greet us. As we passed down the line, each offered his hand, but I just couldn't bring myself to shake their hands after the torture I had just been through for almost four long years. After we passed through the line, we sat in a semicircle on the floor on a soft pillow, our legs crossed in Oriental style. Geishas came in with their heads bowed and served us various types of food. As they left the room, they backed out with their heads bent down low and their arms outstretched in front of them.

None of us ate much of their food. It look delicious, but the doctor advised against it. He said it would be too rich for our bodies. So we took his advice and refrained. However, we all drank a bit of the sake, their wine, and smoked the cigarettes that they had provided. I tried a cigar and almost fell over with the first puff; this was the first cigar or cigarette that I had since the interrogation session on Masonry by the Japanese officers from Tokyo, about a year before. I got a little dizzy, so I switched to the cigarettes. They weren't too bad, but they still made me dizzy.

After dinner, the Geishas put on a beautiful display of Japanese dancing and other entertainment. In all, it was a very pleasant evening. The six families that gave the party for us controlled the finances of Japan in those days. They had all the money. They owned everything from banks to factories. I don't know whether it is still that way today or not. Our camp commander, the colonel, had taken us to the party in town, and when it was over, he suggested that we could either return to the camp, or he would show us some of the town of Ackanobe. We decided to let him show us around town before returning back to camp, knowing that we would never get that chance again.

The camp commander was a real good Joe, so on our way back to camp that evening, we asked him to bring a big truck into camp to carry the food supplies and medicines that would be left over from what the planes had dropped.

I must have been in a trance, because the next morning after the party, it dawned on me that the war was really over and I was not dreaming.

And now that I was relaxed, I started to get very ill, and I collapsed. I weighed only about sixty-five pounds. I was nothing but skin and bones. I guess the only thing that kept me going for so long was the fear of lying down and not getting up again. I knew that my captors would not give anyone any medicine; they just let them die. If you got down sick, they stripped you of your clothing, more precisely, your rags, and threw you in a room about the size of a small bedroom, about nine by nine feet square. They would just toss you in, and if you landed on top of another prisoner, they didn't care. When one was tossed into that room, that was all she wrote, you were never to come out again. You were stripped and were not allowed any food or medicine. You were written off. That was that. Each day, when a guard would go in, and if they couldn't feel any sign of a pulse, out you went to be cremated. I had made up my mind that that wasn't going to happen to me if I could help it. I can truthfully say that it was my strong faith in my God and country that kept me going and standing on my feet.

Now that I finally realized I was a free man, and with the fear gone, I just fell apart and collapsed. Dr. Nardini felt that I and several others should be fed intravenously, so he had us transferred immediately to a Japanese hospital. Before I was put in the ambulance, which Dr. Nardini had requested for those who were bad off, the camp commander came over and actually gave me a big hug and wished me a happy reunion with my relatives and also that I would get better fast. He kept telling me how sorry he was the way his countrymen had treated us. I could see by the expression on his face that he was sincere in what he was saying to me. I told him how much I appreciated the goodness, the kindness, he had meted out to us prisoners. He thanked me, and the ambulance took off.

They told me later that just prior to vacating the prison camp, the Americans and British prisoners with the help of the Japanese guards and some civilians who had come into the camp to try and make friends with the prisoners, loaded all the food and medicines onto the big truck that the camp commander had provided. They had the Japanese driver take it to the commander's home and store it. I would love to have been there that day when they gave the camp commander all that food and medicines, but it wasn't to be. Ironically, on my thirty-ninth birthday 21 August 1945, I was released by the U.S. Army from the hands of the Japanese. What a birthday present. I feel my prayers were heard and answered by my faith in my God in heaven. He made me a free man again.

The American army doctors, upon my release from the Japanese hospital in Ackanobe, felt that due to my being so weak and having lost so much weight, it would not be safe for me to fly home with the other prisoners. I was taken to Yokohama, Japan, where I was put on board the U.S. naval hospital ship, U.S.S. *Benevolence*. I was fed intravenously, not even a bowl of clear broth touched my lips while I was lying in bed on board the hospital ship. After a month or so, the doctors figured I would able to return home to the States. So I was kept on board the hospital ship, the U.S.S. *Benevolence*, when it sailed for the good old U.S.A.

I was told, after I was back in the States, that the Japanese camp commander at Ackanobe came over and shook hands with each of the prisoners as they were set free by the rescue party that came into camp, and that he broke out in tears. As I said before, he was a fine gentleman. Being a prisoner under him allowed me to maintain my faith in mankind. Through him and those who came into camp at Osaka to question us about Masonry, I was made aware that not all the Japanese were rotten back in those days. It made me feel good that there were a few, very few, good ones.

313

84. Back on Good Old United States Soil

Sailing for home on the hospital ship, the U.S.S. *Benevolence,* I tried to shake it all off as a bad dream. As we approached the shores of the United States and were about to go under the Golden Gate Bridge at San Francisco, the nurses and hospital corpsmen helped me to go up on deck, and sat me in a wheelchair in order that I might see the Golden Gate Bridge as we went under it. That was a great treat for me, as they knew I had never seen it, having been out of the country, serving in the Orient for over nine years.

What a thrill it was to go under that great masterpiece for the first time in my life, and also to see America, my country, for the first time in over nine long years. I was overjoyed, thrilled, and I bowed my head and thanked my Heavenly Father for answering my prayers while I was in the prison camps and for His watchful eyes and tender hand that kept me alive and guided me back to freedom. I also thanked Him for being there and watching over me through the many bombings and strafings that I had encountered while serving on the Bataan-Mariveles peninsula and later through that devastating nightmare on Corregidor Island, the Rock, and then again for being in my corner while I was in the prisoner of war camps.

Upon my arrival in California on the hospital ship in early October 1945, I was immediately transferred to Oaknoll Naval Hospital in Oakland, California, to get my strength and weight back. I was now up to about seventy pounds. Before arriving in the United States, I was able to digest a small amount of ordinary, soft foods. The doctors at the Oaknoll Naval Hospital in Oakland watched my intake very closely. The doctors would not allow me to go into town for several months, for fear I would eat something that I wasn't supposed to. They felt that it would not only set me back but could still possibly cost me my life. I was finally given permission to go ashore on liberty on the seventh day of December 1945, Pearl Harbor Day, four years to the day that I finally did get that nip that I had been begging my buddy, Joe Hunter, for in the Philippines.

This was my first liberty in the States since I left for the Philippines and the Orient some nine years before. That first drink was just a sip, as the doctors at the Oaknoll Naval Hospital were still monitoring very closely what I put in my stomach, my vital organs having shrunk so badly.

Upon my release from the hospital in early 1946, I had regained some of my lost weight and was feeling great, but the tortures I had undergone by the hands of the Japanese during those four years were still fresh in my memory. I would wake up several times during the night in a cold sweat and sometimes screaming. That is a part of my life I will never forget.

When I was released from the hospital, I was given fifteen years to live, but God thought differently. That was August 1945. It is now 1998, over fifty years later, and with God's will, I am still going strong at almost ninety-two years young.

My number never came up when we were forced to count off when the Nipponese were losing the war and every *go mae* (fifth man) had to step out and be used for bayonet practice. I will never forget those nights. Lying there, hearing those screams as my buddies were being bayoneted by the Japanese; the torture of those unfortunate prisoners conducted just outside the door of the prisoners' barracks. It seemed that Little Caesar took great joy in making us aware of the screams of our buddies as they were being tortured. It is my utmost hope that never again will the people of this great nation allow any part of their armed forces to get in the position that we were put in out there in the Philippines—no help, no planes, ships, men, or supplies, nothing. The hardest part for me to swallow was that after more than two hundred years of our flag flying high and proud, America went to sleep and allowed a small country like Japan to force that great and heroic General Jonathan M. Wainwright to touch the flag of this great nation to the ground on Corregidor Island in the Philippines. All because our Congress refused to produced material for our boys to fight with. *Wake up, America, your Congress is doing it again.*

The Fil-Americans were a fine group of brave fighting men and deserve all the honor that a nation could give them. Enough credit cannot be given to the brave, courageous Philippine scouts. They were truly the most heroic group of soldiers the world will ever see, barring none. God Bless America, and may she always be the great arsenal of democracy.